3rd Edition

Daniel Muijs and David Reynolds

Effective Teaching

Evidence and Practice

Los Angeles | London | New Delhi
Singapore | Washington DC

First edition published 2001 – Reprinted 2002, 2003
Second edition published 2005 – Reprinted 2006 (twice), 2007

SAGE Publications Ltd
1 Oliver's Yard
55 City Road
London EC1Y 1SP

SAGE Publications Inc.
2455 Teller Road
Thousand Oaks, California 91320

SAGE Publications India Pvt Ltd
B 1/I 1 Mohan Cooperative Industrial Area
Mathura Road
New Delhi 110 044

SAGE Publications Asia-Pacific Pte Ltd
33 Pekin Street #02-01
Far East Square
Singapore 048763

Library of Congress Control Number: 2010920121

British Library Cataloguing in Publication data

A catalogue record for this book is available from
the British Library

ISBN 978-1-84920-075-2
ISBN 978-1-84920-076-9 (pbk)

Typeset by C&M Digitals (P) Ltd, Chennai, India
Printed in Great Britain by CPI Antony Rowe, Chippenham, Wiltshire
Printed on paper from sustainable resources

CONTENTS

INTRODUCTION: EFFECTIVE TEACHING – THE BRITISH RESEARCH REVIEWED

Teaching is, of course, the most important thing that happens in schools. It is of course the most important thing that teachers do. Yet it is only in the last decade that the study of teaching, the generation of agreed teaching 'best practice' and the related policy attempts to improve teaching have really taken root in the United Kingdom. We begin by looking at these matters over the last 35 years.

The British Research

In the United States, there were literally thousands of studies that were from the 'process-product' paradigm (Borich, 1996; Brophy, 1981; Good et al., 1975). These largely involved using a 'pre-test' of some academic achievement like reading, a 'post-test' administered later, and doing in-depth observation of the varying classroom behaviours, attitudes and climates of large samples of different teachers, whose 'gains' in terms of their pupils' achievement levels were related to their characteristics. The studies generated the classic lists of the basic 'effective teacher' characteristics, which were usually seen through the 1970s, 1980s and 1990s as:

- clarity in teaching and in administrative routines
- high opportunity to learn through curriculum coverage
- lesson structure that is well organized
- class management that maximizes pupil attention

- active teaching that 'takes' curriculum content to children
- high levels, and quality, of questioning
- good time management
- frequent feedback.

By contrast, the UK knowledge base was smaller in total and in many ways more rudimentary in its intellectual reach. Early attempts to relate achievement gain to the broad educational philosophies, 'style' and practices of primary school teachers rated as 'progressive' or 'traditional' generated rather little success (Bennett, 1976) and were widely criticized. While in this work 'progressive' teachers had lower achievement gains, interestingly the teacher with what could be called 'structured, consistent progressivism' as a philosophy/practice generated the highest learning gain. In any case, the amount of variation in student achievement explained by variation in the teacher's teaching 'style' was small.

The next major British research was the notable ORACLE secondary school study, which involved a 'process-product' orientation similar to American research (Galton, 1987). Teachers labelled as 'class enquirers' generated the greatest gains in the areas of mathematics and language, but this finding did not extend to reading. By contrast, the group of 'individual monitoring' teachers made among the least progress. It is important to note that the more successful 'class enquirers' group utilized four times as much time in whole-class interactive teaching as the 'individual monitors' (Croll, 1996). Further analyses correlated the academic gain made by the different classes with different patterns of class/teacher interactions, finding a moderate positive correlation between whole-class and small-group interaction and children's progress, showing as Croll (1996) noted 'a positive association of progress and non-individualized interaction'. Croll (1996) also noted two dangers in any rapid translation of ORACLE findings into recommended practice – that the 'whole-class interactive' teachers differed in ways other than in their class teaching techniques, and that teachers utilizing other teaching styles (the 'infrequent changers') that did *not* have high levels of whole-class interaction also scored above average in gain.

The ORACLE study also looked at the children's time on task (or academically engaged time) and found that whole-class interaction was positively associated with high levels of time on task, with the 'class enquirers' having average time on task from their students 10 per cent higher than other teachers. The PACE study (Pollard et al., 1994) also noted high levels of whole-class interaction to be correlated with high pupil 'task engagement'. Further analyses on one of the ORACLE studies (Croll and Moses, 1988) showed a high positive correlation between time in whole-class interaction and time on task. Time in group-based interaction showed no such association. The 'whole-class interactive' effect also applied to types of learning other than in whole-class sessions, with children's time on task also higher in the sections of the lesson when they were working on their own.

Another important historical British study was that of Peter Mortimore and colleagues (Mortimore, et al., 1988), who collected an immensely rich database of information on children, their classrooms, their primary schools and their individual background characteristics, using a cohort of children followed through the four years of British junior school education. Generally, Mortimore found, as had Galton in secondary schools, that teachers were in those days spending much more time communicating with individual children than they were doing whole-class teaching or facilitating collaborative groupwork. At classroom level, the effective teacher characteristics were:

- teachers having responsibility for ordering activities during the day for pupils, i.e. structured teaching
- pupils having some responsibility for their work and independence within working sessions
- teachers covering only one curriculum area at a time
- high levels of interaction with the whole class
- teachers providing ample, challenging work
- high levels of pupil involvement in tasks
- a positive atmosphere in the classroom
- teachers showing high levels of praise and encouragement.

Mortimore and his colleagues also showed that teachers who spent a lot of time with individual pupils were using most of the time in routine (i.e. non-work) matters and there was less use of higher-order questioning, while teachers who used class discussions as a teaching strategy tended to make rather more use of higher-order communication.

Mortimore concluded that the classroom factors contributing to effective student outcomes were structured sessions, intellectually challenging teaching, a work-orientated environment, communication between teachers and pupils, and a limited focus within the sessions.

A further study conducted by Tizard et al. (1988) found low teacher expectations of a sample of inner-city children, with higher expectations on the part of the individual teachers being associated with a wider range of curriculum and learning experiences. There was a wide variation in the curriculum coverage of different teachers, which affected pupil progress, and much of the school day was spent on non-work activities. Indeed, less than half the day, 46 per cent, was devoted to learning activities in the classroom. Children were engaged in their tasks only 61 per cent of the time.

Although it was not research based, as were the above studies, material from OFSTED also addressed issues of teacher effectiveness. Their major report, *Primary Matters* (OFSTED, 1995), outlined a number of general teacher/teaching factors appearing to be associated with positive outcomes in general:

- good subject knowledge
- good questioning skills
- an emphasis upon instruction
- a balance of grouping strategies
- clear objectives
- good time management
- effective planning
- good classroom organization
- effective use of other adults in the classroom.

By the late 1990s and early 2000s, perhaps the major teacher effectiveness research was our own studies built on the evaluation of a specialist mathematics intervention, the Mathematics Enhancement Programme (see Muijs and Reynolds, 1999, 2000b, 2002, 2003; Reynolds and Muijs, 1999a). This work was based upon testing the entire pupil population of 35 primary schools on mathematics, and using a standardized observation instrument that measured teachers' behaviours, pupils' behaviours and lesson structure.

Nearly 60 different behaviours by teachers in classroom concerning their classroom management, management of pupils' behaviour, the quality of their direct instruction of pupils, the interactivity of their teaching, the attention given to individual review and practice, the variation in the teaching methods, the use of 'connectionist' teaching methods and the classroom climate created in lessons were related to improvement in pupil performance over the year. Rather than any one teacher behaviour being strongly related to achievement, lots of small correlations were found, indicating that effective teaching is not being able to do a small number of 'big' things right but is rather doing a large number of 'little' things well. In our more advanced analysis, the factor of 'effective teaching' was the most important determinant of how children did after the influence of their own achievement level, reinforcing what we noted earlier about how important teaching is.

In these studies, though, teaching behaviours were not the only factor of importance to pupil achievement. Teachers' beliefs about teaching, their subject knowledge and their self-efficacy (or their views about their own power as teachers) all also mattered, in the way that they encouraged teachers to adopt the more effective teaching methods that have powerful effects in improving pupils' achievements.

In the last few years, there has been a considerable growth in research, in reviews of research and in models about effective practices in this area (see, for example, Campbell et al., 2004; Muijs et al., 2004). As an example, the Teddlie and Reynolds (2000) review of school effectiveness research had no chapter on teacher effectiveness even though it reviewed over 1500 studies – the new version will have a double length chapter on it.

There have been important new studies in the field. The EPPE (Effective Pre-School and Primary Education 3–11) Project shows, as with our own work, that the influence of overall Teaching Quality upon Maths and Reading outcomes is stronger than the net influence of some background factors such as gender and family disadvantage. In detail, this covers and relates to the richness of instructional methods, a positive classroom climate, productive use of instructional time, the use of feedback to pupils, teacher sensitivity to their pupils and a lack of teacher detachment. An organized classroom where there is a calm orderly climate is also important (see Sammons et al., 2008 for full information).

The VITAE (Variation in Teachers' Work, Lives and Effectiveness) Project has also found an association between teachers' commitment to their jobs, their resilience in resisting stressors and the improvement of their pupils on the English national tests at ages 7, 11 and 14 (Day et al., 2006).

The Neglect of the Teacher Historically

Most of this research, though, has only accumulated comparatively recently. Why is this the case? It may reflect partly the historical belief that teaching was more like a creative subject than a scientific 'technology of practice' that could be learned, in which case there had been little point in studying it because teaching reflected the influence of things 'deep down' in the psyches and constitutions of teachers that determined whether they were effective or not, just as the quality of the work that the artist produces reflected his or her deep structure.

The micro-political difficulties of conducting research in classrooms probably also had an effect. It took perhaps 20 years for the issue of differences in secondary schools' levels of effectiveness to be openly acknowledged among politicians, the public and professionals (Teddlie and Reynolds, 2000), and the issue of the differences between individual teachers in their 'effectiveness', rather than individual schools, is one even more fraught with problems. It strikes at the heart of issues to do with individual professional accountability. It makes professionals vulnerable since they are judged as individuals, rather than as a group which is what happens if their school is evaluated. The outside interventions by politicians and others in this area, about whether teachers need to be monitored more closely by the State for example, have made the profession even more concerned about research in this area and the threat it poses, or is seen to pose.

The nature of British academic life itself has probably also had an effect in restricting the growth of research in this area, seen in the absence of the strong communities of psychologically oriented researchers into learning and instruction that have been central in the educational research communities of the Netherlands, Germany, France, Italy and the Scandinavian countries, as well as the United States.

Lastly, it is likely that the very success of the UK 'school effectiveness movement' may have discouraged the development of a teacher-based focus. In the USA and the UK in the 1960s and 1970s, there was a pronounced pessimism about the prospects of education systems contributing to a fairer world, as shown in the phrase that 'education cannot compensate for society' (Bernstein, 1968). Research evidence suggested that, after all other influences had been controlled out, the effects of individual schools were minimal, as seen in reports by Coleman et al. (1966) and Jencks et al. (1972).

These factors generated, initially in the United States and then worldwide, an international research community in school effectiveness that rejected these views and purported to show that, to use its mantra, 'schools make a difference', yet the focus on only the school was taken not from any logical assessment of its importance compared with that of the teacher, but merely from the focus of the original critics of educational reform. School effectiveness, then, locked itself into a mindset of concern with the school rather than with the teacher, within which, with the notable exceptions of Creemers (1994), Teddlie and Stringfield (1993) and Mortimore et al. (1988), it stayed until ten years ago.

The Costs of Neglect

There is no doubt that the absence until comparatively recently of much focus in the UK upon 'teaching' and 'the teacher' has been very restricting of our educational progress, in a number of ways:

- In the absence of a substantial body of knowledge about effective practices from the research community, much use was made of the definitions of what 'effective' teachers did as judged by OFSTED, the General Teaching Council and/or the Department for Children, Schools and Families, yet these judgments have not always been research based and may be open to political manipulation.
- The absence of a discourse concerning teachers and teaching meant sometimes that highly effective programmes from other countries that have generated teaching-based interventions (e.g. the *Success For All* model of Slavin, 1996) did not root well in the UK educational context because their commitment to improving the 'instructional' or 'teaching' level was not well understood.
- The poverty of the teaching effectiveness literature made it hard to conceptualize, describe and understand the effective teaching practices from other countries that have begun to attract increased interest in UK schools (Reynolds and Farrell, 1996).

The absence of clear descriptions of what effective teachers did meant that professional discussions, and their political equivalents, were often rooted in out-of-date debates about methods that were largely irrelevant, as in the 'progressive against traditional teaching' debate. The absence of research prolonged these essentially 'non rational' discussions.

However, it is clear from a variety of research sources now that teaching matters and that teachers and their methods have very substantial effects on pupils. In our own work (Muijs and Reynolds, 2003), there was a difference of over 20 mathematics 'points' (like a reading score 'point') that resulted from being taught by the most effective and the least effective teachers in our sample of primary schools. If we express this in a different way, the variation between children in their achievement scores (called 'variance' technically) is explicable for the most part by their own achievement characteristics, but the teacher in the class is roughly four times more important than the whole school in affecting how pupils do (see table below, taken from Reynolds, 2006):

Variance at the school, classroom and pupil levels on mathematics achievement

	School	Class	Individual Pupil
Year 1	9.9	14.1	76.0
Year 2	5.6	18.0	76.4
Year 3	4.8	28.8	66.4
Year 4	5.7	22.4	71.9

Note: Year is the year of the study itself.

If we look at the related area of differences between departments – small groups of teachers – and their effects, then contemporary data from the Fischer Family Trust (Reynolds, 2006), on the 65–75 per cent of secondary schools where pupils' progress in Key Stage 3 is roughly in line with national expectations, suggests that if one divides pupils into six groups (boys/girls across three core subjects), then:

- 80 per cent of all schools show value added significantly higher than might be expected for one or more groups
- over a three-year period, 50 per cent of schools have at least one group where their progress is in the top 20 per cent nationally for all schools.

However, it is important to note that it is not just in the research community that teaching is now seen as the key policy 'alterable' variable. In a number of different societies, the evidence has begun to interest and influence policymakers. The OECD recently published their major report on *Teaching Matters* (OECD, 2005), and related this to the need for the improved professional development of teachers since 'at the level of the education system, professional development of teachers is a key policy lever' (p. 20).

More recently still, the massive publicity afforded to the McKinsey report *How the World's Best Performing School Systems Come Out On Top* (Barber and Mourshed, 2007) influenced policymakers worldwide, both with its portrayal of the high-performing Finnish system of education and with its conclusions that 'the quality of an education system cannot exceed the quality of its teachers' and 'that the only way to improve outcomes is to improve instruction' (p. 13). The recruitment, training and continuous professional development of teachers are now attracting greatly increased interest. More than ever, teaching and teachers are seen to 'matter'.

An Outline of the Book

In this book, therefore, we aim to give an accessible introduction to research in this now rapidly expanding field, and in this third edition we have expanded our coverage into many new areas. The book is divided into four Parts. In Parts 1 and 2, we will discuss both learning and generic teaching skills; in Part 3, we consider teaching for specific purposes; and in Part 4, we discuss the teaching of specific subjects and the issue of the assessment and observation of teaching in classrooms.

Part 1, on learning and teaching, contains five chapters looking at research on what can be termed the 'basics of teaching'. After Chapter 1, which outlines what we know about student learning and the development of intelligence, the next two chapters rely heavily on the 'effective teaching' school of research mentioned earlier in this Introduction.

In Chapter 2, the main studies and research methods used in effective teaching research are summarized, and the method identified as the most effective way of teaching basic skills, the direct instruction method, is discussed.

In Chapter 3, research on interactive teaching, an essential component of the direct instruction method and of most other effective teaching methods, is summarized. This research has produced detailed findings on such matters as the appropriate cognitive level of questions, what to do when pupils give a wrong answer and how long optimally to wait for a pupil to answer a question.

In Chapter 4, we will look at the advantages and disadvantages of collaborative small-group work and in Chapter 5 at constructivist teaching, which has been acquiring many adherents in the last ten years.

In Chapter 6, we look at teachers' beliefs – about education, about themselves and about their pupils – since much evidence now exists that shows these factors as important determinants of how children do, in addition to the behaviours of teachers that we have covered in Chapters 2 to 5.

In **Part 2**, we discuss the extensive body of research on classroom and behaviour management, which form part of the basic repertoire of any effective teacher.

In Chapter 7, on classroom management, we will discuss such matters as how to avoid disruption when starting or ending the lesson, or during transitions between lesson parts and when giving homework assignments, and why and how to establish clear rules and procedures.

In Chapter 8, we will discuss research on how to deal with pupil misbehaviour when it does occur, including the most effective ways to use rewards and punishments in the classroom.

In Chapter 9, we look at classroom climate, including such matters as how to create a pleasant classroom climate and the importance of teacher expectations.

In Chapter 10, we discuss homework, including the main types of homework in use, its main goals, what research has to tell us about the effectiveness of homework as a learning tool and how this may differ by age, and how to use homework effectively.

In Chapter 11, we look at the increased emphasis upon the teaching of thinking skills and problem solving in schools, assess its value and outline some of the detailed programmes that have been developed in this area, and their results.

In **Part 3**, we will focus on strategies aimed at teaching for specific purposes for students. Developing students' social skills is the subject of Chapter 12, in which research will be reviewed on the importance of their peer relations to children's development, the characteristics that may lead to children being unpopular with peers, how social skills can be taught or enhanced and what parents can do to help develop their children's social skills.

Another important social outcome is enhancing students' self-esteem, which is discussed in Chapter 13. This is a subject that has received a lot of attention in recent decades, and we will look at what research has found on the relationship between these concepts and school achievement, at whether students' age and gender affect their self-concept, and at what teachers can do to improve their students' self-concept and self-esteem.

In the next three chapters, we look at ways of teaching specific student groups. First, in Chapter 14, we review what is known about teaching students with a variety of special needs, such as learning difficulties, hearing problems, behavioural difficulties and attention disorders, as well as the findings on including students with special needs in the regular classroom.

In Chapter 15, we will look at how to identify a different group of students with special needs – gifted students – and the advantages and disadvantages of different methods of catering for gifted students such as ability grouping, curricular enrichment, cooperative learning and acceleration.

Research on teaching in the early years is reviewed in Chapter 16, in which we will discuss differing views on how to teach in the early years, how best to promote children's school-readiness in pre-school settings, the importance of play and what children learn from it.

In Chapter 17, various ways of dealing with individual differences between students are discussed, including the use of selection, streaming and setting, individualized instruction and other methods. We also describe and evaluate the recent enthusiasm for more 'personalized' forms of educational experiences in UK schools.

In **Part 4**, we will look at the teaching of particular subjects and at other specific classroom techniques such as assessment and classroom observation.

One of the most contentious issues in education over recent years has been the teaching of literacy and in Chapter 18 we will discuss the two methods that have caused so much controversy – 'phonics' and 'whole language' – and review the research on how children learn to read and the best way to teach them this crucial skill.

Chapter 19 focuses on another crucial basic skill – numeracy – and we look at research on how children learn mathematics, and at the implications of this and other research on mathematics teaching.

In Chapter 20, we will outline the various kinds of assessments that are used in schools and pay particular attention to 'formative assessment' which aims to use assessment information to directly improve achievement and understanding, through improving feedback, sharing learning goals, using self-assessment and planning learning.

Cross-curricular or thematically based teaching is the subject of Chapter 21, an interesting collection of methods which were popular during the 'Plowden era' of the 1970s but which have now returned to popularity, especially within primary education. The organizational and logistical challenges of these methods are discussed in detail.

Chapter 22 – our final topic or theme-based chapter – appropriately examines the professional development of teachers, which are the processes whereby they can be encouraged to become more 'effective' in the directions that this book has outlined. Classroom observation of practice, using a variety of methods, is a key mechanism of this and we discuss the various different kinds of systems fully.

In the Conclusion to this volume, we move from reviewing and assessing the knowledge on the subject of effective teaching to speculating about the practices of teaching that will be important in the future. Teaching is likely to become a more and more complex act. It will need to be different in different contexts, subjects and schools, in accordance with their levels of effectiveness and improvement trajectory. It will need to be concerned with a wider range of outcomes, social and affective. It will need to embrace new ideas about how to improve schools – through making each individual school's best practice their universal practice – and about how to potentiate learning, through the new 'brain science' paradigm that is sweeping the world. It will be a challenging world for educators!

We hope that we have provided this overview of research in a wide range of areas related to teaching in an accessible but thorough way. Obviously, it is not possible to treat all these aspects in detail in this volume, and we have probably gone for breadth rather than depth. Hopefully, though, we will have stimulated the reader to go and look for more information in the references provided, and to start to debate with their colleagues the issues about effective teaching that the teaching profession urgently needs to address.

PART 1

INTRODUCTION TO TEACHING AND LEARNING

CHAPTER 1

THEORIES OF LEARNING AND INTELLIGENCE

Key Points

In this chapter, you will learn about:

- the main elements of behaviourist learning theory
- what Piaget and Vygotsky had to say about learning, and its relevance today
- the meaning of IQ and traditional theories on intelligence
- Gardner's theory of multiple intelligences
- the main elements of cognitive and brain research.

Introduction

In this chapter, we will discuss the main theories on how children learn. This is of course an important issue in teaching, as to be effective we need to try and teach in a way that reinforces how people naturally learn. Theories of learning and intelligence are many and diverse, and we can't look at all existing theories in one chapter. What we will do instead, is focus on some of the theories that have been most influential in education over the years.

IQ Theory

One of the first theories on learning to gain widespread currency in education was IQ (Intelligence Quotient) theory.

IQ theory is mainly interested in the concept of intelligence, which is seen as determining people's ability to learn, to achieve academically and therefore to take on leading roles in society. IQ theorists, like William Stern, who was one of the developers of the theory in the early part of the twentieth century, claimed that core intelligence was innate. Many psychologists in the USA and Europe supported that conclusion and psychologists like Terman and Binet developed instruments specifically designed to test people's innate intelligence. These were analysed using the newest statistical methods such as factor analysis, developed by Thurstone and Spearman. These analyses showed that all the items (questions) in those tests essentially measured one big factor, called G, or 'general intelligence'. Therefore, the theory states that people have one underlying general intelligence, which will predict how well they are able to learn and perform at school (Howe, 1997).

A major point of discussion is whether intelligence as measured by IQ tests is innate or learned. The initial theories largely stressed the innate nature of intelligence, seeing it as an inborn property. Subsequent research has, however, clearly shown that IQ can be raised through educational interventions, which means that it cannot be totally inborn. The successful CASE programme in the UK, for example, does just that (Adey and Shayer, 2002). Another fact that points to the 'learnability' of IQ is that average IQ test scores have been increasing steadily over the past decades in all countries where they have been studied (Flynn, 1994). When we are testing someone's IQ, we are therefore testing his or her education level at least as much (if not more) than whatever innate ability he or she may possess. Also, it has become clear that children's IQ test scores are strongly influenced by their parents' so-called cultural capital, that is people's cultural resources (how many books they read, what media they access and so on). This in turn is strongly determined by their socio-economic status, or their position in the social class system (Gould, 1983; Howe, 1997; Muijs, 1997).

As well as the issue of whether IQ is innate or learnt, the whole theory of IQ has been heavily criticized for many years now. These criticisms focus on a number of areas. The first of these is the methods used to measure intelligence, which produced G. While we don't want to go into a discussion of statistics here, it is fair to say that the factor analysis method these researchers developed was specifically designed to come up with one big underlying factor, and usually does. If you use different methods, you are likely to find far more factors. Therefore, in many ways, it is pre-existing theories which led to the development of methods designed to confirm these theories (Muijs, forthcoming). The theory of intelligence also focuses purely on 'academic' intelligence, and so disparages other skills and abilities. As we will see, recent theories have taken a different approach on these matters (Gardner, 1983).

The idea that there is one measurable factor that distinguishes people has also been widely misused. One of the earliest uses of IQ tests was to look at differences in intelligence between particular groups in society, which were then said to be differently intelligent (and by implication more or less suitable to take on leading roles in society). The findings of these studies tell us far more about the societies in which they were carried out than about the 'intelligence of different groups' (which as a matter of fact does not differ significantly). Thus, in the USA, research concentrated on finding differences between racial groups (whites scoring higher than blacks), in France on differences between genders (men scoring higher than women) and in the UK on differences in social class (the higher classes obviously coming out as more intelligent than the working class) (Blum, 1980; Gould, 1983).

Notwithstanding these criticisms, it would be wrong to reject IQ theory. There is evidence that an underlying general aptitude influences how well students perform in a variety of subjects. There is a far stronger correlation between students' performance in maths and English than is often realized, for example. Therefore, the evidence does suggest that such a thing as general intelligence may exist and be a significant predictor of student achievement and learning.

Multiple Intelligences

As we saw in the previous section, the theory of IQ stresses the existence of one overarching intelligence, a view that has become increasingly controversial over time. For many decades, however, no alternative theory was able to overcome the dominance of IQ theory whenever ability and intelligence were studied. This changed in the early 1980s, with the publication of *Frames of Mind* by Howard Gardner (1983), in which he set out his theory of 'multiple intelligences'.

Gardner takes a view that is very different from that of IQ theory. According to him, people do not have one general intelligence, but are characterized by a range of intelligences instead. So, rather than being globally intelligent, I may be particularly strong in certain areas, for example mathematics, while someone else may be particularly strong in another area, for example physical sports.

Gardner (1983, 1993) distinguishes seven main types of intelligence:

1. **Visual/Spatial Intelligence**. This is the ability to *perceive the visual*. Visual/spatial learners tend to think in pictures and need to create vivid mental images to retain information. They enjoy looking at pictures, charts, movies and so on.

2. **Verbal/Linguistic Intelligence**. This is the ability to *use words and language.* These learners have highly developed auditory skills and are generally elegant speakers. They think in words rather than pictures. This is the ability that can be measured by the verbal part of IQ tests.
3. **Logical/Mathematical Intelligence**. This is the *ability to use reason, logic and numbers.* These learners think conceptually in logical and numerical patterns, making connections between pieces of information. They ask lots of questions and like to do experiments. The non-verbal portion of traditional IQ tests largely measures this intelligence.
4. **Bodily/Kinaesthetic Intelligence**. This is the *ability to control body movements and handle objects skilfully.* These learners express themselves through movement. They have a good sense of balance and eye–hand coordination. Through interacting with the space around them, they are able to remember and process information.
5. **Musical/Rhythmic Intelligence**. This is the *ability to produce and appreciate music.* These learners think in sounds, rhythms and patterns. They respond strongly to music and rhythm. Many of these learners are extremely sensitive to sounds occurring in their environment.
6. **Interpersonal Intelligence**. This is the *ability to relate to and understand others*. These learners can empathize and see things from other people's point of view in order to understand how they think and feel. They are good at sensing feelings, intentions and motivations. Generally, they try to maintain peace in group settings and encourage cooperation. They can be manipulative.
7. **Intrapersonal Intelligence**. This is the *ability to self-reflect and be aware of one's inner states.* These learners try to understand their inner feelings, dreams, relationships with others, and strengths and weaknesses. Their strength lies in the ability to be self-reflective (Gardner, 1983, 1993).

A misconception that exists about this theory is that one intelligence is necessarily dominant. This is not really the case, as all of us will possess all intelligences to some extent. It is also important to remember that doing something will usually require use of more than one intelligence.

To some, it might seem that this choice of different intelligences is somewhat arbitrary. Gardner's theories are sometimes seen as somewhat unscientific, a seemingly random selection of intelligences. This is a misconception. In fact, Gardner uses a number of quite stringent criteria for defining an intelligence, taken from a variety of disciplines such as developmental psychology and cultural anthropology:

- Isolation as a Brain Function. A true intelligence will have its function identified in a specific location in the human brain. This can increasingly be determined using the latest brain-imaging techniques.

- Prodigies, Idiot Savants and Exceptional Individuals. In order to qualify as an intelligence, there must be some evidence of specific 'geniuses' in that particular area.
- Set of Core Operations. Each true intelligence has a set of unique and identifiable procedures at its heart.
- Developmental History. A true intelligence is associated with an identifiable set of stages of growth, with a mastery level which exists as an end state in human development.
- Evolutionary History. A true intelligence can have its development traced through the evolution of our species as identified by cultural anthropologists.
- Supported Psychological Tasks. A true intelligence can be identified by specific tasks which can be carried out, observed and measured by clinical psychologists.
- Supported Psychometric Tasks. Specifically designed psychometric tests can be used to measure the intelligence. A psychometric test is a standardized test used to measure a specific psychological facet, such as personality or intelligence.
- Encoded into a Symbol System. A true intelligence has its own symbol system which is unique to it and essential to completing its tasks (Gardner, 2003).

Misuses of Gardner's Theory

Gardner's theory has proved both popular and controversial in education, and both are closely linked. As often happens in education, psychological theories are taken on board by educators or commercial consultants who do not understand them well and produce a low-level vulgarized version for use in schools. Gardner himself for a long time remained silent on the issue of use of MI theory in the classroom, but more recently has pointed to a number of misuses he sees of his theories in education:

1. Sometimes it is inferred that all subjects or concepts need to be taught using all seven intelligences. According to Gardner (1995), while most topics can be taught in a number of ways, it is usually a waste of time to try and teach a topic using all seven intelligences.
2. Going through the motions of using an intelligence does not in itself lead to learning. Gardner gives the example of some teachers getting children to run around as a way of exercising bodily/kinaesthetic intelligence.
3. Gardner (1995) also does not believe that the use of materials associated with a multiple intelligence as background (e.g. playing music in the classroom) will do anything to aid learners who are strong in that area.
4. Sometimes teachers claim they are exercising pupils' multiple intelligences (in this case musical/rhythmic intelligence) by getting them to sing or dance while reciting something like a times table. While this may help them remember it,

(Continued)

(Continued)

Gardner (1995) describes such a use of MI as trivial. What educators should encourage instead is thinking musically or drawing on some of the structural aspects of music in order to illuminate concepts in other fields (like maths).

5. The use of various measures or instruments that grade intelligences is seen by Gardner as being directly in opposition to his views of intelligence as something that occurs when carrying out activities within cultural settings.

While Gardner's theories have been widely influential in education recently (although, as mentioned above, not always in the most helpful way), they have also been subject to criticism. One criticism focuses on what is seen as a lack of testability of Gardner's theories. This is seen to result from an ambiguity of the theory, in that it is not clear to what extent the intelligences are supposed to operate separately or interconnectedly. The fact that the existence or not of an intelligence is not testable experimentally and cannot be accurately psychometrically assessed is also critiqued (Klein, 1997), although Gardner would argue that this critique misunderstands the theory which sees intelligences as operating in cultural action. Critics claim that Gardner doesn't provide a clear definition of intelligence and some authors state that what Gardner is studying are in fact cognitive styles rather than intelligences (Morgan, 1996). The criteria he uses have been described as somewhat arbitrary (White, 1998), and Gardner is seen as not providing a clear explanation as to why these and not other possible criteria were chosen (Klein, 1997). Furthermore, the continual addition of new intelligences by Gardner has to lead to doubts as to the rigour of this framework. A number of recent studies have also led to questions over the validity of this theory. Visser et al. (2006), for example, found that when tests were developed for each intelligence, there was evidence of a global G factor underlying them, as would be predicted by intelligence theory. This view is also supported by findings from neurological research that show significant overlap between neural pathways controlling different brain functions (Waterhouse, 2006). In general, a lack of empirical evidence is a major problem with this theory, as over 25 years after its initial publication we should by now have been able to collect evidence to support it (Waterhouse, 2006). Arguments made to counter this problem, are that new tests are required for these domains, that theories don't necessarily require empirical data to be useful. Some test of real-world relevancy is necessary, and until this is forthcoming we have to conclude that this theory is not supported.

Behaviourism

One of the earliest theories to focus explicitly on learning rather than on intelligence is called behaviourism. Behaviourism was developed in the 1920s and

1930s by psychologists such as Skinner, Pavlov and Thorndike. While obviously somewhat outdated now, this theory still has a strong influence on educational practice, if not theory.

Behavioural Learning Theory emphasizes change in behaviour as the main outcome of the learning process. Behavioural theorists concentrate on directly observable phenomena using a scientific method borrowed from the natural sciences. The most radical behaviourists, such as Skinner, considered all study of non-observable behaviour ('mentalism') to be unscientific (Hilgard, 1995; O'Donohue and Ferguson, 2001). In recent years, however, most researchers and psychologists in the behaviourist tradition, such as Bandura (1985), have expanded their view of learning to include expectations, thoughts, motivation and beliefs.

Learning, according to behaviourists, is something people do in response to external stimuli. This view was an important change over previous models, which had stressed consciousness and introspection, and had not produced many generalizable findings about how people learn.

When they studied learning, behaviourists usually did so using experiments conducted with animals like dogs as well as humans. This is because, being against 'mentalism', behaviourists think that it is largely external factors which cause our behaviour. The basic mechanism through which this happens is conditioning. According to behaviourists, there are two different types of conditioning:

Classic conditioning occurs when a natural reflex responds to a stimulus. An example of this comes from Pavlov's experiments with dogs. In order to process food, dogs need to salivate when they eat. As all dog owners will know, what happens is that dogs will start to salivate even before eating, as soon as they have smelt or seen food. So, the external stimulus of food will cause the dog to salivate. It has become a habit that is conditioned. When confronted with particular stimuli, people as well as animals will produce a specific response.

Behavioural or **operant conditioning** occurs when a response to a stimulus is reinforced. Basically, operant conditioning is a simple feedback system: if a reward or reinforcement follows the response to a stimulus, then the response becomes more probable in the future. For example, if every time a pupil behaves well in class s/he gets a reward, s/he is likely to behave well next time.

Rewards and punishments are an important part of behaviourist learning theory. Initial experiments with dogs and rats convinced these psychologists of the importance of the use of rewards and punishments to elicit certain desired behaviours such as pushing a lever, in these animals. Over ensuing decades, these findings were further tested and refined with human subjects, and became highly influential in education. Pleasurable consequences, or *reinforcers,* strengthen behaviour, while unpleasant consequences, or *punishers,* weaken behaviour. Behaviour is influenced by its consequences, but it is influenced by its antecedents as well, thus creating the A(ntecedents)–B(ehaviour)–C(onsequences) chain. Skinner's work concentrated mainly on the relationship between the latter two parts of the chain (O'Donohue and Ferguson, 2001; Skinner, 1974), and these findings still form the basis of many behaviour management systems in schools, as well as much of the research on effective teaching (e.g. Muijs and Reynolds, 2003).

While this movement remains highly influential, behaviourism has come to be seen as far too limited and limiting to adequately capture the complexity of human learning and behaviours. The idea that learning occurs purely as a reaction to external stimuli has been proved wrong. Activities such as recognizing objects (this is a ball), sorting objects (this is a rugby ball, this is a football) and storing information are clearly 'mentalist' activities – they occur in the head. While of course an external stimulus (perception of an object) is present, behavourist theory cannot account for the information processing that occurs when we are confronted by stimuli. Behaviourism also cannot account for types of learning that occur without reinforcement – in particular, the way children pick up language patterns (grammar) cannot be explained using a behaviourist framework. Behaviourism also presents problems when the learner is confronted with new situations in which mental stimuli s/he has learnt to respond to are not present. The fact that behaviourism does not study the memory in any meaningful way (they only talk about acquiring 'habits'), is another major problem if we want to explain learning. If we want to really understand how people learn, we have to be 'mentalists' and look at what is going on inside the brain as well as measuring reactions to external stimuli.

However, not all the criticism of behaviourism is justified. Some of it seems to emanate from a dislike of the findings rather than a close look at the evidence. Behaviourism has little place for the role of free will and human individuality. This is never a popular view, and as we have seen this determinism is clearly overdone in behaviourist theories. However, that does not mean that it is entirely inaccurate. While we always like to believe that we are entirely free, our behaviours can to an extent be predicted, in some cases by behaviourist models. That this is true is attested to by the continued usefulness of behaviourist methods in teaching, such as the use of rewards. Not liking certain research findings does not make them wrong, and it is not the job of research and science to simply tell us what we want to hear. Recently, it is fair to say that many neo-behaviourist theories have become popular among scientists looking at the role of evolution in the way we behave. If you read the work of Richard Dawkins (1989), for example, there are clear links with behaviourist psychology.

Piaget and Vygotsky

Piaget and the stages of cognitive development

As well as the behaviourists like Skinner, two other pioneering psychologists who have had a continuing influence on how we view learning are Piaget and Vygotsky.

Jean Piaget was a Swiss psychologist, who started his important work on how children develop and learn before the Second World War. In contrast to the behaviourists, who developed most of their theories using laboratory experiments and rarely looked at the real-life behaviours of children, Piaget's theories were developed from the observation of children.

What these observations taught him was that in order to understand how children think, one has to look at the qualitative development of their ability to solve problems. Cognitive development, in his view, is much more than the addition of new facts and ideas to an existing store of information. Rather, children's thinking changes qualitatively; the tools which children use to think change, leading children of different ages to possess a different view of the world. A child's reality is not the same as that of an adult (Piaget, 2001).

According to Piaget, one of the main influences on children's cognitive development is what he termed **maturation**, the unfolding of biological changes that are genetically programmed into us at birth. A second factor is **activity**. Increasing maturation leads to an increase in children's ability to act on their environment, and to learn from their actions. This learning in turn leads to an alteration of children's thought processes. A third factor in development is **social transmission**, which is learning from others. As children act on their environment, they also interact with others and can therefore learn from them to a differing degree, depending on their developmental stage.

According to Piaget (2001), learning occurs in four stages:

The sensori-motor stage (0–2 years) – the baby knows about the world through actions and sensory information. S/he learns to differentiate her/himself from the environment. The child begins to understand causality in time and space. The capacity to form internal mental representations emerges.

The pre-operational stage (2–7 years) – in this stage, children take the first steps from action to thinking, by internalizing action. In the previous stage, children's schemes were still completely tied to actions, which means that they are of no use in recalling the past or in prediction. During the pre-operational stage, the child starts to be able to do this, by learning how to think symbolically. The ability to think in symbols remains limited in this stage, however, as the child can only think in one direction. Thinking backwards or reversing the steps of a task are difficult.

Another innovation that starts to take place during this phase is the ability to understand conservation. This means that the child can now realize that the amount or number of something remains the same, even if the arrangement or appearance of it is changed (for example, four dogs and four cats is the same amount). This remains difficult for children in this phase. Children here still have great difficulty freeing themselves from their own perception of how the world appears. Children at this age are also very egocentric. They tend to see the world and the experiences of others from their own standpoint.

The concrete operational stage (7–12 years) – the basic characteristics of this stage are: (1) the recognition of the logical stability of the physical world; (2) the realization that elements can be changed or transformed and still retain their original characteristics; and (3) the understanding that these changes can be reversed.

Another important operation that is mastered at this stage is *classification*. Classification depends on a child's ability to focus on a single characteristic of objects and then to group the objects according to that single characteristic (e.g. if one gives a child a set of differently coloured and differently shaped pens, they will be able to pick out the round ones). Students can now also understand seriation, allowing them to construct a logical series in which A is less than B is less than C and so on. At this stage, the child has developed a logical and systematic way of thinking which is, however, still tied to physical reality. Overcoming this is the task of the next phase.

The formal operational stage (12+) – in this stage, which is not reached by all people, all that is learned in previous stages remains in force but students are now able to see that a real, actually experienced situation is only one of several possible situations. In order for this to happen, we must be able to generate different possibilities for any given situation in a systematic way. Students are now able to imagine ideal, non-existing worlds. Another characteristic of this stage is adolescent egocentrism. Adolescents tend to incessantly analyse their own beliefs and attitudes, and often assume that everyone else shares their concerns and is in turn analysing them.

Piaget's theory has been hugely influential, but has been found wanting in a number of areas. His stages of learning are clearly too rigid. A number of studies have found that young children can acquire concrete operational thinking at an earlier age than Piaget proposed, and that they can think at higher levels than Piaget suggested. Piaget also underestimated the individual differences between children in how they develop, and the fact that some of these differences are due to the cultural and social background of the child. Piaget also did not take much notice of the way children can learn from others, seeing learning as largely dependent on their stage of development. Notwithstanding that, Piaget's theories have stood the test of time well, and are still a useful way of looking at children's development.

Vygotsky and the role of the environment in child development

Vygotsky was a Russian psychologist, who worked at around the same time as Piaget (although he died younger) and was influenced by Piaget's work. During his lifetime, he was not well-known in the West, but after his death (in particular since the 1960s) he has become increasingly influential.

Vygotsky's main interest was the study of language development, which he believed initially develops separately from thought, but starts to overlap with thought more and more as the child grows up. According to Vygotsky, a non-overlapping part still remains later in life, some non-verbal thought and some non-conceptual speech existing even in adults (Moll, 1992; Vygotsky, 1978).

A major disagreement between Piaget and Vygotsky was that Vygotsky did not think that maturation in itself could make children achieve advanced thinking skills. Vygotsky, while seeing a role for maturation, believed that it was children's interaction with others through language that most strongly influenced the levels of conceptual understanding they could reach (Vygotsky, 1978).

Vygotsky strongly believed that we can learn from others, both of the same age and of a higher age and developmental level. One of the main ways this operates is through **scaffolding** in the **zone of proximal development**. This latter concept, one of Vygotsky's main contributions to learning theory, refers to the gap between what a person is able to do alone and what s/he can do with the help of someone more knowledgeable or skilled than her/himself. It is here that the role of teachers, adults and peers comes to the fore in children's learning, in that they can help bring the child's knowledge to a higher level by intervening in the zone of proximal development. This can be done by providing children's thoughts with so-called scaffolds, which once the learning process is complete are no longer needed by the child. Not all children are as *educable* in this respect, some being able to learn more in the zone of proximal development than others.

Thus, for Vygotsky, it is *cooperation* that lies at the basis of learning. It is formal and informal *instruction* performed by more knowledgeable others, such as parents, peers, grandparents or teachers that is the main means of transition of the knowledge of a particular culture. Knowledge for Vygotsky, like for Piaget, is embodied in actions and interactions with the environment (or culture), but unlike Piaget, Vygotsky stresses the importance of *interaction* with a living representative of the culture.

While Piaget has been criticized for being too strongly focused on developmental learning, Vygotsky's work is seen as suffering from the opposite problem. Vygotsky wrote little about children's natural development and the relationship of that to their learning (Wertsch and Tulviste, 1992). Vygotsky's theories are also in many ways rather general and overarching, and have not been fully worked out (that Vygotsky died at the age of 37 is one reason for this). Vygotsky's contribution lies mainly in his attention to the social aspects of learning, which clearly need complementing by what current research is teaching us about brain functions.

This view of learning as socially constructed strongly influenced the so-called constructivist theories that have followed since then, and has influenced classroom practice. His ideas about pupils' learning in their zone of proximal development have been influential in the development of collaborative learning programmes.

Learning Styles

Recently, a lot of attention has focused on differences in pupils' learning styles. While this concept is often evoked, what exactly is meant by different learning styles is not always clear.

Kolb's Learning Styles Theory

One of the most clearly elucidated theories of learning styles is that of Kolb (1995), according to whom learning styles can be ranked along a continuum running from:

1. concrete experience (being involved in a new experience) through
2. reflective observation (watching others or developing observations about our own experience) and
3. abstract conceptualization (creating theories to explain observations) to
4. active experimentation (using theories to solve problems and make decisions).

As is clear from the above, Kolb saw these different styles as a cycle through which all learners should move over time. However, more recently, learning theorists have conceptualized these styles as ones which learners come to prefer and rely on, most learners thus preferring one of these four styles. Litzinger and Osif (1993) called these different types of learners *accommodators, divergers, convergers and assimilators*, and arraigned them along Kolb's continuum as depicted in Figure 1.1.

Accommodators prefer an active learning style. They tend to rely on intuition rather than on logic and like to connect learning to personal meaning and experiences. They enjoy applying their knowledge to real-life situations and don't like to analyze too much. When teaching these learners, it is recommended to

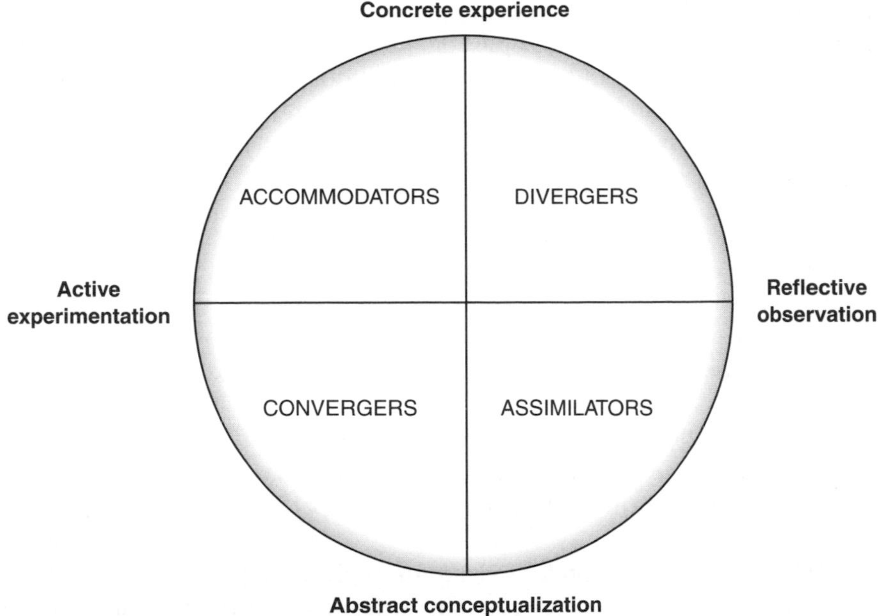

FIGURE 1.1 Kolb's learning styles (from Litzinger and Osif, 1993)

encourage independent discovery and to let learners participate actively in their learning. Interpersonal aspects are important to accommodators, so they will tend to enjoy cooperative learning and group work.

Assimilators like accurate, organized delivery of knowledge and tend to respect the views of those they consider to be experts on the subject. They think logically and prefer abstract ideas. Logic is more important to them than a practical explanation. They will prefer lecture-style lessons or carefully prepared exercises which they will follow closely. However, they also enjoy independent analysis of data and research.

Convergers are mainly interested in the relevance of information. They want to understand in detail how something operates, so they can use it in practice. These learners prefer technical information and are not very interested in social and interpersonal issues. Lessons that suit these learners are interactive, and it can be useful to provide them with real-life problems to explore. Convergers will enjoy doing hands-on tasks, use manipulatives, etc.

Divergers are mainly interested in the 'why' of a system. They like to reason from concrete specific information and to explore what a system has to offer. They like to see things from a variety of viewpoints and like categorizing information. These learners like to use their imagination when solving problems. Divergers enjoy self-directed learning and like independent study, simulations and role play. Information should be presented to them in a detailed, systematic manner.

Kolb's theory is far from being the only learning styles classification in existence. Another classification looks at pupils' different sensory preferences. According to this theory, learners can be classified as preferring either visual, auditory or tactile/kinaesthetic learning (Benzwie, 1987; Dunn and Dunn, 1978), while others add print, interactive and olfactory learners to this typology, leading to the following typology:

- Visual learners learn best by looking at pictures, graphs, slides, demonstrations, films, etc. Colourful, bright graphics can help these learners retain information.
- Auditory learners like to learn through listening both to others speaking and to audio tapes. They will benefit, for example, from preparing listening tapes for review.
- Tactile/kinaesthetic learners learn best through touch and movement, and will therefore like to work with hands-on manipulatives. They will also like role plays and activities which employ body parts as a mnemonic device, such as hand-signals.
- Print-oriented learners prefer to learn through reading.
- Interactive learners enjoy discussions with other pupils in small groups or during paired work.
- Olfactory learners benefit from the use of smell during learning. Associating certain lessons to particular smells can benefit these learners.

The distinction between inductive and deductive learners has also been looked at by learning styles researchers (Hodges, 1994). Inductive learners begin with observations or data and then infer governing rules and principles from these observations. They work from particulars to general principles, and want to know (1) what will the results to be derived help me know?; (2) what are the results?; and (3) how do I derive them? Deductive learners begin with general principles, then deduce consequences and phenomena from these. They work from generalities to particulars and want to know: (1) what are the results to be derived?; (2) how do I derive them?; and (3) how do I use them?

A final distinction that is sometimes made is of that between sequential and global learners. Sequential learners learn one thing at a time. They function well with partial understanding, are good at analysis and convergent thinking, but may sometimes miss the big picture. Global learners, on the other hand, learn in large chunks, don't function well with partial understanding, are good at synthesis and innovation, but are fuzzy on details and may appear to learn more slowly, especially at the beginning of a topic.

The evidence on learning styles

As can be seen from the above, there are a whole number of learning styles, one recent study finding a total of 71 different learning styles frameworks (Coffield et al., 2004). There are a number of commercial tools on the market designed to measure learning styles among pupils of various ages, such as the Learning Style Inventory (Dunn et al., 1985). However, while a number of these tips make intuitive sense, there is very little research that suggests that teaching to different learning styles actually aids pupils' achievement.

While some studies show a relationship between learning style and achievement (e.g. Burns et al., 1998; Uzuntiriyaki et al., 2003), in general there is very little evidence to support learning styles. In a large scale review of the evidence, Coffield et al. (2004) found that learning styles had weak theoretical grounding and close to no empirical support. Davis (1990) measured the learning styles of a group of second-grade pupils and changed the classroom environment to reflect their preferred learning styles. She found that a control group of pupils whose learning styles had not been taken into account outperformed the experimental group. Similar findings are reported by O'Sullivan et al. (1994), who found mixed effects of an intervention to help at-risk ninth graders through learning-style-based instruction. As well as a lack of evidence on the relationship of Kolb's learning styles to achievement, doubt has been cast on the validity of the concept, with Garner (2000), for example, finding no evidence of the existence of stable learning styles in his study using Kolb's Learning Styles Inventory.

Stahl (1999: 27), reviewing a number of studies on the effects of teaching different learning styles, concluded that: 'These five research reviews, published in well-regarded journals found the same thing. One cannot reliably measure children's learning styles and even if one could, matching children to reading programs by learning styles does not improve their learning.'

Cognitive Theory and Brain Research

What many of the older learning theories (like behaviourism and the theories of Vygotsky) were not able to incorporate was any theory of how the brain works (due to limitations in research methods at the time). More recently, however, brain research and the neurosciences have progressed greatly, and are informing learning theory and education to an ever-greater extent. To some extent, these new methods are confirming theories that we discussed earlier, like Vygotsky's views on learning, but they are also offering us important new insights.

Cognition and memory

One of the first major theories of learning that explicitly based itself on our emerging knowledge of the brain was cognitive information processing theory.

Especially important in this theory is the role of memory in learning processes. The memory consists of three parts: the sensory buffer, the working memory and the long-term memory.

The memory works as follows: one's experiences (tactile, visual or auditory) are registered in the sensory buffer, and then converted into the form in which they are employed in the working and long-term memories. The sensory buffer can register a lot of information, but can only hold it briefly. Some parts of the information in it will be lost, while other parts will be transmitted to the working memory. The working memory is where 'thinking gets done'. It receives its content from the sensory buffer and the long-term memory but has a limited capacity for storing information, a fact that limits human mental processes. The working memory contains the information that is actively being used at any one time.

The long-term memory has a nodal structure, and consists of neural network representations, whose nodes represent chunks in memory and whose links represent connections between those chunks. As such, nodes can be equated with concepts, and links with meaningful associations between concepts. Together these form schemata, or clusters of information. Activating one item of the cluster is likely to activate all of them (Best, 2000).

This means that memorization and making connections are two crucial components of learning, according to cognitive information processing theory.

Brain research

Brain research is also telling us that the brain is a pattern maker. The brain takes great pleasure in taking random and chaotic information and ordering it. The implications for learning and instruction are that presenting a learner with random and unordered information provides the maximum opportunity for the brain to order this information and form meaningful patterns that will be remembered. Setting up a learning environment in this way mirrors real life, which is often random and chaotic (Lackney, 1999). The brain, when allowed to express its pattern-making behaviour, creates coherency and meaning. Learning is best accomplished when the learning activity is connected directly to physical experience. We remember best when facts and skills are embedded in natural, real-life activity. We learn by doing. The implications of applying the findings of neuroscience related to coherency and meaning suggest that learning is facilitated in an environment of total immersion in a multitude of complex, interactive experiences which could include traditional instructional methods as part of this larger experience (Kotulak, 1996; Lackney, 1999).

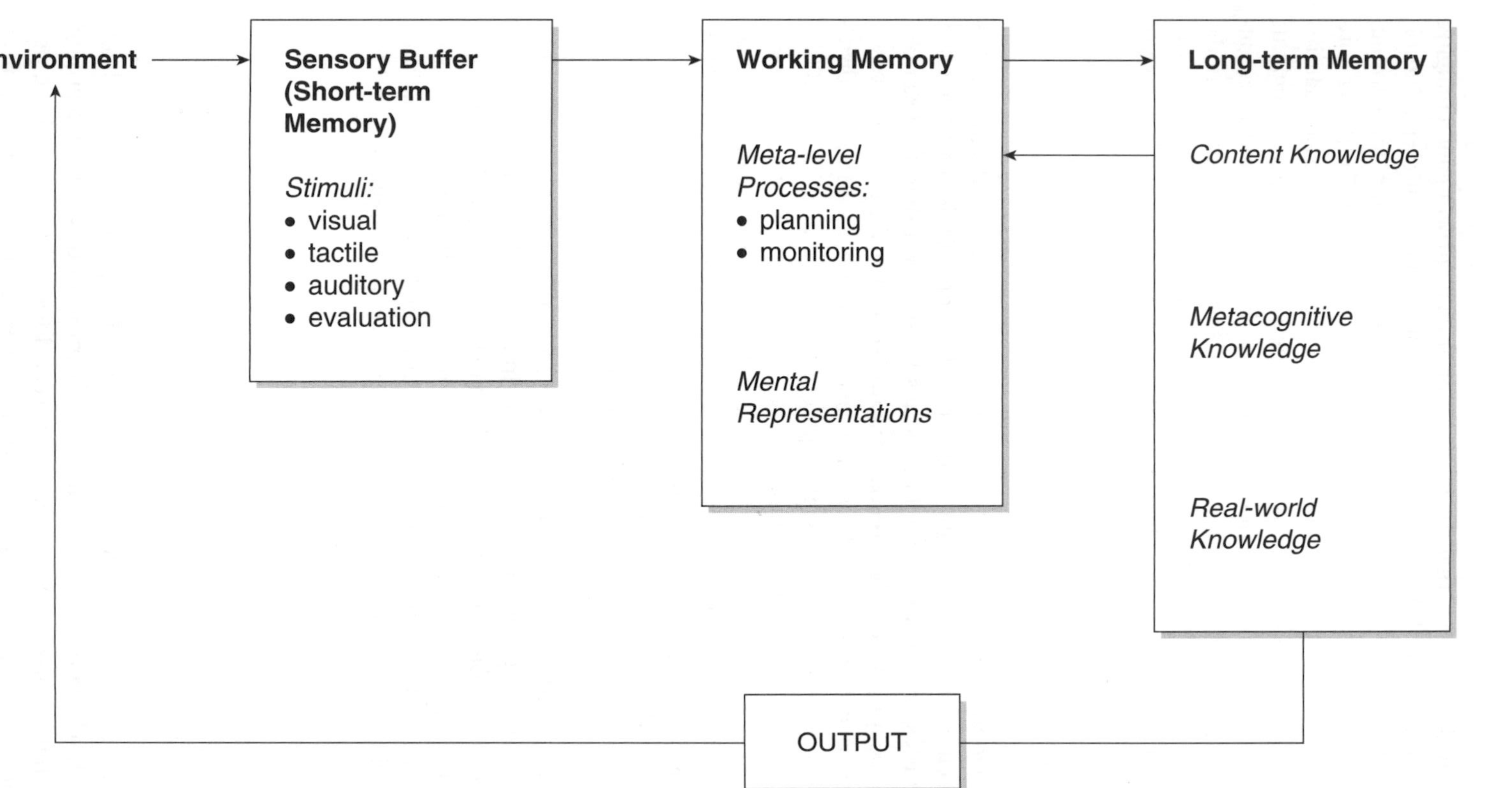

FIGURE 1.2 The structure of memory

Brain research also suggests that the brain is continually growing and changing throughout our life, but that this process is more pronounced at certain developmental stages, which can be seen as a 'window of opportunity' for learning. During childhood, this process of selectively strengthening and pruning connections in the brain is at its most intense, and it is therefore fair to say that this is a crucial period in development. Although this process continues throughout our lives, it seems to be most pronounced between the ages of 2 and 11, as different developmental areas emerge and taper off. During these critical periods, the brain demands specific and extensive (stimulating) inputs to create or consolidate neural networks, especially for acquiring language, emotional control and learning to play music. While one can learn outside of this period, what one has acquired during these windows of opportunity is crucial to what can subsequently be learned (Sousa, 1998).

Another important finding relates to the strong evidence of individual differences between the brain functioning of different learners. While the basic brain architecture is essentially the same, brain scans have shown that, for example, 'while most people, when they recognize an object visually, show increased activity in the back part of their brains, the exact magnitude, location, and distribution of that increased activity varies quite a bit' (Rose and Meyer, 2002). Similarly, learners differ in the strategies they employ to make connections in the brain (Dall'Alba, 2006). This is important for teachers, as it means both that, as constructivist educators have long claimed, each learner will construct knowledge in a slightly different way, and that teaching should be varied to address the different needs and strategies of learners, a finding that confirms the views of those who take a 'multiple intelligences' approach.

The final critical finding from recent brain research relates to the importance of emotion in learning. Emotions can both help and hinder learning. On the positive side, emotions help us to recall information from the long-term memory, through allowing any information received through the sensory buffer to be perceived as positive or a threat. Research suggests that the brain learns best when confronted with a balance between high challenge and low threat. The brain needs some challenge to activate emotions and learning. This is because if there is no stress the brain becomes too relaxed and cannot actively engage in learning. Too much stress is also negative, however, as it will lead to anxiety and a 'fight' response which are inimical to learning. A physically safe environment is particularly important in reducing overly strong levels of stress (Sousa, 1998).

Brain research is a constantly developing research field, and it is highly likely that further developments will in future strongly inform our views on learning, and our teaching strategies. However, one caveat does apply: while I have presented a number of basic findings, this research area is diverse. Findings from different studies do not always agree with one another, and are usually far more subtle than I have been able to outline in this introductory text. Also, it is always dangerous to try and directly translate findings from brain research into the classroom. This type of research should clearly inform us, but we need to take into account that it has been conducted for very different purposes, and will always need to be matched to educational research findings on effective classroom teaching before it can be translated into effective classroom strategies.

Summary

In this chapter, we have looked at some educationally influential theories of learning and intelligence.

Behaviourism was mainly concerned with how we learn from external stimuli. Using experimental methods, behaviourists looked at how behaviour can be conditioned, for example by providing rewards and punishments.

Piaget used observation to come to his theories of learning. He was particularly interested in the ways children develop. This happens through *maturation*, whereby our genetic growth creates change, and through *activity,* whereby children act on their environment and learn from this. An important finding of Piaget's is that growing up does not just mean knowing more, it actually entails a change in how we think.

Vygotsky concentrated on the ways in which learning is a social process. We learn through interaction with others, both of the same age and of a higher age and developmental level. This process operates through *scaffolding* in the *zone of proximal development*. The ZPD is the gap between what a person is able to do alone and what s/he can do with the help of someone more knowledgeable or skilled than him/herself. Scaffolding refers to the way others can help us to bridge that gap.

IQ theory focuses on the concept of intelligence. According to IQ theorists, there is one underlying, general intelligence that determines our capacity for learning. More recently, Gardner developed his theory of multiple intelligences. Rather than just the one intelligence, Gardner claims that there are a number of different intelligences, such as musical and visual/spatial intelligence. For most tasks, we need to use more than one intelligence.

Brain research is a fast-developing area in psychology, which is producing valuable findings for educators. One of these is that we learn best when challenged but not stressed. Another is the importance of pattern making in the brain. This implies that we need to provide children with the opportunity to create patterns. Finally, brain research confirms that while we can learn throughout our life, early childhood is a key period in developing (the capacity for) learning.

Reflective Questions

1. Thinking about your own practice, in what ways do you think learning theories influence the way you teach?
2. Thinking about your own learning, how well do you think learning theories describe how you learn?
3. What elements of behaviourist theories might be useful to the way we teach?
4. What elements of learning styles theory might be useful to the way we teach?

CHAPTER 2

DIRECT INSTRUCTION

Key Points

In this chapter, you will learn about:

- direct instruction and what it means
- evidence for the effectiveness of this strategy
- specific behaviours that have been found to enhance pupil learning
- some models of direct instruction
- limitations and criticisms of the direct instruction model
- how to use seatwork effectively.

Introduction

In this and the following chapters, we will discuss what research has to say about one of the most widely used and most effective teaching methods: direct instruction.

'Direct instruction', also known as 'active teaching' or 'whole-class teaching', refers to a teaching style in which the teacher is actively engaged in bringing the content of the lesson to pupils by teaching the whole class directly. This has long been found to be an important aspect of effective teaching, and a number of studies have shown that what the teacher does has a strong influence on pupil outcomes (for a recent study of the impact of teachers on pupil performance, see Nye et al., 2004).

Whole-class teaching has been employed in schools for a long time, but the effectiveness of whole-class teaching methods hasn't been scientifically studied until quite recently. Interest in this style of teaching took off with the 'teacher effectiveness' school of research, which started in the late 1960s, following the failure of attempts to explain differences in the performance of teachers by looking at their personalities. In contrast, teacher effectiveness researchers decided to look at the actual behaviours of teachers in classrooms, observing lessons and linking the behaviours they observed to pupil outcomes such as scores on standardized tests. This research school started in a period in which policy was moving towards 'child-centred' strategies in many countries (such as the USA and the UK), which often degenerated into lessons in which pupils spent most of their time working from worksheets on their own, while the teacher would sit at her desk marking pupils' work.

The early teacher effectiveness researchers in the USA gradually started to find patterns which indicated that more effective teachers (that is, teachers whose pupils made stronger gains on standardized achievement tests) tended to actively teach the whole class, spending significantly more time explicitly lecturing, demonstrating or interacting with the class than less effective teachers (Rosenshine, 1979a). As well as actively teaching the whole class for more of the time, effective teachers used a number of behaviours that will be identified in this and the next three chapters.

After this initial research had identified a number of behaviours that were effective, researchers decided to put theory into practice by training teachers to use these effective methods and subsequently testing whether this would actually make a difference to pupil achievement. One of the first and most important of these programmes was the Missouri Mathematics Effectiveness Study conducted by Good and Grouws (1979) in the late 1970s. In this study, 40 teachers were divided into two groups. One group of teachers received training in the effective direct instruction behaviours identified in previous research, while the other group continued to teach as before. It was found not only that the 'trained' group did indeed use the strategies they were taught, but that their pupils made more gains on the test than did those taught by the control teachers. A similar study was conducted by Fitzpatrick (1982) for English teaching, and he similarly found that these behaviours could successfully be taught to teachers, and that teachers using them were more able to engage pupils in their classroom. A recent study which used a quasi-experimental method where pupils were divided into two groups also found that those taught using direct instruction methods outperformed those in the comparison group (Nye et al., 2004). Reviews of school improvement programmes similarly support the use of direct instruction models (Stringfield et al., 1997).

A number of studies outside the USA reported the same positive findings for whole-class teaching methods. In the UK, three major (non-experimental) studies of teacher effectiveness have been conducted in the last few decades. The first of these, Galton's ORACLE project, found that teachers labelled as 'class enquirers' generated the greatest gains in mathematics and language, but that this finding did not extend to reading. By contrast, the group of 'individual monitoring' teachers made amongst the least progress. It is important to note that the more successful 'class enquirers' group spent four times as much time using whole-class interactive teaching than the 'individual monitors' (Croll, 1996; Galton and Croll, 1980).

The second important British teacher effectiveness study is the Junior School Project of Mortimore et al. (1988), based upon a four-year cohort study of 50 primary schools, which involved collecting a considerable volume of data on children and their family backgrounds ('intakes'), school and classroom 'processes' and 'outcomes' in academic (reading, mathematics) and affective (e.g. self-conception, attendance, behaviour) areas. This study reported on factors that were associated with effectiveness both across outcome areas and within specific subjects such as mathematics. Significant positive relationships were found with such factors as structured sessions, use of higher-order questions and statements, frequent questioning, restricting sessions to a single area of work, involvement of pupils and the proportion of time utilized in communicating with the whole class. Negative relationships were found with teachers spending a high proportion of their time communicating with individual pupils (Mortimore et al., 1988), which once again suggests that use of whole-class teaching is beneficial to pupils.

More recently, a classroom observation study of over 100 mathematics teachers in England and Wales also found that the effective behaviours we will discuss below were able to distinguish effective from ineffective teachers, and that it was teachers who spent more time teaching the whole class as opposed to teaching individual pupils whose pupils showed stronger gains in mathematics achievement (Muijs and Reynolds, 1999, 2001, 2002).

Studies in continental Europe tend to support this viewpoint (Creemers, 1994). However, a review of Dutch research found disappointing results, with whole-class teaching being positively related to pupil outcomes at the primary level in just 4 studies out of 29 (and negatively related in none), while differentiation and cooperation were negatively related to outcomes in 2 and 3 studies respectively, and positively related to outcomes in none (Scheerens and Creemers, 1996). However, where significant results are obtained, they tend to support the conclusions of the American and British studies (Creemers, 1994; Westerhof, 1992).

More evidence comes from international comparative research, such as the 'Worlds Apart' report (Reynolds and Farrell, 1996) in the UK, which compared teaching methods in England to those employed in countries that did better in international studies of pupils' achievement such as Singapore. The authors found that one of the main factors that distinguished these more successful countries from England was a more widespread use of whole-class interactive teaching.

There are several reasons why this whole-class approach has been found to be more effective than individualized learning approaches. One of these is that studies have found that whole-class teaching actually allows the teacher to make more contacts with each individual pupil than individual work. And, as we will discuss further on in this book, interaction between pupils and the teacher is a crucial aspect of successful teaching and learning. Pupils have also been found to be more likely to be on task during whole-class sessions than during individualized instruction. This is mainly because it is easier for the teacher to monitor the whole class while teaching than to monitor individual pupils. Whole-class teaching also allows the teacher to easily change and vary activities and to react quickly to signs that pupils are switching off, either through lack of understanding of the content or through boredom. It also allows mistakes and misconceptions made by pupils to be illustrated to the whole class. Furthermore, some other arrangements, in particular those in which different pupils or groups of pupils are doing different activities within the classroom, are more complex, and therefore more difficult to manage effectively than a whole-class setting in which pupils are mainly doing the same thing (Brophy and Good, 1986; Rosenshine and Stevens, 1986). Whole-class teaching also fits in with some of the theories of learning we discussed in the previous chapter. As for behaviourist approaches, the need for direct instruction of pupils fits in with what we know about the structure of memory. In particular, as we discussed in Chapter 1, the long-term memory is key to learning, in that a number of studies suggest that learning happens through making connections in the long-term memory and between new knowledge stored in the short-term memory and what knowledge is already available in the long-term memory. Also, research has shown that problem solving relies strongly on being able to access a variety of strategies stored in the long-term memory. This means that the more information we have stored in the long-term memory, the easier we are likely to assimilate and use new knowledge. Therefore, direct instruction, as the most rapid way of attaining new knowledge, is important to developing our ability to learn (Kirschner et al., 2006).

Evidence suggests that direct instruction is particularly helpful for pupils from low SES backgrounds and low-attaining pupils (Muijs and Reynolds, 2006; Schippen et al., 2005).

This, however, does not mean that teachers should spend the whole lesson teaching the whole class. Individual or group practice remains an essential part of the lesson if pupil learning is to be maximized, as pupils have to have the opportunity to reinforce their learning. It would also be wrong to equate whole-class teaching with passive reception of learning by students. The theoretical underpinning of this type of teaching stresses the fact that learners need to be active to learn, and active engagement in the lesson is necessary.

The Main Elements of Effective Direct Instruction

It is not enough merely to teach the whole class in order to have an effective direct instruction lesson. A number of conditions need to be met in order to ensure this. These will be discussed here.

Clearly structured lessons

The lesson should have a clear structure, so pupils can easily understand the content of the lesson and how it relates to what they already know. Many researchers recommend starting the lesson with a review and practice of what was learnt during the previous lesson, for example by going over homework, as this will allow the teacher to find out to what extent pupils have grasped the content of previous lessons, and therefore to what extent this content will need to be *retaught.*

The objectives of the lesson should be made clear to pupils from the outset, with examples such as 'today we are going to learn about …', or through writing the objectives on the board or on a flipchart. During the lesson, the teacher needs to emphasize the key points of the lesson, which may otherwise get lost in the whole. A certain amount of repetition will certainly do no harm here. At the end of the lesson, the main points should once again be summarized, either by the teacher or, preferably, by the pupils themselves, such as through asking them what they have learnt during the lesson. Subparts of the lesson can usefully be summarized in the same way during the course of the lesson. Teachers must also clearly signal transitions between lesson parts such as the start of a new topic or practise of the previous topic. All this ensures not only that pupils will remember better what they have learnt, but will help them to more easily understand the content as an integrated whole, with recognition of the relationships between the parts. This emphasis on explaining the goals of the lesson – not just what was to be done during this lesson, but how that related to what pupils could learn longer term – was found to be typical of effective teachers from the start of the school year in one study of primary classrooms (Bohn et al., 2004).

It is also recommended that teachers build a certain amount of redundancy into the lesson, in the form of repeating and reviewing general rules and key concepts, in order to facilitate pupil retention and understanding of the topic. This is particularly important for more demanding topics or rules. Teachers would also do well to explain such demanding topics using a variety of media and methods, in order to help pupils with different learning styles (Borich, 1996; Brophy, 1992; Reynolds and Muijs, 1999b; Rosenshine and Stevens, 1986).

Clear, structured presentations

Within this overall structure, it is recommended that material should be presented in small steps pitched at the pupils' level, which are then practised before going on to the next step. This allows pupils to gain a sense of mastery over the content and will stop pupils getting bored or losing the thread of the lesson. Information should be presented with a high degree of clarity and enthusiasm. Teachers need to focus on one point at a time, avoid digressions and avoid ambiguous phrases or pronouns.

There are a number of ways to enhance the clarity of presentations. Two traditional models of presenting a topic are the *deductive* model and the *inductive* model.

- In the *deductive* model, the presentation starts with general principles or rules and goes on to more detailed and specific examples. An example of this is teaching comparative democracy. One could start with the general principle of what democracy means, and then attempt to apply this to the political system of a variety of countries.
- In the *inductive* model, the presentation starts with (real-life) examples and moves on to general rules or principles. Using the same examples, one could look at the system of government in a number of different countries, and then work out some general principles of what makes for democratic government.

Borich (1996) suggests a number of other methods for structuring content:

- The *part–whole format*. A topic is introduced in its most general form, and then divided into easily distinguishable (and digestible) subparts. The teacher should make sure that the subparts are clearly and explicitly related to the whole. Borich gives the example of teaching the possessive by first explaining what a possessive is, and then dividing it into rules for 'of' phrases (the daughter of) and 's' phrases (the holiday of).

- A second method is *sequential ordering*. With this method, the content/rule is taught in the order in which it occurs in the real world. This method is often used in teaching mathematical rules. Another example is teaching how the steel making process works, by going through the different stages from iron ore to finished product.
- It is also possible to use *combinatorial relationships*. In this method, the teacher brings together the various decisions or elements that influence the use of rules, facts or sequences in a single format. For example, in teaching law, you could draw together all the influences on the process of making a particular law.
- Finally, in the *comparative relationships* method, different elements are placed side by side so that learners can compare and contrast them. One could, for example, compare two different beliefs in religious studies in this way.

Another recommended practice in presentation is to break up the lesson into smaller component tasks, linked to clear goals. Activities within these components need to be designed so that students can clearly develop mastery of what they are intended to learn, before moving on to the next part of the lesson (Joyce et al., 2000).

Pacing

Pacing of the lesson is an important, but not wholly uncontroversial, part of effective direct instruction. Initially, researchers suggested that lessons need to be fast-paced, and a recent study of effective primary teaching in maths and literacy has found that the more effective teachers used a higher pace than the less effective teachers (Smith et al., 2004). The advantages of this are seen to lie in maintaining momentum and the interest of pupils, and in allowing a relatively large amount of content to be processed. However, it has been found that while this seems to be the best way to teach lower-level basic skills and younger pupils, in higher grades and for more demanding content, the pacing often needs to be slower to allow pupils more time to develop understanding. It is recommended by teacher effectiveness researchers that lessons designed to teach basic skills are paced in such a way that during weekly or monthly reviews pupils are able to respond correctly in 90–95 per cent of cases.

Modelling

A useful procedure to follow when teaching certain topics is to explicitly model a skill or procedure. Modelling means demonstrating a procedure to learners. This can be more effective than using verbal explanations, especially with younger learners or those who prefer a visual learning style. Modelling follows the following sequence: the teacher (or another person who is perceived to be an expert) demonstrates the behaviour by doing it, linking the behaviour to skills or behaviours that learners already possess. S/he needs to go through the different parts of the behaviour in a clear, structured and sequential way, explaining what s/he is doing after each step. Then learners need to memorize the steps seen, and imitate them (Ausubel, 1968). To be effective, modelling needs to be followed by practice, and effective teachers have been found to carefully monitor how well new practices or methods are used by their pupils and to provide appropriate feedback (Bohn et al., 2004).

Use of conceptual mapping

A strategy that can help to structure the lesson in pupils' minds is the use of conceptual mapping. A conceptual map is a framework that can be presented to pupils before the topic of the lesson is presented, providing the pupil with an overview linking different parts of a topic and with a ready-made structure (or schema). This helps pupils to store, package and retain the concepts, and to link different lessons to one another. This is especially useful for more complex topics, which take several lessons to cover. An example of this is the conceptual map for a history topic given in Figure 2.1.

Interactive questioning

A crucial part of the direct instruction lesson is interactive questioning. Because of its importance to effective teaching, and as there is a lot of research on this element, it will be discussed separately in the next chapter.

While direct instruction can be a very effective teaching method, it will not work without the inclusion of an element of practice, as it is essential for pupils to be able to practise what they have learnt so they can retain it. Individual practice is usually called seatwork. As we will see in the next chapter, an increasingly popular alternative to individual practice is group work.

The main elements of effective seatwork are summarized below.

Preparing seatwork

A first essential element to bear in mind when preparing seatwork is to make sure that there is enough material available for pupils to use during individual practice. If worksheets are used, it is imperative not only to prepare enough worksheets so each child has one, but also to have some work as a 'backup' in case some or all pupils finish the task faster than expected. If the task requires

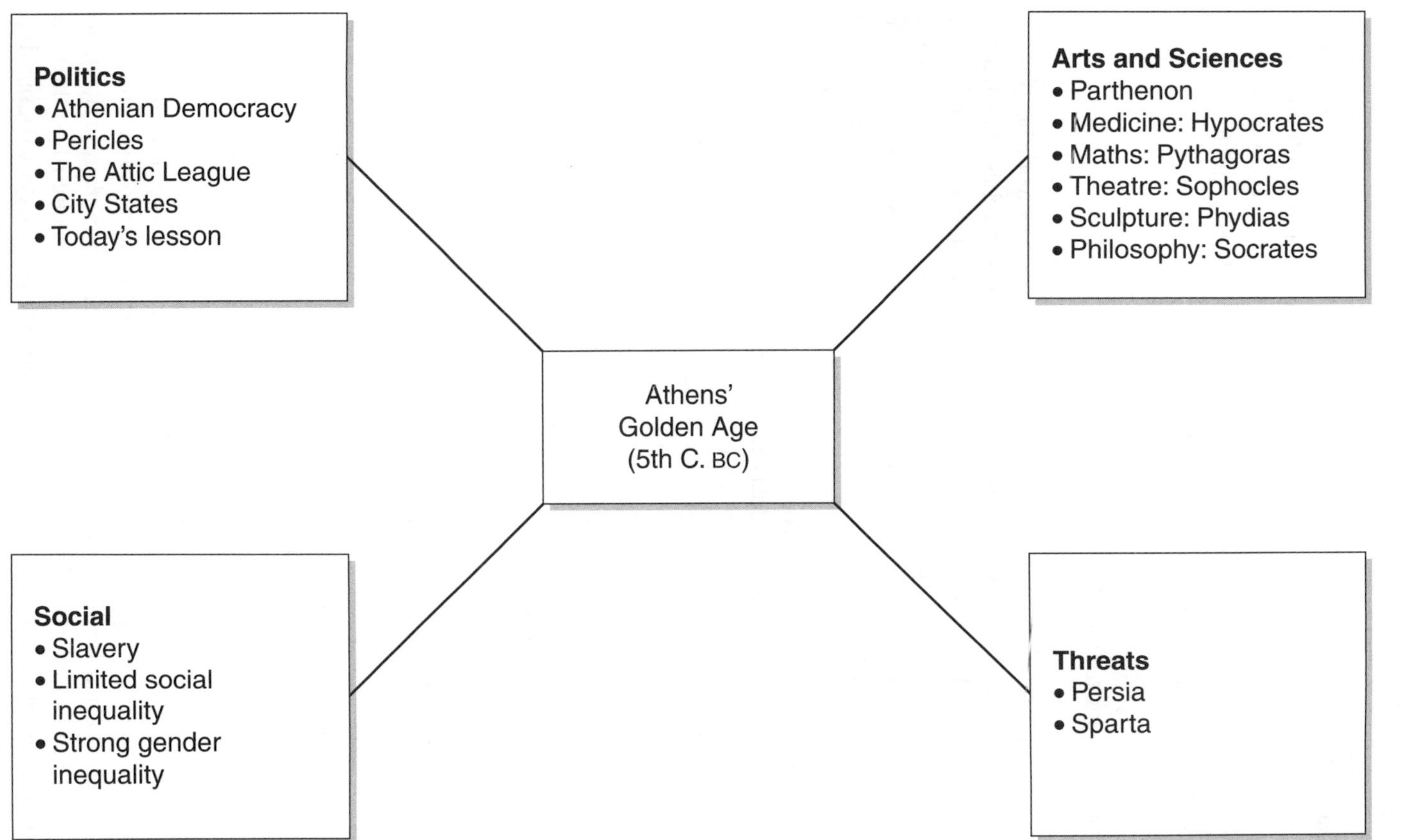

FIGURE 2.1 Conceptual map: the Golden Age of Ancient Athens

use of manipulatives or materials, such as number lines or scissors, the teacher must make sure that enough of these are available as well.

The seatwork task needs to tie in with the objectives of the lesson and previously learnt material, and needs to be tailored to pupils' ability levels. Seatwork needs to take place as soon as possible after the questioning (guided practice) part of the lesson. In this way, pupils will make fewer mistakes, enhancing their feelings of mastery over the content of the lesson.

Use of workbooks/textbooks

Frequently, seatwork will consist of exercises from workbooks or worksheets. Both can be effective and have advantages and disadvantages. Using published schemes, textbooks and workbooks makes preparation for seatwork less time-consuming, and attractively illustrated books can motivate (especially younger) pupils. However, teachers need to ensure that the exercises in the workbook are suitable for their pupils and tie in with the goals of the lesson and the content taught. If using a direct instruction approach, it is also advisable to use a scheme that has been designed with such an approach in mind rather than one that has been designed to accommodate an individual learning approach. Worksheets are usually less attractively presented and can be a lot of work, in particular if the teacher has to devise the exercises herself. The major advantage of worksheets is that they can be tailored accurately to reflect the goals of the lesson, and allow the teacher to lift content from a variety of sources. Generally speaking, slavishly following a particular scheme of work is not to be recommended as this may not suit the pupils or the content of the lesson and also because the use of a variety of schemes and workbooks gives access to a wider range of good ideas for teachers to use.

Organizing seatwork

As with the lesson as a whole, teachers need to clearly state the goals of seatwork to pupils. It can be necessary to make clear exactly what the (cognitive) reasons are for doing seatwork so pupils do not perceive it as merely filling time. The process goals need to be explained as well, as pupils can easily see the goal of seatwork as merely giving the right answers to specific questions (Arends, 1998).

The task needs to be clearly explained and needs to be unambiguous. If during seatwork monitoring it appears that the task has not been well understood by many pupils, the teacher may need to stop the work and explain it again. To ensure that pupils understand what they need to do, it is useful to go through the first task with the whole class. The teacher needs to make clear to pupils that the task is one they can succeed at.

During seatwork, pupils need to be continually monitored by the teacher. S/he has to go round checking pupils' work, both to ensure that pupils remain on task and to check for pupils' understanding. If pupils seem to be having difficulties with the task, the teacher needs to intervene to help them. If a substantial part of the class seems to be having a particular problem, the teacher may need to stop seatwork and go over the problem with the whole class before letting the pupils return to the assignment. The teacher needs to be approachable; pupils must feel they can ask the teacher for help.

A problem that can occur during seatwork is that the teacher ends up spending quite a bit of time helping a particular pupil or group of pupils and as a result fails to monitor the rest of the class. To avoid this becoming a problem, it is necessary when helping a pupil to occasionally stop to monitor the rest of the class, to check whether other pupils are having problems or getting off task. Emmer et al. (1997) recommend giving roughly an equal amount of time to all pupils, and not spending too much time with one or a group of pupils. During some lessons, it can be useful for teachers to mark pupils' work as they go round the class. Seatwork requires active teacher involvement that cannot be limited to sitting behind the desk waiting for pupils to come to her/him with problems.

The teacher also needs to be clear on whether and when talking is allowed during seatwork. Obviously if seatwork is meant to be collaborative, talking will be allowed but if the task is not supposed to be collaborative, it may be necessary to restrict talking or, in some cases, to prohibit it altogether. Seating arrangements can either facilitate or hinder pupil talk, i.e. seating pupils in groups around tables will encourage talk, while seating pupils in rows will make this more difficult (Arends, 1998; Johnson and Johnson, 1994).

Feedback on seatwork

In order for seatwork not to be perceived as a time-filler, pupils need to receive feedback on the tasks they have been doing. Feedback can be provided in a number of ways. During seatwork, the teacher can go round marking pupils' work and giving some verbal feedback to pupils while they are working. During seatwork, the teacher can also get pupils to check on each other's work. Alternatively, she can collect in workbooks or worksheets and mark them outside of teaching time. A useful approach can be to go over seatwork during the final whole-class section of the lesson. Pupils can be asked for their answers or, if seatwork was differentiated, pupils can be asked to tell the class what their group has been doing. The teacher should aim for a high success rate in seatwork aimed at basic skills instruction, with most learners getting at least 60–80 per cent of answers right.

Differentiating seatwork?

A further decision that needs to be made before assigning seatwork is whether or not to differentiate tasks. There can be two different reasons for doing this. Firstly, the teacher can decide to tailor the task to different ability levels in the classroom. Whether or not to do this will depend on the spread of ability in the classroom. This ability spread may be particularly large in mixed-ability (as opposed to set) classrooms, and can be more pronounced in deprived areas, where the spread of ability appears to be greater as, although due to social disadvantage the average levels are lower in these areas, there are usually some highly able pupils even in schools in these areas (Muijs and Reynolds, 1999). Another reason to differentiate seatwork can be to let pupils do different parts of a task which can then be brought together during a whole-class session. This can help illustrate to pupils the advantages of collaboration and interdependence and help maintain interest during the whole-class review, as what other pupils have done will be directly relevant to their own work. If seatwork is differentiated, the teacher needs to make sure that seating arrangements reflect this, in particular if pupils are allowed to discuss their work with each other.

Why Practice is Important for Pupil Learning

The main learning goals of independent practice are *automaticity* and *unitization*.

Automaticity refers to processes becoming so well embedded in pupils' long-term memory that they no longer require conscious attention. For example, when first learning handwriting, the formation of every word requires careful and thorough attention. However, once it has been thoroughly learned, the process becomes *automatic*. It is important that processes like that become automatic in order to free space in the short-term memory for the execution of more complex tasks (Woolfolk, 1997).

Unitization is a different process, and refers to the bringing together of facts and procedures into sequences that can be used for actual problem solving. Independent seatwork allows pupils to do this under the teacher's guidance in a controlled environment. To make sure that unitization occurs, the teacher must ensure that pupils have to consider all these disparate facts and procedures to be able to solve the problem, and have to connect them into one fluent sequence of action.

Some Examples of Direct Instruction

Several models of direct instruction have been developed over the years. We will discuss a number of them here, in order to provide a clearer view of what direct instruction means in practice. One of the first models to be put into practice was the Active Teaching Model, developed for the Missouri Mathematics Effectiveness Project (Good et al., 1983). On the basis of extant research findings, a primary school teaching model was designed, which teachers were trained to implement. Lessons were to be structured as follows:

(a) Daily Review (+/– 8 minutes, except on Mondays)
   1. Review concepts and skills associated with yesterday's homework
   2. Collect and deal with homework assignment
   3. Provide several mental computation exercises

(b) Development (+/– 20 minutes) (introducing new concepts, developing understanding)
   1. Briefly focus on prerequisite skills and concepts
   2. Focus on meaning and promoting pupil understanding by lively explanations, demonstrations etc.
   3. Assess pupil competence
      a. Using process and product questions (active interaction)
      b. Using controlled practice
   4. Repeat and elaborate on the meaning portion as necessary

(c) Seatwork (+/– 15 minutes)
   1. Provide uninterrupted successful practice
   2. Momentum – keep the ball rolling – get everyone involved, then sustain involvement
   3. Alerting – let pupils know their work will be checked at the end of each period
   4. Accountability – check the pupils' work

(d) Homework assignment
   1. Assign on a regular basis at the end of each maths class except Fridays
   2. Should involve about 15 minutes of work to be done at home
   3. Should include one or two review problems

(e) Special reviews
   1. Weekly review
      a. Conduct during the first 20 minutes on Mondays
      b. Focus on skills and concepts covered during the previous week
   2. Monthly review
      a. Conduct every fourth Monday
      b. Focus on skills and concepts covered since the last review

As mentioned above, this programme was highly successful, and a slightly revised secondary version of the Active Mathematics Teaching model was also found to be effective. Programmes based on the same teacher-effectiveness principles but with modifications suited to the particular contexts, have been implemented on a smaller scale in the USA, such as Griffin and Barnes' (1986) CTP project, which also showed good results (Schaffer, 1997).

One of the most ambitious applications of a direct instruction model was developed in England in the form of the National Literacy and National Numeracy Strategies developed in the second half of the 1990s. These were developed as a result of worries about the performance of English pupils in these two subjects, and have been strongly inspired by research showing the effectiveness of direct instruction.

The English 'National Numeracy Strategy' for the teaching of primary mathematics was also inspired by the direct instruction model, but takes a less prescriptive approach, outlining general teaching strategies rather than setting out a strictly delineated time for each part of the lesson. This influence is clearly evident on the education ministry (Department for Education and Employment) website, where teachers are advised to 'spend as much time as possible in direct teaching and questioning of the whole class, a group of pupils, or individuals'. It is further stated that 'Direct teaching and good interaction are as important in group work and paired work as they are in whole-class work but organising pupils as a "whole class" for a significant proportion of the time helps to maximise their contact with you so that every child benefits from the teaching and interaction for sustained periods' (DfEE, 1999). Suggested teaching guidelines illustrate this further:

- **Directing**: sharing your teaching objectives with the class, ensuring that pupils know what to do, and drawing attention to points over which they should take particular care, such as how a graph should be labelled, the degree of accuracy needed when making a measurement, or how work can be set out.
- **Instructing**: giving information and structuring it well – for example, describing how to multiply a three-digit number by a two-digit number, how to interpret a graph, how to develop a mathematical argument.
- **Demonstrating**: showing, describing and modelling mathematics using appropriate resources and visual displays – for example, showing how to scribe numerals, showing how to measure using a metre stick or a protractor, demonstrating on a number line how to add on by bridging through 10, using a thermometer to demonstrate the use of negative numbers.
- **Explaining and illustrating**: giving accurate, well-paced explanations, and referring to previous work or methods – for example, explaining a method of calculation and discussing why it works, giving the meaning of a mathematical term, explaining the steps in the solution to a problem, giving

examples that satisfy a general statement, illustrating how the statement $7 - 3 = 4$ can represent different situations.

- **Questioning and discussing**: questioning in ways which match the direction and pace of the lesson and ensure that all pupils take part (if needed, supported by apparatus or a communication aid, or by an adult who translates, signs or uses symbols), listening carefully to pupils' responses and responding constructively in order to take forward their learning, using open and closed questions, skilfully framed, adjusted and targeted to make sure that pupils of all abilities are involved and contribute to discussions, allowing pupils time to think through answers before inviting a response.
- **Consolidating**: maximizing opportunities to reinforce and develop what has been taught, through a variety of activities in class and well-focused tasks to do at home, asking pupils either with a partner or as a group to reflect on and talk through a process, inviting them to expand their ideas and reasoning, or to compare and then refine their methods and ways of recording their work, getting them to think of different ways of approaching a problem, asking them to generalize or to give examples that match a general statement.
- **Evaluating pupils' responses**: identifying mistakes, using them as positive teaching points by talking about them and any misconceptions that led to them, discussing pupils' justifications of the methods or resources they have chosen, evaluating pupils' presentations of their work to the class, giving them oral feedback on their written work.
- **Summarizing**: reviewing during and towards the end of a lesson the mathematics that has been taught and what pupils have learned, identifying and correcting misunderstandings, inviting pupils to present their work and picking out key points and ideas, making links to other work in mathematics and other subjects, giving pupils an insight into the next stage of their learning.

All the examples above are essentially 'three-part lessons' starting with a whole-class session, followed by individual/group practice and a final whole-class session at the end of the lesson. This is not the only model possible in direct instruction. Alternatives have been developed, such as short whole-class presentations followed by individual practice, which is followed by the next short whole-class session, etc. There is no evidence that this is either more or less effective than the three-part lesson strategy.

A recent development is the use of this type of model for the design of online instruction. Programmes such as SuccessMaker are clearly predicated on this basic model, as are many applications of online learning that follow the steps of going through sequences of information, practice to mastery and then on to the next step (Magliaro et al., 2005).

Weaknesses and Limitations of Direct Instruction

While, as illustrated above, direct instruction is one of the most effective teaching strategies available, it is not necessarily the best strategy to use in all circumstances.

Direct instruction has been found to be the best method to teach rules, procedures and basic skills, especially to younger pupils (Good and Brophy, 1986). However, when the goals of the lesson are more complex or open-ended (e.g. developing pupils' thinking skills, or discussing the merits of different electoral systems), the structured and teacher-directed approach that characterizes direct instruction is less effective. More open-ended models may be more appropriate for achieving these goals (Joyce and Weil, 1996).

The effectiveness of direct instruction also seems to depend on the characteristics of the pupils taught. The highly structured approach seems to be particularly effective for pupils from disadvantaged backgrounds, or pupils starting from a low level of achievement in a particular subject. For example, in a recent study in England and Wales, relationships between pupil achievement and direct instruction-style teacher behaviours were twice as high in schools with a high or average percentage of pupils from deprived backgrounds than in schools with a low percentage of pupils from deprived backgrounds. This suggests that these pupils are more in need of explicit teaching (Muijs and Reynolds, 2000c).

A further problem with direct instruction is that the role of pupils may become too passive, leading to overdependence on the teacher and underdevelopment of independent learning skills (Gipps and McGilchrist, 1999).

The evidence on direct instruction is also skewed towards primary-age pupils and the subjects of mathematics and English. More research in other subjects and in secondary schools is needed to see whether this method is supported in those settings as well (Campbell et al., 2004).

Further, it has to be remarked that it is entirely possible to use effective direct teaching strategies to teach undemanding and unchallenging content, or to teach in a way that does not suitably connect material. Finally, in some cases, direct instruction can degenerate into ineffective lecture-style ('chalk and talk') lessons with little interaction with pupils.

Therefore, deciding whether or not to use a direct instruction model must depend on the goals of the lesson, and must be linked to good subject knowledge and suitable lesson content in order to be effective. Moreover, as we saw in Chapter 1, there is increasing evidence from brain research and constructivist learning theory that traditional direct instruction methods may not be those that fit most closely with the way we learn.

Summary

In this chapter, we have learnt more about one of the most widely used and also most effective teaching strategies at the disposal of teachers: direct instruction.

Direct instruction is based on an active role for the teacher, who is central in bringing the content of the lesson to pupils by teaching the whole class. This teaching method was found to be effective in a large number of studies that linked findings from classroom observation to measures of pupil outcomes.

There are a number of elements that need to be in place for a direct instruction lesson to be effective.

Firstly, the lesson as a whole needs to be well structured, with the objectives of the lesson clearly laid out, key points emphasized, and main points summarized at the end.

Teachers need to present the material they are teaching in small steps. Pupils need to fully master these before going on to the next part. Each step itself needs to be well structured and clear.

The pace of the lesson needs to be fast for lower-level skills, while leaving more time for reflection when the goal of the lesson calls for higher-level skills.

The use of advance organizers and modelling can help aid lesson clarity.

Examples of direct instruction models were given, one of the first being the Missouri Mathematics Enhancement model, and two of the most recent being the English National Literacy and Numeracy Strategies.

Direct instruction does have its limitations. It is not effective with all differential pupils and is more suited to teaching basic skills than to teaching higher-order thinking skills.

Individual practice, also known as seatwork, is an important part of direct instruction, but again certain conditions need to be in place to make it effective. Seatwork needs to be well prepared and needs to tie in clearly with the objectives and goals of the lesson. While it is normal that seatwork will often take the form of doing exercises in a workbook or on worksheets, it is important not to slavishly follow a publisher's scheme, but to tailor seatwork to the objectives of the lesson and the pupils being taught.

Teachers need to monitor the whole class during seatwork to ensure all pupils stay on task. They need to go round the class helping pupils experiencing problems without staying with one or a group of pupils for too long.

Reflective Questions

1. In what circumstances do you think it would not be useful to use direct instruction? When wouldn't it be the right approach?
2. Think of a presentation you have used or encountered in teaching. How could you make it more effective?
3. How do you think direct instruction relates to the learning theories we discussed in Chapter 1?
4. Can you design a direct instruction lesson to teach a topic of your choice?
5. What do you think the most important limitations of the direct instruction approach are?
6. Think of the last time you used or encountered seatwork. What aspects could you improve on?

CHAPTER 3

INTERACTIVE TEACHING

Key Points

In this chapter, you will learn about:

- the importance of interaction in direct instruction
- what are seen as the main elements of effective questioning techniques, according to research in this area
- how class discussion is related to questioning
- how you can avoid disadvantaging girls and shyer pupils.

Introduction

As we saw in the previous chapter, in order to be effective, direct instruction has to be far more than lecture-style delivery of content to pupils. Almost all researchers agree on the importance of interaction between teachers and pupils, and the studies reviewed in the previous chapter pointed not only to the importance of spending a substantial part of the lesson teaching the whole class, but also to the importance of teaching in an interactive way.

For example, in their study of primary school pupils in England, Mortimore et al. (1988) found positive effects for the use of frequent questioning, communicating with the class and the use of 'higher order' questions and statements. Another study in England and Wales also demonstrated the importance of interaction to effective teaching, again factors such as using a high frequency of questions, use of open-ended questions, asking pupils to explain their answers and using academic questions being significantly related to pupil achievement. In this study, interactive teaching overall was one of the factors most strongly related to pupil outcomes (Muijs and Reynolds, 1999). More recently, effective teachers were seen to ask more questions than less effective teachers in English primary classrooms (Smith et al., 2003). Similarly, Veenman (1992) found this to be a crucial element of direct instruction in his research in the Netherlands.

American researchers had already demonstrated the importance of interaction in their research prior to these European studies. Rosenshine and Furst (1973) found the use of a wide variety of questions to be a crucial factor in their research from the 1960s and early 1970s. This was confirmed in later studies, such as those mentioned in the previous chapters (Brophy, 1992; Brophy and Good, 1986; Creemers, 1994; Good et al., 1983; Rosenshine and Stevens, 1986).

American researchers have done more than merely demonstrate the importance of interactive teaching. They have studied in detail what constitutes effective interaction and questioning techniques. These findings will be discussed in the next section.

Questioning

Due to its importance, questioning is one of the most widely studied elements in teaching research. Therefore, we know quite a bit about what effective questioning entails. This evidence, taken from the research discussed earlier (Bennett et al., 1981; Brophy and Good, 1986; Cooper et al., 1987; Rosenshine, 1983; Rosenshine and Stevens, 1986), will be discussed here.

When and how often to use questioning

As one of the most important elements of effective instruction, questioning should take up a large part of the lesson. In the previous chapter, we mentioned that a lot of researchers believe the lesson should start with a review of what was learnt previously. This is the first part of teaching where interaction and questioning are crucial as they are the best way of checking pupils' retention of material taught earlier. Once new content is presented in small steps, each step should be followed by *guided practice,* to allow pupils to practise what they have learnt, and to allow teachers to check how well pupils have understood the lesson. This will help the teacher to decide whether all or part of it needs to be retaught. The same goes for the review at the end of the lesson. While it is possible for the teacher to list what was learnt in the lesson, it is usually more effective to ask pupils to explain this themselves. Overall, then, questioning will take up much of the direct instruction lesson, and will be one of the main teaching activities for the teacher.

Eliciting a pupil response

Saying that interaction is crucial obviously begs the question of how to get pupils to answer the questions posed. This can be a problem, especially with older and shyer pupils. The first thing to note here is that this problem will be attenuated if pupils are used to interactive lessons, which will be the case if there is a school- , or at least subject-wide teaching strategy that is based on interactive teaching. A non-evaluative, positive atmosphere is important as well. Pupils are more likely to get involved if they feel that a wrong response will not elicit criticism or ridicule from the teacher (or fellow pupils). A strategy that can be used to get all pupils to answer a question can be to make pupils write down their answers before the teacher shows the correct answer on the board, or to get them to find the answer using answer cards (such as number cards in mathematics) which they show to the teacher after first hiding their answer from the teacher and other pupils (e.g. by holding the cards to their chest).

The cognitive level of questions

The cognitive level of questions refers to the difficulty of the questions, in particular whether they require relatively sophisticated thinking skills from pupils ('higher' level) or more basic application of rules or retention of facts ('lower' level). Lower-level questions should be relatively easy to answer, and should in most cases elicit a correct response. As higher-level questions require more thinking from pupils, they will be more difficult to answer. Research has shown that effective teachers use more higher-level questions than less effective teachers, although the majority of questions used are still lower level. Obviously, the exact balance of the two must depend on the content taught. A topic requiring factual recall, such as multiplication facts in mathematics, would require lower-level questions than one which probes for higher-level content, such as asking pupils to design an experiment in science. It is, however, important to ask higher-level questions whenever possible to help develop pupils' thinking skills.

Open and closed questions

A related distinction is that between open and closed questions. Closed questions have one clear answer (e.g. 'how much is 4 times 8?'), while open questions have open-ended answers (e.g. 'what do you think makes a country democratic?'). Again, effective teachers have been found to ask more open questions than less effective teachers, although a large proportion of questions used by effective teachers are still closed questions. However, as with cognitive level, the right mix of open and closed questions will depend on the topic and goals of the lesson. Not using any open questions, however, may be ineffective as it may result in the teacher providing insufficient cognitive challenge to pupils. In many lessons, open questions are underused, with one study of classrooms in English finding that no open questions were asked in over a third of lessons observed (Smith et al., 2004).

Process and product questions

Another distinction is that between process and product questions. Product questions are designed to find the answer to a particular problem, while process questions are meant to elicit procedures, processes and rules used to get to the answer. The importance of product and process is a subject that has been debated quite a lot in education recently, and in a lot of countries there is a move towards emphasizing process more strongly, as obtaining generic skills (such as 'problem solving') is seen as more important in a rapidly changing world than accumulating factual knowledge. Research bears out that it is important not to limit questioning to product questions, effective teachers having been found to ask more process questions than ineffective teachers, within a mix that contains product questions as well. Obviously, once again, the exact mix should depend on the topic and goals of the lesson, and more generally the overall mix will depend to an extent on the emphasis of the curriculum on process or product. Generally speaking, product questions are closed, and often lower level, while process questions are often open, higher-level questions. Some differences have been found between more and less effective teachers in how much emphasis there is on product and process. While all teachers are found to ask product questions, more effective teachers use a greater number of process questions as well (Muijs et al., 2010). There are also cultural differences in this, with teachers in England, for example, seeming to use more product questions than teachers in Russia (Wilson et al., 2004).

Process and product questions can often be combined in one teaching moment. Thus, the teacher can ask a pupil a product question (e.g. 'what is the area of this room?'), and then ask the pupil to explain how she worked out that answer.

What to do when a pupil answers a question correctly

When a pupil makes what Rosenshine (1983) referred to as a correct, quick and firm response, the correctness of this response must be acknowledged in all cases, and this must be done in a businesslike way. Effusive praise is usually unnecessary, and slows down the lesson. Often, depending on the pupil's self-confidence, age and background, a nod or gesture will be sufficient (although young pupils, pupils lacking self-confidence and lower-ability pupils may need more praise and positive reinforcement). According to research, it is a good idea to ask another question to the pupil who has just answered correctly, which will permit further feedback.

What to do when a pupil answers a question correctly but hesitantly

When a pupil answers a question correctly but hesitantly – something that can occur frequently when a topic has just been introduced – it is essential that the pupil receives positive feedback. Feedback in this case needs to be more explicit than when the answer is firm and unhesitant to help the pupil remember that the response was indeed correct. When a similar question next comes up, s/he will hopefully be able to answer it less hesitantly as a result. If many pupils seem hesitant, it may be worth finding out the reasons for this hesitancy and if necessary reteaching the material.

What to do when a pupil answers a question incorrectly

Two types of incorrect answers can be identified: incorrect answers due to carelessness or lack of effort, and incorrect answers due to lack of understanding. In both cases, teachers need to acknowledge that the answer is incorrect in a businesslike way without resorting to personal criticism of the pupil. In the case of incorrect answers due to carelessness, this may be difficult at times, but research has clearly shown that personal criticism is ineffective and may be harmful rather than helpful, turning the pupil against the teacher and leading to less subsequent effort. Once the teacher has pointed out that the answer is incorrect, s/he must move swiftly on to the next pupil. The denial of possible praise is the best response to this problem.

A different strategy needs to be followed when the answer is incorrect due to lack of understanding or knowledge. When this occurs, it is best to prompt the pupil, simplify the question (e.g. by breaking it down into a series of small steps) or provide hints so s/he can find the answer and think things through. If this fails to elicit the correct response, one can go to the next pupil, and ask her to correct it. If possible, it is always better for the teacher to try to get another pupil to correct the answer rather than for the teacher to do it her/himself.

What to do though, if many pupils seem to be having problems with answering the question, even after prompting? A number of strategies have been proposed, such as reviewing the key facts or rules needed to get to the right answer, explaining the steps used to reach the solution, prompting with clues or hints representing a partially correct answer, or using a similar but different problem to guide a pupil to the correct answer (Borich, 1996). Doing this will not only help the pupil who has been asked to answer the question, but will help pupils more generally.

What to do when a pupil answers a question partially correctly

When a pupil answers a question partially correctly, it is necessary first of all to acknowledge that part of the answer that was correct, making it very clear which part was and which wasn't, so as not to create confusion among either the responding pupil or the other pupils. Then the teacher should prompt the pupil who answered the question towards correcting that part of the answer that s/he answered incorrectly. If prompting in this way still doesn't elicit the correct response, one may need to ask another pupil to correct the part-answer. However, in all cases, the teacher should first try to get the pupil who first partially answered the question to find the right answer.

Prompting

On a couple of occasions above, we have referred to giving prompts in order to help pupils answer questions. There are three types of prompts which teachers can use for this purpose. The most obvious of these are *verbal prompts*. These can take the form of cues, reminders, instructions, tips, references to previous lessons or giving a part sentence for pupils to complete. Examples of this are: 'What was the first step for solving this type of problem?', 'Can you remember what we did yesterday during the experiment?', 'Don't forget to add the comma' and so on. *Gestural prompts* are also used very frequently in lessons, allowing the teacher to model the behaviour of pupils early before they actually make the mistake. This can be done by pointing to the object one wants a pupil to use, such as a number line or microscope, or by modelling a behaviour such as holding a pen correctly. Among young learners, *physical prompts* may be necessary. This can be the case when the pupil does not yet grasp the motor skills needed to, for example, hold a crayon or form letters or numbers. One can then take the pupil's hand and guide her/him explicitly *hand over hand*. This method is also used during physical education.

Cooper et al. (1987) recommend using the least intrusive prompts first. They consider the least intrusive to be verbal prompts, followed by gestural prompts and physical prompts. The reason for this is to stop the learner becoming overly dependent on the teacher's guidance as, according to these researchers, verbal prompts will fade from memory faster than (especially) physical prompts, and will therefore be more effective 'scaffolds' to pupils' learning, leading them to be able to perform the behaviour independently.

What is the correct wait-time?

How long should one wait for a pupil to answer the question? This is an important matter, as one needs to ensure the smooth flow of the lesson and avoid embarrassing silences, but also allow pupils enough time to think through their answers. Therefore, wait-time has to depend on the type of question asked. If the question is a closed, lower-level, factual recall question, three seconds or slightly longer is the optimal wait-time. However, for open-ended, higher-level questions, a longer wait-time (up to 15 seconds) is required, though some studies have shown that teachers rarely wait this long, usually giving students only up to seven seconds to answer (Smith et al., 2003). Waiting much longer than this may lead to the other pupils becoming restless. Prompting the pupil after the acceptable wait-time has been passed is therefore necessary. When asking a complex question requiring a lot of thought, it can be a good idea to allow the pupils some time to work the answer out on their own (on paper, for example) before asking them to provide the answer. Research has found that among beginning teachers leaving insufficient wait-time is more common than allowing too much wait-time (Rowe, 1986).

What percentage of questions should be answered correctly?

At the end of a topic, the majority of questions asked should elicit a correct, firm and quick response. If 95 per cent of pupils are able to answer the question correctly, the content has been well mastered. For lower-level content (such as mastering of facts), it is suggested that 60–80 per cent of questions following a presentation (in small steps) should be answered correctly before moving on to the next step. Obviously, for some types of open questions, the concept of 'right' or 'wrong' answers may be less appropriate (e.g. when asking pupils for their opinion), and understanding must then be probed by means of the logical and consistent use of arguments by the pupil for which s/he needs to be prompted if necessary. Many questions have more than one correct answer (process questions such as how a pupil has worked out an answer in mathematics, for example), and all correct answers must be acknowledged even if the teacher was looking for another answer or a faster method. The pupil can then be prompted for the answer or method the teacher was looking for (e.g. 'That's correct. Do you know any other ways of doing that?')

Students' Responses to Questioning

If questioning is to function as an integral part of student learning, students need to play an active role in the process. Language plays an important role in learning and in the formation of concepts and understanding in the brain. Pupils' own responses are part of the process through which they make sense of their own thinking about a topic.

However, there are many other ways in which pupils use questioning in their learning. Research has shown that the most common way pupils themselves see the role of questioning is listening out for the correct answer. Rather than fully engaging with the dialogue between teacher and class, what they do is wait until the right answer is given and then memorize that answer. While they can obviously learn correct responses in this way, this passive role will tend to lead to surface learning of correct answers rather than any in-depth understanding of the topic. Students also often see listening as more important than talking, even though it is through talk that a lot of understanding develops (Pratt, 2006).

Making sure students are truly engaged in questioning may be helped by not too obviously telegraphing right and wrong answers, by getting pupils themselves to try and respond to each other's responses and by holding group discussions.

Classroom Discussion and Its Relationship to Questioning

While questioning is the most widely used form of teacher–pupil interaction, it is not the only form of interaction possible, and indeed in some cases is not the most desirable form. Questioning is inevitably teacher-led which in some cases may not be appropriate to the goal of the lesson.

Discussion can occur in the classroom in two settings: between pupils in small groups during cooperative small group work, or with the teacher and other pupils in a whole-class setting. Small group work will be discussed in the next chapter; in this section we will limit ourselves to whole-class discussion.

Classroom discussion can help fulfil three major learning goals: promoting pupil involvement and engagement in the lesson by allowing them to voice their own ideas; helping pupils to develop better understanding by allowing them to think things through and verbalize their thinking; and, lastly, helping pupils to obtain communication skills (not least the self-confidence to voice their own opinions in public and the ability to do so in a clear and concise way).

Discussion needs to be carefully prepared and usually needs to follow on from some prior activity such as a previous lesson on a certain topic. Alternatively, the teacher can get pupils to read up on a particular topic before the lesson. Discussions can also follow brief presentations on a topic by the teacher or other pupils.

In order for a discussion to be effective, it is important to keep it focused and to the point. As with direct instruction, teachers need to clearly set out the purpose of the discussion from the start. It can be useful to provide pupils with a couple of 'pointer' questions in order to focus the discussion, and to link the discussion to pupils' prior knowledge. During the discussion, the teacher needs to keep pupils firmly on task, and avoid them wandering off to different subjects. Writing down the main points to emerge from the discussion on the board or a flipchart can help focus pupils and also emphasize the fact that the discussion is a learning activity and not a just a way of filling time.

During the discussion, the teacher needs to respond to pupil ideas in such a way as to encourage them to clarify and be more conscious of their thought processes. This can be done by seeking clarification ('Could you clarify that for me…'), by reflecting on pupil ideas ('That's a novel idea, what I think you're trying to say is…'), and by getting pupils to consider other points of view.

At the end of the discussion, it is once again useful for the teacher to briefly summarize the main points to have come out of the discussion, followed by a debriefing focusing on the process and how well the discussion did or did not proceed. Both can be done by the teacher or (often more appropriately) by asking for the pupils' comments.

Whether or not to use class discussion once again depends on the subject of the lesson, and also on the maturity of the pupils as well as their communication skills. A classroom climate in which mutual respect exists and in which the views of all pupils are valued is essential. All these factors will also determine the amount of teacher direction and structure given to the discussion.

One of the tensions that have been found to exist in lessons is that between questioning and discussion. Research has found that in some cases teacher questions can function in such a way that they abort classroom discussion, by imposing the teacher's views on the pupils (Askew et al., 1994).

Gender, Shyness and Interactive Teaching

A criticism of direct instruction, and particularly the interactive part of the whole-class lesson, has been that it may advantage boys and be disadvantageous to girls and to shyer pupils.

The reason for this is seen to lie in the more assertive nature of boys, and the (obviously) less assertive nature of shy pupils in the classroom. This means that boys will be more likely to volunteer to answer questions and to dominate lessons, and that shyer pupils will avoid doing so. In this way, the more assertive boys may start to dominate the lesson at the expense of other pupils. A further potential problem in whole-class interactive teaching is deliberate non-involvement by certain pupils – the so-called 'free rider effect'. This refers to the fact that certain pupils may choose to avoid actively taking part in the lesson and let others do all the work, either because they are unsure or unwilling.

These problems can easily be avoided by judicious teacher action, however. Thus, when questioning, teachers need to make sure that all pupils get to answer questions, not just the pupils who volunteer or are the most persistent. A way to make sure this is done is to go round the class in a certain (varying) order, or to have a list of pupils on the teacher's desk on which names can quickly be ticked off. Teachers also need to make sure that girls get as much chance to answer questions as boys. Among younger pupils, it is important to stop pupils shouting out answers, as it will usually be the most assertive pupils who do this.

Another thing the teacher must avoid is the temptation to target mainly those pupils who s/he thinks are most likely to answer the question correctly. In order to avoid weaker pupils getting answers wrong too often, which will not help them to attain a feeling of mastery, it may be necessary to vary the difficulty of questions according to the pupil they are directed at. It is important to involve all pupils in the lesson.

Summary

In this chapter, we have learnt about interaction between teacher and pupil, which is one of the most important aspects of direct instruction. Questioning can be used to check pupils' understanding, to 'scaffold' pupils' learning, to help them clarify and verbalize their thinking and to help them develop a sense of mastery.

Effective questioning is also one of the most widely studied aspects of teaching, and therefore a solid body of knowledge exists on which strategies are most effective.

In direct instruction lessons, questions need to be asked at the beginning of the lesson when the topic of the last lesson in that subject is being reviewed, after every short presentation and during the summary at the end of the lesson. Teachers need to mix both higher- and lower-level questions, product and process questions, and open and closed questions. The exact mix depends upon the lesson topic, but teachers need to ensure that enough open, higher-level process questions are posed.

Correct answers need to be acknowledged in a positive but businesslike fashion. When a pupil answers a question partially correctly, the teacher needs to prompt that pupil to find the remaining part of the answer before moving on to the next pupil. When a pupil answers a question incorrectly, the teacher needs to point out swiftly that the answer is wrong. If the pupil has answered incorrectly due to inattention or carelessness, the teacher must move swiftly on to the next pupil. If the answer is incorrect due to lack of knowledge, the teacher needs to try and prompt the pupil to answer correctly.

Another form of interaction that may be effective in certain lessons is classroom discussion. In order for discussion to be effective, it needs to be carefully prepared. The teacher needs to give pupils clear guidelines on what the discussion is about. During the discussion, pupils need to be kept on task, and the teacher needs to write down the main points emerging from the discussion. After the discussion, these main points (the product of the discussion) can be summarized, and pupils can be debriefed by asking them to comment on how well the discussion went (the process of the discussion).

Teachers need to make sure that girls and shy pupils, who may be less assertive, get the chance to answer questions.

Reflective Questions

1. Can you think of any lessons you have been part of (as teacher or pupil) that could have been more interactive? Where and how would you have added interaction?
2. What would you do if pupils consistently answer a question incorrectly?
3. How would you organize a classroom discussion? Can you give an example?
4. Do you think whole-class interactive teaching is disadvantageous for girls?
5. When teaching basic skills, should the teacher refrain from using open-ended or process questions? Why (not)?
6. In your experience, do teachers wait long enough for an answer to a question? If not, how would you help them to improve that aspect of their teaching?
7. When would you reteach a particular topic?

CHAPTER 4

COLLABORATIVE SMALL GROUP WORK AND PEER TUTORING

Key Points

In this chapter, you will learn about:

- the main benefits of collaborative small group work
- the main disadvantages of collaborative small group work
- how to effectively use small group work
- how to assess collaborative work
- the benefits of peer tutoring
- the key characteristics of effective peer tutoring.

Introduction

As we mentioned in Chapter 2, an alternative approach to individual practice in the direct instruction lesson is the use of cooperative small group work during the review and practice part of the lesson. This method has gained in popularity in recent years, and has attracted a lot of research interest in a number of countries, such as the USA (Johnson and Johnson, 1994; Slavin, 1996). In other countries such as the UK, this method is still underused, however. In a recent study in primary schools, we found that less than 10 per cent of lesson time was spent doing group work (Muijs and Reynolds, 1999, 2002).

Benefits of Small Group Work

The use of small group work is posited to have a number of advantages over individual practice. The main benefit of small group work seems to lie in the cooperative aspects it can help foster. One advantage of this lies in the contribution this method can make to the development of pupils' social skills. Working with other pupils may help them to develop their empathic abilities, by allowing them to see others' viewpoints which can help them to realize that everyone has strengths and weaknesses. Trying to find a solution to a problem in group also develops skills such as the need to accommodate others' views.

Pupils can provide each other with scaffolding in the same way the teacher can during questioning. The total knowledge available in a group is likely to be larger than that available to individual pupils, which can enable more powerful problem solving and can therefore allow the teacher to give pupils more difficult problems than s/he could give to individual pupils. Small group work can also help students to restructure their own thinking through talking to others, talk being an important part of the way students develop their thinking, and help them to understand their own strengths and weaknesses better (O'Donnell, 2006).

There is a lot of evidence that collaborative small group work is related to higher student achievement. Veenman et al. (2005), for example, found a relationship between providing explanations in small groups and students' mathematics achievement, while Webb and Mastergeorge (2003) have found that receiving explanations is related to better achievement, especially if students then put the received explanation into their own words.

Making Small Group Work Effective

Effective small group work does require a significant amount of preparation, and a number of preconditions have to be met beforehand in order for it to be effective. Firstly, pupils must be able to cooperate with one another, and to provide each other with help in a constructive way. A number of studies have found that while small group work is positively related to achievement when group interaction is respectful and inclusive, use of group work is actually negatively related to achievement if group interaction is disrespectful or unequal (Battistich et al., 1993; Linn and Burbules, 1993). This is by no means a given, as many (especially young pupils and pupils from highly disadvantaged backgrounds) have been found to lack the social skills necessary to interact positively with peers.

Thus, pupils often lack *sharing skills,* which means that they have difficulty sharing time and materials and can try to dominate the group. This problem can be alleviated by teaching sharing skills, for example by using the 'round robin' technique in which the teacher asks a question and introduces an idea that has many possible answers. During round robin questioning, a first pupil is asked to give an answer, and then pass his turn to the next pupil. This goes on until all pupils have had a chance to contribute.

Other pupils may lack *participation skills*. This means that they find it difficult to participate in group work because they are shy or uncooperative. This can be alleviated by structuring the task so that these pupils have to play a particular role in the group (see below) or by giving all pupils 'time tokens', worth a specified amount of 'talk time'. Pupils have to give up a token to a monitor whenever they have used up their talk time, after which they are not allowed to say anything further. In this way, all pupils get a chance to contribute.

Pupils may also lack *communication skills*. This means that they are not able to effectively communicate their ideas to others, obviously making it difficult for them to function in a cooperative group. Communicative skills, such as paraphrasing, may need to be explicitly taught to pupils before small group work can be used.

Finally, some pupils may lack *listening skills.* This can frequently be a problem with younger pupils who will sit waiting their turn to contribute without listening to other pupils. This can be counteracted by making pupils paraphrase what the pupil who has contributed before them has said before allowing them to contribute.

The role of the teacher is important, not just in preparing students for group work but in preparing the task and monitoring what students are doing. Tasks for small group work need to be sufficiently open-ended and challenging to engage students in higher-order thinking without being too confusing, which may require quite a bit of preparation. The teacher also needs to monitor what is going on in the groups. S/he will have to make sure that students are on task, and that they are engaging with the task. Giving task-specific advice and instructions have been found to be effective, as has asking students to explain their thinking. More general questions such as 'How is it going?' are less effective (Webb, 2009).

Giving and Receiving Help

One of the main advantages of cooperative small group work lies in the help pupils give one another. Not all kinds of help are necessarily useful, however. Just giving the right answer is not associated with enhanced understanding or achievement. In her review of research, Webb (1991) reports a positive relationship between giving content-related help and achievement. Giving non-content-related help did not seem to improve pupil achievement, though. Receiving explanations was found to be positive in some studies, and non-significant in others, this presumably because the receiver has to understand the help given and be able to use it. This may well require training pupils to give clear help. Receiving non-explanatory help (e.g. being told the answer without being told how to work it out) was negatively or non-significantly related to achievement in the studies reviewed, while being engaged in off-task activities (e.g. socializing) was negative. In a more recent study of grade 3 to 5 pupils, Nattiv (1994) found that giving and receiving explanations was positively related to achievement, giving and receiving other help was slightly positively related to achievement, while receiving no help after requesting it was negatively related to achievement. Webb and Moore Kendersky (1984) report similar findings among high-school pupils. Asking for help is also important, and in particular students need to be encouraged to ask specific rather than general questions (e.g. 'How does that work?') or stating general lack of understanding ('I don't understand') (Webb, 2009).

How to Structure Group Work Tasks

For small group work to be effective, a number of elements need to be taken into account in the structuring of the task. Before commencing the task, the goals of the activity need to be clearly stated and the activity needs to be explained in such a way that no ambiguity can exist over the desired outcomes of the task. The teacher needs to make clear that cooperation between pupils in the group is desired. According to Slavin (1993), these goals need to be group goals, in order to facilitate cooperation, which need to be accompanied by individual accountability for work done in order to avoid free-rider effects. Some form of competition with other groups can help pupils work together, as can using a shared manipulative or tool such as a computer.

Avoiding free-rider effects can be aided by structuring the group work in such a way that every group member is assigned a particular task. One way of doing this is by making completion of one part of the task dependent on completion of a previous stage, so pupils will pressure each other to put the effort in to complete the stage before them. Johnson and Johnson (1994) suggest a number of roles that can be assigned to pupils in small groups, such as:

- the *summarizer*, who will prepare the groups' presentation to the class and summarize conclusions reached to see if the rest of the group agrees
- the *researcher*, who collects background information and looks up any additional information that is needed to complete the task
- the *checker*, who checks that the facts the group will use are indeed correct and will stand up to scrutiny from the teacher or other groups
- the *runner*, who tries to find the resources needed to complete the task, such as equipment and dictionaries
- the *observer/troubleshooter*, who takes notes and records group processes. These may be used during the debriefing following the group work
- the *recorder*, who writes down the major output of the group, and synthesizes the work of the other group members.

For group work to have the positive effects on learning and achievement that we have mentioned above, students must engage in genuine conversation, where they react to, restate and think about each other's ideas. Too often that is not the case, with pupils talking over one another rather than listening. This means that in many cases groups need to be tightly structured, for example by having pupils take on different roles as above or by making sure every comment is responded to and all comments relate to the task goal (Barron, 2003). In many cases, it can also be useful to give students specific prompts to get them to engage in higher-order thinking (e.g. 'Can you explain why you think that answer is right?'). Students can also be taught to ask each other this type of question (Webb, 2009).

Giving both individual grades (for the pupil's work in reaching the group goal) and collective grades (for the group as a whole) is an effective strategy for ensuring both group goals and individual accountability.

After finishing the group task, the results need to be presented to the whole class and a debriefing focusing on the process of the group work (the effectiveness of the collaborative effort) should be held. A useful way of starting a debriefing session is by asking pupils what they think has gone particularly well or badly during group work (the observers mentioned above should be able to do this). The teacher can then give feedback on which elements s/he thought went well or less well, and ask pupils how the process could be improved.

Research has shown that cooperative groups should be somewhat, but not too, heterogeneous with respect to pupil ability. Groups composed of high- and medium- or medium- and low-ability pupils gave and received more explanations than pupils in high–medium–low ability groups. Less heterogeneous groupings were especially advantageous for medium-ability pupils. When pupils of the same ability are grouped together, it has been found that high-ability pupils thought it unnecessary to help one another while low-ability pupils were less well able to do so (Askew and William, 1995; Webb, 1991).

All in all, it is clear that collaborative small group work requires a lot of thought and preparation, and is far removed from merely seating pupils around a table and hoping effective collaboration will follow.

The Disadvantages of Cooperative Small Group Work

While cooperative group work can be a powerful teaching and learning strategy, it does have a number of disadvantages which mean that it needs to be used in conjunction with, and not as a replacement of, individual practice.

One of these disadvantages lies precisely in the cooperative nature of group work. A problem with this is that it does not naturally promote independent learning and can foster dependency on certain dominant members of the group. If this happens, the pupil will not easily be able to develop the skills s/he needs to use independently in other situations. Furthermore, small group work can easily lead to 'free rider effects' whereby certain members of the group do not effectively contribute and rely on the work of others.

A further problem can be the fact that misconceptions can be reinforced if they are shared by several pupils in the group.

The complexity of small group work can also make it harder to manage for the teacher. Collaborative group work requires a significant amount of preparation as teachers need to have a sufficient amount of tasks ready and need to prepare tasks that make for effective interaction in the group. Some research has also found that small group work can result in more time spent on lesson transitions.

Overall, while small group work can be a powerful method for teaching higher-level cognitive tasks, it can be less useful when teaching basic skills where automaticity and overlearning are paramount.

Small Group Work as an Alternative to Direct Instruction

In this chapter, we have so far treated collaborative small group work as a potentially powerful part of a direct instruction lesson. However, many educators consider small group work to be so advantageous that they have advocated structuring the whole lesson around cooperative small group work (e.g. Slavin, 1996). Within the approach discussed here, collaborative group work can take up a large part of the lesson (around 30 minutes out of a one-hour lesson would seem to be a minimum), with the whole-class session being limited in time if the teacher thinks that would help improve the effectiveness of teaching that particular topic. Most of the lesson should be spent on collaborative tasks, with only brief introductions by the teacher at the start of the session, and plenary, whole group work at the end.

A number of authors see cooperative learning as part of a new paradigm of teaching and learning, based on constructivist principles (see Chapter 5). Learning is seen as a process whereby knowledge is constructed and transformed by pupils, and cannot just be 'transmitted' from teacher to pupil. Teaching is then seen as developing the conditions in which learning can occur through interaction between pupils and teacher, and, especially, through interaction between pupils (Johnson et al., 1998).

An example of the use of collaborative small group work is the *Jigsaw* technique, developed by Aronson and associates in the 1970s, around which whole lessons can easily be structured (Aronson and Patnoe, 1997). *Jigsaw* works by dividing the class into groups of five or six pupils. Pupils are then each given a specific task, or a specific issue to research. Pupils go off to research their topic, and then meet up with those pupils from other groups who have been doing the same task (for example, if the task was to look at what different intelligences mean according to Gardner, all pupils from each group charged with researching visual-spatial intelligence will meet up and discuss their findings). This will ensure that the quality of information found by any group member is increased. They will also rehearse their presentation with these other 'experts'.

Once they have done that, pupils go back to their groups and present their findings to the group in a well-organized and structured way. All pieces of the jigsaw will be necessary to complete the task set to the group by the teacher, so each pupil will have to attend to and is dependent on the others. In this way, the method can help develop empathy and listening skills, as well as producing positive academic outcomes.

Collaborative group work does not have to take place in one lesson. Collaborative tasks can be set over a longer period of time, with tasks continuing for several lessons, making it a very flexible method with regards to curriculum coverage.

Some disadvantages to collaborative work as a basic teaching structure are also obvious, however. One is the fact that it can take a lot longer to cover a particular topic when using collaborative learning than when using direct instruction methods. However, the obverse of that may be that deeper learning will take place. Shyer pupils, or those that need to work at a different speed (faster or slower) than that of the group, may feel that they are not benefiting as much. Some pupils may prefer to work individually, and the fact that different pupils are doing different tasks may disadvantage some. A further question has been raised as to whether collaborative small group discussions are a good way to develop higher-order thinking. In one study, it was found that teacher-guided discussions were more efficient for attaining higher reasoning levels and higher quality explanations, but peer discussions were more generative and exploratory (Hogan et al., 1999).

Therefore, while collaborative work is clearly a potentially highly effective teaching method, like any other method, it is probably best to use it in combination with others, depending on the topic taught. However, it is fair to say that this method is currently under- rather than overused in most schools.

A model that integrates collaborative work with whole-class instruction is provided by Good et al. (1995: 140). They suggest the lesson structure shown in Figure 4.1.

As you can see, this model switches from teacher-directed whole-class activities to pupil-directed tasks, allowing for both direct instruction and group work elements, with an emphasis on active learning.

Assessing Collaborative Work

One question that can come up when doing collaborative work is how to assess the work done.

One possibility is obviously to use traditional knowledge tests at the end to see what pupils have learnt from group work, but this is often seen as a somewhat impoverished way of assessing the multiple outcomes of group work, not least as it does not assess the group contribution, which may lead to individual competition between group members. Therefore, other methods are proposed.

Panitz and Panitz (1996) suggest that observation, using a structured taxonomy based on Bloom, can be helpful. They suggest looking at five elements: knowledge of the basics needed to solve the problem; an application of this knowledge to solve the problem; the ability to extend pupils' reasoning to new problems or situations; the ability of pupils to create their own questions or problem statements based on the concepts being studied; and the ability of pupils to explain their reasoning to peers. Observation has the big advantage of looking directly at the processes of group work rather than just at the outcomes, and will allow the teacher to make an assessment of how well the group is functioning and of each individual's contribution to the group.

Evaluating the actual tasks pupils have done (a research report, essay, presentation) is another method that will value the group element of the task. The problem can be that because individual contributions are not assessed, the temptation for

Approximate time	Activity	Locus of control
10 minutes	**Introduce, explore, investigate or reinforce concepts** – explore new concepts and skills – provide problematic situations and modelling of strategies – guide meaningful discussions – assign tasks – clarify expected outcomes	Teacher
5–10 minutes	**Work group: task 1** Inquiry, reinforcement or extension of concept using task – exploration – investigation – application – reinforcement	Group
5 minutes	**Assess progress/Process and clarify** – utilize active question/answer interaction – discuss problem situation – discuss strategies/process/findings – provide new development – provide new tasks	Teacher
10–15 minutes	**Work group task 2**	Group
5 minutes	**Assess progress/Process and clarify**	Teacher
10–15 minutes	**Work group task 3**	Group
5 minutes	**Review/Summary of task** – brief review of objectives – review of tasks – review of findings – connections to future/past study	Teacher

FIGURE 4.1 Lesson based on group work

some pupils to become 'free riders' may be strong. Therefore, some combination of this method with individual tests may be more appropriate.

Another form of assessment that can be effective when assessing collaborative group work is peer assessment, in which students evaluate each other's work. This is especially so as it is hard for the teacher to fully assess processes occurring in a number of small groups, and the contribution made by group members. The fact that in real life students will be required to evaluate themselves and others is another justification for developing this skill in the classroom (Gueldenzoph and May, 2002). Of course, as with other elements of collaborative work, peer assessment needs careful structuring. Students need, firstly, to be clear on what the goals of the assessment are, and criteria need to be clear and quantifiable (e.g. did he/she collect complete his/her part of the task on time?). Things which are typically part of peer assessment include:

- attendance
- an ability to deal constructively with conflicts that arise
- active participation in the group task
- how good the work is that students do.
  (Gueldenzoph and May, 2002).

Clear tools need to be prepared that students can use for the assessment which incorporate the elements you think are important, and in many cases students can help develop these.

Peer Tutoring

Peer tutoring, where students help each other to learn, is another method that has been found to be very effective. Typically, one student takes on the role of tutor and the other the role of tutee, though these roles will often be swapped later, so that all students have the opportunity to act in both roles. While traditionally it has been common to use pupils of higher ability as tutors and pupils of lower ability as tutees, it has become increasingly clear that a lot of the most effective tutoring involves pupils of similar abilities, but where the 'tutor' has previously gained knowledge of a particular aspect of the curriculum and is only more knowledgeable in this particular area.

The main differences with peer tutoring are that students take on specific roles as either tutor or tutee, and that the groups are usually smaller, typically students working one-to-one (Topping, 2005).

There is a lot of evidence on the effectiveness of peer tutoring, in studies in a range of countries (e.g. the USA: Powell, 1997; Kamps et al., 2008; the UK: FitzGibbon, 1988; Topping, 2005; Germany: Grossen and Bachman, 2000; Australia:

Topping et al., 2006.) A key advantage of peer tutoring is that learners of similar ages may identify more easily with one another, and possibly understand each other's ways of thinking more clearly than adults. As with cooperative small group work, there is the advantage of talk as a way of developing thinking, especially for the tutor who will need to have a good understanding of whatever s/he is trying to explain and be able to put this into words.

As is the case for collaborative small group work, peer tutoring needs to be carefully structured and prepared (and there are a number of structured programmes in existence), with attention paid to aspects like context (the specific class and learners involved), clear objectives, who the participants will be and how they will be prepared for the activity, what training is needed for the pupils and possibly for teachers or classroom assistants, and what resources and materials are necessary to make the activity successful.

A number of things that are necessary for effective peer tutoring are:

- Good preparation and training of tutors. This training will need to include teaching strategies (e.g. how to set up a specific task, how to explain something clearly) and use of praise (when and when not to praise). It is a good idea to give tutors some practice with one another before getting them to work with tutees. It can be helpful for teachers to demonstrate peer tutoring to the class by two teachers taking on the roles of tutor and tutee. Tutees need to be prepared to accept tutoring from peers and not to get defensive or angry when they make mistakes.
- A careful selection of activities for peer tutoring. Peer tutoring works best as an addition to and not a replacement of classroom teaching. Helping tutees develop skills they are struggling with that have been previously taught to the whole class is a particularly effective way of using peer tutoring. The materials selected must be well understood by peer tutors, and must be well-defined and clear. Open-ended tasks do not lend themselves to peer tutoring as well as to collaborative small group work.
- A careful selection of tutors and tutees. While tutors and tutees don't need to differ in ability, they do need to have different levels of overall knowledge of the area that is being tutored. Pre-testing can be used to make sure this is the case. In many cases, cross-age tutoring is used, where an older student (typically around two years older) will tutor a younger student. This has a number of advantages. There will not be a perceived status or ability difference between tutor and tutee, as differences will be attributed to age. The difference in knowledge is also likely to be clear. However, there are examples of effective peer tutoring with pupils of the same age group, though if that strategy is used, it is recommended that all students in a class get the opportunity to be both tutors and tutees.
- Proper preparation of the space and any materials. Tutors and tutees need a space where they can work one-to-one without too much disturbance, which

can often be a problem in schools. They may also be helped by having some materials prepared beforehand, such as flash cards with questions and answers on. It is best for the teacher to take a lead role in preparing these materials, especially with younger students.

- Peer tutoring is a well-supported method, that deserves greater use in our schools and classrooms, and, if implemented well, can be an important part of the teacher's arsenal of strategies.

Summary

In this chapter, we have looked at the use of collaborative small group work.

The use of small group work can foster collaborative skills and social skills and is therefore seen as an important part of developing pupils. Pupils can also provide each other with scaffolding in the same way the teacher can during questioning. Group work enables more powerful problem solving, because the total knowledge available in a group is likely to be larger than that available to individual pupils.

Making collaborative small group work effective requires a lot of preparation, and attention to a number of factors.

Pupils must be able to cooperate with one another, and to provide each other with help in a constructive way. Not all pupils possess the necessary collaborative skills when they come to school, and these will need to be developed before group work can take place.

The goals of the activity need to be clearly stated and the activity needs to be explained in such a way that no ambiguity can exist over the desired outcomes of the task.

Teachers need to avoid free-rider effects. This can be helped by giving all pupils defined roles, and by assessing individual as well as group contributions.

After finishing the group task, the results need to be presented to the whole class and a debriefing focusing on the process of the group work should be held.

Some researchers advocate the use of collaborative group work as the main teaching activity in lessons. A number of models, such as the *Jigsaw* model, have been developed that allow teachers to do this.

Another form of collaborative work that has strong support from research is peer tutoring, where one student takes on the role of tutor and the other the role of tutee. Often, older students will tutor younger ones. Like collaborative small group work, peer tutoring requires a lot of preparation, including the training of tutors and tutees.

Reflective Questions

1. What types of topics do you think are best taught using collaborative small group work?
2. What are the main benefits of small group work compared to direct instruction?
3. What are the main disadvantages of small group work compared to direct instruction?
4. What method of assessment do you think would be most effective to evaluate collaborative group work?
5. How would you group pupils in a small school with mixed-age classes?
6. Can you think of a topic you could teach using the *Jigsaw* method?
7. How do you think collaborative small group work relates to the theories of learning we saw in Chapter 1?

CHAPTER 5

CONSTRUCTIVIST TEACHING

Key Points

In this chapter, you will learn about:

- the main elements of constructivist philosophy
- the main elements of constructivist teaching
- a constructivist lesson and what it might look like
- evidence for the claim that constructivism improves pupil outcomes.

Introduction

A teaching philosophy that has been becoming increasingly popular in teaching over the past few decades is constructivism. Constructivism is a broad movement, which is as much a philosophical position as an educational strategy. Constructivism has been highly influential in education, and has led to a variety of new teaching methods and strategies. In this chapter, we will look at what constructivism is, and how it relates to teaching.

The Philosophy of Constructivism

The basic principle underlying constructivist philosophy is that all knowledge is constructed rather than directly perceived by the senses (smell, sight, touch, etc.). According to Von Glasersfeld (1984), one of the founders of the constructivist movement, constructivism starts from the assumption that knowledge, no matter how it is defined, is in the heads of persons, and that the thinking subject has no alternative but to construct what he or she knows on the basis of his or her own experience. All our thinking is based upon our own experience, and is therefore subjective.

We can't objectively observe things, as we are all part of what we are observing. Reality is not 'out there' to be objectively and dispassionately observed by us, but is at least in part constructed by us and by our observations. There is no pre-existing objective reality that can be observed. Each of us generates our own (rules) and (mental models), which we use to make sense of our experiences. The process of our observing reality changes and transforms it, and therefore subjectivists are relativistic. All truth can only be relative, and is never definitive.

This view stands in contrast to that of the so-called 'realist' position, which states that 'The truth is out there' and that we can objectively observe reality as long as we use the 'right' (accurate, reliable) methods. Positivism is the most extreme form of this worldview. According to positivism, the world works according to fixed laws of cause and effect. Scientific thinking is used to test theories about these laws, and either reject or provisionally accept them. In this way, we will finally get to understand the truth about how the world works. By developing reliable measurement instruments, we can objectively study the physical world. This view that there is a true reality out there that we can measure completely objectively is problematic. We are all part of the world we are observing, and cannot completely detach ourselves from what we are researching. Historical research has shown that what is studied, and what findings are produced, are influenced by the beliefs of the people doing the research and the political/social climate at the time the research is done. Saying that, it's clear that the extreme relativist position is as problematic as the extreme positivistic one, denying, for example, that anything more distinguishes witchcraft and modern science than social consensus and power.

The extreme view of constructivism I mentioned above is what is known as 'radical constructivism'. Most educators, while subscribing to the basic constructivist idea that all knowledge is constructed, take a less radical position, which lies somewhere between the constructivist and realist positions outlined above (Bruner, 1962; Piaget, 1970).

Principles of Constructivist Teaching

Within education, these constructivist ideas are translated as meaning that all learners actually construct knowledge for themselves, rather than knowledge coming from the teacher and being 'absorbed' by the pupil. This means that every pupil will learn something slightly differently from a given lesson, and that as teachers we can never be certain what our pupils will learn. To most teachers, this will seem like quite a commonsensical idea, something they have all observed in their lessons already. However, a lot of other teaching approaches, such as direct instruction (see Chapter 2), are premised on learning theories that are far closer to a stimulus (teacher input)–response (pupil output) model.

The fact that pupils are active knowledge constructers has a number of consequences:

- Learning is always an active process. The learner actively constructs her/his learning from the various inputs s/he receives. This implies that the learner needs to be active to learn effectively. Learning is about helping pupils construct their own meaning, not about 'getting the right answer', as pupils can be trained to get the right answer without actually understanding the concept. Children learn best by resolving cognitive conflicts (conflicts with other ideas and preconceptions) through experiences, reflection and metacognition (Beyer, 1985).
- Learning, for the constructivist, is a search for meaning. Pupils actively try to construct meaning. Therefore, teachers should try to construct learning activities around big ideas and explorations that allow pupils to construct meaning.
- The construction of knowledge is not just an individual thing. Learning is also socially constructed, through interaction with peers, teachers, parents and so on. Therefore, it is best to construct the learning situation socially, by encouraging group work and discussion.
- Another element that follows from the fact that pupils individually and collectively construct knowledge is that in order to be effective, teachers will have to have a good knowledge of child development and learning theory, so they can judge more accurately what learning can occur.
- Something else that follows from this is that learning is always contextualized. We don't learn facts in a purely abstract way, but in relationship to what we already know. We also learn in relation to our preconceptions. This means that we learn best when new learning is explicitly connected to what we already know (Schunk, 2000).
- Real in-depth learning means thoroughly constructing knowledge, by exploring and revisiting material rather than quickly moving from topic to topic like in the direct instruction approach. Pupils can only construct meaning if they can see the whole, not just the parts.
- Teaching is about empowering the learner, and allowing the learner to discover and reflect on realistic experiences. This will lead to authentic learning and deeper understanding, compared to the surface memorization that often characterizes other teaching approaches (Von Glasersfeld, 1989). This also leads constructivists to believe that it is better to use hands-on and real-life materials than textbooks.

Constructivism in Practice

Constructivist authors have developed a number of teaching strategies, which, though varied and often subject-specific, have many common elements. The following elements are often present:

Connecting new ideas to prior knowledge can be done at the start of a new topic, but should not be limited to that part of the lesson. The teacher will need to find out what the pupils know about the topic before teaching starts (De Jager, 2002).

During **modelling**, another key aspect of constructivist teaching, the teacher carries out a complex task and shows pupils the processes needed to carry out that task; alternatively, the teacher can tell the pupils about her thinking and strategies while solving a problem. The teacher will also provide the reason for doing it the way she did, and will demonstrate the key steps. Modelling exists in two forms: behavioural modelling of the overt performance and cognitive modelling of the covert cognitive processes. The idea is that while the teacher might initially model a process, the pupils will become increasingly independent over time, and modelling will decrease. This process is known as **scaffolding**, and is an important part of constructivist methodology as it helps to develop independent learners.

During **scaffolding**, the teacher gives assistance to pupils to achieve tasks that they cannot yet master on their own, and then gradually withdraws her support. Scaffolding from the teacher can take on a variety of forms, including questions, prompts, suggested tasks, available resources, challenges and classroom activities. Scaffolding, however, does not mean guiding and teaching a learner towards some well-defined goal but supporting the growth of the learner through cognitive and metacognitive activities (Hannafin et al., 1997). Scaffolding also does not have to come from the teacher. Pupils can often effectively scaffold each other's learning. For example, in small group tasks, discussion between pupils can help provide the necessary scaffolding.

Coaching is a process of motivating learners, analysing their performance, and providing feedback on their performance. Teachers help the pupils while they are solving problems independently or in group, which will motivate and support them. One form of coaching is called cognitive coaching. Cognitive coaching is designed to make pupils more aware of their own thinking processes, which will help them be more reflective about their learning. This will build up their problem-solving skills, by giving them tools they can use in a variety of situations. This type of coaching involves helping pupils think about the way they are solving problems. It involves them in self-reflection, internalizing and generalizing (Costa and Garmston, 1994).

An important element of the constructivist lesson is **articulation**: encouraging pupils to articulate their ideas, thoughts and solutions. Pupils should not just be given the chance to construct meaning and develop their thinking, but can deepen these processes through expressing their ideas. To enable them to do this, they should be given complex tasks, which include opportunities to talk about their ideas, and present them to other pupils and the teacher. Group work, where pupils are encouraged to discuss problems and strategies with peers, presents many opportunities for articulation. Allowing pupils the opportunity to present their ideas and arguments and defend them publicly will help sharpen their thinking about the topic (Fosnot, 1996).

Reflection happens when pupils compare their solutions to those of 'experts' or other pupils. This is one of the key learning moments, and can be encouraged by the teacher providing counter examples to the views put forward by other pupils, and by allowing pupils to discuss their findings, ideas and strategies (Duffy and Jonassen, 1992). Reflection also means getting pupils to think about the way they solve problems, the strategies they use, and whether or not these are effective. This is called 'metacognition', reflecting on one's own learning. In Chapter 11, we will look at a number of strategies than can help this kind of reflection to happen. Self-reflection is an important part of this, and one strategy that has been found to help learning is self-explanation, whereby students verbalize their own learning and understanding (Rittle-Johnson, 2006).

Another element of much constructivist teaching is **collaboration**. This clearly comes from the social side of the constructivist movement, which stresses the ways in which children can learn from each other when they collaborate with each other or with the teacher. While collaborative learning can be stressed by educators and researchers who do not have strong constructivist backgrounds (see Chapter 4), it is particularly relevant within constructivism. Constructivists believe that our practical knowledge is located within relations among practitioners, social structures and organizations. For this reason, learning should involve a strong social dimension (Gredler, 1997; Lave and Wenger, 1991). Constructivist approaches to collaboration include reciprocal teaching, peer collaboration, cognitive apprenticeships, problem-based instruction, webquests, anchored instruction and other methods that involve learning with others (Schunk, 2000). A key concept in constructivist collaboration is that of 'purposeful talk', talk that allows opportunities for pupils to examine, elaborate, assess and build their knowledge in a social context.

Exploration and problem-solving activities are key parts of the constructivist lesson. Both allow pupils to develop their thinking and meaning making, by developing novel combinations of ideas and thinking about hypothetical outcomes of imagined situations and events (De Jager, 2002). In the constructivist classroom, pupils will often search for data or information that answers a question or helps solve a problem (Glasser, 1998). This seems more in tune with views of the modern, complex world which requires people who can find and process information rather than have a large store of knowledge.

A related element is that constructivist teachers will give their pupils **choices** and **options**. They are allowed to have a say in what tasks, projects or assignments they are doing. Rather than the lesson and assignments being teacher-designed, teachers work with pupils to design projects and activities. This will not only be more motivating to pupils, but is also more meaningful, and therefore likely to lead to more learning.

Flexibility is important. Rather than having a fixed and unvarying lesson plan, constructivist teachers are reactive, in the sense that they let pupils guide where the lesson is going (to an extent at least). Teachers can react to pupils' responses and ideas, and the lesson can go in a different direction from that originally planned. This means that if a pupil comes up with a good idea or question, rather than saying something like 'That's interesting, but we can't go into that today', the teacher should follow up the question. Some of the most cognitively and motivationally rewarding lessons are said to occur when pupil questions or comments lead to the discovery of new knowledge and ideas in the classroom.

Teachers also need to be **adaptive**. The individuality of pupils must be taken into account, not only with respect to their academic ability, but also with respect to their learning styles. This means that teaching needs to be varied, to appeal to pupils' different ways of learning. It also means that pupils may vary in the time it takes them to gain understanding of a particular concept. They need to be given that time, by allowing concepts to be explored in full. Teachers need to continually observe pupils' learning, and adapt their teaching/curriculum where necessary.

Stressing the existence of **multiple realities** is a good way of moving pupils away from the conception that there is always a right answer, and will help them become more thoughtful and to engage in deeper learning. This may sound a bit abstract, especially for younger pupils, but can be as simple as allowing different ways of solving a problem, or pointing out that different answers are possible.

Constructivism has implications for **curriculum** and **assessment** as well as for classroom practice. The view that one needs to work with pupils' prior knowledge and individual and collective meaning making means that standardized curricula, that are the same for all pupils, do not fit well within the constructivist model. Curricula need to focus on big ideas that are treated in depth rather than a breadth of topics treated in a superficial way (Brooks and Brooks, 1999).

Standardized tests are not seen as promoting pupils' construction of meaning. Formative, learning-focused assessment is seen as more appropriate. If learning happens as pupils give meaning to experiences building on their existing knowledge and understandings, assessment techniques must allow pupils to express their personal understanding of concepts in individual ways (Dana and Davis, 1993). That standardized testing does not necessarily promote learning is illustrated, according to constructivist educators, by the fact that pupils who score well on a standardized test may fail to answer the same questions correctly a couple of months later. Clearly, in those cases, learning has been surface rather than deep. Use of portfolios and observation of pupils by the teacher are seen as useful alternatives to traditional testing. An alternative that some constructivist writers promote is the use of **rubrics**. Rubrics are statements that describe different levels of accomplishments for a specified outcome, often developed jointly with pupils. This is said to help pupils gain a deep understanding of what is expected of them, and means that assessment can be used for learning rather than just as an accountability measure.

These views might make you think that in constructivism everything goes, and that constructivist teaching is not focused on outcomes. This is not accurate, however. Constructivist teachers have a clear understanding of where pupils are coming from, and what their learning goals are, and try to construct a learning environment in which those goals can be met.

Constructivist Versus Traditional Classrooms: a Comparison

Brooks and Brooks (1999) give us an interesting comparison between constructivist and traditional classrooms:

Traditional	Constructivist
Activities rely mainly on textbooks	Activities rely on hands-on materials
Presentation of material starts with the parts, then moves on to the whole	Presentation of material starts with the whole, then moves to the parts
Emphasis on basic skills	Emphasis on big ideas
Teacher emphasizes following fixed curriculum	Teacher follows pupils' questions
Teacher presents information to pupils	Teacher prepares a learning environment, where pupils can discover knowledge
Teacher tries to get pupils to give the 'right' answer	Teacher tries to get pupils to give their point of view and understandings, so they can understand pupils' learning
Assessment is seen as a separate activity, and occurs through testing	Assessment is seen as an activity integrated with teaching and learning, and occurs through portfolios and observation

The Structure of Constructivist Lessons

What would a constructivist lesson look like?

It will be clear, from all we have said above, that it won't be possible to create a 'generic' constructivist lesson that would hold for all situations. By its very nature, constructivism should encourage experimentation, contingency and fluidity in lessons and cannot be prescribed in the way a direct instruction lesson can be. However, certain key factors will be similar, which allows constructivist authors to suggest a number of possible structures. One example is the four-step model presented here.

1. Start phase

The teacher might want to start by teasing out pupils' prior knowledge and setting up activities. The teacher can start off with a broad open question (e.g. 'What do you think biology is about?'), and then encourage open answers and discussion on this subject. An alternative is to start with a problem that is relevant to pupils' daily lives. The topic of the lesson could then be introduced. The teacher may also decide to introduce a puzzling or surprising situation, which causes pupils to think about the situation. Rather than introduce pupils directly to definitions or concepts, the teacher will try to get pupils to discover rules and definitions, and will set up an activity that allows them to do this.

2. Exploration phase

The pupils can now do the activity set up by the teacher in phase 1. This activity will typically be exploratory, involve real-life situations or materials, and allow group work. The activity should be structured in such a way that pupils confront issues which allow them to develop understanding, and should be challenging (though not beyond their abilities, obviously). It is a good idea to remind pupils of metacognitive processes they might want to employ when solving problems.

3. Reflection phase

During this phase, pupils may be asked to look back at the activity, and analyse and discuss what they have been doing, either with other groups or with the teacher. The teacher can provide useful scaffolding during this phase, through questions and comments designed to link the exploration to the key concept being explored.

4. Application and discussion phase

Following this, the teacher can convene the whole class to discuss findings, and come to conclusions. Next steps can be identified, by either teacher or pupils, and main points can be recapped.

While this is one example of a possible structure, we have to reiterate that there is no such thing as 'the' constructivist lesson structure and that, because concepts are studied in depth, an exploration can go on for several lessons.

The Evidence Base for Constructivism

While constructivism has been making strong inroads among teachers and teacher educators, some researchers urge educators to exercise caution before going down this road. According to some authors, because our view of how the mind works is continually being revised, the best strategy may be to reserve judgement about constructivism while monitoring how it compares with new theories of learning and the findings of cognitive science. Good and his colleagues, for example, state that 'learning may be more than just "carpentry" and teaching may be more than just "negotiation" and "building inspection"' (Good et al., 1993).

Up until recently, the effectiveness of constructivist teaching methods has been underresearched, constructivism to many authors being close to a 'belief system' that is a-priori 'right' and not particularly in need of empirical verification (see, for example, Ernest, 1999 and Von Glasersfeld, 1989). Those studies that did exist tended to be small-scale qualitative studies, that give a useful insight into constructivist teaching as it occurs in the classroom, but do not usually incorporate rigorous methodology using comparator groups or measures of pupil learning. This has led to scepticism about the validity of these findings, not least by proponents of the direct instruction model.

Recently, however, the volume of research on the effectiveness of constructivist approaches has increased.

An example of this is a Dutch study that has attempted to compare constructivist approaches to direct instruction using quasi-experimental methods. Teachers were trained in either the direct instruction or a cognitive apprenticeship model based on the principles mentioned above, with a control group of teachers remaining untrained. Pupils were tested on reading comprehension, metacognition and attitudes towards school and learning pre- and post-implementation, while follow-up tests were also administered later on to see whether learning had been retained. Compared to the comparison group, the pupils taught under the direct instruction model scored better on metacognition on the post-test, but not the follow-up. Pupils taught using cognitive apprenticeship scored better on some aspects of reading comprehension, metacognition and focus on learning on the post-test. Only the effect on metacognition was sustained in the follow-up study, however. When compared directly to one another, pupils receiving the cognitive apprenticeship model did better than those taught under the direct instruction model on aspects of reading comprehension (including in one instance the follow-up), the follow-up test of metacognitive skills, and the follow-up tests of perception of skills and focus on learning (attitudes). While these results are somewhat patchy, they are clearly suggestive of the possible strength of the cognitive apprenticeship model and constructivist strategies (De Jager, 2002).

Another experimental study, that explicitly compared third-grade (6–7-year-old) pupils taught using constructivist experiential methods in a traditional expository way found that the experimental (experiential) group did significantly better on the post-test than the control group (McDavitt, 1994). A similar result was found in a study in Korean classrooms (Kim, 2005), though in both cases it is not entirely clear to what extent the traditional model related to effective direct instruction approaches.

Evaluation of the MathWings project in the USA, a programme to improve mathematics teaching and learning which uses a constructivist approach to teaching, has shown positive results in a number of different school districts. Comparison of schools using the programme to matched schools that did not use the programme showed positive programme effects on standardized tests. The tests used differed from state to state, but in all cases children in the programme schools on average did better than those in the matched schools. The different tests focused on basic skills as well as higher-order skills (Madden et al., 1999). A small but positive effect of constructivist methods on achievement in standardized test scores was also found in a study that used a survey of over 4000 teachers to measure teaching behaviours (Wilson et al., 2002). Implementation of a constructivist literacy curriculum had a positive effect on pupils' writing in another study (Au and Carroll, 1997). A US study found positive effects on pupils' motivation, in that pupils in a constructivist classroom were more internally motivated, and saw the task itself as a reward, rather than being motivated mainly by external factors (Koebley and Soled, 1998).

Not all studies show positive results though. One US study looking at the implementation of a science teaching reform programme that used a constructivist framework reported no effects on either achievement or pupil attitudes to science, while research that used data on the level of implementations of constructivist teaching within the same programme likewise found no effects (Shymansky et al., 1999, 2000). Another study reanalyzed US data from the Third International Maths and Science Study (TIMSS), an international study of maths and science achievement and teaching, and found that pupils taught by teachers who had a behaviourist, direct instruction approach did significantly better than those taught by teachers with constructivist beliefs (Gales and Yan, 2001). A reanalysis of TIMSS data to find out whether using constructivist methods was associated with better performance on those test items that measured conceptual understanding found this to be the case for some items, but the relationship was quite weak (Walker, 1999). In a study of primary science teaching, Klahr and Nigam (2004) found that children taught using direct instruction acquired the concepts more easily than those using discovery approaches, and that they had equally strong levels of understanding as the minority of children who had discovered the knowledge for themselves.

A major critique of constructivist methods relates to the translation of theories of learning into methods of teaching. According to Mayer (2004), active learning doesn't necessarily equate to discovery-type approaches as often advocated by constructivist educators. Rather, evidence reviewed by the author suggests that in most cases teacher-led approaches appear to be more effective, though they can often include constructivist elements. A similar conclusion is reached by Kirschner et al. (2006), who conclude from their review of research that overly discovery-oriented approachcs to tcaching are inefficient as they put too strong an emphasis on searches using short-term memory while failing to teach strategies and knowledge that can be stored in the long-term memory.

Research on constructivist teaching is therefore inconclusive. What is clear, however, is that pure discovery approaches don't appear to be effective. Some form of teacher guidance and direction needs to be a part of these approaches, and in practice most effective implementations of constructivism mentioned above employ a form of mixed approach where elements of direct instruction are melded with constructivist approaches like coaching. There is also a clear need to consider the context and goals of teaching in deciding what methods to choose. Constructivist teaching may work better when the subject is an unstructured situation (such as diagnosing a patient in medicine) rather than a well-structured situation (like a mathematics problem) (Spiro and DeSchryver, 2009).

An additional issue with introducing constructivist teaching methods is that a number of studies show that many teachers find these methods quite hard to implement. In one study, informal interviews prior to implementation of a programme designed to introduce constructivist methods indicated that teachers viewed a constructivist approach to teaching as a challenge and a concept that is difficult to grasp in a short period of time (Dharmadasa, 2000). In another study, teachers saw constructivist methods as burdensome, and were concerned about its effect on classroom discipline. They were not confident about providing appropriate materials, promoting experimentation and initiating children's construction of knowledge (Au and Carroll, 1997). One German study appears to show that in order to be able to implement constructivist strategies, teachers must reach a certain prior level of effectiveness. In other words, they need to be effective teachers before they can be effective constructivist teachers (Klieme and Clausen, 1999). Certainly, good classroom management and a positive classroom climate are essential to making constructivism work in the classroom. It can be argued that the added motivation the constructivist strategies can engender in pupils may encourage better and more attentive behaviour among pupils, however.

Summary

Constructivism is a teaching philosophy that has made strong inroads among teachers and teacher educators in recent decades. It is based on the premise that pupils actively construct knowledge, rather than receiving it from the teacher. Learning is a search for meaning. Teachers should encourage pupils to construct meaning by structuring learning activities around big ideas and explorations, giving them enough time to thoroughly explore concepts, and connecting new knowledge to what pupils already know.

These principles have led constructivists to propose a number of methods that can helpfully be used in the constructive classroom. These include modelling (showing pupils how to do or think about a difficult task), scaffolding (providing a lot of support at the outset, which is gradually withdrawn), coaching (helping pupils while they are solving a problem), articulation (getting pupils to express their ideas), reflection (getting pupils to reflect on their activities), collaboration (with other pupils), exploration and problem-solving activities, giving pupils choices, encouraging them to come up with multiple options and answers, and being flexible and adaptive rather than sticking to a fixed lesson plan.

While initially there was a lack of evidence on the effectiveness of constructivism in encouraging pupil learning, the amount of research has increased, though results are mixed and controversial. Teachers often find constructivist methods hard to implement, however.

Reflective Questions

1. Do you agree with constructivist philosophy? How does it differ from a realist view of the world?
2. Think of the direct instruction lesson we discussed in Chapter 2. How do you think this differs from a constructivist lesson?
3. In Chapter 1, we presented evidence in favour of the direct instruction model. Do you think this contradicts evidence for the constructivist model we have presented here?
4. Do you think it is possible to integrate direct instruction and constructivist teaching models? Why/why not?
5. Can you design a lesson structure that integrates both constructivist and direct instruction models of teaching?
6. How well do you think constructivist teaching models fit with the theories of learning discussed in Chapter 1?

CHAPTER 6

TEACHER BELIEFS, VALUES AND KNOWLEDGE

Key Points

In this chapter, you will learn about:

- why teacher beliefs matter
- the main types of teacher beliefs that affect teaching
- the relationship between teacher beliefs and student achievement
- forms of knowledge that teachers should have.

Introduction

In previous chapters, we have talked mainly about what teachers *do* in the classroom, known in the jargon as teacher behaviours. These are, as we have seen, of critical importance to pupil learning (or not learning for that matter). However, what teachers do in the classroom isn't the only thing that matters. Teachers' planning of lessons is of course important, but alongside that there is what teachers *think*. Of course, what teachers think, and in particular for us what they think good teaching is, what they think about pupils, and what they think about learning, will not normally affect pupils in the same direct way as what they do in the classroom, and because of that some of the teacher effectiveness researchers whose work we reviewed in previous chapters may not have taken too much notice of teacher beliefs and values. However, it would be wrong to think that these don't matter, just because a teacher doesn't directly communicate her beliefs about what good teaching is to pupils. In all parts of life, what we believe influences what we do. Think, for example, about your own beliefs about global warming. If you believe that this is the greatest challenge of our times, that it is a man-made problem and that our emissions are a key part of the problem, you are more likely to modify your behaviour by, for example, travelling in a more fuel-efficient hybrid car or by using public transport than if you believe that global warming is simply a part of the natural cycle of temperature change on Earth. In the same way, what you believe about teaching and learning will influence how you teach, and what you think your pupils can actually learn. That is why beliefs and values are important to effective teaching, and some beliefs are associated with more effective teaching behaviours than others.

What beliefs?

Belief systems are dynamic and permeable mental structures, susceptible to change in light of experience. The relationship between beliefs and practice is not a simple one-way relationship from belief to practice, but a dynamic two-way relationship in which beliefs are influenced by practical experience (Thompson et al., 1992).

A difference with research on teachers' behaviours is that while most researchers working in that area have focused on a similar set of behaviours, the belief structures that have been studied are more wide-ranging, as the universe of teacher beliefs is larger than the universe of in-class behaviours. One of the problems with talking about teacher beliefs and values is therefore that there is a lot of disagreement about what they are and how we should look at them.

A number of different types of beliefs exist that can have an impact on teaching. In an early study in this area, Clark and Petersen (1986) identified three types of teacher thought processes: teacher planning, teacher thought processes and teachers' theories and beliefs. To include planning as a thought process would seem a bit arbitrary, as one could equally see these as an action by teachers.

More recently, most researchers have settled on some version of three main types of beliefs that matter to teaching: beliefs about what effective teaching is (for example, do teachers believe in a constructivist approach to teaching?), beliefs about how children learn (e.g. do children have to reach a particular stage of maturity before they can learn certain concepts? Do they need to have a particular ability level before they can learn certain concepts?) and more general beliefs about pupils (e.g. do pupils from disadvantaged backgrounds require school to provide them with discipline they lack in the home? Do children require freedom of choice and involvement in determining curricular goals to flourish?). These three sets of beliefs are, however, interconnected. Askew et al. (1997) have described the relationship between them. These English researchers see the key distinction as one between connectionist, transmission and discovery orientations. These ideal types can be distinguished on the basis of teachers' beliefs about what it means to be a student, their beliefs about how best to teach and their beliefs about students and how they learn. We will discuss these three aspects in turn.

According to Askew et al. (1997), *connectionist* teachers believe that mastering the subject involves being both efficient and effective, being able to choose an appropriate problem-solving method and being able to make links between different parts of the curriculum. Connectionist teachers stress the importance of the application of learning to new situations by encouraging students to use realistic problems. *Transmission*-oriented teachers believe in the importance of students obtaining fluency in a number of standard procedures and routines, and they believe that students need to learn to do routine procedures before applying them to problems. The *discovery*-oriented teacher believes that all methods are equally acceptable as long as the answer is obtained, whether or not the method is efficient. They emphasize students' creation of their own methods.

When the researchers looked at teacher beliefs about students and how they learn, they found the following differences. *Connectionist* teachers believe that most students are able to learn given effective teaching, and that students come to school already possessing a lot of prior knowledge. The teacher's role is then to work with the students to introduce more efficient strategies. Misconceptions are seen as important teaching tools. For *transmission*-oriented teachers, who emphasize set rules and methods, what students already know before they come to class is less important. Students' own methods do not form the basis of teaching. Students are believed to differ in ability, with failure to learn once the teacher has explained the procedures to students resulting from lack of ability. *Discovery*-oriented teachers believe that learning is an individual activity, which happens once students are 'ready' to learn a certain concept. Learning takes precedence over teaching, and students' own strategies are paramount.

Finally, teachers were found to differ in their beliefs about what the most effective teaching methods are. *Connectionist* teachers believe that teaching is based upon dialogue between teacher and students. This helps teachers to better understand their students and allows students to gain access to teachers' knowledge. This leads to interactive teaching, with an extensive focus on discussion to help students explore more efficient strategies. *Transmission*-oriented teachers emphasize teaching over learning, and focus on introducing students to routines or knowledge through clear verbal explanations. Interaction consists largely of the teacher checking whether the student can reproduce the taught procedure or knowledge using mainly closed questions. *Discovery*-oriented teachers believe in letting students discover methods for themselves, through extensive use of practical experience.

Teacher Beliefs and Pupil Achievement

Beliefs therefore seem to be important to what teachers do. But is there any actual evidence that beliefs influence pupil achievement?

Quite a few studies have looked at this issue. In their study of 90 mathematics teachers, Askew et al. (1997) found that highly effective teachers were characterized by connectionist beliefs, while transmission and discovery orientations tended to characterize some of the less effective teachers. Similarly, in her overview, Fang (1996) reports on a number of studies that suggest that teachers' beliefs about literacy teaching affect outcomes. However, as beliefs aren't directly experienced by pupils, and we said earlier that it is what pupils directly experience that influences them, how do beliefs influence achievement? Unsurprisingly, they do this through changing behaviour. One study that looks at this was conducted by Muijs and Reynolds (2003). Teacher behaviours, teacher beliefs, teacher self-efficacy and teachers' (self-rated) subject knowledge were measured in a sample of 103 British primary school teachers for that purpose, and linked to student achievement controlled for prior achievement and background factors. The researchers proceeded from a theoretical model that hypothesized that these factors would have an influence on student achievement proportionate to their proximity to student experience, with more distant factors influencing outcomes indirectly through their impact on the most proximal factor – teacher behaviours in the classroom. They found that teacher behaviours significantly affected achievement at the end of the school year, controlling for prior achievement and background factors. A connectionist orientation was important as well, however. Indirectly, this set of teacher beliefs had a significant influence on achievement, through their impact on teacher behaviours, of which they were the strongest predictor. Teacher self-efficacy and subject knowledge also impacted on teacher behaviours, and thus affected student achievement indirectly.

Not all studies show that beliefs influence behaviour. In one overview, it was found that a number of studies report inconsistencies between what teachers believed and what they actually did in the classroom (Fang, 1996). This is not entirely surprising, and can happen for a number of reasons. The first is that teachers' individual beliefs may not be the same as those held by their head teachers or the government, so that they may be forced to use approaches that they themselves would not feel are the most effective. For example, in systems where high-stake national tests are used to rank schools and pupils, many teachers spend a lot of time on test preparation, even though they believe that this may be detrimental to pupils' real learning. There is also the problem that teachers may use particular concepts when talking to researchers but understand them differently. The term constructivist may be an example of this. It is a popular term to use when discussing teaching, but that doesn't mean that everyone understands the term in the way it was originally framed by people like Von Glasersfeld (1987). What has also been found is that teachers aren't necessarily the best judges of their own teaching practice, so that they may act differently than they believe they do, as it is often hard for any of us to really understand what we are doing in the classroom while we are doing it (Muijs, 2008). An example of this can be found in a study of nursery activities. All four adult supervisors expressed strongly child-centred beliefs to the interviewer, stating that the children had to have ownership of the activities. However, when observed, only two of the four conducted the activity in a way that allowed children that freedom of initiative, with the other two being much more directive (Blay and Ireson, 2009).

Teachers' Self-efficacy Beliefs

Other areas of teacher belief that are of importance to their effectiveness are teachers' self-concept and teachers' self-efficacy. Self-concept can be defined as 'a person's perceptions of him/herself, formed through interaction with the environment, interactions with significant others and attributions of behaviors'. (Shavelson et al., 1976). The self-concept is multidimensional, which means that one can have different self-concepts about different life areas. For example, a primary teacher could have a self-concept of herself as a math teacher, and a different self-concept of herself as a PE instructor. Teacher self-efficacy has been defined as 'a teacher's judgement of his or her capabilities to bring about desired outcomes of student engagement and learning, even among those students who may be difficult or unmotivated' (Henson, 2001). It is clear that the two concepts overlap to a certain extent.

Teacher self-efficacy has been linked to student outcomes in a number of studies. A variety of studies have found that students with teachers who score highly on self-efficacy did better on standardized tests of achievement than their peers who are taught by teachers with low self-efficacy beliefs (Moore and Esselman, 1992; Anderson et al., 1988; Watson, 1991, cited in Henson, 2001). Low teacher self-efficacy beliefs have also been linked to low expectations of students, an important factor in student achievement as mentioned above (Bamburg, 1994). Teacher self-efficacy was found to be related to student self-efficacy in a study by Anderson et al. (1988).

Therefore, just as pupils' academic self-concept is related to their achievement, it would seem that teachers' beliefs in their own self-efficacy is related to their effectiveness. This doesn't, of course, necessarily mean that self-efficacy is the cause of teacher effectiveness, as the causal direction may go the other way. Most likely, as with the relationship between self-concept and achievement among pupils, the relationship goes both ways.

Changing and Influencing Teacher Beliefs and Values

Teacher beliefs are shaped by a number of different factors, which can make them hard to change. They can in part be formed by teachers' underlying ideological beliefs and beliefs about what matters and how the world works, which will influence what teachers see as important values they need to express in their teaching, such as an emphasis on equity which may lead people to want to teach in schools in disadvantaged areas. As to teaching methods and practice, a key influence has been found to be the teacher's own experiences as a school pupil, which will tend to be what they see as the 'normal' way of teaching. These sources of beliefs about teaching are then modified through teacher training, where teachers will experience new sets of beliefs and practices regarding teaching, both from their trainers and through their classroom practice during training. The latter is an especially strong influence, that can shape teachers for the rest of their careers. The culture of the schools they work in will also shape teacher beliefs, as whenever we become part of an organization we will start to take on the norms and values of the place. Life experiences and professional development may modify beliefs over time, as in one study of two science teachers who had received very similar teaching as pupils themselves, but whose very different life experiences had led them to, respectively, a direct instruction and constructivist approach to teaching (Smith, 2005).

It is often said in school improvement that it is necessary to change beliefs to affect change in classroom practice. And, certainly, when we look at the importance of beliefs to behaviours as shown in the research mentioned earlier, this would seem a sensible strategy. The problem with this, though, is that it is hard to do. Beliefs are deeply ingrained, especially where they touch on deeply held values and ideologies, as mentioned above. Therefore, it has become apparent that in order to change teachers' beliefs, what we need to do in many cases is to first change behaviours, for example by developing a new teaching strategy and equipping teachers with the skills to apply that in practice. Behaviour change can then lead to change in beliefs if the new strategy is seen to work. A practical result has been found to lead to modifications in beliefs in this way, as teachers are keen to use strategies that work in their classrooms. If these new successful practices go somewhat against existing beliefs, this creates what is known as 'cognitive dissonance', a discrepancy between previously held beliefs and new actions. This will lead the individual to seek to reconcile behaviours and beliefs again, typically by looking for evidence to support the successful behaviours, and change beliefs accordingly. This tendency to change beliefs based on changing behaviours can be strengthened by clearly laying out the rationale for the proposed change in behaviour, i.e. the evidence for the new practice. This needs to be done in such a way that the change can be seen as complementing rather than directly contradicting existing beliefs, which makes it important to know what those beliefs are.

Teacher Knowledge

As well as teacher beliefs, it is of course also the case that what teachers know can make a real difference to how well they teach. It is a bit of a no-brainer to say that teachers' knowledge matters, but that still leaves a number of questions, like what exactly do teachers need to know, and how strong does that knowledge need to be?

Generally speaking, researchers identify three main types of teacher knowledge: teachers' subject knowledge (what they know about the subject they are teaching), teachers' pedagogical knowledge (what they know about effective teaching) and teachers' pedagogical subject knowledge (what they know about the effective teaching of their specific subject). Beattie (1995) adds another dimension of teacher knowledge – personal practical knowledge – which is a teacher's knowledge of her students, in particular their individual learning needs, strengths and weaknesses, and interests.

Of course, all these types of knowledge are potentially important to effective teaching. If teachers don't have any knowledge of the principles of effective teaching, then they are unlikely to fully apply them, and the same goes for knowledge of the pedagogy of teaching their own subject.

The topic of actual subject knowledge has been somewhat more controversial. It seems obvious that teachers need to know about what they teach, but the extent to which they need to know their subject is a bit less clear. Not all studies have shown that teacher subject knowledge affects achievement. In particular, a number of American studies on the relationship between teachers' scores on the National Teacher Examinations and the performance of their students have found little or no effect, while studies on the impact of teacher certification are also mixed (Darling-Hammond, 2000). This, however, has a lot to do with the way these variables are measured. Teacher certification (whether or not teachers have a teacher training qualification) is a pretty weak measure of subject knowledge, as trained teachers can differ strongly in their backgrounds in this respect. The same is true of national examinations, which tend to set a lower threshold for knowledge without testing it in full. When better measures of teacher knowledge are used, stronger effects are found. Muijs and Reynolds (2004) asked teachers themselves to state their subject knowledge in mathematics and found that teachers who were observed to be more effective and had higher levels of pupil achievement also reported stronger subject knowledge. Other studies show similar results. In a study of British early years (infant) teachers, Aubrey (2007) found that teachers' lack of deep subject knowledge stopped them from bringing into practice their knowledge of how children learn. In Askew et al.'s (1997) study, in which informal 'concept mapping' interviews with teachers were used to gauge their subject knowledge, it was found that the connectionist teachers, who were the most effective, had a wider knowledge of practical and formal methods of representation and of students' mental strategies than transmission- or discovery-oriented teachers. Teachers who made few conceptual links showed fewer student gains in achievement, although the relationship was weak. There was no relationship between gains and other content knowledge variables, such as fluency, scope, explanation or understanding. Teachers did not differ in their understanding of mathematical concepts, although connectionist teachers seemed more inclined to link different numeracy concepts. Formal mathematics qualifications were likewise not linked to student gains.

Still the question remains as to how much knowledge is needed. It is certainly not the case that all teachers need a PhD in the subject they teach to be effective, and certainly experience of university subject teaching shows us that this is by no means a guarantee of effective teaching! Rather, the exact amount of knowledge necessary will differ by age group and level taught, and there may well be a ceiling effect on the necessary amount of knowledge. An interesting example of this was found in a study of over 2800 students using data from the Longitudinal Study of American Youth. Monk (1994) found a positive but curvilinear relationship between teachers' subject knowledge as measured by courses taken and student achievement. This suggests that there may be a threshold effect operating, in that a minimal level of subject knowledge is necessary for teachers to be effective, but that beyond a certain point, a law of diminishing returns may operate, which may explain the mixed findings in other studies.

Summary

While previously we have mainly discussed teacher behaviours, it is clear that what teachers believe is also important to their effectiveness. In particular, their beliefs about effective teaching, beliefs about how children learn and beliefs about children's development in general are important. There is disagreement on how exactly to classify beliefs, but a well-supported classification was made by Askew et al. (1997) who distinguished *connectionist, transmission-oriented and discovery-oriented* teachers. Connectionist teachers were found to be most effective in a number of studies.

While beliefs are important, they are hard to change, as they are deeply ingrained and linked to values and personality. It is often more effective to first change behaviours. If these are experienced as effective, teachers are then more likely to adapt their beliefs.

As well as beliefs and values, teachers have different levels of knowledge they bring to their teaching. The key elements of teacher knowledge are their subject knowledge, their pedagogical knowledge and their knowledge of teaching their specific subject, known as pedagogical subject knowledge.

Reflective Questions

1. Thinking about your own teaching, what beliefs about how pupils learn do you think underlie your practice?
2. What do you think have been the main influences on what you believe to be effective teaching?
3. How do you think your own beliefs influence the way you teach?
4. What contradictions do you think exist between what you believe about teaching and learning and the way you teach? What is the cause of these contradictions?
5. Have you ever felt that gaps in your subject knowledge limited the effectiveness of your teaching? Why/why not?

PART 2

CREATING A FRAMEWORK FOR LEARNING

CHAPTER 7

CLASSROOM MANAGEMENT

Key Points

In this chapter, you will learn about:

- the main studies on classroom management
- how to avoid disruption during lesson transitions
- why and how to establish clear rules and procedures
- what seating arrangements are most effective for different teaching situations.

Introduction

One of the main features to emerge from teacher effectiveness research as a correlate of pupil achievement and attainment is *opportunity to learn*. This refers to whether or not the content tested for (on whatever test is used to measure pupils' achievement) has actually been seen by the pupils during the course of the year. The main factors to influence opportunity to learn are curriculum coverage (the extent to which the content covered by the teacher actually matches the content covered by the test) and the related factor of how many hours are actually pencilled in to study the subject tested. However, another major factor influencing opportunity to learn within the lesson is *time on task*, that is the amount of time within a lesson that pupils spend engaging with the curriculum rather than on other activities such as socializing, moving around the classroom and being disciplined (Brophy and Good, 1986; Reynolds and Muijs, 1999a).

Time on task in turn is crucially dependent on the quality of both classroom and behaviour management, in that ensuring a smooth flow of the lesson is important to both. Classroom management (Lemlech, 1988) has consistently been found to distinguish more from less effective teachers (e.g. Muijs and Reynolds, 1999) and has also been found to distinguish expert teachers, who appear able to manage classrooms very smoothly by ensuring that activities blend into each other seemingly without effort, from novice teachers for whom classroom management appears to present significant difficulties. A major study of classroom management was undertaken in the 1970s at the Research and Development Center for Teacher Education at the University of Texas, by a team led by Edmund Emmer and Carolyn Evertson. Coming from a teacher effectiveness research perspective, they looked at differences between teachers in their pupils' on and off task behaviour and related these to the teachers' classroom management strategies (Emmer et al., 1997; Evertson, 1995). Many of the findings from that study have influenced subsequent practice as well as the recommendations given below.

A different perspective is that of 'classroom ecology' research, initiated by Kounin in the late 1960s and continued in research undertaken by Doyle and Carter from the 1980s onwards. Kounin was one of the first to realize, after extensive studies, that pupils' behaviour was not just, and indeed not primarily, influenced by teachers' disciplining techniques, but by their classroom management (Kounin, 1970). Classroom management is closely connected to and often discussed in conjunction with dealing with pupil misbehaviour. In this book, we will discuss the two separately, viewing classroom management as creating conditions under which pupil misbehaviour is less likely to occur. How to deal with misbehaviour when it does occur will form the subject of Chapter 8.

Classroom management is crucially linked to preparation. In one study of effective teachers, for example, they were found to strongly emphasize effective planning and organization as prerequisites for effective teaching, not least as good planning facilitates classroom management (Watson et al., 2007), and as a general rule it can be stated that effective classrooms are managed through procedures and rules, not through punishment. Therefore, procedures need to be planned and implemented early on, from the first lesson of the new school year.

Elements of Effective Classroom Management

Starting the lesson

An obvious but often neglected element of effective classroom management is starting the lesson on time. Reasons for lessons starting late are various, amongst others prior lessons running late, playtime going on for too long, chaotic transitions from playtime to lessons, and ineffective management of pupils coming into the classroom. While the teacher can her/himself help to alleviate these problems, a whole-school policy aimed at maximizing lesson time is essential as well (Creemers, 1994).

The start of the lesson can involve several classroom management difficulties that the teacher needs to take into account. The main problem is that pupils will often be coming from the playground or lunch where different, more lax rules apply, and therefore the transition to appropriate classroom behaviour may cause difficulties. The teacher can keep disruption to a minimum by instituting a number of set procedures for dealing with lesson starts. The teacher can, for example, write instructions on the board before the pupils come in so they can get started with the lesson immediately, train pupils to take the register and read instructions or have certain set activities that pupils can start doing as soon as they come into the classroom, such as chanting times tables. Having a seating arrangement from the start of the year so all pupils know where to go every lesson is also important.

Appropriate seating arrangements

Another important aspect of classroom management is providing appropriate seating arrangements in the class. One general principle is that pupils should have sufficient space to work comfortably. If movement in the class is desired or necessary, pupils should be able to do this easily and without too much pushing and shoving. There should be enough room between seats for the teacher to be able to move around the classroom without bumping into or disturbing pupils. How exactly to arrange pupils and desks depends on the space and resources available.

There is also a pedagogic aspect to this in that choice of the exact seating arrangements will need to match the formats and goals of the lesson, as the

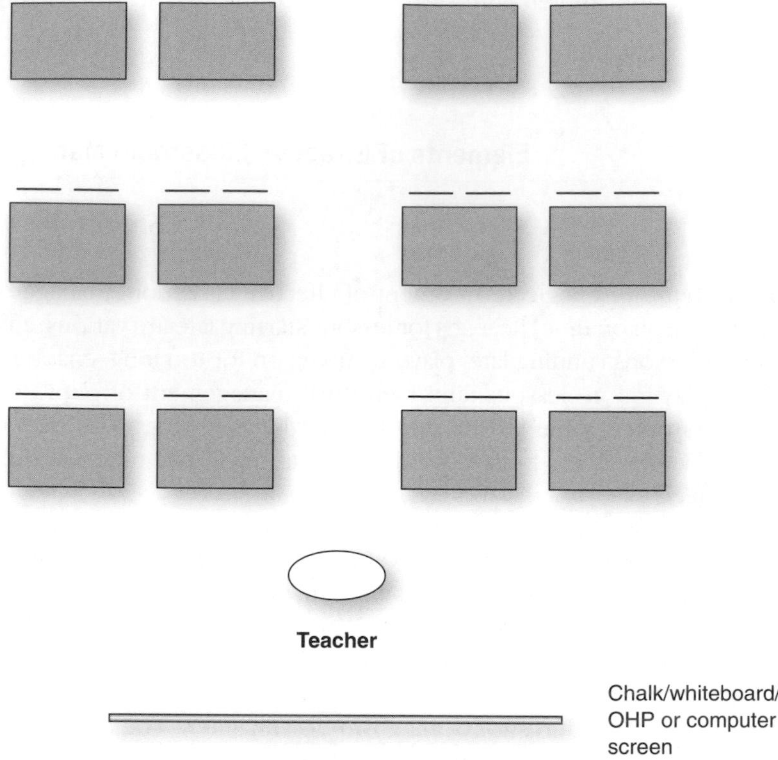

FIGURE 7.1 Seating in rows. This seating arrangement is effective for whole-class teaching, but not for small group work or classroom discussion

way pupils are positioned can influence the effectiveness of different types of delivery (see Figures 7.1 to 7.3). If a direct instruction style lesson is to be used in which the teacher will spend a substantial amount of time delivering content to and interacting with the whole class, all the pupils should be able to see the teacher and the tools s/he is using (black/whiteboard, OHP screen, number line) without straining. No pupils should be sitting with their backs to the teacher. This still leaves a number of seating arrangements open to the teacher, such as seating pupils in rows facing the teacher, seating them in a semi-circle or horseshoe or, with younger pupils, letting them sit around the teacher on the rug.

Other lesson plans may require different seating arrangements, however. For cooperative small group work, for example, it is recommended to place the groups around tables to allow them to interact easily with one another. If individual work is required where pupils aren't supposed to interact with each other too much, this seating arrangement should on the contrary be avoided.

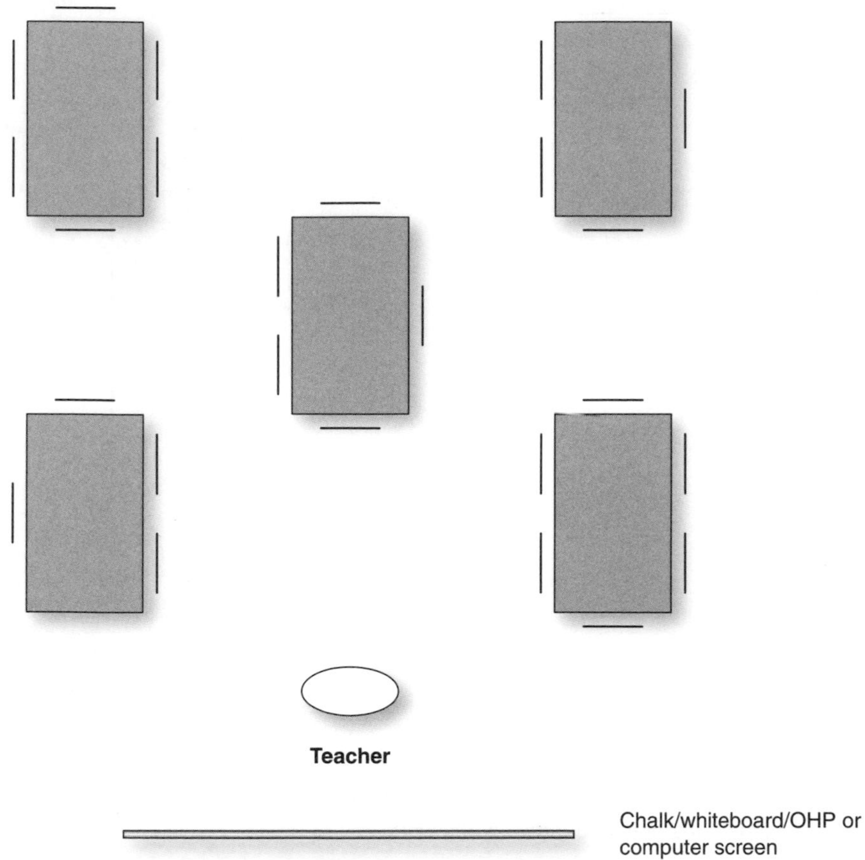

FIGURE 7.2 This seating arrangement is suitable for small group work, but less suitable for whole-class teaching and class discussion

Whole-class discussion can be facilitated by seating pupils around a big table or seating them in a circle or semi-circle, while seating them in rows will impede discussion. A possible compromise (for young pupils) involves pupils sitting round the teacher on the carpet during the whole-class part of the lesson and then moving them to sit around tables for small group work afterwards. Using a semi-circle seating arrangement can stop pupils trying to 'hide' and not take part in interactions (Joachim, 2002).

Dealing with external disruptions

Disruptions from outside the classroom can take up valuable teaching time. These can take several forms such as the head coming in to make announcements,

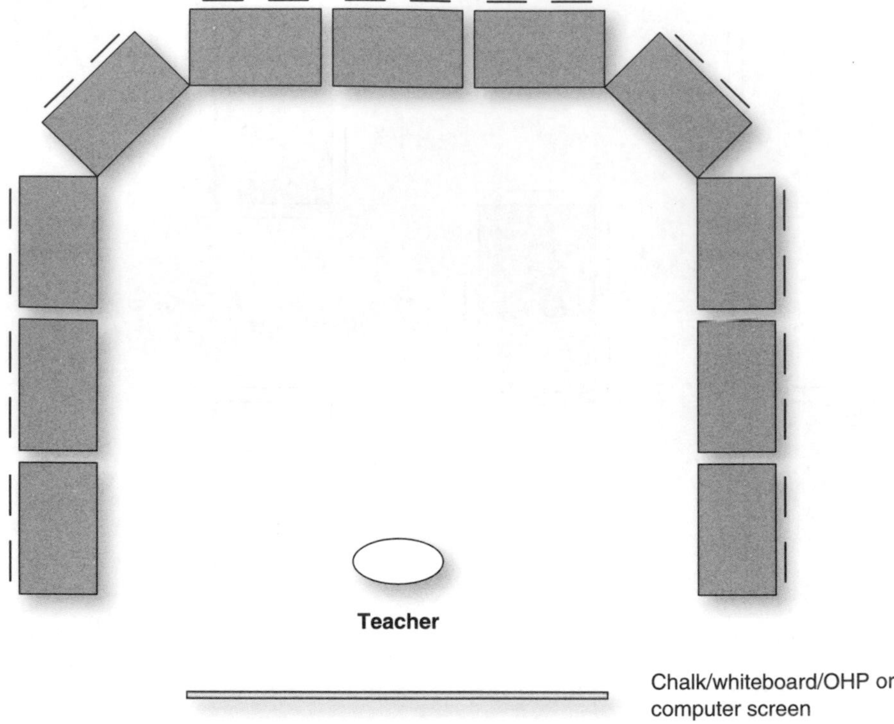

FIGURE 7.3 This seating arrangement is suited for class discussion and whole-class teaching, but is not suitable for small group work

teachers from other classrooms coming in with questions and pupils coming in with various requests. While a whole-school strategy to limit this kind of interruption is desirable, some interruptions are inevitable. The teacher needs to make sure that interruptions cause minimum disruption to the lesson by having clear rules for pupils' behaviour during such disruptions (such as sitting quietly or getting on with seatwork) and by dealing with them quickly, if necessary telling the teacher or pupil who has come in to leave and come back later.

Establishing clear rules and procedures

One of the main factors for ensuring smoothly run lessons is to establish clear rules and procedures from the start. *Rules* are more formal, usually written, statements that specify what pupils are allowed to do or expected not to do. *Procedures* are more informal arrangements that specify how things are to be done in a particular classroom. Rules are often specified school-wide, and have been identified in school effectiveness research as distinguishing more from less effective schools. Procedures can in many cases also be school-wide, but are often specified by the teacher for his or her class. Effective teachers have been found to spend a considerable amount of time and effort on specifying and clarifying procedures at the beginning of the school year (Wong and Wong, 2004). While this may seem to be at odds with the principle of maximizing opportunity to learn and time on task (spending as much time as possible on academic teaching), the additional time spent on this at the beginning of the year is more than made up for by the time won through less time-wasting during the rest of the year. Also, pupils do actually want rules, they want to know what is expected of them, and will behave better the clearer that is. Below, we will discuss a number of elements for which clear rules and procedures need to be established.

For rules and procedures to work, they need to be actively taught to pupils. As in the school as a whole, it is better to stick to a small number of clearly understood and consistently enforced rules rather than a large number of (therefore) more difficult to enforce regulations. The rules taught need to become a routine and automatic part of pupil behaviour. This requires a good deal of reinforcement at the beginning of the school year. It is important that the teacher not only tells pupils what the rules are, but explains the reasons why they exist as well. Thus, when telling young pupils not to shout out answers, the teacher should explain that the reason they shouldn't do this is to give all pupils a chance of answering the question. Likewise, when telling them to be quiet while another pupil is answering the teacher needs to explain the reasons for this, such as showing respect to other pupils and being able to learn from their answers. Reasons for being careful with laboratory equipment need to be explained as being a matter of pupil safety (and not merely the school's insurance policy!).

A lot of rules have to do with movement around the class, such as sitting in a circle in an orderly way. These situations obviously need to be practised a number of times before they will run smoothly and, like other motor skills, they need to be automatized as much as possible. Other rules that need establishing relate to things like how to pass round material, what to do when arriving late and how to ask for help.

One of the main factors to take into account when setting up classroom rules and procedures is to ensure they are consistently implemented. If consistency is not enforced, rules will soon break down. For example, if the teacher has decided to prevent pupils shouting out answers to questions, this rule must be constantly enforced and as soon as a pupil shouts out an answer, s/he must be told off. If this does not happen and one pupil is allowed to shout out an answer, soon more and more pupils will start doing this and the teacher will have to take strong action to restore the rule.

Smooth transitions between lesson segments

One of the main ways to ensure maximum time on task is to ensure that not too much time is wasted during transitions from one part of the lesson to the next part of the lesson, for example when going from teaching a new topic to the whole class to individual practice of the new topic. This can be a particularly difficult problem if pupils need to move from one part of the classroom to another, like when they have to move from the carpet to their tables or need to get materials such as workbooks and pencils. If not managed appropriately, such transitions can easily lead to time-wasting and can take up a significant part of the lesson (in our own research, we found this to be up to 15 per cent of lesson time in some lessons!) (Muijs and Reynolds, 1999).

Transitions need to be as short and smooth as possible. In order to make this easier, effective teachers establish clear procedures for lesson transitions. These can include rules limiting how many pupils can move around at any one time (for example, by letting one table move at a time), or assigning a particular child to clear away papers and pencils left on the table (it is a good idea to give this role to different pupils at different times). The best way to do this is to think of transitions as a set of steps that need to be executed by pupils. These can be put up on a wall chart, and be taught to pupils. For example, the transition from whole-class work during which pupils sit in a circle around the teacher to seat-work at their desks could be as follows:

1. Pupils go to their tables in order, i.e. first table 1, then table 2 etc.
2. At their tables, they take a worksheet from the middle as well as their pencil.
3. Pupils write their name and the date at the top of the worksheet.
4. Pupils start working (Arends, 1998; Borich, 1996).

Another useful technique is cueing. This is a technique used to alert pupils to the fact that a lesson transition is about to occur. An example that is often used during seatwork is to tell pupils that they have five minutes left to work and to repeat this one minute before the end of seatwork. Cueing can help prevent the problem of pupils who continue to work on the preceding activity after they are supposed to have moved on to the following activity.

Pupil talk

Inappropriate pupil talk can disrupt lessons. Pupils talking during the lesson are off task themselves and can distract other pupils. Correcting this misbehaviour will slow down the lesson and make the classroom climate less pleasant. Therefore, clear rules on when pupil talk is or is not allowed are important. This does not mean that talking should be prohibited at all times. During small group work and some other types of seatwork, low-level talk can be appropriate, but this is clearly not the case during whole-class presentations. Clear rules also need to be established for pupil behaviour during questioning. Pupils should not usually be allowed to shout out answers (except during quick-response games) and should be made to listen to each other's answers and ideas. A period when loud talk can occur is during lesson transitions. According to Borich (1996), it is best to institute a no-talking rule during transitions, as allowing low levels of talk is difficult and often unsuccessful.

Giving homework assignments

Giving (homework) assignments can be one of the more difficult parts of the lesson, not least because not all pupils will be keen to do them. In order to minimize these problems, effective teachers give assignments immediately following related in-class activities. This ensures that the homework assignment often appears to be a natural part of the lesson and not something 'tacked on' afterwards. It is also important that the teacher makes it clear that homework is important and not just an obligatory time filler. For example, the teacher saying 'It is important that you practise this aspect, so you can use it well when we get to more difficult exercises, so I'll give you some homework on this' creates different expectations than the teacher saying something like: 'I have to assign you homework, so do exercises 10 and 11 on page 32.' Homework should not be used or presented as a punishment.

Maintaining momentum during the lesson

One of the most fruitful ways of preventing pupil misbehaviour during lessons is to ensure the smooth flow of the lesson. Kounin (1970) described a number of ways in which teachers themselves can slow down the momentum of lessons. Two of these refer to the teacher stopping an activity already begun:

- A *dangle* occurs when the teacher starts to do a particular activity, but then stops it halfway, leaving it 'dangling in mid-air'. This can happen when a teacher starts preparing a seatwork activity and then suddenly decides s/he needs to teach something else first, for example.
- A variation of this is a *flip-flop*, in which a teacher starts an activity but goes to another activity before finishing it, after which s/he goes back to the original activity once again. Both dangles and flip-flops can cause confusion among some pupils, and can trigger misbehaviour among the naughtier pupils. Both can be prevented by good lesson planning on the part of the teacher.

- Another way in which teachers can impede lesson flow is through *overdwelling*. This occurs when a teacher goes on explaining instructions to pupils after they have totally grasped what they need to do. This will lead to boredom and restlessness among pupils, and thus to a higher chance of misbehaviour.
- *Fragmentation* occurs when the teacher breaks down activities into too many different steps. An example would be where the teacher hands out papers in the following steps: 'Take the pile of handouts', 'Take one off the top and hand the pile to your neighbour', 'now take one off the top'. It has to be noted, however, that what constitutes overdwelling or fragmentation may differ from group to group, depending amongst other things on the age and ability level of the class.

Downtime

Downtime refers to those parts of the lesson during which one or more pupils (or the whole class) have time to fill because they have finished seatwork early, because the lesson has finished early and there is no point starting a new topic, or because pupils have to wait for materials to be fetched, the computer to load and so on. These situations can easily lead to disruption if clear procedures do not exist to deal with them. Effective teachers have clear rules, such as 'If you finish early, go into the reading corner and silently read a book' or 'If you've finished your work, come and ask me for the answer sheet and mark your answers'.

The best way to avoid downtime problems is to limit the amount of it that occurs. This can be done by, for example, making sure that there are enough additional tasks available for pupils who finish quickly and by making sure that all materials to be used are in class before the start of the lesson. It is better to have more exercises available than everyone will be able to do during the allotted time than to be left with unproductive time which has to be 'filled'.

Ending the lesson

A final moment during which management problems are likely to occur is at the end of the lesson. Problems that can occur at this point include not leaving enough time for finishing the planned activities (research has shown that the end-of-lesson summary is especially likely to get shortened or even completely cut out), lessons running over time, and instructions for homework getting lost as pupils rush to collect their belongings and go off for lunch or playtime. Effective teachers experience fewer problems with ending the lesson than less effective teachers, through methods such as planning and pacing the lesson to leave sufficient time for activities at the end, giving out homework early so that no confusion occurs, establishing a set of rules for leaving the classroom (letting pupils go out one by one after answering a final question can be effective) and cueing so pupils know how long the lesson still has to go.

Summary

In this chapter, we have learnt about what research has found to be effective classroom management techniques.

Research on classroom management started in the late 1960s, and identified a number of points to help teachers avoid pupil misbehaviour.

Pupil misbehaviour is most likely to occur during the start of the lesson, at the end of the lesson, during downtime (which should be limited as much as possible) and during transitions. In all four cases, it is important to establish clear procedures for pupil behaviour. More generally, spending some time on establishing clear rules and procedures at the beginning of the year can save teachers a lot of time later in the year.

The teacher should limit the number of rules and procedures used, however, and rules must be rigorously enforced otherwise they will soon be ignored by pupils. The reasons for enforcing particular rules need to be explained to pupils, and it can be helpful to engage pupils in the process of making rules.

The teacher needs to maintain momentum during the lesson and has to avoid actions that can impede momentum such as 'dangling', 'flip-flops', 'overdwelling' and 'fragmentation'. Teachers will often need to limit or prohibit pupil talk.

When giving out homework assignments, teachers need to make clear the educational value of the assignment and avoid giving the impression that it is a punishment.

Reflective Questions

1. You are planning a lesson using whole-class teaching and individual pupil practice. What seating arrangements could you use?
2. How would you avoid disruption during lesson transitions?
3. You are starting the year teaching a new class. How would you go about setting up classroom rules?

(Continued)

(Continued)

4. Think of a lesson you have recently taught, observed or been a pupil in. When did disruptions occur? What could have been done to avoid those?
5. Think of a lesson you have recently taught, observed or been a pupil in. Were there any occasions when you felt the teacher her/himself was causing the lesson to lose momentum? How could this have been avoided ?
6. Do you think it is better for a school to instigate a whole-school behaviour policy, or to leave this to individual teachers? Why?

CHAPTER 8

BEHAVIOUR MANAGEMENT

Key Points

In this chapter, you will learn about:

- the main causes of pupil misbehaviour
- when to deal most effectively with pupil misbehaviour
- some models for dealing with pupil misbehaviour
- effective and ineffective uses of praise, rewards and punishment
- assertive discipline
- behaviourist psychology and what it has taught us about reinforcers and punishers.

Introduction

In the previous chapter, a number of techniques were discussed which should contribute to the orderly and smooth conduct of the lesson. Applying these techniques should help avoid pupil misbehaviour occurring. However, as every teacher will tell you, even the best classroom management in the most effectively taught lesson will not avoid misbehaviour occurring at all times. The issue of discipline and what to do when pupils misbehave is therefore one of the main issues for beginning teachers, and several studies have shown that classroom misbehaviour is the main concern of many teachers, and one of the key stressors in their job, this across a range of countries (Akin-Little et al., 2007; Gaby, forthcoming; Ritter and Hancock, 2007).

It is therefore not surprising that the issue has received plenty of attention from researchers as well, often in conjunction with research on classroom management more generally (as discussed in the previous chapter).

Causes of Pupil Misbehaviour

Pupil misbehaviour can result from a variety of causes, some of which are external to the classroom situation and some of which may be caused, or at least reinforced, by the classroom situation.

Home circumstances can predispose pupils to misbehaviour. Pupils who have just experienced or are experiencing parental divorce can often become either withdrawn or, conversely, disruptive in school. Pupils from unstable backgrounds tend to be more disruptive in school, especially as some children may experience a lack of authority or caring at home. Schools in areas likely to suffer from these problems therefore need to provide a disciplined, structured and caring environment, in order to help compensate for what pupils are missing at home. A further problem may be that the values pupils are exposed to in the home may not be the same as those that are encouraged at school. Some parents have themselves found schooling to be a negative experience from which they have not benefited, and are therefore unlikely to take a strong interest in their children's performance at school. It is important that the school tries to develop a more positive relationship with these parents.

Developmentally, pupils at certain ages (particularly early adolescence) will feel the need to rebel and seek attention in the classroom.

Schools and teachers themselves can precipitate misbehaviour. Lessons which are perceived as boring or irrelevant by pupils may provoke misbehaviour more easily, while schools and teachers that are either too authoritarian or too lax on discipline are more likely to encounter disruptive behaviour.

Finally, there is a clear relationship between pupils' school achievement and their behaviour in school, low achievement often leading to misbehaviour as pupils become disenchanted with school. Therefore, misbehaviour can be limited by providing a relevant curriculum that allows all pupils to experience success.

Preventing Misbehaviour

While most approaches have traditionally dealt with correcting misbehaviour once it occurs, it is obvious that the best way to stop misbehaviour is by trying to prevent it before its starts.

This is of course far more easily said than done, and some misbehaviour will occur even in the best lessons. However, it is clear that there are a number of ways that schools and teachers can try to help pupils be more motivated and therefore behave better.

Starting with teaching and learning

While many beginning teachers (and indeed many schools, especially in disadvantaged areas) think that you need to create an environment in which there are no serious behaviour problems before moving on to tackling teaching and learning, there is increasing evidence that this may be misguided.

Quite a lot of misbehaviour actually appears to be caused by poor teaching, or at least teaching that is poorly adapted to the interests and abilities of the pupils in the school and classroom (Muijs et al., 2004). A focus on improving teaching and learning can therefore be a very effective way of improving behaviour in a school.

One issue here is that learning and teaching in the school need to be adapted to the needs and developmental levels of pupils. Boys in particular often prefer active learning styles and may not react well to prolonged periods of having to sit still and listen. Introducing hands-on activities during lessons can help. It has also been found to be effective, from time to time, to introduce a pause during which students can engage in a physical activity.

Looking at the curriculum

Connected to the issue of improving teaching and learning is that of having a suitable curriculum. In many cases, a curriculum that is not adapted to pupils' interests can lead to boredom and rebellion, and therefore to behaviour problems.

Changing the curriculum to give pupils more choice, or allowing them to engage in activities that better meet their needs, may be one way to help prevent misbehaviour before it occurs. This does not mean taking out all the 'difficult' subjects, or giving up on key subjects that may not be popular (such as maths and literacy). Doing that would mean offering some pupils an impoverished curriculum, which may hinder their chances and achievement later in life (Guthrie et al., 1989; Leithwood and Steinbach, 2002). What it does mean, however, is trying to accommodate pupils' interests within core subjects, and allowing them broad choices in other areas.

Whole-school Behaviour Policies

School effectiveness research has long pointed to the importance of school-wide behaviour policies in creating the academically oriented, high-achieving school (e.g. Reynolds, 1992). Having a school-wide policy has an important advantage over teacher-made classroom rules in that it ensures consistency, with pupils knowing what rules they have to follow in all lessons. For individual teachers, this means less time spent teaching pupils the rules their classrooms. In order to reinforce these rules, they can be put up in all classrooms and in halls.

It can often be fruitful to involve pupils in the making of these rules in order to encourage a sense of ownership and shared responsibility over them, and to involve (especially older) pupils in policing rules and procedures. These rules can be more or less extensive but they should never be too numerous, otherwise pupils will start to perceive them as being petty. A limited number of well-understood and enforced rules will be more effective than a large number of detailed rules and procedures that are therefore more difficult to police.

An example of whole-school rules are:

- Use indoor voices at all times.
- Listen to others.
- Always do your best.
- Listen to and respect other pupils.
- Don't run in the corridors.

Listening to pupil voice

Saying teaching and curriculum need to be adapted to the needs of pupils is easy, but how can this be achieved in practice?

Involving pupils in the work and in leadership of the school has been found to be an effective way of combating disaffection. Rudduck and Flutter (2003) suggest that pupils can become 'pupil leaders', who, as well taking responsibility for their own learning, are actively playing a role in the running of their schools. This needs to be more than merely symbolic, and encompasses consultation on important as well as trivial decisions. The pupil council is usually a suitable forum for this consultation process (Heath and Vik, 1994). Pupil councils can help organize activities, plan pupil events, and help solve problems involving discipline, teaching and learning. However, as not all pupils will be involved in the council, and in particular more disaffected pupils may not want to be involved, it is a good idea to regularly survey the whole cohort of pupils on their views or to conduct interviews and focus groups with pupils you particularly want to reach.

One argument made strongly by advocates of pupil leadership is that the lack of pupil voice in schools is one of the elements that leads to pupil disaffection (Rudduck and Flutter, 2003). This is seen as a problem that is increasing in scope, as society as a whole is tending towards providing young people with ever more choice (in terms of consumption and lifestyle) and freedom in other areas (less authoritarian parenting, for example). The contrast with the school environment is then substantial, and frustrating to pupils.

Allowing pupils more say in school is likely to lead to a stronger identification with the school community, and can improve pupil motivation and consequently learning. There are several research studies that indicate that pupil leadership results in improved attitudes to school and enhanced self-efficacy among pupils (Goldman and Newman, 1998; Mosher, 1994). In one study of four schools in the USA, it was found that pupils who had participated in school leadership felt an increased responsibility for the school, and started seeing themselves as members of the 'school team' (Short and Greer, 1993). A programme requiring adult school staff and pupil leaders to form a community of learners in which all participated in improving the school, saw a significant decline in truancy and improvements in behaviour (Furtwengler, 1996).

Pupils, especially teenagers, attach a strong importance to the concept of 'respect' (Rudduck and Flutter, 2003). In many cases, they feel that they are not respected, causing resentment and anger towards the school. While teenagers in particular are quick to take offence in these areas, it is undoubtedly true that in many cases they are treated with a lack of respect.

Involving pupils certainly doesn't mean slacker discipline. One interesting finding from research is that pupils themselves appreciate clear behaviour rules, and when consulted will tend to support their implementation. While some humanist commentators have claimed that rules and stricter forms of classroom management by definition limit intrinsic motivation of students, research actually shows the opposite to be the case, with rule clarity and teacher monitoring being positively associated with interest in the subject taught (Kunter et al., 2007).

Dealing with Inappropriate Behaviour

While dealing with the causes of misbehaviour such as those outlined above is important, in actual classroom situations it is often better to focus on the misbehaviour itself in order to allow the lesson to proceed smoothly and not impede pupil learning. It can be a good idea to ask the pupil to see the teacher after the lesson to discuss what problems s/he may be having that could be causing her/him to misbehave. In most cases, it is crucial for teachers to spot the misbehaviour as quickly as possible and deal with it immediately (Arends, 1998; Borich, 1996).

A first rule for correcting misbehaviour is *not to overreact*. Minor off-task and attention-seeking behaviour should be dealt with quickly and with a minimum of fuss. After all, it would be counterproductive if dealing with the misbehaviour disrupted lesson flow more than the actual misbehaviour itself. One way to do this is through what is known as *overlappingness*, a term that refers to teachers' ability to nip misbehaviour in the bud in an unobtrusive way. Invading a pupil's physical space by moving close to the pupil or lightly touching him or her can quickly stop off-task behaviour, while allowing the teacher to continue teaching. One way to do this more effectively is by *scanning* the classroom, looking back and forwards through the class to try and spot any (emerging) problems.

An important skill that comes to some extent with experience is what Kounin (1970) referred to as *with-itness*. This is the ability to spot all misbehaviour quickly and accurately and to identify the right pupil as the culprit. This skill is quite difficult to learn for beginning teachers but once picked up, it will significantly help the smooth flow of the lesson as trouble will be snuffed out before it can grow into anything more serious. Targeting the right pupil will stop possible resentment from pupils wrongly singled out.

In some cases, it might be better to ignore minor misbehaviour altogether, as correcting every single occurrence of misbehaviour will disrupt lesson flow and may worsen classroom climate as pupils could perceive the teacher as being overly authoritarian. However, it is important to maintain a large degree of *consistency* in deciding which minor misbehaviours not to correct. If this is not the case, pupils will see the teachers' interventions as arbitrary, and may start to become more resistant.

Culturally Appropriate Behaviour Management

One issue with correcting misbehaviour is to be sure that you are sensitive to the different cultural backgrounds of pupils in your classroom, and don't misinterpret behaviours due to a lack of cultural understanding. Examples of these are the fact that while in Western cultures we expect eye contact during interactions, in parts of Asia it has traditionally been seen as polite to avert one's eyes when interacting with elders and people in authority. This is not therefore necessarily impolite or a sign of avoidance. Among many Chinese pupils, deference to authority might have been a value given to them by their parents, and they may be reluctant to express opinions.

Similarly, forms of 'ribbing', seemingly aggressive verbal interactions between boys, are part of culturally appropriate adolescent behaviour, like a sport, in some African American cultures, and do not constitute bullying (Weinstein et al., 2004).

As a teacher, it is therefore important to find out as much as you can about culturally normal behaviours among the pupils in your class. While of course not everyone from a particular culture will behave in a similar way, it is important to be aware of what different norms to your own may exist, and not to inappropriately sanction behaviour. However, we must of course be careful that differentiation doesn't lead to discrimination and perceived inconsistency.

However, the teacher will often have to deal with misbehaviour in order to stop it from escalating and causing increasing problems. Kounin (1970) refers to this as *desist incidents*. Evertson and Emmer (1982) suggest the following sequence for dealing with this type of behaviour:

1. The teacher should ask the pupil to stop the inappropriate behaviour. The teacher should maintain contact with the pupil until the behaviour has ceased.
2. The teacher should make eye contact with the pupil until appropriate behaviour returns.
3. The teacher needs to remind the pupil of what the appropriate behaviour is.
4. The teacher may need to ask the pupil to explain the correct behaviour to him/herself. If the pupil doesn't understand, s/he should be provided with feedback.
5. The teacher needs to impose the penalty for breaking the rule. This will usually consist of performing the procedure until it is done correctly. However, when the pupil understands what s/he needs to do but is doing it incorrectly on purpose, the teacher can use some mild form of punishment, such as withholding privileges.
6. Often, off-task behaviour occurs when pupils are doing repetitive, boring tasks which they have already mastered. Varying activities, for example by going from seatwork to interactive teaching or by going on to another type of exercise or another topic, can refocus pupils on the lesson.

Another model for dealing with misbehaviour is the LEAST model, which suggests five steps for dealing with desist behaviours:

1. **L**eave it alone. If the behaviour is not going to become troublesome, leave it alone.
2. **E**nd the action indirectly. This can be done by distracting the pupil from her/his misbehaviour through giving him/her something else to do.
3. **A**ttend more fully. Teachers should try to get to know pupils, so they can get to the heart of the problem. Has s/he got problems at home? Is s/he being

bullied? Does s/he have learning difficulties etc.? This will help the teacher decide what to do.

4. **S**pell out directions. Remind the pupil of what he or she should be doing and, if necessary, warn her/him of the consequences of not complying.
5. **T**rack the behaviour. If there appears to be a recurring problem with misbehaviour of one or more pupils, it is useful to keep systematic records of the behaviour, by using pupil tracking records, for example. These can then be connected to a reward system: pupils who do not appear on the tracking sheet for a certain length of time receive a reward, while those that are marked for a certain number of times receive some form of punishment (Arends, 1998).

In general, both approaches suggest three main phases once the decision has been made to correct a certain misbehaviour. Initially, one can try to divert the misbehaviour by, for example, distracting the pupil by asking a question, picking up the pace, boosting interest by starting a new activity, or removing certain tempting materials with which pupils can fiddle. If that does not help, more explicit correction may be needed, by moving close to the disruptive pupil, making eye contact with the pupil, using verbal cues such as naming the pupil (e.g. 'and, Daniel, the next topic is…'), pointing out in general that the class should be engaged with the lesson, or praising a particularly well-behaved pupil. If this still does not succeed in preventing misbehaviour, the teacher needs to go on to more severe warnings and, if necessary, punishment.

Behaviourism and Punishment/rewards

Behaviourist learning theory, which we discussed in Chapter 1, has a lot to say on the use of rewards and punishments in changing behaviour.

Skinner's theories are particularly relevant here. According to Skinner, who built on the work of Pavlov and Thorndike, a prime element of behavioural theory is the emphasis on consequences. Pleasurable consequences, or *reinforcers,* strengthen behaviour, while unpleasant consequences, or *punishers,* weaken behaviour.

With regards to reinforcers, it is important to know that no consequences are of necessity fixed to be reinforcers or punishers. Thus, while sending a child to see the head will be a punisher for most children, for some it may enhance their desired status as rebels and therefore on the contrary be a reinforcer of unwanted behaviour. What constitutes a reinforcer is an empirical question, not a given.

There are two broad types of reinforcement: *positive reinforcement* and *negative reinforcement.* Positive reinforcement occurs when a (positive) stimulus is given following a particular behaviour. In school, such stimuli include giving stars and praise. *Negative reinforcement* occurs when an aversive (unpleasant) stimulus is removed or averted. In the classroom, this can refer to releasing a pupil from having to perform an unpleasant task. Thus, good behaviour and a good workrate can result in pupils not having to do additional homework. Negative reinforcement is thus not the same as *punishment*. Negative, like positive, reinforcement strengthens a behaviour, while punishment (e.g. sending a child to the head) weakens a behaviour. Like reinforcement, *punishment* comes in two forms: *presentation* and *removal* punishment. Presentation punishment is the use of unpleasant consequences, e.g. a pupil has to write 'I will not misbehave in class' 50 times. Removal punishment refers to the removal of reinforcers, such as when a pupil must stay in class at break. Use of punishment is controversial among behaviourist researchers, some researchers claiming that it only has temporary effects. The majority of behaviourists claim that punishment is less effective than reinforcement.

If people are learning a new behaviour, they will learn it faster if they are reinforced for every correct response. This is called a *continuous reinforcement schedule*. However, once the behaviour has been mastered, it is better only to reinforce it *intermittently*. The main reason for this is that this helps the pupil not to expect reinforcement of behaviour every time, and of course it is also rather time-consuming for the teacher to reinforce each and every behaviour (Muijs and Reynolds, 2000a).

Using Rewards and Punishment

Behavioural psychological theory and classroom practice point to the importance of using rewards and punishments in classroom management. Using a reward may help to reinforce certain (desired) behaviours, whereas using punishment may deter certain behaviours. The basic principle in using rewards is to first identify what behaviours you want to reinforce, then decide what rewards would be appropriate to reinforce these behaviours, and finally to use these rewards in such a way that they can most effectively reinforce the desired behaviour.

There are a number of rewards that can be used to reinforce desired pupil behaviours.

The first is using *praise* in the classroom. This is probably one of the most frequently used behaviour management tools in classrooms and can be highly effective, although it should not be overused. However, a number of guidelines need to be taken into account to ensure the effectiveness of praise. Some further findings, largely from Brophy's (1981) research, are summarized below.

Teachers can also use specific *rewards, incentives and privileges* to reinforce desired behaviours. Rewards can take various forms such as house points resulting in a letter of praise to parents or entry into a prize draw, badges or symbols such as happy faces which children can wear and which can be used in conjunction with house points, honour rolls (listing 'pupils of the month', for example), sweets and so on. Privileges can include being excused from some forms of work or being given special responsibilities in class or in the school (which can range from being allowed to wipe the chalkboard to becoming form captain). It is often useful to involve pupils themselves in deciding what rewards to use, as in that way the teacher can ensure that the rewards given are indeed valued by the pupils. It is important to remember that what is valued by pupils can differ according to such factors as age and gender.

However, one needs to be careful of overusing external rewards as these can interfere with the pupil's own intrinsic motivation to learn. For this reason, an increasing amount of research has turned to the use of so-called *natural reinforcers*. These are reinforcers which are naturally present in the classroom. While for some pupils these may lie in their motivation to learn, for others these can be elicited by using reinforcement. The way one can do this – once the behaviour one wishes to reinforce has been selected – is to think about what natural consequences result from that behaviour. For example, writing an essay has consequences such as writing sentences, being able to express one's ideas, filling up a page, etc. The teacher then needs to choose which behaviour s/he wants to reinforce. In the case of essay writing, a desirable consequence may be enhancing the ability of the pupil to express his/her ideas. In order to be effective, this consequence should be obvious to the pupil. The teacher then needs to design the lesson in such a way that these desirable outcomes are made conspicuous. Focusing on how the task is done, as well as on outcomes, may help. The teacher also has to select a *backup reinforcer*. Unlike natural reinforcers these are extrinsic. These are essentially rewards, but must have educational value. The teacher may start off using such backup reinforcers, but once the pupils have started doing the task, the teacher should give feedback pointing out the natural consequences which should (hopefully) become natural reinforcers. The backup reinforcers should be given initially, but should over the course of time be removed. The natural reinforcers should be pointed out for a longer time, but it should hopefully become less and less necessary to do this explicitly as they become internalized (Horcones, 1991, 1992).

While using rewards is one of the most effective behaviour management tools, in some cases it will be necessary to use *punishment* as well. Punishment is designed to create an avoidance response, in that pupils should avoid behaviours which result in punishment in future. Such punishments usually include taking house points away for misbehaviour, making pupils stay in after school or during play, removing privileges, expelling the pupil from class (or, in the worst instances, from school) or giving verbal warnings in the classroom. Usually, the teacher should start off by giving a verbal warning for non-major misbehaviour, before going on to more serious punishments. However, after giving two or three warnings, some punishment should follow to avoid damaging the teacher's credibility in the eyes of pupils, who could otherwise start to believe that the teacher is not really serious about preventing this misbehaviour.

In general, though, research has found that punishment is less effective than praise in most cases. There are a number of reasons for this:

- The effects of punishment are usually specific to a particular context and teacher. They are less likely to be carried over to other teachers or classrooms, or to other types of misbehaviour. For example, if a pupil is punished for talking during the lesson of teacher A, this may stop her/him from talking in that teacher's lesson again, but not from talking in other teachers' lessons or from engaging in other misbehaviour during the lessons of teacher A.
- Punishment does not always guarantee that the desired response will occur. Because punishment is seen by pupils as specific to a particular context, it may keep the pupil from engaging in behaviour that gets her/him punished while not necessarily getting the pupil to engage in desired behaviour instead. For example, in the above situation, the pupil may refrain from further talk during the lesson, but that does not mean that s/he will instead engage in on-task behaviour. Instead, s/he may daydream or fiddle as long as this doesn't get her/him punished.
- The punishment may also become associated with the punisher rather than with the behaviour of the punished pupil. Teachers who use punishment too often may find that the punishment becomes associated with themselves rather than with the behaviours they are trying to avoid.
- Likewise, punishment that is designed to stop an undesired behaviour, but that is not associated with a desired behaviour, seldom has long-lasting effects. Pupils may not understand what the desired behaviour is, and therefore they will not start engaging in the desired behaviour.
- Punishment can also sometimes have negative side-effects. For example, in the above case, the pupil may decide not to risk talking at all any more, and may become less willing to make substantive contributions during lessons.
- Occasionally, punishment can lead to aggressive or violent reactions from pupils (Arends, 1998; Borich, 1996).

Effective Use of Praise

Brophy (1981) developed the following guidelines for the effective use of praise, based on extensive research:

Effective praise:	Ineffective praise:
• is delivered contingently	• is delivered randomly or unsystematically
• praises the particular behaviour it wants to reinforce	• is non-specific and global
• is perceived as credible by pupils, through signs that it is non-routine and spontaneous	• is blandly uniform, suggesting that it is an automatic reaction made with minimal thought

(Continued)

(Continued)

Effective praise:	Ineffective praise:
• rewards attainment of specific performance criteria (which can include effort)	• rewards mere participation, without consideration of processes or outcomes
• provides the pupils with specific information about their accomplishments	• provides no information to pupils, or information about their status
• orients pupils towards better appreciation of their own task-related behaviour and thinking about problem solving	• orients pupils towards comparing themselves with each other and thinking about competing
• uses pupils' own prior accomplishments as the basis for comparison	• uses the accomplishments of peers as the basis for comparison
• is given in recognition of noteworthy effort or success at difficult tasks (for this pupil)	• is given without regard to the effort expended or the meaning of the accomplishment
• attributes success to effort and ability, implying that similar success can be expected in future	• attributes success to ability alone or to external factors such as luck
• encourages internal attributions (gets pupils to believe they expend effort on the task because they enjoy it and/or want to develop task-relevant skills)	• encourages external attributions (gets pupils to believe they expend effort on a task for external reasons, such as to please the teacher, to get a reward, etc.)
• focuses pupils' attention on their own task-relevant behaviour	• focuses pupils' attention on the teacher as an external authority figure who is manipulating them
• fosters appreciation of, and desirable attributions about, task-relevant behaviour after the process is completed.	• intrudes into the ongoing process, distracting attention from task-relevant behaviour.

Therefore, while punishment is sometimes necessary, it should be used as a last resort and not as an automatic reaction to pupil misbehaviour.

An important aspect of effective use of rewards and punishment is consistency, both within the practices of one teacher and across the school. If the use of rewards and punishment is inconsistent, it will be perceived by pupils as unjust and arbitrary, and lead to a resentment that may ultimately lead to more rather than less misbehaviour.

The Assertive Discipline Programme

A classroom and behaviour management programme that has received a lot of interest, is the 'assertive discipline' programme developed by Lee and Marlene Canter (1976, 1989). This is based around the principle that teachers should react assertively towards pupil misbehaviour.

To adopt an assertive discipline approach, teachers and pupils (who need to be involved for this approach to be more effective through pupils feeling ownership of the rules) need to design at the outset a set of rules for school and classroom, along with clear procedures for dealing with infringements of these rules. Rules and consequences need to be communicated to parents, and stringently followed through by teachers.

Teachers should react assertively to misbehaviour, according to the procedures agreed, and should not accept any excuses from pupils. Teachers should not react in a hostile, angry or guilt-inducing way (e.g. 'You'll be sorry . . .') or in a passive way.

While popular, this approach has not been well researched for effectiveness, may put too much emphasis on punishment and may disrupt lesson flow if procedures to deal with misbehaviour are too complicated or take too much time to administer.

Summary

In this chapter, we looked at behaviour management, defined as what to do when pupils misbehave.

Elements that can predispose pupils to misbehave can lie both in situations outside school, such as pupils' psychological development, and in school and classroom factors such as boring, irrelevant lessons and curriculum or overly lax or authoritarian rules.

Therefore, tackling teaching and learning can help prevent misbehaviour occurring in the first place. Giving pupils a say in the running of the school can also help combat disaffection, as many pupils feel that the school environment is more restrictive and gives them less voice than other parts of their life.

When misbehaviour occurs, the teacher should not overreact to minor misbehaviour but try to deter it in the most unobtrusive way possible. Constant scanning of the classroom and overlapping can help nip problems in the bud.

If the behaviour is serious enough to warrant intervention, there are a number of models that have been proposed to deal with misbehaviour, such as the Evertson and Emmer model and the LEAST model.

(Continued)

(Continued)

One of the most common and effective ways of correcting behaviour is the use of rewards and punishment. A frequently used form of reward is teacher praise. However, not all praise is effective. In order for praise to work, it should not be an automatic reflex. Praise needs to be specific, credible and oriented towards both effort and ability, encapsulating the expectation that similar performance can be attained in future. Rewards can also take the form of house points, stars, badges and privileges such as responsible roles in the school. While effective, these rewards can lead to pupils becoming externally oriented rather than valuing learning for its own sake. To counter that, some researchers advocate the use of 'natural reinforcers', which are educational and available in the classroom.

Punishment is sometimes inevitable, but should not be overused, as it has been found to be less effective in engendering desired behaviours than the use of rewards.

Reflective Questions

1. In what ways do you think you as a teacher can contribute to the occurrence of pupil misbehaviour? Can you think of any examples you have experienced or observed?
2. What are the disadvantages of relying too strongly on punishment in behaviour management?
3. Why, according to behaviourist learning theory, are rewards and punishment effective?
4. Do you believe pupil leadership can make a contribution to decreasing misbehaviour?
5. Think of a lesson you have recently taught, observed or been a pupil in. How did you or the teacher use praise? Was this done in the most effective way? Why/why not?
6. Can you think of any natural reinforcers you could use during lessons?
7. Would you consider using 'assertive discipline'? Why/why not?

CHAPTER 9

CLASSROOM CLIMATE

Key Points

In this chapter, you will learn about:

- how to create a pleasant and productive classroom climate
- the uses, advantages and disadvantages of three types of classroom climate: competitive, cooperative and individual
- the importance of teacher expectations
- how to avoid negative expectations of pupils
- the importance of taking into account cultural differences in the classroom.

Introduction

Classroom climate as defined here is quite a wide-ranging concept encompassing the mood or atmosphere that is created in the teacher's classroom through the rules set out, the way the teacher interacts with pupils, and the way the physical environment is set out (Creemers and Reezigt, 1999; Freiberg and Stein, 1999).

Classroom climate has been widely studied since the 1960s. Most of these studies have identified it as an important factor in pupil achievement, both in Europe (Mortimore et al., 1988; Muijs and Reynolds, 1999) and in the USA (Brophy and Good, 1986; Rosenshine, 1979b). A large-scale meta-analysis conducted by Wang et al. (1997) found classroom climate to be one of the most important factors to affect pupil achievement. Learning environment was also found to be related to achievement in Fraser's (1994) review of 40 studies on the effects of classroom climate. Apart from this relationship with pupil achievement on tests, a warm, supportive classroom climate has also been linked to a number of other factors, such as pupils' self-esteem (Fraser, 1994), pupils' participation in the classroom, and even pupils' democratic values (Cotton, 1997). A classroom climate emphasizing warmth and support was associated with lower levels of bullying and victimization in one study in Israel (Shechtman, 2002). One dimension of classroom climate is affiliation, the level of friendship that students feel for each other. This factor has been found to be related to pupils' motivation in the classroom (Anderson et al., 2004). Classroom climate is also related to pupil well-being, according to Van Petegem et al.'s (2008) study in Belgium. More generally, pupil emotions play a role in learning, and in particular whether or not they feel safe and comfortable, which are clearly influenced by classroom climate (Meyer and Turner, 2006). Classroom climate has also been found to be a strong predictor of pupil aggression, with better relations with teachers and peers being related to lower levels of aggression (Shechtman, 2002). Creating a positive climate was identified as a prime characteristic of quality teachers in a study of teaching in 11 countries (OECD, 1994).

School climate and classroom climate

While in this book we are focusing on classroom teaching, it is clear that certainly with respect to classroom climate, teachers do not operate within a vacuum. School climate will strongly influence classroom climate, and in order to be effective the two need to be complementary. A teacher going against the prevailing school climate will find it difficult to change pupils' established habits. If, for example, pupils are not used to contributing ideas in other lessons, they will find it hard to change their habits for one particular teacher.

The school can do a number of things to help create a warm, supportive atmosphere. As in the classroom, the use of pleasant, bright displays will help, with pupils' work put up in hallways and dining areas. Schools should have strong and strictly enforced anti-bullying policies and should be open and receptive to problems pupils are having outside school. Good support services can help all pupils reach their potential. Minimizing noise and clean and pleasant communal spaces (hallways, dining room) will make a difference as well (Freiberg, 1999).

Measuring school and classroom climate

In order to be able to improve school and classroom climate, it is necessary first of all to find out what the climate in school is like, and where possible problems may lie. A number of direct and indirect measures have been proposed, which can involve teachers, pupils, parents and other members of the community. Getting information from pupils as well as teachers is important, as they can often have a somewhat different perspective on school and classroom climate. Fraser (1999), for example, has found that teachers have a more positive perception of the climate in their classrooms than their pupils. Involving pupils by getting them to give feedback on classroom climate has the further advantage of making them feel valued and important, and can contribute to school and classroom climate in and of itself.

A number of checklist and rating scales have been proposed that can be used with either teachers, pupils, school management or parents, such as that proposed for Dutch primary schools by Creemers and Reezigt (1999) or Fraser's (1999) Learning Environment Questionnaires. Fraser proposes measuring both pupils' and teachers' perceptions of school climate and measuring both actual and preferred climate among pupils. This can allow teachers and heads to see where the main discrepancies between actual and preferred climate lie and to target interventions specifically at those areas. Questionnaires aimed at parents and other members of the community have also been designed. A useful suggestion is the use of entrance and exit questionnaires. Pupils entering secondary school could be asked questions such as:

- What do you like about your current school?
- What is one concern you have about going to this school?
- What will you do to improve your success in school?
- What is one message you would like to give to your teachers?

Pupils leaving the school could be asked:

- What do you like about this school?
- What was your most memorable experience in this school?
- What area would you like to have improved in this school?
- What is one message you would like to give your teachers? (Freiberg, 1999)

With very young pupils, the use of questionnaires is inappropriate. One way of collecting classroom climate measures from these pupils is to ask them to draw a picture of their classroom. This can provide valuable insights into how much distance they perceive from their teacher, how formally or informally the classroom is run and what parts of the classroom (such as the blackboard or the reading area) are perceived to be important (Freiberg and Stein, 1999).

Data such as the number of referrals of pupils to the head by a particular teacher or the number of absences in the school as a whole are also useful indicators of school and classroom climate. In order for these measures to be of practical use, however, the results they generate need to be used to improve the school climate. As many of the measures mentioned above are quite fine-grained and look into various areas in some detail, specific points can be targeted. Feedback on the results can be discussed, on the basis of which an improvement plan can be drawn up. Some time after the reform has been implemented, the same form can be used to measure school/classroom climate again to see whether the reform has had any effect (Fraser, 1994).

Creating a Pleasant Classroom Environment

Classroom relationships

The most important aspect of classroom climate is the *relationship between teacher and pupil*s. This relationship can range along a continuum from formal to informal, and from warm to cool. A warm, supportive environment has been found to be important to teacher effectiveness, especially in encouraging pupils to contribute constructively to the lesson. Teachers who are perceived as being understanding, helpful and friendly and show leadership without being too strict have been found to enhance pupils' achievement and their affective outcomes, while teachers who come across as uncertain, dissatisfied with their pupils and admonishing produce lower cognitive and affective outcomes (Anderson et al., 2004; Wubbels et al., 1991).

Teachers should create an unthreatening environment in which pupils' opinions are valued, respected and solicited. Wrong answers should not provoke negative reactions on the part of the teacher, but need to be perceived as part of pupils' learning processes. This can be done by reacting positively to wrong answers and by trying to emphasize what was right about the pupil's thinking process.

Teachers who are concerned with pupils' emotional and social as well as academic needs have been found to engender more pupil involvement in lessons. Research has also pointed to the role of classroom climate in encouraging pupils with problems to request help. Often, it can be the case that it is precisely those pupils who need help most who are most reluctant to request it, the most able pupils having been found to be the most likely to request help. Research has found, however, that this gap can be reduced if not closed by teachers who value the emotional needs of their pupils and create a warm and not overly competitive environment (Deci et al., 1999).

A basic, but often overlooked, element in creating good classroom relations is the *use by the teacher of pupil names*. This can appear trivial, but not knowing pupils' names can create the impression that the teacher does not care about her/his pupils as people. Therefore, the teacher should address pupils by name as often as possible. At the beginning of the year, when faced with a new class (and, especially in secondary school, with one of several new classes), this can be more difficult than it sounds, however. A number of ways of making this easier can be the following:

1. Have pupils give their name each time before they speak, until the teacher feels s/he knows everyone.
2. Have pupils make name tags they can put on their table, so every time the teacher looks at the pupil s/he can associate the face with the name. It can be helpful to ask pupils to write down some memorable characteristic or hobby, which the teacher can associate with the pupil and which will help her/him to get to know the pupils better.
3. Have a list of names with the pupils' photos on the teacher's desk.
4. Try and memorize one row of pupils a day.
5. Ask pupils to introduce themselves to the class, giving their names, likes and dislikes, and other personal information.

An important component of classroom climate is the *enthusiasm* shown by the teacher. If the teacher him/herself is unenthusiastic about the subject or lesson being taught, this attitude is likely to rub off on pupils. Teachers who enjoy teaching and their subject and can put their enthusiasm across are more likely to motivate their pupils, and research has found a positive association between teacher enthusiasm and pupil involvement during lessons. It is no coincidence that most people, when they are asked to describe their favourite school teacher, will tend to pick out a teacher who managed to inspire them through their enthusiasm about the subject. Of course, no teacher can be equally enthusiastic about all subjects or on all days. It is, however, important to avoid expressing overt dislike of the subject or topic through comments such as, 'I know this is boring, but we have to do it because it is in the curriculum'.

Two aspects of classroom climate that are important when it comes to relationships are emotional support for pupils and providing relevant and quick performance feedback. Both act to create an environment that is warm and supportive, but with sufficient academic press to allow achievement to be optimized. An emotionally supportive environment in which the teacher also supplies plenty of evaluative feedback has also been found to have a positive influence on pupils' social competence (Wilson et al., 2007).

The physical environment

An aspect of a pleasant classroom that the teacher has a large amount of control over is creating attractive and pleasant *displays*. Colourful and bright displays can cheer up the classroom and make it a more pleasant environment, while also giving the teacher the opportunity to allow peripheral learning to occur. This can be done by displaying learning materials on classroom walls which can aid learning in an almost subliminal way by drawing pupils' attention to the displayed educational materials. Classroom climate can also be improved by displaying pupils' own work on the wall, as this can encourage pupils to take pride in their work and can motivate them. It is, however, important to give all pupils the chance to have their work displayed and not just to display the 'best' work, if this means constantly displaying work from the same pupils.

Other aspects of the physical environment of classrooms and schools can also impact on school climate. Clean and tidy classrooms, hallways and toilets can create a better atmosphere across the school. Small things matter. High noise levels in, for example, the dining room or the hallways can have a strong negative effect on school climate and pupil behaviour but can often be quite easily reduced (Freiberg, 1999).

According to some authors, *class size* can affect classroom climate, with smaller classes often showing a warmer and more supportive atmosphere (Harman et al., 2002).

Some of what has been said in this chapter about the need for classrooms to be warm, relaxed environments may appear to contradict what was said in earlier chapters about the need for the classroom to be a disciplined, work-centred environment. If one veers to the extremes of either position, this can indeed be the case. The best teachers, however, are able to create a classroom that is all these things, rather than being either overly authoritarian or undisciplined (Wilson et al., 2007). In our own research (Muijs and Reynolds, 1999), we found that good classroom discipline and a positive classroom climate were strongly related to each other, which suggests that in practice effective teachers are able to strike the right balance between the two.

Sometimes it can be necessary to put in place a strategy to improve school and classroom climate. The best way to do this is to do something that can be quickly implemented and is highly visible, for example greeting all pupils when they come to school in the morning. Pupils should be involved in the improvement effort as much as is possible as this will mean the climate is improved in ways that are important to them, and because it will help them feel involved and valued which in itself can improve school climate. Giving pupils authority in the classroom can improve classroom climate and encourage them to take responsibility for their environment. This has been identified as one of the differences in favour of Japanese schools when compared to American schools (Linn et al., 2000).

Three Types of Classroom Climate

Borich (1996) defines three types of classroom climate that the teacher may wish to use in different lessons. These are the competitive, cooperative and individualistic types. These three types are arranged along a continuum where the authority ceded to the pupils by the teacher ranges from none to quite extensive, and where teaching and learning move from being very teacher-led to being very pupil-centred.

In a *competitive* classroom, pupils will compete among themselves to give the right answer or to attain a standard set by the teacher. The teacher is the sole arbiter of the correctness of the response, and no authority is given to pupils. The teacher leads the class, presents and organizes the material and evaluates the correctness of the pupils' responses. In whole-class lessons, this can take the form of pupils competing by having the turn to give the right answer. In collaborative work, groups can compete against each other, for example through group games. During individual work, the teacher can get pupils to compete by giving a prize to the pupil who has correctly completed answers on a worksheet most quickly or for having the largest number of correct answers. A competitive climate can motivate pupils, especially boys, and can enhance pupil achievement because of this. This type of classroom also allows for a large amount of teacher guidance, which can be important to pupil learning. Structured, whole-class teaching has been found to be effective in raising pupils' achievement. The possible negative effects are damaging the self-confidence of less able pupils through the constant comparison involved, which may lead to them becoming disengaged from the lesson and possibly school and learning in general, and the fact that this method will not inculcate cooperative skills in pupils.

In a *cooperative* classroom, pupils engage in dialogue that is monitored by the teacher. They are allowed to discuss and bring up their own ideas, but the teacher intervenes to help them sharpen up and clarify their ideas and to encourage higher-order and creative thinking. In this type of classroom, pupils have more authority than in the competitive classroom, in that they are allowed to present their own opinions and ideas, and discuss these freely with one another. The teacher's role is to stimulate discussion, arbitrate the discussion and make sure disagreements between pupils do not get out of hand. At the end of discussions, the teacher will summarize and organize the ideas presented by pupils. In whole-class lessons, this can take the form of pupils being allowed to call out hints or clues when another pupil is having difficulties. During individual work, pupils can be made to cooperate with their neighbour by exchanging papers, checking each other's work or sharing ideas. This climate type lends itself particularly well to group work, in which pupils can cooperate by discussing a topic or working out problems with all pupils being allowed to contribute. A major advantage of this type of classroom is that it will help develop pupils' social and cooperative skills, which are becoming more and more important in the workplace. Pupils often enjoy working with one another, which means that cooperative work can be highly motivating. Being able to articulate their own ideas can help develop pupils' thinking skills. Disadvantages are that exchanges can easily become dominated by one or two highly self-confident individuals, with others allowing them to do all the work – the so-called 'free-rider' effect. Also, pupils can strengthen each other's misconceptions, and there is a risk of classrooms getting out of hand with pupils shouting out answers if not managed well.

The final type of classroom climate is the *individualistic* type. In that type of classroom, the emphasis will be on pupils getting through work independently and testing themselves. Pupils will complete assignments monitored by the teacher, and are encouraged to give those answers that they think are best, rather than answers that are considered to be 'right' or 'wrong'. The pupils' role will then be to complete the assignment with the best possible responses, while the teacher's role will be to assign the work and make sure that orderly progress is made towards completing it. In a whole-class setting (not the most natural one for this type of classroom), this can take the form of the entire class chanting out answers in unison. When group work is used in the individualistic classroom, subgroups will complete their own assigned topic which will be independent of topics done by other groups. Results are not shared with the class. During individual work, pupils will complete seatwork on their own without direct teacher intervention. Advantages of this type of classroom are the freedom it allows for pupils to work at their own level and develop their own answers to questions. This will encourage pupils' individual problem solving and independent learning skills. Negative effects can be that particularly less and averagely able pupils will suffer from lack of teacher guidance and make insufficient progress when left to learn in this way. Pupils will also not have the opportunity to develop cooperative skills, and for most pupils using too much individualized instruction has been found to be ineffective.

Teacher Expectations

What are teacher expectations?

Important to consider, both in classroom climate and in school and teacher effectiveness more generally, are the teacher's expectations of her/his pupils. From the late 1960s onwards (see box), research has found that teachers' expectations of their pupils can become a self-fulfilling prophecy. Pupils that teachers expect to do well tend to achieve better, while pupils who are expected to do badly tend to fulfil their teachers' expectations as well. School effectiveness research has paid a lot of attention to this factor, which has been found to be one of the most consistently important factors in this type of research (Mortimore et al., 1988; Reynolds et al., 1996; Rutter et al., 1979).

Of course, one could argue that the relationship between teachers' expectations of their pupils' achievement and pupils' actual outcomes is merely the result of teachers having accurate perceptions of their pupils' ability. However, research has shown that although this is the case to a large extent, there is more going on. The initial research came about as a result of finding that teachers form expectations of pupils even before they have any evidence for their performance. These expectations have been found to be related to pupils' ethnic, gender and background characteristics. Thus, teachers tend to have lower expectations of working-class pupils than of middle-class pupils, they tend to have lower expectations of pupils from ethnic minorities, and in the past they tended to have lower expectations of girls, although there is some evidence that this has changed to the extent that gender expectations in many cases may have become reversed (Covington and Beery, 1976; Rosenthal and Jacobson, 1968).

These expectations can affect pupils in a variety of (often subtle) ways. Teachers communicate their expectations of certain pupils to them through verbalizations (which according to Burns, 1979 are fraught with evaluatory statements), by paying closer attention to high-expectancy pupils and spending more time with them, by failing to give feedback to responses from low-expectancy pupils, by criticizing low-expectancy pupils more often and praising them less often, by not waiting as long for the answer of low-expectancy pupils, by calling on them less to answer questions, by asking them only lower-order questions, giving them more seatwork and low-level academic tasks, and by leaving them out of some learning activities (Brophy and Good, 1986). These expectations are then internalized by the pupils and the peer group, who start to behave in the way expected of them by the teacher. Sometimes these expectations can be communicated more directly than this as well. In our own research, we observed a teacher say to her class with an air of resignation: 'I know this topic is too difficult for you, but it is in the National Curriculum, so we have got to do it'.

Negative teacher expectations can be a particular problem in schools in disadvantaged areas, where an ethos of negative expectations can take over the whole school, creating an atmosphere in which teachers will say things like 'Well, what can you expect with pupils like ours'. This will often lead to less effort being made to help these pupils achieve and can lead to a negative spiral in which teacher expectations and pupil expectations feed on each other. This becomes even more problematic in low-ability sets, as there seem to be some differences depending on pupil background and ability, in that teacher expectations appear to have their strongest impact on pupils in the low-ability stream (Liu and Wang, 2008).

Even where teacher expectations are unbiased and accurately reflect a pupil's ability in a particular subject, a form of expectation effect can occur, in that when a pupil's achievement suddenly improves (or goes backwards), the teacher's expectations remain unchanged. For example, a pupil who usually gets high marks for a subject may continue to receive high marks on a bad essay s/he has done. Another example occurred with a pupil in our university who had not achieved well in French classes when at school. At one point, this pupil returned to his old school for a reunion. When asked what he was doing, he (truthfully) told his former French teacher that he had just got a first at university. The teacher furiously accused him of being a liar.

Rosenthal and Jacobson's Research on Teacher Expectations

The first major study on the teacher expectancy effect was undertaken by Rosenthal and Jacobson (1968) in the 1960s. At the start of the school year, teachers were provided with a list of pupils who were said to be expected to bloom intellectually in the coming years on the basis of a test, but who in fact did not differ from their peers in this respect. Pupils were retested on Three occasions during that school year and during the following year. Results indicated that 'bloomers' gained more in IQ than did control group children, although the effect wore off among the younger subjects, while growing in strength among older pupils. Grades in reading ability also improved significantly among the experimental group children, who were also rated more positively by their teachers on factors such as intellectual curiosity. Since then, the effect has received considerable empirical support (Burns, 1979; Covington & Beery, 1976).

Strategies for avoiding negative expectations

The question then is how best to avoid these negative expectation effects. The first thing is for teachers to be aware of their own (unwanted) biases. Pupils from a different ethnic group and social class may look and act somewhat differently from the teacher's norms. S/he should be aware of this, and not treat this as a sign of low ability. However, changing unconscious beliefs is no easy task. There are, however, a number of things teachers can do to help overcome this problem.

- The first is to remember that all pupils can learn, and communicate that belief to pupils.
- Teachers should make sure all pupils get the chance to answer questions, contribute to discussions and so on.
- Teachers should try and be aware of how often they call on girls and boys and pupils from different ethnic groups. It can be useful to have a colleague observe the lesson to point out if there are problems in this respect. The

observer's report needs to take account of both verbal and non-verbal interactions.

- Teachers should try to use objective criteria when marking pupils' work. To check whether this is the case, one can occasionally have pupils' work double-marked by a colleague who doesn't know the pupils.
- Teachers should monitor how they distribute rewards and punishments. It is important to remember that expectancy effects can manifest themselves through allowing pupils of whom the teacher has low expectations to behave worse and be off task and disengaged from the lesson more often than high-expectancy pupils, as well as through giving them more punishments and fewer rewards than high-expectancy pupils.

Summary

Classroom climate can be defined as the mood or atmosphere created by a teacher in her/his classroom, the way the teacher interacts with pupils, and the way the physical environment is set out.

Research has shown the importance of classroom climate, not only to pupil achievement, but to self-esteem and lesson participation as well.

One of the main elements in developing a positive classroom climate is creating a warm, supportive environment in which pupils feel unthreatened and are therefore willing to make a positive contribution to the lesson. The enthusiasm of the teacher has likewise been found to be an important factor. Therefore, even if the teacher is not feeling that enthusiastic on a particular day, s/he should avoid communicating negative feelings about the subject, lesson or curriculum to pupils. Creating a bright and pleasant classroom with displays of pupil work and educational materials can motivate pupils and create peripheral learning as well.

Teacher expectation effects occur when teachers attribute certain characteristics to pupils (usually ability) based on factors such as class, gender and ethnicity. These expectations can easily turn into self-fulfilling prophecies, and must therefore be avoided as they can damage the achievement of pupils from these groups. While this is difficult, being aware of the problem is a first important step. Teachers should also carefully monitor their own behaviour, or have a colleague observe them, to see whether they are, for example, giving more attention to boys than girls.

As societies are becoming increasingly multicultural, it is important that teachers are aware of this, and don't allow inevitable culture shock to turn into prejudice. When teaching a group with pupils from different cultural backgrounds it can be useful to try and find out more about the pupils' culture at the outset.

Reflective Questions

1. Think of a lesson you have recently taught, observed or been a pupil in. Were low expectations of any pupils evident? How do you know?
2. What would you do to encourage low ability pupils to request more help?
3. Which of the three types of classroom climate would you prefer to use? Why?
4. Have you ever experienced culture shock? How do you think it can be overcome?
5. What do you think can be done through school policies to counter teachers' low expectations of pupils?
6. Do you think classrooms can be both businesslike and warm environments at the same time? How could that be achieved?

CHAPTER 10

EFFECTIVE USE OF HOMEWORK

Key Points

In this chapter, you will learn about:

- the main types of homework and the purposes for which it can be set
- research on the effectiveness of homework as a learning tool
- how the setting of homework can be used effectively by teachers
- the importance of establishing a school-wide homework policy
- the role of parents in homework and how the school can help them.

Introduction

Homework is one of the most widely used but also one of the more controversial aspects of teaching. Unpopular with pupils, and often with teachers and parents as well, it remains a central part of school life. In this chapter, we will review research that has looked at whether or not homework is an effective learning tool, and research that has looked at how to use it most effectively.

Homework can be defined as 'tasks assigned to students by school teachers that are meant to be carried out during non-school hours' (Cooper, 1989: 67). It can be either individualized or assigned to the whole class. LaConte (1981) classified the three main types of homework as:

- *Practice assignments*, which reinforce newly acquired skills or knowledge. An example of this can be when pupils have learnt about different types of leaves, and are asked to look for examples in their environment.
- *Preparation assignments*, which are intended to provide background to particular topics. For example, pupils can prepare for a lesson by reading texts or by collecting material in advance.
- *Extension assignments*, which are designed to practise learnt material or extend the pupil by encouraging them to do more research on the subject after the topic has been studied in class.

While describing what types of homework exist is useful, it is probably more important to take account of what homework is actually for. Homework can be designed to meet a variety of purposes, such as:

a. Increasing pupil achievement
b. Reinforcing and strengthening topics taught in class
c. Completing unfinished work
d. Developing independent study skills
e. Developing self-discipline
f. Developing time-management skills
g. Involving parents in helping their children's learning
h. Allowing preparation for future lessons and topics
i. Developing pupils' research skills
j. Reviewing and practising topics taught in school
k. Extending the school day.

The precise form that homework will take will depend on the goals that the teacher is trying to accomplish. However, the bottom line of all these goals is aiding pupils' learning. This leads us to the question of whether homework is an effective learning tool.

Is Homework Effective?

There is quite a bit of research that has attempted to answer this question, often with ambiguous results, however. The main reason for this ambiguity is that it is very difficult to isolate the effects of homework from a variety of other factors affecting pupils' achievement.

A major overview of research was published by Cooper (1989, 1994) who looked at 120 studies categorized into three subsets:

- experimental studies comparing homework to no homework
- experimental studies comparing homework to in-school supervised work
- non-experimental correlational studies that looked at the statistical relationship between the amount of homework done and achievement, as found through questionnaires of pupils and teachers.

Looking at 17 studies that have compared homework with no homework, he found that homework can strongly benefit pupil achievement. Seventy per cent of the studies he looked at found that pupils who did homework made more progress than pupils who didn't. Furthermore, pupils who did more assignments per week achieved better than those who did fewer assignments per week, as measured by how both groups differed from pupils who did no homework. However, if a homework assignment spanned a long period of time, such as several weeks, the impact was less strong. Studies comparing homework with in-school supervised study also found homework to be more beneficial, although the difference was not as large as with pupils who did no homework. A follow-up study of more recent research published between 1987 and 2003 was conducted by Cooper and associates (Cooper et al., 2006). This review confirmed the earlier findings of a positive influence of homework on achievement, which was consistent across subjects and outcome measures used. However, the relationship was significantly stronger in secondary than in primary schools.

According to Cooper, the following positive effects for homework have been put forward: in the short-term, homework can lead to better retention of facts and knowledge, increased understanding, improved critical thinking skills, improved information-processing skills and the possibility of extending the curriculum. Long-term effects include the development of better study habits, the development of more positive attitudes towards school and studying, and the encouragement of learning outside of school hours. Non-academic, long-term effects include the development of greater self-direction, greater self-discipline, more independent learning and problem solving, better time organization and more inquisitiveness. Finally, homework can be used to complete tasks that pupils were not able to complete in class.

Negative effects posited include satiation, as pupils become tired of studying, which can lead to a loss of motivation and interest in academic work; cheating, copying either from fellow pupils or from published work; and lack of time for out-of-school leisure activities. In her review of research, Hallam (2004) found that homework can lead to tensions and rows between pupils and parents, and can cause resentment among pupils who feel their free time is taken away from them. This could eventually lead to them becoming disaffected from school.

Other American reviews have also provided support for the view that setting homework can improve pupils' achievement (e.g. Faulkner and Blyth, 1995;

Foyle and Bailey, 1988; Keith, 1987). Keith found that homework was particularly effective for pupils from disadvantaged backgrounds.

Rutter et al. (1979), studying British secondary schools, found a strong positive relationship between the number of minutes of homework assigned and pupils' achievement, attitudes towards school and attendance.

A more recent study in Israel likewise found a positive effect for homework. Pupils who were said by their teachers to complete more homework received higher teacher grades (Chen and Ehrenberg, 1993). However, it is clear that this could be as much the result of higher-achieving pupils having more positive attitudes to school and therefore completing more homework than the other way round. Similarly, an analysis of German data from the international PISA study found a positive relationship between homework assignment and achievement (Trautwein, 2007).

One recent study looked at mediating factors between homework and achievement. The authors found that successful completion of homework led to higher ratings of self-efficacy and perceived responsibility for their own learning among secondary school students, which in turn led to higher grades (Zimmerman and Kitsantas, 2005).

Some studies do not find positive effects. For example, in a study of secondary schools in England, Tymms and Fitz-Gibbon (1992) reported no positive effects on achievement in classrooms in which more homework was assigned.

Slightly different findings are reported by Hallam (2004) in her overview of research. While some studies, according to her, show positive effects, in a lot of cases results are negligible. She points to an overemphasis on the amount of homework as a cause of this, pointing out that quality and purpose of homework matter more strongly. When effective, homework can have a positive benefit on achievement, but the effect is far smaller than that of pupils' social background and other elements such as time on task and motivation. According to her review, homework is more effective when set in moderate amounts than when used to excess.

These differential effects are confirmed by a study using an international data set (from the PISA study on secondary mathematics). Dettmers et al. (2009) found that while there was a positive relationship between time spent on homework and achievement in mathematics at the school level (i.e. schools which gave more homework did better), this was not the case at the individual pupil level (i.e. pupils who spent more time doing homework didn't do better than pupils who spent less time on homework). There were also differences between countries, with the relationship generally being stronger in Asian than in European countries.

Overall, then, homework does seem to be an effective learning tool, especially for pupils in the higher grades (upper secondary school). However, this conclusion leaves many questions unanswered, such as how homework should be most effectively employed. These will be looked at next.

The Effective Use of Homework

In order for homework to be an effective learning tool, it needs to adhere to a number of principles.

The first principle, which goes against a lot of present classroom practice, is *not to use homework as a punishment*. Doing so will lead to pupils resenting homework, and to homework not being seen as a learning activity. Pupils will get the impression that the teacher does not value homework as a learning tool, and will attempt to complete it as quickly and perfunctorily as possible. As a way of motivating pupils or extending learning outside the classroom, this practice can be positively harmful (Cooper, 2006).

That the teacher is taking homework seriously is indicated to pupils by the way s/he does or does not provide *feedback* on homework. Homework should be marked and returned as soon as possible. It should always be properly corrected, as uncorrected homework gives pupils the impression that all that matters is completing the task, no matter how. This will obviously not encourage them to make an effort to produce correct or quality work, and will thus not aid pupil learning. One way to do this that saves marking time is to let pupils correct each other's homework. As pupils are usually asked to complete homework within a set time frame, marking and returning homework speedily will set the right example and not give pupils the impression that different rules apply to pupil and teacher. One of the findings of Cooper's (1989) overview was that homework that is checked contributes more to pupil achievement than homework that is assigned but not checked. Ornstein (1994) suggests that it is better to give less homework but correct it, rather than give more homework that remains uncorrected. Cooper (2006) suggests that feedback on homework should consist of instructional feedback rather than grades. This is because grading homework might lead to pupils losing intrinsic motivation to do homework and lead to them completing it out of fear of bad grades instead.

Corrected homework can also provide helpful feedback to teachers on pupils' progress in the subject. One way of increasing the usefulness of homework as a feedback tool for teachers is to log beforehand how long s/he expects the homework to take. Pupils can then be asked to write on the homework sheet how long it has actually taken them to complete it. If this period is particularly long, this could be an indication that the pupil is having problems understanding that particular topic.

To be effective, homework should be *integrated* into the lesson or topic studied. One way to do this is to review homework at the start of the lesson. When routinely done, this will ensure that homework is seen as an integral part of the lesson and may also be a good way to link previous and current lessons.

While practice of skills during homework can be necessary, research does suggest that homework is most effective when it *reinforces major curriculum ideas* (Black, 1997). Homework should be challenging, but pupils should be able to complete it successfully. It should not be confusing or frustrating for pupils. According to Cooper, almost all pupils should be able to successfully complete homework, which should therefore not be used as a way of testing pupils. One way to help achieve this, which can also help overcome some of the problems involved with teaching a heterogeneous set of pupils, is to individualize homework, so that it is tailored to pupils' levels in the subject.

A way of making homework more relevant to pupils is to connect what they have learnt in the classroom to their *everyday life*, for example by using TV guides to help them learn the time, by measuring their room and estimating how much paint would be needed to paint it and how much that would cost, or by interviewing relatives to learn something about local history or media use habits. Preparing new topics by asking pupils to bring in material they have collected, such as leaves of different types for a biology lesson, can also help achieve this aim. Researching something on the internet can likewise be both useful and enjoyable, though in-school provisions need to be provided for those pupils who do not have a computer or internet link at home. Apart from heightening the relevance of homework, using real-life experience and materials in homework can help pupils to more easily remember what they have learnt in school (Boers and Caspary, 1995).

Homework planners can help pupils develop independent learning and organizational skills. Homework planners can, for example, take the form of a small calendar, in which pupils have to note what homework they need to be doing and when they have to complete it. Pupils will need to be taught how to use homework planners initially, but will find them very useful once taught. Using homework planners can help pupils develop good study habits, and use of planners is recommended practice for other forms of independent study as well.

If homework is not completed, consequences need to be attached to this, such as making pupils complete homework during breaks, giving them a negative mark in a behaviour log, withdrawing privileges, etc. If no negative consequences follow non-completion of homework, pupils will soon start to take it less seriously, which may turn non-completion into an endemic problem.

Homework does not have to be a solitary activity as it is possible to set *cooperative homework tasks*. These can take the form of cooperative research assignments or tasks which require two or more pupils working together to complete. As with cooperative work in general, it is necessary to ascertain that pupils have the necessary social skills to work cooperatively and, if this is not the case, to teach them these skills first (see Chapter 4). Both joint goals and individual accountability are likewise necessary for cooperative homework to be successful.

As was remarked in the overview of research above, the effectiveness of homework seems to differ according to grade level. Also, it is a well-known fact that as they get older, pupils' concentration levels and independent learning abilities increase. This leads to the question of how much homework to assign at the different grade levels.

For the youngest children, too much homework can be harmful as they are already tired when they come home from school, and homework can put extra pressure on them. Thus, in primary school, some researchers advocate not assigning homework, and the research reviewed above does suggest that homework has a smaller impact on achievement in primary schools. There are arguments in favour of assigning at least some homework to primary-age pupils, though. The main one is to help pupils develop their independent learning skills and help them to attain the attitude that learning can take place outside of school as well as in school. However, it is clear that young children should not be overburdened by homework. It is generally recommended that children from nursery to the first three or four years of primary school should spend at most 20 minutes a day doing homework, and no more than 30–40 minutes a day in the upper primary years. These should be seen as upper limits.

As children move to secondary school, the evidence on the positive effects of homework becomes stronger, and there is clear support for setting homework at this level. The development of young people allows for more time to be spent on homework and, as the pupil becomes older, the development of independent learning skills becomes ever more important in the light of the move to higher education and the workforce. Therefore, daily homework of up to 90 minutes a day is recommended for secondary school pupils. In both primary and secondary schools, it is important not to overdo the amount of homework given. Research certainly doesn't support a view that more is necessarily better (e.g. Trautwein, 2007).

Apart from differences in the amount of time to be spent doing homework, homework at different grades will also serve different purposes and may therefore take different forms. As pupils grow up, more complex tasks can be assigned, including writing papers based on some kind of extended research.

School-wide Homework Policies

In order for homework to be most effective, a school-wide approach is recommended.

One of the benefits of school-wide policies is that they can create an ethos in which all pupils feel they are treated the same, as all teachers apply the same rules. Also, school-wide coordination can help avoid the problems that can occur when different teachers give large amounts of homework to be completed during the same period. Furthermore, school-wide policies on homework, as on other aspects of school life, help create equity within the school, with all pupils benefiting from the same level of homework, whomever is their teacher.

School-wide policies can take a variety of forms. A set amount of homework per week in different subjects can be helpful, as can establishing set nights to do homework in different subjects (e.g. Monday is maths homework day). Developing some form of standardization for such things as homework headings can save time and effort, as can the use of standardized school-wide homework planners. Homework policies should also contain guidelines for teachers on systematically correcting and returning homework within a specified time frame. The policy should also set out what is expected from parents.

Use of homework clubs and opening the school library after hours can help pupils who have difficulty completing homework at home. School-wide coordination of such activities is necessary, though, so that facilities do not become too full and a sufficient number of support staff are available.

Parental Involvement in Homework

The attitude of parents to homework is often ambiguous. On the one hand, they may believe it will aid their children's school achievement, and they may see homework as a good way of finding out more about what their children are actually doing at school, while on the other hand, they may feel that it takes time away from other worthwhile activities, and some parents may be at something of a loss as to how best to help their children to do their homework successfully.

Parental support in their children's homework is important, however. This has been found to be positively related to achievement and social outcomes, especially support from the mother (Murray et al., 2006). In one review of research, parental involvement in their children's homework was related to higher levels of completion of homework tasks and fewer problems with homework (Patall et al., 2008).

One of the main things that parents can do to help their children complete their homework is to provide a quiet and private space where the child can do her/his homework. This does not necessarily mean that parents should make sure that children turn the radio off or don't listen to music. On the contrary, according to some research, listening to music can aid concentration (Hallam and Cowan, 1999). This will probably differ from child to child and children should be allowed to listen to music while studying or completing homework if they feel comfortable doing so.

Parents should encourage their children to complete their homework and should support their children when they ask for help without (obviously) actually doing the homework for them (Hallam, 2004). Showing an interest in homework will help give children the feeling that homework is important and valued. Parents can also help by establishing a routine in which a certain time of the day is set aside for homework completion. If possible, parents can help pupils develop their time management and organizational skills, although some guidance from the school can be necessary to help parents to do this. This is particularly important with younger children, who need more parental help to successfully complete their homework assignments. Secondary school children should by and large be able to complete homework independently. What parents should not do is be overly controlling or interfering with their children's completion of homework, as this can negatively affect motivation (Patall et al., 2008). They should, however, set clear rules on when and where homework needs to be done.

The school can help parents by giving them the information they need and regularly communicating with them on homework. If there is a school-wide homework policy, parents should be made aware of this. Teachers should let parents know how much homework they plan to assign and approximately how long assignments should take. The homework planner, mentioned above, can be used to communicate to parents what homework has been assigned, and it might be useful to ask parents to sign the planner as well. If there are consistent problems with a child not completing assignments or completing them to a standard that is well below what one would expect or what the child seems able to do in class, teachers should discuss this with parents to ascertain whether there are circumstances at home, such as lack of a quiet working space, that may stop the child from completing homework satisfactorily. If possible, teachers should involve parents in developing a strategy to solve the problem. It is important to remember, though, that parents may not be aware of what is happening while pupils do their homework due to them returning late from work, for example (Hoover-Dempsey et al., 1995). It is also important to provide support to parents on how to help pupils because confusion can result from pupils receiving different advice or methods from parents than they do from teachers at school. Findings from research suggest that providing parents with training about what the school expects and how they can help with their children's homework has significant positive effects on completion rates and quality of homework completion of pupils (Patall et al., 2008). This training should focus on improving the learning environment, helping students improve homework habits, and supervising the homework processes rather than monitoring homework.

Especially with younger children, parents should be encouraged to do some homework activities with their children such as reading aloud to them or playing games with them. Explaining to parents at the beginning of the school year how they can help in this way will be helpful to them, as will designing certain homework assignments for pupils to work on with parents. One method that can help involve parents in their children's homework is to give homework in the form of games that can be played with parents and siblings, while reinforcing principles that need to be learnt (Bryan and Sullivan, 1995).

For some parents, especially if they suffer socio-economic deprivation, it may be impossible to provide the calm, supportive space needed for children to be able to successfully complete homework. A small minority of parents may not even be willing to do so. Here, the school can help out by providing pupils with the space they need, for example by setting up in-school homework clubs where pupils can come to study and complete homework outside of school hours, as has successfully been done in schools in a wide number of countries, such as the UK.

A further problem may be the differential access that children have to material in the home that they can use or need to use to complete homework. This can be a particular problem with homework assignments that do not provide merely practice of the day's lesson, but ask pupils to do research on a topic or find out something to prepare for coming topics. Here again, the school can help out by providing library facilities that pupils can access outside of school hours.

Hallam (2004) suggests that homework clubs can also lead to a more positive attitude to homework among pupils, as they appear to find them more enjoyable than doing work at home, and feel that homework clubs can benefit them. Working in homework clubs can also help alleviate the tensions between parents and pupils that can result from homework.

Summary

Homework can fulfil a number of different goals, such as increasing pupil achievement, reinforcing and strengthening topics taught in class, completing unfinished work, developing independent study skills and involving parents in helping pupils' learning.

Most studies have found homework to be an effective way of improving pupils' achievement. However, this positive effect is not uniform across grades, being strongest in the latter years of secondary school and weakest in primary school. Homework can still be useful for primary-age pupils, however, as it may help develop independent learning skills, may foster the attitude that learning can occur outside as well as in school, and may help develop pupils' organizational skills.

In order for homework to be effective, a number of elements have to be in place. It is imperative that homework should not be used as a form of punishment. Pupils should receive feedback on homework as soon as possible so they will realize that homework is valued and important. For this reason, homework should also be an integral part of the lesson. One goal of homework can be to allow pupils to connect school work to life outside of school. This can be done by making sure that assignments use real-life experience and materials collected in the pupil's environment as much as possible. Use of homework planners can help pupils to develop their organizational skills and can provide useful practice for other forms of independent learning. The amount of time pupils should spend doing homework increases as pupils get older, from no more than 20 minutes per day in the early primary years to up to 90 minutes a day in the higher secondary grades.

Parents can help their children by providing them with a quiet space to complete their homework, by encouraging them to complete their assignments, and, especially for younger pupils, by helping them if necessary. Teachers can help parents by regularly communicating with them on what homework has been assigned and what is expected from pupils. Training parents in how they can help pupils has been found to increase homework completion and quality.

Some parents may not be able to help their children or provide them with a quiet study environment. Homework clubs, where pupils can come to school to do homework after school hours and teachers are available to help them, can help solve this problem.

Reflective Questions

1. Do you think homework is an effective learning tool for primary school pupils?
2. How would you train parents to help their children with homework?
3. What do you think teachers at the school you were a pupil at could have done to help your parents?
4. Do you think homework should be graded? Why/why not?
5. What are the possible disadvantages of homework? Are these outweighed by the advantages, or do they provide a strong argument against using homework?
6. How can teachers help ensure that pupils value homework?
7. Can you think of any particularly effective examples of homework you have come across in teaching or as a pupil? What made them so effective?

CHAPTER 11

PROBLEM SOLVING AND HIGHER-ORDER THINKING SKILLS

Key Points

In this chapter, you will learn about:

- why there is an increasing focus on thinking skills in education
- the main elements of the heuristic approach to problem solving
- how thinking skills can be improved through metacognitive approaches
- why constructivist teaching has been said to improve thinking skills
- some programmes based on a formal operations-based approach to thinking skills.

Introduction

In recent years, there has been an increased emphasis on teaching thinking skills and problem solving in school. This has been caused in part by research that has pointed to the link between pupils' generic thinking skills and their achievement in school subjects (there is evidence that thinking skills development can improve pupil achievement, with one study even finding that thinking skills were more important to learning difficult concepts than ability (Prins et al., 2006)), but also by changes in society, especially the move towards a society in which knowledge and information are becoming ever more complex and ever more quickly redundant, and the migration of information onto the World Wide Web makes research skills possibly more important than factual knowledge. This means that, increasingly, possessing a large amount of knowledge is insufficient. Children and adults will need to possess the skills to make choices and to solve problems using logical reasoning.

Thinking skills are varied, but a useful summary of the main ones was developed by Swartz and Parks (1994):

- ordering data and finding meaning in information, i.e. ordering; sorting, classifying, grouping; comparing and contrasting data
- making predictions, hypothesizing; drawing conclusions
- critical thinking: questioning information and making judgements about it
- creative thinking: brainstorming, thinking of new connections and ideas
- problem solving; defining problems, thinking up and evaluating solutions, testing solutions
- planning
- making decisions; generating options, weighing up the advantages and disadvantages, and choosing a course of action.

Because of the growing importance of thinking skills, an increasing number of programmes have been developed that aim to improve them in pupils (e.g. Hamers and Csapo, 1999; Nickerson et al., 1985). While these are increasingly popular, there is still evidence that many teachers are confused about how to teach them (Barak and Shakman, 2008). The four main types of thinking skills programme follow:

1. A popular approach is to teach pupils a number of problem-solving skills – the so-called **heuristic** approach. The task will first be analysed so that it can be broken down into manageable subsets. These can then be tackled using problem-solving strategies that have been taught previously. Programmes based on this approach will often be content-free.
2. The **metacognitive** approach starts from the premise that performance can be improved through a better understanding and awareness of one's own thought processes. Teaching pupils this self-awareness is the mainstay of this approach.
3. Some educators believe that the open-ended, active learning encouraged by **constructivist** teaching methods will in itself be sufficient to develop pupils' higher-order thinking skills.
4. Based on Piagetian theories, the **formal thinking** approach aims to help pupils make the transition between the various stages they are supposed to pass through – according to Piaget's theories – more easily. Thinking skills programmes taking this approach will tend to integrate their programme with regular classroom teaching.

These four types have all given birth to programmes aimed at improving pupils' thinking skills. We will discuss approaches based on each of these four types in the following sections.

Heuristic Problem-solving Strategies

In the heuristic approach, the aim is to teach specific problem-solving skills, which pupils can use when they have to solve any particular problem. To do this more easily, the problem-solving process needs to be deconstructed into its composite parts. A lot of research in this paradigm has been done on solving word problems, for example mathematical questions in context. For example, a bus, travelling from Antwerp to Brussels (40 km), sets out at the same time as a car travelling in the other direction. The bus travels at 90 km/hour, the car at 120km/hour. After how many km will they pass one another? The following sequence has been proposed for solving problems:

1. understanding and representing the problem
2. selecting or planning the solution
3. executing the plan
4. evaluating the results (Polya, cited in Orton, 1992).

1. Understanding and representing the problem

The first step in problem solving is finding out exactly what the problem means. This entails finding the relevant information in the problem and disentangling what is relevant to solving the problem from those elements that aren't. This is typically a situation that is created in mathematical word problems, in which pupils have to find the relevant mathematical problem from within the contextual information that surrounds it. As well as identifying the problem, it is necessary to develop an accurate representation of the problem. This requires two main elements. The first is *linguistic understanding*, which means that the pupil needs to understand the full meaning of all sentences in the problem. This entails more than just understanding the words, as pupils need to understand the logical structure of the sentences. Pupils usually have more problems with relational propositions (i.e. bus A goes 10 miles per hour faster than bus B) than with assignment propositions (i.e. a bus ticket costs 35 pence). Once all sentences have been understood, pupils have to assemble them into a whole, and have to be able to understand the whole problem. Many pupils tend to decide too quickly what the problem is, based on observable cues. It is therefore important that they are taught to unravel problems thoughtfully, reading the whole problem before deciding what the question is (Woolfolk, 1997).

One way of helping pupils to do this is by letting them see many different kinds of worked-out examples. This has been found to be more effective than just giving a few examples and then having pupils solve problems on their own. Teachers can also help pupils by teaching them to recognize and categorize different problem types and to select relevant and irrelevant information contained in the problem. The teacher needs to make sure that pupils understand the problem by asking them to explain it to other pupils, by asking them to verbalize the assumptions they are working under, and by asking them to make clear what they think is relevant and irrelevant information in the question. The teacher also needs to encourage pupils to look at the problem from a variety of perspectives. This can be done by asking them to offer different or unconventional solutions, in order to help them to move away from conventional ways of looking at things.

2. Selecting or planning the solution

Once the problem has been understood, the second part of the process consists in designing a plan to solve the problem. In order to do this, pupils need to have a general problem-solving strategy – a so-called *heuristic.* One of the best strategies is to break down the problem into a number of smaller steps and then find a way to work out these different steps. There are a number of different ways of doing this. One is *working backwards*, from the goal to the unsolved initial problem. Solving mathematical proofs can often usefully be tackled in this way. Another strategy is to use *analogical thinking*. This means limiting one's search for solutions to strategies already used to solve problems that resemble the problem faced at present. Explaining strategies selected can help as well, as it can lead to pupils more clearly understanding the problem-solving sequence. Research has shown that pupils who were asked to explain each step in their problem solving were more successful than pupils who were not asked to do this (Gagne, 1965).

Having done this, pupils should be able to choose an effective *algorithm* for each part of the problem. An algorithm is a step-by-step procedure to achieve something, which is usually subject (or topic) specific. A problem that occurs when pupils have not carefully selected a heuristic is that they will tend to randomly apply algorithms, based not on understanding of the problem but on the understanding that, for example, certain algorithms have been used in maths lessons before so they think they might as well try them here. Pupils will then go through a number of standard algorithms in a random way. In some cases, this may even lead to the right result eventually, but obviously no real understanding will have been achieved. This is another reason to make pupils explain their answers.

Teaching heuristics can be aided by asking pupils to explain the steps they are taking as they are solving the problem. The different types of heuristics mentioned above can be explicitly taught.

3. Executing the plan

The third part of the process involves finding the actual solution to the problem. If the heuristic chosen in the previous step has led to the right plan with respect to which algorithm to use, this step is usually straightforward, entailing merely the application of the chosen algorithm. However, a lot of pupils do make algorithmic mistakes, so a good knowledge of the basic algorithms is necessary for effective problem solving.

4. Evaluating the results

The final step is checking the answer. A common-sense, but often forgotten, check is simply to look and see whether the answer makes sense. For example, an answer of 7000 miles per hour when calculating the speed of a car clearly indicates a mistake in either calculation, choice of algorithm or heuristic. Estimation can help here. For example, if the answer involves calculating 101×31, it can easily be estimated that the answer will be somewhat over 3000. Also, pupils need to check for all evidence and data that could contradict (or confirm) their answer.

To be effective in developing higher-order thinking skills, problems need to follow a number of rules. Problems should be new activities, which are meaningful to the pupils and which must be sufficiently close to their current level of knowledge to be assimilated, and yet sufficiently different to force them to transform their methods of thinking and working and develop their understanding. This means that such problems are by definition 'difficult', though not too difficult (Grugnett and Jaquet, 1996; Sosniak and Etherington, 1994). Problems can be made easier for pupils by using familiar, real-life contexts and by the use of pictures (Hembree, 1992).

That heuristic training can be effective was shown in a meta-analysis of problem-solving studies conducted by Hembree (1992), who reports that children who had received instruction in problem-solving skills performed significantly better than children who had not. Heuristic instruction appears to be most helpful for younger and under-achieving students and is most effective when it combines several interrelated strategies (Schraw et al., 2006).

The Metacognitive Approach

An important element in problem solving is metacognition. This term basically encompasses knowledge about one's own thought processes, self-regulation and monitoring what one is doing, why one is doing it and how what one is doing helps to solve the problem (or not). This allows one to ascertain whether the strategies one is using are effective, and thus to change strategies if necessary (Schoenfeld, 1992). It is clear that metacognitive skills are of great importance to children, not only to develop their problem solving but to develop thinking skills more generally. Developed metacognition will also lead pupils to be more aware of their own strengths and weaknesses (Lester, 1994; Schoenfeld, 1987). Lack of metacognition leads to children using ineffective (correct but slow or inefficient) problem-solving strategies. In order to learn more effectively, therefore, metacognitive processes must be brought into the open and self-regulation needs to become a conscious process. The direct teaching of metacognitive skills has been found to be an effective method, providing teachers are properly trained to deliver this (De Jager et al., 2005).

Schoenfeld (1987) suggests a number of techniques to teach children metacognitive strategies:

- Develop awareness of thinking processes among pupils. To do this it is important to explain why problem-solving strategies are important. Schoenfeld suggests activities such as showing a video of other pupils engaged in cooperative problem solving, so that pupils can see others using ineffective problem-solving strategies. This can impress upon them the importance of awareness of what one is doing.
- Work problems through on the blackboard by presenting the whole problem resolution rather than just the neat solution. Both this technique and the one previously presented are useful because they bring certain behaviours to centre stage and highlight the importance of metacognitive skills.
- Let the class as a whole work on a problem, with the teacher taking the role of moderator of pupil discussion. The pupils will choose to do certain things which may or may not be right. If their strategy doesn't turn out well, new solutions should be tried until the right solution has been found. This should be followed by a debriefing conducted by the teacher. This activity has been found to help self-regulation.

Developing metacognitive skills can also be aided through specific activities. Cooperative group work can be used to this effect, not least because of the scaffolding that it makes possible. It has been suggested that pupils working in small groups can be given cards containing a number of basic questions that should help them to think about their own thinking. These include: 'What am I doing now?', 'Is it getting me anywhere?' and 'What else could I be doing instead?' (Perkins and Salomon, 1989). This will help them reflect on their problem solving, until in due course this 'scaffold' (the cards) can be removed once pupils have internalized metacognitive thinking.

Heuristics Intervention Programmes

Apart from applying the general guidelines given here, a number of researchers have put into place specific intervention programmes aimed at improving pupils' thinking skills.

One of the best known is De Bono's CoRT programme. This is a content-free thinking skills programme for secondary school pupils (and adults). This approach sets out to teach a number of heuristics such as looking for the plus points, minus points and interesting points in any situation (PMI), considering all factors in a situation (CAF), exploring the consequences of decisions (consequence and sequel, C & S), and looking at goals, orders and objectives (AGO). In total, CoRt consists of 60 lessons. The effectiveness of the programme has been evaluated in a number of studies, but results have been inconclusive (Edwards, 1991).

Feuerstein's Instrumental Enrichment programme tries to address a range of thinking skills, such as seriation, classification, verbal reasoning, numerical ability and spatial relations. While this programme, like CoRT, is not subject-specific and is taught in specific IE lessons, it differs from the former in that rather than directly teaching heuristics, it attempts to teach strategies designed to help pupils find their own heuristics when they are confronted with a particular problem. Pupils will, for example, learn strategies to gather information, use information gathered, and express the solution to a programme.

Evaluations carried out in Israel, where the programme was developed, showed positive effects on school achievement and general intelligence (Feuerstein et al., 1980; Rand et al., 1981). However, an American study showed no effect (possibly due to weaknesses in study design). Two different studies were carried out in the UK, one showing positive effects, the other no effects (Shayer and Beasley, 1989).

A major criticism of thinking skills programmes like those discussed above, is that they are content-free. Some research has suggested that it is better to teach heuristics and problem solving in a highly contextualized way, because it is seen as important to connect the techniques to pupils' existing knowledge (Perkins and Salomon, 1989). Teaching heuristics or thinking skills in a decontextualized, stand-alone fashion has shown rather mixed effects in teaching thinking skills.

As a response to these criticisms, approaches have been developed that attempt to integrate thinking skills and metacognitive development and teaching with particular subject topics. So-called immersion approaches such as the 'Activating Children's Thinking Skills' approach (McGuinness, 2000) look for specific curricular topics that lend themselves to the teaching and development of thinking skills among pupils. Examples of these are causal thinking in a science lesson or decision-making skills through the studying of a historical personage in history. The benefits of this infusion approach are seen as matching thinking skills directly with topics in the curriculum; invigorating content instruction leading to deeper understanding; using classroom time optimally; directly supporting teaching for thoughtfulness across the curriculum; and facilitating transfer and reinforcement of learning. This approach has shown gains in metacognitive skills for experimental over control groups in a number of studies (Dewey and Bento, 2009; McGuinness, 2006).

Improving Thinking Skills Through Constructivist Teaching

In Chapter 5, we looked at the main theories and method underlying constructivist teaching methods. We mentioned the advantages that many educators see in these methods, one of which includes the promotion of thinking skills.

Constructivist teaching might help to develop thinking skills through the open-ended, problem-based style of teaching used. Constructivist classrooms provide opportunities for educators to implement active learning and to challenge learners to look for further knowledge in the learning environment. Learners are encouraged to actively take knowledge, connect it to previously assimilated knowledge and make it theirs by constructing their own interpretation (Hanley, 1994). Use of analogies has been suggested as one way of enhancing the teaching of thinking skills in constructivist lessons (English, 1993). If it is to be effective in developing thinking skills and metacognition, contructivist teachers need to make sure their activities are authentic, i.e. as close to real-life problem-solving situations as possible. This means, for example, encouraging pupils to develop their own research questions rather than the teacher providing them. The problem with this, of course, is ensuring curriculum coverage, and the high demands on teachers in ensuring that effective learning occurs (Schraw et al., 2006).

That constructivist methods show promise in this area is demonstrated by a number of studies. De Jager et al. (2005) looked at a cognitive apprenticeship approach with limited teacher structuring as one constructivist approach to teaching metacognitive skills. They found that they did not perform better than teachers using direct instruction in developing metacognition. Both groups had been trained in developing pupils' metacognitive skills, however, and both groups did better than a control group of untrained teachers. A programme using constructivist methods to improve the thinking skills of bilingual pupils showed positive results (Thomason, 2003), as did an even smaller study of one dance teacher (Chen, 2001). In one programme, constructivist-based discussions were used in a science classroom. Pre- and post-test measures indicated that the experimental class experienced significantly greater gains in scientific reasoning than did the control group (Sprod, 1998). In a larger-scale study of over 350 pupils, it was found that high school pupils taught in a constructivist way did not score higher on measures of higher-order thinking than pupils taught using direct instruction (Chang et al., 1994). These findings leave some doubt as to whether constructivist teaching alone would be sufficient to develop higher-order thinking skills in pupils.

Group work and peer tutoring have increasingly been used in schools, and have also been considered potentially effective in improving thinking skills of pupils, as the interaction with peers, working on problems as a group, and the verbalization of learning can help develop metacognitive skills. In one study, a whole class of seven-year-olds were tutees, while a whole class of 11-year-olds were the tutors, with another class of seven-year-olds the control group. In Phase 1, a paired reading intervention was implemented for six weeks for all groups. In Phase 2, the experimental classes of tutors and tutees engaged in the 'paired thinking' (PT) method for 10 weeks, while the comparison group continued with paired reading. Pre- and post-test assessment of thinking skills and attitude to reading was conducted, and the experimental tutees showed significantly better performance in thinking skills than comparison tutees (Topping and Bryce, 2004), suggesting that peer tutoring approaches aimed at developing thinking skills may have potential.

The Improving Formal Thinking Approach: Cognitive Acceleration in Science and Maths

In the light of the problems involved in teaching pupils heuristics and thinking skills out of context, a number of intervention programmes have been designed to teach thinking skills within a particular subject.

One of the most effectively worked out cognitive intervention programmes is the CASE (Cognitive Acceleration in Science Education) project, designed by Adey and Shayer (1994) in the UK. This project is based on Piagetian and Vygotskian thinking in that the aim is to bring pupils up to the formal operational thinking stage, in part through making them in their zone of proximal development work as much as possible. The programme is subject-specific, developed for science and contains specific science topics in each lesson. More recently, a related Cognitive Acceleration in Mathematics (CAME) project has been developed as well, which has similarly shown very positive outcomes (Shayer and Adhami, 2007).

The project, containing 52 lessons, has five main elements:

1. Concrete preparation to introduce the necessary vocabulary and clarify the terms in which the problem is to be set. This means that the teacher needs

to set the problem in context, and explain the meaning of the vocabulary that the pupil will need. An example given by Adey and Shayer (1994) is that of introducing the concept of relationships. First, the pupils must be introduced to the concept in a simple way, not least by giving examples in which no relationship exists.
2. The teacher needs to introduce 'cognitive conflict'. This occurs when pupils are introduced to an experience which they find puzzling or which contradicts their prior knowledge or understanding. This can lead to pupils moving towards their zone of proximal development, but only if the activity is well managed by the teacher. Otherwise, the danger exists that the discordant information will simply be dismissed or distorted to fit pupils' existing schemata.
3. Pupils then need to move on to a *construction zone* activity. This is an activity which ensures that pupils go beyond their current levels of understanding and competencies. This has been facilitated by the cognitive conflict, which has forced pupils to challenge their own preconceived notions and thought processes. Teachers can help pupils do this by helping them to build up step by step the higher-level reasoning patterns they need to access.
4. Pupils need to reflect consciously on their problem solving (metacognition) in ways similar to those described above.
5. Pupils then need to 'bridge' their new skills or knowledge, i.e. be able to apply it in different contexts. A number of the methods proposed above can be used to facilitate this.

CASE lessons typically involve a lot of pupil–teacher and pupil–pupil interaction, and often collaborative group work as well. The teacher's role is obviously an important one, and a lot of what has been described here may sound somewhat daunting to beginning teachers. While this method does indeed require good classroom management and interactive teaching skills and the self-confidence to allow a lot of pupil direction in the lesson, the programme developers provide worked-out material for each lesson as well as professional development training activities.

Some highly positive effects of this method have been reported, in that pupils involved in the project performed significantly better on the age-16 national science examination in the UK (GCSE exams) than a matched control group, not just in science but in other subjects as well. This would suggest that the thinking skills obtained do transfer to other subjects as well. Interestingly, no effects were found on a post-test given to pupils following the intervention, suggesting that the effects may lag and be long-term rather than having strong short-term effects.

Recently, the cognitive acceleration approach has been extended to other areas of the curriculum and to other age groups than the secondary pupils it was designed for, with programmes now existing for subjects like arts and for pupils aged five upwards (Shayer and Adey, 2002).

Transfer of Thinking Skills

One of the difficulties with both the heuristic and the metacognitive methods is transfer of the skills learned outside of the classroom. An issue can be that the techniques and heuristics learned can be applied easily to classroom problems that are very similar to the problems that the heuristic was first learnt with, but that when they are confronted with new situations in or outside of the classroom, pupils will revert to inefficient random application of algorithms or guessing. While it is hard to totally counter these difficulties, there are a number of strategies teachers can follow to make transfer more likely.

Actively involving pupils in their learning is one such strategy. Pupils who have been actively involved in learning, through discussion, interactive teaching, independent research or experiments have been found to be more likely to transfer their knowledge to other situations.

When teaching new concepts, it is important that they are practised in a wide range of different problems. Simply repeating similar problems is likely to lead to the pupil only transferring the skills learned to the same type of problem. Practice should include some unstructured, complex problems of the type the pupil may encounter in real life.

Forms of simulation in which the learning takes place in an environment similar to that in which it will be applied also aid transfer. An example of this is driving lessons, which usually take place at least partly along the routes to be followed during the driving test.

Overlearning, practising a skill until it becomes automatic, has also been found to aid transfer. For example, most people taught times tables at school can still use them in later life when confronted with multiplication problems.

Finally, teachers can draw pupils' attention to the thinking skills learnt in previous lessons when during a lesson a situation occurs in which use of these skills will be useful.

A number of methods that can encourage pupils' thinking skills were discussed in Chapters 2 and 3 on direct instruction. These include asking pupils higher-order and open questions, making sure they have to verbalize their answers and explain their thought processes, and allowing pupil discussion and input into the lesson. Teachers can also make sure that lessons (and tests) focus on processes as well as, or more than, on outcomes. This can be aided by giving marks for incorrect solutions if the processes used are good.

However, not all the recommendations given in the chapters on direct instruction are in accordance with those recommended by thinking skills researchers. One of these is pace. Obviously, if pupils are to develop problem-solving and thinking skills by doing demanding problems, they need to have the time to solve the problem. This may necessitate giving over a large part of the lesson to individual or group work. When presenting a problem, the teacher must not give too many clues as pupils need to be encouraged to think about the problem for themselves. Therefore, while the effective teaching methods discussed under direct instruction are the best way to teach basic skills or topics which necessitate transfer of content, an exclusive reliance on this technique could lead to neglect of another important and basic part of teaching – developing pupil's higher-order cognitive skills.

Summary

In this chapter, we looked at ways in which we can enhance pupils' thinking skills and problem solving, something which has received increasing attention in education in recent years.

Four main approaches to teaching thinking skills exist.

Heuristics programmes like CoRT aim to teach specific problem-solving skills which pupils can use when they have to take on any particular problem. To do this more easily, the problem-solving process needs to be deconstructed into its composite parts.

Metacognitive strategies aim to improve pupils' conscious self-regulation. The term refers to knowledge about one's own thought processes and monitoring what one is doing, why one is doing it and how what one is doing helps to solve the problem (or not). This allows one to ascertain whether the strategies one is using are effective, and thus to change strategies if necessary. A number of strategies have been proposed to enhance pupils' metacognitive strategies.

Finally, strategies based on Piagetian and Vigotskyan thinking include the successful CASE programme, which is a subject-specific programme built around 52 science lessons.

A number of methods that can aid easier transfer of knowledge to different contexts include practising problem solving in different contexts, using complex real-life examples, reminding pupils of learnt thinking skills during relevant parts of other lessons and actively involving pupils in learning, and overlearning.

Reflective Questions

1. Which of these four approaches do you think would be most effective? Why?
2. Why can we say CASE has been influenced by Piagetian and Vigotskyan thinking?
3. How would you go about helping pupils to more easily transfer thinking skills to new problems?
4. Do you think metacognition is important when we try to solve problems? Can you give an example from your own experience?
5. How would you help pupils to find effective heuristics for problem solving?
6. What do you think teachers can do to help develop pupils' thinking skills during regular lessons?

PART 3

TEACHING FOR SPECIFIC PURPOSES

CHAPTER 12

DEVELOPING PUPILS' SOCIAL SKILLS

Key Points

In this chapter, you will learn about:

- the importance of peer relations to children's development
- characteristics that may lead to children being unpopular with peers
- how social skills can be taught or enhanced
- what parents can do to help develop their children's social skills
- how to help children suffering from persistent shyness.

Introduction

Peer relations are highly important to children's development. Friends provide companionship and support, allow children to take part in social recreational activities they cannot do on their own, and are important to children's social skill development. By interacting with peers, children will learn to join a group, make new friends, manage conflict and learn to cooperate. Therefore, there is a vicious circle for some children, in that lack of social skills makes it difficult for them to join a peer group, which in turn hinders the development of their social skills.

A lot of research has been done into pupils' peer relations and social skills in recent decades, often using so-called sociometric methods. Sociometric research involves asking children to nominate peers they like or dislike. Children can then be categorized as more or less popular or unpopular based on the number of positive or negative choices they have received, and the characteristics of the popular and unpopular children can then be compared on a number of factors, such as school achievement. Another fruitful research method in this area is ethnographic research, in which the researcher spends a long period of time in the child's social setting, for example the school, and directly observes what social groupings exist and which children participate in which ways in those groups.

Research has shown that children tend to fall into one of four categories with respect to their popularity in school (Kupersmidt and Coie, 1990):

- *Popular children* have successfully established relationships with a variety of peers and social groups. They are well-known and well-liked in school and other social settings.
- *Controversial children* are well liked by a group of peers with whom they have successfully established social relations, but are unpopular with other groups of children.
- *Isolated children* are not openly unpopular, but are often ignored by their classmates, and are not always a part of existing social groups.
- *Rejected children* are actively disliked and are often subjected to bullying or harassment from peers.

Why Social Skills Matter

Social skills are not just important in and of themselves, but are also linked to other desirable outcomes. For example, among adolescents, a lack of social skills has been found to be related to depression and anxiety (Merrell, 2001; Tryon et al., 2001), and to low academic achievement (Elliott et al., 2001; Malecki and Elliott, 2002), with pro-social behaviour and a lack of aggression being related to achievement in literacy in primary schools (Miles and Stipek, 2006). Teachers are clearly concerned at a perceived lack of social skills in some pupils, especially when it comes to appropriate behaviour in the classroom and interaction with peers. A lack of self-control was frequently mentioned as a big problem in one study of teachers across primary and secondary schools (Lane et al., 2006).

Children who experience rejection by peers are likely to be lonely and exhibit low self-esteem, as well as being more likely to drop out of school, to be involved in delinquent activities and to have lower school achievement (Parker and Asher, 1987). Isolation from peers is associated with a whole number of social and psychological adjustment problems such as low self-esteem and perceived competence (Moran and Eckenrode, 1991; Newcomb and Bagwell, 1996), and unpopular children are at risk of academic failure, mental health problems and later delinquency (DeRosier et al., 1994).

Once a child is rejected by peers, s/he tends to stay rejected across settings. Early rejection also has a continuing impact on anti-social behaviour, DeRosier et al. (1994) reporting that aggression among their subjects was stronger the more times they had been rejected by peers in the past and the closer in time the last rejection. Furthermore, one rejection at an early age was still significantly associated with later aggression. In a study of 881 fifth graders, Parker and Asher (1993) report that children who are not accepted by peers have fewer best friends than average or highly accepted children. Low accepted children's friendships were qualitatively less satisfying than high accepted children's friendships, and low accepted children were lonelier than high or averagely accepted children. Roe (1983) found isolated adolescents to be very high television viewers, as a result of both lack of peer-related leisure time activities and of the use of television as a companion. Muijs (1997) found unpopular children to be higher users of most electronic media, including television, computer games and music.

What Makes Children Popular?

A question then is what causes friendships to develop, and what causes some children to become isolated from their peers. In one overview of research that looked at what factors seemed to cause children to develop strong social relationships in adolescence, it was found that a positive parent–child relationship, low family discord, no parental divorce, and proximity to adults and peers who were not part of the child's family appeared to help (Hair et al., 2001). An important aspect of this is a child's social skills. According to Hair et al. (2001), developing social skills is related to having a warm and friendly personality, good nonverbal intelligence, responsive parenting, and regular contact with siblings. Poverty has also been found to be linked to a lack of social skills in children (Bates et al., 2003).

Children are looking for friends who are fun to be with, make them feel good and are perceived as trustworthy. Similarity is also important, children with similar interests and backgrounds being more likely to form friendships. Which of these aspects is the most important changes as children get older. Young children are largely concerned with whether or not their friends are fun to be with, while adolescents strongly value trustworthiness and loyalty. Williams and Asher (1993) give the following list of characteristics for childhood and adolescent friendship choices (Figure 12.1):

Acceptance	Rejection
Is this child fun to be with?	
Sense of humour	Aggressive/mean
Resourceful/skilful	Disruptive
Participatory/readily involved	Bossy/domineering
Cooperative	Withdrawn/apprehensive
	Low cognitive skills
Is this child trustworthy?	
Reliable	Aggressive/mean
Honest	Dishonest
Loyal	Betrays confidence
Do we influence each other in ways I like?	
Cooperative	Aggressive/mean
Responsive	Bossy/domineering
	Resistant/rigid
Does this child facilitate and not undermine my goals?	
Cooperative	Disruptive
Helpful	Impulsive
Does this child make me feel good about myself?	
Supportive/kind	Insulting/demeaning
Responsive	Non-responsive
Likes me	Dislikes me
Is this child similar to me?	
Common values and interests	Different values and interests
Respect for peer conventions	Non-conformity to peer conventions
Same gender, race, age	Superior manner
	Handicapped

FIGURE 12.1 Characteristics for childhood and adolescent friendship choices (Williams and Asher, 1993)

Recent research points to the importance of emotional intelligence, the extent to which people are able to empathize, show social adeptness and adaptability and are self-aware with respect to their impact on others. This factor has been found to be related to friendship choices at all ages (Schutte et al., 2001).

Of course, having one or two 'rejection characteristics' will not necessarily cause rejection. Rather, it is a collection of all these characteristics that is likely to be problematic. Research does show, however, that for a number of children many of these characteristics do indeed coalesce (Muijs, 2000).

Developing Children's Social Skills in School

While a lack of social skills is clearly a big problem for some children, there is, luckily, quite a lot of evidence that school intervention programmes can help to improve social skills (Anderson-Butcher et al., 2003; Lane et al., 2003; Taylor et al., 2002). However, while many intervention programmes exist, not all are successful. One meta-analysis of outcomes of social skills programmes identified the following aspects as necessary for success: programmes must devote ample time to skills enhancement, be explicit about what they wish to achieve, use activities that are coordinated and sequenced to achieve their purpose and require active involvement of all participants (Durlak and Weissberg, 2007).

It is important, when trying to improve the socials skills of unpopular children, not to just focus on behaviours that seem to make them unpopular with other children (such as starting fights). We need to try to develop their social skills more generally, as apart from these overt behaviours, they may lack other social skills and find it difficult to know how to respond in social situations.

A question is how to find out what (less immediately obvious) skills the child may lack. In order to do this, most researchers say it is best to use observation. The child will need to be carefully observed in her/his interactions with peers and adults in order to ascertain both what skills the child already has and what skills s/he may be lacking. The observer needs to take account of what situation is being observed (is the child trying to maintain a conversation, join a group, play a game?) and make notes on what is going on in order to be able to intervene where necessary. These observations can then be grouped under one of the six categories mentioned in Table 1 (is the child fun to be with, resourceful/ skilful, participatory/readily involved, cooperative? Does the child possess a sense of humour?) so both the child's strengths and weaknesses can be listed and the weaknesses can be addressed (Williams and Asher, 1993). Looking at the behaviour of children during organized games can be a good guide to their social skills in general (Dodge et al., 1986).

As well as observation, self-report checklists have been used to measure pupils' social skills. Instruments like the CS4 (Children's Self-Report Social Skills Scale – Danielson and Phelps, 2003) can be given to children to complete. This is easier to do than observing children, but may be less reliable (Merrell, 2001). Teacher rating scales have also been used, and these have been found to be consistent with ratings by pupils themselves. However, the results seem to differ a bit depending on what rating scale is used (Hall and Bramlett, 2002; Ogden, 2003).

One way of improving pupils' social skills is through social skills coaching. The underlying principle of social skills coaching is that children's social skills problems are often caused by the fact that children do not know what to do in social situations, and that they can be taught to overcome these deficiencies. The coaching thus involves direct instruction in crucial social skills. Williams and Asher (1993) suggest a three-part coaching session. The first part involves the coach (a responsive adult, for example the child's teacher) talking to the child about how to interact better with peers. The coach needs to focus on what the child should do, rather than what s/he shouldn't do when explaining this concept. The second part of the coaching involves practising the activity with other children. Finally, the coach and the child can discuss the use of the social concept during that activity with the child. McIntyre (2003) suggests that the following elements need to be developed in social skills training:

A social skills training programme might include (among other things):

- manners and positive interaction with others
  - approaching others in socially acceptable ways
  - asking for permission rather than acting
  - making and keeping friends
  - sharing toys/materials
- appropriate classroom behavior
  - work habits/academic survival skills
  - listening
  - attending to task
  - following directions
  - seeking attention properly
  - accepting the consequences of one's behaviour
- better ways to handle frustration/anger
  - counting to 10 before reacting
  - distracting oneself through doing a pleasurable task
  - learning an internal dialogue to cool oneself down and reflect upon the best course of action
- acceptable ways to resolve conflict with others
  - using words instead of physical contact
  - seeking the assistance of the teacher or conflict resolution team.

He suggests a direct instruction approach to teaching these skills, specifically in small groups, with opportunities for practice.

Another approach to developing social skills is through the use of so-called 'social skills autopsies' (LaVoie, 2005). This technique is based on analyzing errors children make in social situations in realistic environments, and is best used as a response in instances where a child has made a social faux pas. This technique has five stages:

1. *Ask the child to explain what happened*. The child needs to explain in some detail what happened.
2. *Ask the child to identify the mistake that he made*. In many cases, the child will not realize that s/he made a mistake, but this is in itself an important finding that can lead to the next step.
3. *Discuss what mistakes the child made in the social situation*, and coax and present alternatives to the way the child reacted. It is best to present a range of alternatives rather than just one 'right' solution, to demonstrate that social situations can have different positive outcomes.
4. The next activity is the *scenario*. The scenario is *the part of the process wherein the adult creates a brief social story that has the same basic moral or goal as the social faux pas.* The scenario should have the same basic solution as the incident, and should allow for generalizability to other situations.
5. Finally, it is a good idea to *set some homework*, where the child is encouraged to apply the techniques learnt to another setting, and then report back to the teacher.

When a child is unpopular, one of the most useful things teachers can do is make the child aware of those things that are likely to increase her/his popularity, such as smiling, laughing, greeting others, complimenting others and starting conversations. Making the child feel valued by the teacher is also important.

It is important that social skills instruction should not just consist of a description of the skill and why it is important, but also explain and demonstrate how to implement the skill and when and why to implement it. Practising the skill is vital (Brophy, 1996). Sometimes it can be useful to practise the skill in a role play before applying it to real-life situations. Modelling the desired behaviour by the teacher or other professionals in the school can contribute to the child's understanding of pro-social behaviour.

According to Williams and Asher (1993), four basic concepts should be taught in social skills coaching:

- cooperation (e.g. taking turns, sharing materials and making suggestions during games)
- participation (e.g. getting involved, getting started and paying attention during a game)
- communication (e.g. talking with others, asking questions, talking about yourself, listening skills, making eye contact, using the other child's name)
- validation (e.g. giving attention to others, saying nice things to other people, smiling, offering help or suggestions).

Individual children may need additional coaching in specific areas as well. For example, some children may be excluded from games and activities because of their lack of basic games or sports skills. Some training in these skills can therefore help such children become better integrated into existing peer groups.

As well as specific social skills, there are a number of other things classroom teachers can do to help unpopular children. The first of these is to try and find out what hobbies, interests or talents the unpopular child has and to publicly 'advertise' them, by encouraging them to bring objects relating to their hobbies into the class or letting them give a presentation on their hobby. This should help position the child as an expert on something, which can strengthen her/his prestige in the group.

Giving the child a responsible role in the class can also help to increase peer acceptance, but among adolescents in particular one must beware of positioning the child as a 'teacher's pet' (Lavoie, 1997).

Among pre-school children, visible acceptance of the child by the teacher may be helpful, in that this behaviour may be imitated by the other children (Lavoie, 1997).

Collaborative group work, while requiring good social skills from pupils, can also help develop them. Making a rejected child work with a high status peer in paired work can increase her/his acceptance, but the teacher has to ensure that the child is accepted by this peer first. Grouping less socially skilled pupils with their more skilled peers in both collaborative group work and games can help them learn through observing these more socially able peers. Grouping all pupils lacking in social skills together has been found to be less effective (Ang and Hughes, 2002; Kemple, 1992; Lavoie, 1997). Using collaborative group work in a way that emphasizes and targets social skills has been found to increase these in a number of studies (Carter et al., 2001; Gut and Safran, 2002). Doing this will also allow collaborative group work to proceed more effectively in future. There is increasing evidence that approaches that combine direct instruction on social skills with collaborative group work are effective in developing pupils' social skills. In one recent project in primary schools, a combination of direct coaching in social skills and collaborative group work was used. The researchers found that the group work in which the skills was practised was particularly important, but that direct coaching was also needed to change pupil behaviour (Dohrn et al., 2001). An evaluation of a similar intervention, that used a combination of direct instruction in social skills and group work, found that following the intervention, pupils' ability to work together and their ability to resolve conflicts in a positive way had increased. The researchers also found that pupils were on task more during lessons (Brandt and Christensen, 2002). Other studies have reported similar successful findings (Kolb and Weede, 2001), although it has to be said that all these studies are pretty short-term, which makes it hard to tell whether or not these effects last over time.

Some rejected children behave aggressively, because they do not possess any other conflict-resolution skills. These children need to learn different ways of dealing with conflict (such as taking one's turn or sharing), which can be done either through direct instruction in these methods or through activities such as role plays and discussions in which other solutions are presented. Once these have been learnt, the teacher may still need to initially give the child on-the-spot guidance when conflict does occur in class (Kemple, 1992).

In order to avoid the unpopular child always being 'picked last' for games, the teacher could assign children to teams her/himself, for example by random selection.

Some research suggests that unpopular and rejected children may be less well able to interpret others' emotions than popular peers, and may therefore respond to others' emotions in inappropriate ways. These children can be helped by giving them clues on other children's emotions, such as 'look at Jane, what do you think she is thinking? Do you think she is happy with what you have done?'

When children are having problems expressing their feelings and thoughts, it can be necessary to explain what they want to the other children, for example 'John would like to join in'. However, one must be careful not to force other children to play with an unpopular child as this may cause resentment and make the child even more unpopular.

Helping pupils to get to know each other at the beginning of the year, for example by asking all pupils to tell the class something about themselves including hobbies and interests, can show children that they have some things in common with children who might otherwise be unpopular.

Throughout the year, primary pupils can learn about friendship and acceptance of different pupils through various activities. Children's literature, for example, provides many examples that can be fruitfully used to encourage pupils to interact with all other children. Many books treat the theme of making friends, and can be used as a starting point for discussions, role play and lessons about making friends. Other books explicitly look at making friends with 'unusual' children or adults, or discuss themes such as handling rows.

It is important to start developing pupils' social skills early on. Hartup and Moore (1990) found that if children have not developed social skills by age six, they are at risk of experiencing problems throughout their life.

The Role of Parents in Developing Children's Social Skills

Parents and siblings have an important role to play in helping to develop children's social skills.

Children's social skills development has been linked to the parenting style used most often by the child's parents. Parenting styles can be defined along two continua: parental warmth or responsiveness and parental control or demandingness (Baumrind, 1991). This leads to four distinct parenting styles:

- *Permissive* parents are warm and accepting. They are non-traditional and lenient, and allow their children a lot of leeway. They avoid confrontation with their children.
- *Authoritarian* parents, on the other hand, are highly demanding and restrictive, and expect their orders to be obeyed without question or explanation. They score low on the warmth dimension.
- *Authoritative* parents are both warm and demanding. They expect discipline, but are supportive of their children as well.
- *Uninvolved* parents are low on both dimensions, being neither demanding nor accepting.

Children from both authoritative and permissive households have been found to have better social skills than children of uninvolved and authoritarian parents. Children of authoritative parents do better in school and are less likely to show problem behaviour than children of permissive parents, however. This means that though children of permissive parents tend to be friendly and sociable, they tend to lack knowledge of appropriate behaviour in different social situations and don't take responsibility for their own actions.

Lack of social skills can also partly be caused by more extreme family circumstances. Children whose parents have a disruptive relationship, in which antisocial and aggressive behaviour are common, or whose parents don't converse with them regularly will tend to develop antisocial behaviour.

There are a number of things parents can do to help their children's social skills development. One is providing children with opportunities to play with peers. Encouraging children to participate in out-of-school recreational groups or hobbies that involve other children will help them develop their social skills as well as hopefully being fun.

Shy children can benefit from interaction in small groups, so encouraging children to invite other children over one at a time to do something may help them.

Parents playing with their young children can help their children to develop the skills they will need for play with peers. Research has shown that children whose parents have played with them in this way have more advanced social skills than children who have not had this experience, especially if the play was 'peer-like' and for the sake of having fun (Linsey et al., 1997). The parent must not try to dominate the play, or to correct the child, but should attempt to play as equals. In this way, the child will learn a lot of the social skills needed to interact successfully with children their age.

Talking with children about peer relationships has also been found to enhance their social skills (Laird et al., 1994). This usually takes the form of a conversation about daily activities the child has done.

Parents must take children seriously when they come to them with peer-related problems and help them to consider various options and solutions to the problem, always encouraging friendly, pro-social solutions.

When children do get excluded from, for example, a play situation, as inevitably happens on some occasions even to children that are not unpopular, parents should avoid defeatist comments like 'Maybe they don't like you', and instead say something more constructive like 'Maybe they're just having a bad day, they might want to do something tomorrow'.

Shyness

A related but different problem to lack of social skills is shyness. Shyness is a feeling that all children have at some point, but if it becomes too prevalent, shyness may hinder children's social development. Shyness in children can be recognized quite easily through such signs as an averted gaze and physical and verbal reticence. Shy children often speak softly and hesitantly. Young children sometimes suck their thumb or act coyly .

In normal doses, shyness is not a problem, and can even be a healthy form of social adaptation. Young children will usually be quite shy with strangers, but this shyness will diminish as they get older and get more used to interacting with different people. However, when shyness is not limited to new social situations or new encounters, or if it does not diminish over time, it can become problematic. Shy children can have problems making friends and fitting into peer groups, and often have low self-esteem. The fact that they do not integrate into peer groups can further hinder their social skill development.

Shy children can be helped in a number of ways. Frequent praise can build up their self-esteem. Being sensitive to the child and trying to get to know her/him slowly can help build up a relationship. Pushing them into new situations too rapidly is not a good idea, though, because this can exacerbate their social anxiety. Finally, some

(Continued)

(Continued)

social skills training can be useful, such as teaching the child entry strategies, for example how to use questions like 'Can I join your game?', or role playing entry techniques (Hyson and Van Trieste, 1987). Brophy (1996) found that effective teachers use a variety of strategies to help shy children, such as changing their environment by seating them with friendly children or assigning them to a sociable partner, encouraging increased responsiveness from them, minimizing their exposure to stress, engaging them in special activities and involving them in frequent private talks. Giving them roles that force them to communicate, such as being a messenger, is another strategy that has been found to be effective.

Shy children may perceive large groups as threatening, and can therefore benefit from initially interacting with peers in small groups.

Summary

Research into children's relationships with same-age peers is often done using sociometric techniques, asking children to nominate peers they like or dislike. This research has led to the identification of four types of children: popular, controversial, isolated and rejected.

Being isolated or rejected can be harmful to children's development in a number of ways and has been linked to low school achievement, school drop-out and mental health problems. One of the reasons pupils can become isolated from or rejected by peers is through a lack of social skills. In order to be accepted by peers, children must be perceived as being fun to be with, as having an influence that is perceived as positive, as facilitating the others' goals, as making peers feel good about themselves and as being similar to peers in a number of ways.

In order to determine where the problems of an unpopular child lie, an adult can observe the child (in structured play settings, for example). The child can then be coached in the social skills s/he is missing. The four basic skills that will most often need to be addressed are cooperation, participation, communication and validation. Teachers can also help unpopular children by 'advertising' their interesting hobbies or specialist knowledge and structuring cooperative work with popular peers.

Increasingly, the evidence suggests that a combination of direct instruction in social skills and collaborative small group work in which pupils lacking social skills are grouped with their more socially adept peers and engage in activities specifically designed to enhance social skills may be an effective way of developing pupils' social skills.

Parents can help by encouraging their children to participate in out-of-school group activities and hobbies, playing with them in a peer-like way when they are young, and discussing their social life with them.

Reflective Questions

1. Why do you think developing healthy peer relations is important?
2. Can you remember any very shy children from your time teaching or being a pupil? Do you think more could have been done to help that child in the school?
3. Do you think the research we discussed on the relationship between parenting styles and children's social skills is valid? Why/why not?
4. What would you do if you saw a child who seemed unpopular in your class?
5. Think of the four types of children identified by sociometric research. From your experience, does this seem accurate, or are there other types of children?
6. Do you think social skills coaching can help make unpopular children more popular? Why/why not?
7. What do you think are the most important factors that can cause a child to be rejected by peers?

CHAPTER 13

ENHANCING PUPILS' SELF-ESTEEM AND SELF-CONCEPT

Key Points

In this chapter, you will learn about:

- the meaning of the terms self-concept and self-esteem
- research on the relationship between these concepts and school achievement
- whether pupils' age and gender affect their self-concept
- what some pioneering psychologists of the self had to say about self-concept
- what teachers can do to improve their pupils' self-concept and self-esteem.

Introduction

Self-concept and self-esteem are concepts that are often discussed not just in the context of schooling but in the context of solving various problems of young people's behaviour in society. Having low self-esteem (or a negative self-concept) has been said to have a detrimental effect on pupils' achievement and life chances, and low self-esteem has been implicated as a cause of factors as diverse as eating disorders and juvenile delinquency. It is therefore not surprising that developing pupils' self-esteem and self-concept has been put forward as a goal that schools and teachers need to pursue.

In this chapter, we will look at what research has to say about the effect of pupils' self-concept and self-esteem on achievement, and what schools and teachers could do to improve both. First, however, we need to clarify what is meant by these two concepts, which are frequently confused with each other.

What are Self-concept and Self-esteem?

Shavelson and Bolus (1982) and Shavelson et al. (1976) define self-concept as *a person's perceptions of him/herself, formed through experience with the environment, interactions with significant others and attributions of his/her own behaviour*. As such, it is both evaluative and descriptive, referring to both what one thinks about oneself in a certain dimension, and how one feels about that.

Self-concept, according to this theory, which is well supported by research (e.g. Marsh et al., 1983; Muijs, 1997), is both *multidimensional* and *hierarchical*. The multidimensional aspect refers to the fact that one can have a different self-concept about different aspects of one's life. In school, for example, one can feel that one is good at English, but not particularly good at mathematics. Likewise, one can feel that one has excellent social skills, but is not a good athlete. The number of aspects that one can have a self-concept about is virtually unlimited. However, Shavelson hypothesized that among children and adolescents, seven dimensions were the most important: self-concept about school subjects, self-concept about English, self-concept about maths, self-concept about relations with peers (other children), self-concept about relations with parents, self-concept of appearance and self-concept of athletic ability. These factors are arranged in the mind in a hierarchical manner, meaning that the three school-related factors go together to form an *academic self-concept* (e.g. I'm generally a good pupil) while the other four factors go together to form a *non-academic self-concept*. These then form the overall or global self-concept, as depicted in Figure 13.1.

Self-esteem is usually used to refer to a person's view of him or herself in a similar way to Shavelson's global self-concept, and can be defined as *a personal judgment of worthiness that is expressed in the attitudes the individual holds towards him/herself* (Coopersmith, 1967). While in Shavelson's model, it is formed out of the different self-concepts a person can hold on different aspects, different people can consider different aspects to be more or less important. For a professional footballer, for example, self-concept of physical ability is likely to be particularly important to global self-esteem, while academic self-concept may

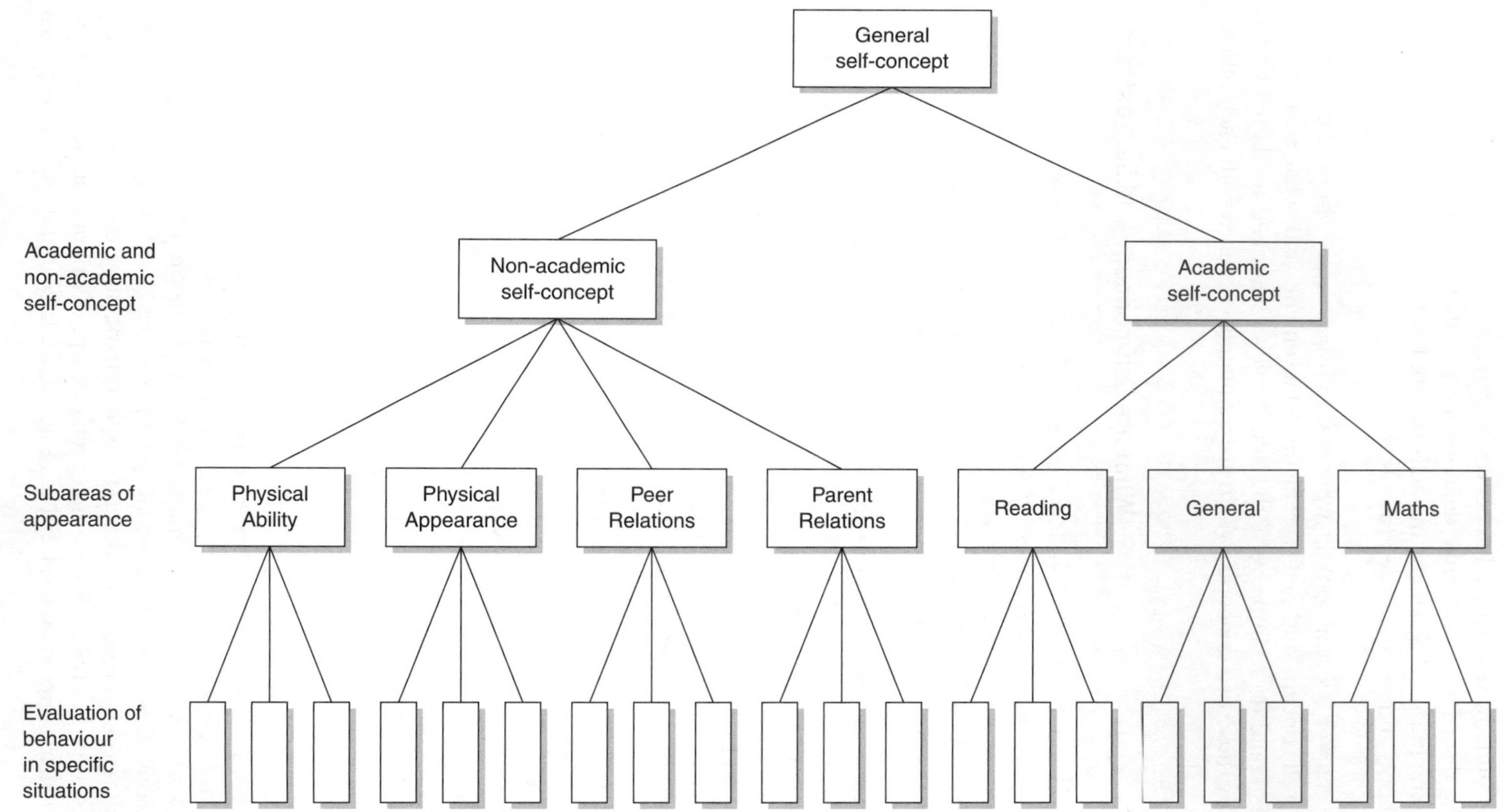

FIGURE 13.1 Shavelson's multifaceted, hierarchical self-concept model (Byrne and Shavelson, 1986: 476)

be less important. For the authors of this work, self-concept of 'research ability' will strongly influence global self-esteem. There is also some evidence that shows that people tend to set more store on aspects of self-concept that they feel positive about when forming their global self-esteem. One can often see that pupils who are not doing well at school will try to diminish the importance of school achievement to their self-esteem through compensation strategies (for example, by attaining expertise in music, or by dismissing high achievement as uncool). This does not mean that people are entirely free to choose what aspects they will value. Society imposes certain values such as physical attractiveness or, for school-age pupils, academic achievement, which are disseminated through parents, peers and media, and therefore self-concept problems in key areas like that will almost inevitably impact on self-esteem.

Is Self-concept Related to Pupils' Achievement?

The global picture

The existence of a self-concept–school achievement relationship, and a stronger school achievement–academic self-concept association is supported by a large body of research. This is a longstanding and established finding. In his review of research up to 1970, Purkey (1970) concluded that a significant relationship existed between self-concept and school achievement, noting that the unsuccessful pupil as opposed to his successful peers was characterized by low self-concept. Burns (1979) in his review reports average correlations of .3 to .4 of school achievement with general self-concept and higher correlations with academic self-concept. West et al. (1980) cite correlations ranging from .18 to .5 between general self-concept and achievement, and correlations of .27 to .70 between academic self-concept and achievement. In a meta-analysis of 128 studies, Hansford and Hattie (1982) found a mean correlation coefficient of .21 Correlations are measures of the relationship between two variables. A Correlation of 0 means there is no relationship, a correlation of that there is a perfect relationship. While these reviews focused mainly on American research, recent studies support the existence of this relationship in a large number of other countries such as Flanders (De Fraine et al., 2006; Muijs, 1998a), Sweden (Johnsson-Smaragdi and Jonsson, 1995), Norway (Skaalvik and Hagtvet, 1990), Israel (Orr and Dinur, 1995), Boputatswana (Maqsud and Rouhani, 1991), Australia (Marsh et al., 1985), Germany (Pekrun, 1990), Finland (Keltikangas-Jarvinen, 1992) and Taiwan (Hong et al., 2002).

What is far less clear, however, is whether there is a relationship between self-esteem and achievement. One review concluded that no such relationship exists, and that there is in fact somewhat more evidence of a negative than of a positive relationship, if any (Baumeister et al., 2003). By contrast, the evidence for the relationship with academic self-concept remains strong (Marsh and O'Mara, 2008). The key finding is therefore that what matters to achievement is self-concept in those areas closest to it rather than more general psychological feelings of self-esteem. This is confirmed by findings that show that the relationship with achievement becomes even stronger when one looks at specific subjects, such as the relationship between maths self-concept and achievement in maths, correlations reaching .6 between Dutch language self-concept and achievement in reading and spelling in a Flemish study, for example (Muijs, 1997). Similar results are also reported in a number of studies in England, Australia and the United States with children and adolescents, in which subject achievement in English and maths was consistently found to be most highly correlated with self-concept in that area, less highly correlated with self-concept in other academic areas, and not (or very slightly) correlated with non-academic self-concept facets (Marsh, 1990; Marsh and Craven, 2006; Marsh et al., 1983, 1985). Self-concept has also been found to be related to specific aspects of pupil achievement and behaviour. One study of adolescents, for example, found that pupils with low self-concepts were less persistent and more easily distracted (Arsenault, 2001), while another found that pupils with a more positive self-concept reported higher levels of classroom involvement (Byer, 2001). Achievement and self-concept are also related to interest. In one study, students showed both high self-concept and interest in domains where they achieved well, and were interested in domains where they perceived themselves as being strong (Denissen et al., 2007).

Differences by age and gender

The relationship has been found to differ by age in some studies. Hansford and Hattie (1982) found significant *age* differences in the mean relationship between general self-concept and achievement, the relationship being lowest in preschool, then climbing in primary and in secondary school, to go down again in university pupils (possibly because pupils at university are likely to be higher achievers, and therefore have a more positive self-concept than the population as a whole). This seems to be consistent with Chapman and Tunmer's (1995) finding that different subcomponents of reading self-concept were more strongly related to reading achievement each year between the first and fifth year of primary school among their school children in New Zealand. A more recent longitudinal study among adolescents found that the relationship between academic achievement and academic self-concept increases over time, becoming stronger as the pupils move through school (Arsenault, 2001), though a study in secondary schools in Flanders found the opposite (De Fraine et al., 2006). Another age effect is that pupils' self-concept tends to start off by being very positive in the lower primary grades. It then tends to dip among many pupils, as they become better able to integrate feedback about their performance into their views of themselves, and drops again just after the transition to secondary school. Thereafter, it usually tends to stabilize or drop further (De Fraine et al., 2006).

Boys and girls have also been found to have different levels of self-concept in a number of studies. These differences are not particularly pronounced when looking at global self-esteem, for which different studies have reported different findings. But when we look at self-concept in different areas, clear patterns do emerge. Girls have more positive self-concepts in the area of peer relations, while boys have a more positive self-concept in the area of physical ability (Marsh et al., 1985). Differences are also apparent in academic self-concept. From primary school onwards, boys tend to develop a more positive self-concept in mathematics, while girls develop a more positive self-concept in English. This has been found to be the case in a number of different countries, and a number of studies have found that this occurs whether or not boys actually outperform girls in the subject or vice versa (e.g. Cloer and Dalton, 2001; Dai, 2001; Thomson and Zand, 2002). Muijs (1997) found that among Flemish primary school children, boys had a more positive mathematical self-concept, although their grades in maths were no better than those of girls. This points to the importance of not letting societal prejudices about 'male' and 'female' subjects influence teaching and the way teachers interact with pupils of different genders, as this may influence self-concept and ultimately achievement. One study of secondary school pupils in Flanders found that the academic self-concept of girls decreased more rapidly than that of boys over time, and that this was unrelated to changes in academic achievement amongst the two genders (De Fraine et al., 2006). There is evidence from some studies that the relationship between achievement and self-concept is weaker amongst girls (Denissen et al., 2007).

The Development of Self-concept Research in Psychology

Interest in the self started early in the history of psychology, William James being the major contributor. He divided the global self into two parts: the Me, or the self as object and the I, or the self as subject. The Me represented the contents of experience, which could be studied by empirical psychology, while the I subjective experience could only be the subject of philosophical thought. James saw the empirical Me as composed of four selves: the spiritual self, the social self, the material self and the bodily self (hierarchically ranked in order of importance for the individual) which are combined in unique ways to constitute a person's view of himself (Burns, 1979; Wylie, 1974).

Cooley was the first to stress the interaction of self and society, and the importance of subjective feedback in self-formation. The self-concept, he believed, arises out of symbolic interaction between an individual and his various primary groups (= a group characterized by face-to-face interaction, relative permanence and a high degree of intimacy). The self-concept is influenced by what you believe others think of you – the so-called looking-glass self (Burns, 1979). According to Mead (1934), the self arises in interaction as an outgrowth of the individual's concern about how others

(Continued)

(Continued)

react to him or her. The process of communication has an important role in this theory, as communication means anticipating the other's reaction through language in order to elicit a reaction in those others. It is through the internalization of these others' expected reactions, necessary for an effective communication, that the individual learns to see his or her environment as others see it. This is how society exerts its influence on the individual.

By the 1940s, interest in the self in psychology started to rise again, as the limits of behaviourism became clear. The necessity of introducing intervening variables in behaviourist models was becoming obvious and the exclusion of many domains vital to human experience from psychology was becoming frustrating to a number of theorists and researchers. New theoretical schools, such as Neo-Freudianism and Phenomenology, reserved an important place for the self.

One of the main post-war theorists on the self was Carl Rogers. Behaviour, according to Rogers (1967), is not directly influenced by organic or cultural factors but by the individual's perception of them. Self-concept is developed and maintained through perceptions of the external world. Once it has been formed, it is difficult to alter, as maintenance of the self-concept is one of the most fundamental human motives. In this way, the self-concept can act as a screen, blocking out perceptions which are in conflict with the established self-concept (= selective perception). The self-concept, being the way a person sees and feels about himself, can only be studied from the standpoint of the individual. It includes both real and ideal self (Burns, 1979; Rogers, 1967).

What comes first? Studies on cause and effect

Finding a relationship doesn't tell us what causes what, however. Do pupils who start off with a negative self-concept then start to do worse in school, or do pupils who do worse in school start to get a more negative academic self-concept? A number of researchers have attempted to unravel this so-called 'causal chain', using path analysis and structural equation modelling.

While early results had been contradictory, research using more sophisticated statistical methods is starting to present more uniform results. Hoge et al. (1995) found paths from grades to specific and general academic self-concept to be stronger than those in the other direction, though none of the paths were strong. Skaalvik and Hagtvet (1990) found achievement to be predominant over academic self-concept amongst third- to fourth-year primary school pupils, while by the sixth year the relationship had become reciprocal, both influencing each other more or less equally. This was also the result of a model using data on 2000 grade 10 boys conducted by Rosenberg et al. (1995). Marsh and O'Mara (2008) likewise found a reciprocal relationship in a seven-year longitudinal study using US data. Muijs (1998a), studying 1000 fourth and fifth grade pupils in

Flanders, found achievement and self-concept to both influence one another, but the effect of achievement on self-concept was stronger than the other way round. Similar findings were reported by Guay, Marsh and Boivin (2003) in Canada and Marsh, Hau and Kong (2002) in Hong Kong. Overall, then, self-concept and achievement influence each other, but the effect of achievement on self-concept is the strongest. Thus, it would seem that getting low grades causes pupils' self-concept to decline, which in turn leads them to achieve less well.

The importance of pupils' frame of reference

A complication in the relationship between self-concept and achievement is that the relationship depends on what is known as the pupils' 'frame of reference'. This means that when pupils form their self-concept, they compare their achievement not with some absolute standard, but with those kids they interact with day-to-day in their class or school. What this means is that a low-performing pupil in a class or school with mainly lower-performing pupils will usually have a more positive academic self-concept than an averagely performing pupil in a class or school with high-performing pupils, even though in absolute terms the latter is the higher achiever. There are many examples of this phenomenon in self-concept research. A study by Marsh and Craven (2002), for example, found that pupils with special educational needs had higher self-concepts in special schools (where they mixed only with other pupils with special needs) than in regular mainstream classrooms where they mixed with a majority of pupils who did not have special educational needs, a finding confirmed by Erlbaum (2002) in her overview of studies in this area.

Enhancing Pupils' Self-esteem in School and Classroom

Teacher behaviours that enhance self-esteem

As self-concept affects school achievement, and self-concept is in turn hierarchically related to global self-esteem, improving pupils' self-esteem could improve their school achievement. Low self-esteem is also related to depression and other mental problems, and enhancing self-esteem is therefore a positive psychological outcome in its own right. Many commentators also believe that improving pupils' self-esteem could strongly benefit society, as low self-esteem is posited to be related to such factors as juvenile delinquency. The evidence for this latter assertion is weak, however. Delinquent youths have not necessarily being found to suffer from low self-esteem (Baumeister et al., 2003; Muijs, 1997). There is, however, a relationship between low achievement at school and delinquency, which means that the indirect effect of improving pupils' self-esteem may be significant. Many pupils come to school with negative self-esteem already developed, often due to the circumstances they have grown up in. There is evidence that school environment can affect this. One study, for example, found that in classroom environments in which competition is encouraged and which show a meritocratic approach to learning, there was a stronger relationship between academic self-concept (which in turn was strongly related to achievement) and self-esteem than in classroom environments that showed an approach that was more focused on protecting pupils' ego and self-esteem (Trautwein et al., 2006).

A number of elements have been proposed to enhance pupils' self-esteem in school. The main thing teachers can do is to create a supportive and loving environment with clear boundaries. This type of environment has been found to be the most beneficial to improving self-concept not just in school, but in the home as well (Coopersmith, 1967). This means that while supportive and caring, schools that foster self-esteem should also be disciplined, orderly environments with clear, though not stifling, rules and procedures.

One of the main factors in improving self-concept is having high *expectations* of all pupils. This element was discussed in Chapter 6, but one way in which self-fulfilling prophecies can occur is through low expectations being expressed by teachers which will then negatively impact on pupils' self-concept for that subject. This may in turn lead to lower achievement. That this is the case is another reason to maintain high expectations of pupils. Teachers should beware of the hidden messages that they are sending out. Verbal and non-verbal cues can send out the message that the teacher is not interested in the pupil, doesn't trust her/him, or doesn't value the pupil. Examples are giving responsibility only to a small group of pupils, giving out the message that the others can't be trusted, or saying something like 'You're now in secondary school, you should be able to do secondary work', which implies that the pupil is stupid. Some studies have found that when adults and teachers praise pupils, they often unconsciously sandwich this praise between instances of criticism which dilutes positive effects, and that in many cases negative feedback could be phrased in a more positive way (Podesta, 2001).

Another element that has already been touched on is *correcting misbehaviour*. This should be done in such a way that pupils' self-concept is not damaged. It is important to avoid personal criticism. The teacher should focus on the misbehaviour, giving reasons why the behaviour is inappropriate, and criticize the behaviour, not the person. As you can see, these recommendations follow those mentioned in the chapter on behaviour management. Teachers should avoid name calling (stupid…), belittling, put-downs or deliberately embarrassing pupils in front of classmates. They should refrain from labelling pupils (e.g. 'you're irresponsible'), and label the behaviour instead (Burns, 1979).

Giving pupils responsibilities helps build up a sense of personal power, which will enhance self-esteem. Pupils should be given the opportunity to make choices and should be allowed to make an active contribution to lessons. Younger pupils should be given responsibility over small tasks, such as keeping the classroom tidy, wiping the board etc., while older pupils should be actively involved in developing classroom rules. Teachers should be supportive of pupils and create a climate in which their contributions are valued. Praise is useful, but should not be overused, because otherwise it will be perceived to be insincere. Praise must also be realistic. Praising a pupil for something s/he has done wrong will not be taken seriously by the pupil and will lead to future praise being devalued.

Teachers should emphasize pupils' successes rather than their failures. They should draw attention to those parts of a task that were done well, and emphasize that learning occurs through trial and error and that making mistakes is a way of learning rather than something to be ashamed of. Teachers should let pupils know what they are doing right as well as correcting their mistakes. Pupils should be encouraged to strive for their own personal best, rather than competing with others or constantly comparing their results with those of classmates.

Specific programmes and activities

A number of specific activities to develop pupils' self-esteem have also been proposed. One such activity is the so-called 'magic circle'. This is an activity during which one child receives a badge, saying something like 'I'm great'. S/he will then be asked to leave the room, while the other pupils are asked to think of all the nice things they can say about her/him. These are then conveyed to the pupil when s/he comes back into class. All comments have to be preceded with the words 'I think …' or 'I believe …' in order to make it easier for the recipient to accept them as opinions which can't be contradicted. At the end of the exercise, the pupil is asked to say something positive about him/herself, something of which s/he is proud (Mosley, 1999). The effectiveness of this type of activity is unproven, however. Another activity that has been proposed is positive self-talk. Getting children to talk positively to themselves internally (saying things to themselves like 'I'm going to do well in maths today') is supposed to improve self-esteem. This is based on the psychological theory that what we repeat internally to ourselves can affect our moods and beliefs. Again, the effectiveness of this method, though strongly supported by some psychologists, remains unproven.

At the end of the day, though, the research reviewed above has shown that the effect of achievement on self-concept is stronger than the effect of self-concept on achievement. Therefore, the best way to improve self-concept is probably to improve pupils' achievement. Just improving achievement for all pupils across the board may not be sufficient, however, as research has shown that self-concept is developed by comparison. Therefore, even a well-performing pupil may have a negative academic self-concept if s/he is not performing as well as other pupils in the school. One way to overcome this would seem to be not to publish pupil grades. However, apart from the positive benefits of performance feedback on pupil achievement (see Chapter 20), an admittedly small-scale study by Muijs (1997) showed that self-concept differences were as pronounced in two schools in which grades were not shown to pupils as in two matched schools in which they were. Pupils thus seem very well able to judge their own competence through classroom interaction. One must also beware of shielding pupils too much from reality, or of building up unrealistic expectations, as this will catch up with them in the long term and can potentially be harmful (Begley and Rogers, 1998). This is another argument for the use of formative feedback aimed at improving pupils' weak points rather than just publishing pupil grades (Black and William, 1998).

The most effective way of doing something about pupils' self-concepts thus seems to be to make sure that all pupils have the opportunity to experience success (Covington and Beery, 1976; Nunn and Parish, 1992). This can be done through teaching that ensures that pupils reach a high level of mastery in a given sub-topic or skill before moving on to the next part of the lesson. Presenting information in small chunks and working towards mastery also ties in well with other research on effective teaching, as discussed in Chapter 2. Giving pupils the chance to participate in a wide range of extracurricular activities (not just sport!) can also help them experience success.

Summary

Self-concept is defined as *a person's perceptions of him/herself, formed through experience with the environment, interactions with significant others and attributions of his/her own behaviour*. People have self-concepts in a variety of areas, including their competence in various school subjects, and in school subjects in general. Self-esteem is a more global concept, referring to people's general view of their own worth.

Research has clearly established that there is a relationship between pupils' self-concept and self-esteem and their school achievement. This relationship is strongest with academic self-concept, and lower with global self-esteem. The relationship is reciprocal, meaning that self-concept affects achievement, but achievement affects self-concept as well. Thus, low achievement will lead to negative self-concept, which will in turn lead to lower achievement. The effect of achievement on self-concept is stronger than the effect of self-concept on achievement.

There are a number of things teachers can do in the classroom to improve their pupils' self-esteem. Having high expectations of pupils will improve their self-concept as well as their performance. When correcting misbehaviour, it is important to correct the behaviour, rather than criticizing the pupil. To build up pupils' self-worth, they should be given some responsibilities in the classroom. With younger pupils, this can take the form of being responsible for things like keeping the classroom tidy, while older pupils should be involved in decision making. Teachers should emphasize pupils' successes by telling them what they are doing right as well as correcting their mistakes, and should show that their contributions are valued.

The most important aspect, however, is to ensure that all pupils experience success. This can be achieved by teaching to high levels of mastery and by teaching content in small steps and making sure that pupils have grasped a concept before moving on to the next part of the lesson. Providing them with a range of extracurricular activities can help them experience success in other areas as well.

Reflective Questions

1. Shavelson's model posits seven self-concept dimensions. Can you think of some others that are important to you?
2. What dimension of self-concept would you expect to be most strongly related to a pupil's performance on a History test?
3. Do you agree that mastery learning helps pupils' self-esteem? Why/why not?
4. Why might using a magic circle help improve pupils' self-esteem, and why might it not?
5. How might non-verbal cues affect pupils' self-concept?
6. What could a teacher do to help pupils attain a positive self-concept?
7. What areas of pupil self-concept do you think might be related to gender?

CHAPTER 14

TEACHING PUPILS WITH SPECIAL EDUCATIONAL NEEDS

Key Points

In this chapter, you will learn about:

- the characteristics of a number of types of special educational needs (SEN) which teachers may encounter
- what research has to say about the effects of inclusion of pupils with special needs in 'mainstream' classrooms
- what teaching methods are most effective in teaching pupils with a variety of learning difficulties
- how best to deal with pupils with different special needs
- what parents can do to help children with learning difficulties.

Introduction

Special needs is a broad term, referring to very different pupils with a wide range of different needs and problems. The Education Ministry in the United Kingdom (known at the time of writing as the Department for Children, Families and Schools (DCSF) – the actual name tends to change every few years) defines special needs as follows: 'A child is defined as having special educational needs if he or she has a learning difficulty which needs special teaching. A learning difficulty means that the child has significantly greater difficulty in learning than most children of the same age. Or, it means a child has a disability which needs different educational facilities from those that schools generally provide for children of the same age in the area. The children who need special education are not only those with obvious learning difficulties, such as those who are physically disabled, deaf or blind. They include those whose learning difficulties are less apparent, such as slow learners and emotionally vulnerable children. It is estimated that up to 20 per cent of school children may need special educational help at some stage in their school careers' (DfEE, 2000a).

One group of pupils with special needs that we will discuss in the next chapter are *gifted pupils*. At the opposite spectrum of academic achievement we find pupils with *learning disabilities*.

Types of Special Needs

The DCSF (2008), in a useful classification, identifies the following types of special educational needs:

1. Cognition and learning needs

Specific Learning Difficulties (SpLD)

Pupils with specific learning difficulties have general difficulties with learning. Pupils with SpLD may have a particular difficulty in learning to read, write, spell or manipulate numbers so that their performance in these areas is below their performance in other areas. Pupils may also have problems with short-term memory, with organizational skills and with coordination. Three of the most common SpLDs are dyslexia, dyscalculia and dyspraxia. Pupils with dyslexia have difficulty in acquiring accuracy or fluency in learning to read, write and spell, even though they may be able and perform well in other subjects. Pupils may have poor reading comprehension, handwriting and punctuation. They may also have difficulties in concentration and organization and in remembering sequences of words. They may mispronounce common words or reverse letters and sounds in words. Pupils with dyscalculia have similar difficulties, but with mathematical rather than reading skills. Pupils may have difficulty understanding simple number concepts, lack an intuitive grasp of numbers and have problems learning number facts and procedures. Pupils with dyspraxia have motor skills difficulties. Gross and fine motor skills are hard to learn and difficult to retain and generalize. Pupils may have poor balance and coordination and may be hesitant in many actions. They may also have poor awareness of body position.

Moderate Learning Difficulties (MLD)

Pupils with moderate learning difficulties will have attainments well below expected levels in all or most areas of the curriculum.

Pupils with MLD have much greater difficulty than their peers in acquiring basic literacy and numeracy skills and in understanding concepts. They may also have associated speech and language delay, low levels of concentration and under-developed social skills. They will be behind other learners in the school.

Severe Learning Difficulties (SLD)

Pupils with severe learning difficulties have severe and complex learning needs, and in addition they often have other significant difficulties, such as physical disabilities or a sensory impairment. These pupils require a high level of adult support, both for their learning needs and also for personal care. They are likely to need sensory stimulation and a curriculum broken down into very small steps. Some pupils communicate by gesture, eye pointing or symbols, others by very simple language.

Profound and Multiple Learning Difficulties (PMLD)

These pupils suffer even greater learning difficulties than pupils with severe learning difficulties, and are very unlikely to benefit from mainstream education.

2. Behaviour, emotional and social development needs

Pupils with behavioural, emotional and social difficulties show problematic behaviours that present a barrier to learning and persist, despite the implementation of an effective school behaviour policy and personal/social curriculum. They may be withdrawn or isolated, disruptive and disturbing, hyperactive and lack concentration, have immature social skills or present challenging behaviours.

Pupils with a range of difficulties, including emotional disorders such as depression and eating disorders; conduct disorders such as oppositional defiance disorder (ODD); hyperkinetic disorders including attention deficit disorder or attention deficit hyperactivity disorder (ADD/ADHD); and syndromes such as Tourette's fall into this category.

3. Communication and interaction needs

Speech, Language and Communication Needs (SLCN)

Pupils with speech, language and communication needs have difficulty in understanding and/or making others understand information conveyed through spoken language. Their acquisition of speech and their oral language skills may be significantly behind their peers. Their speech may be poor or unintelligible.

Pupils with language impairments find it hard to understand and/or use words in context. They may use words incorrectly with inappropriate grammatical patterns, have a reduced vocabulary or find it hard to recall words and express ideas. They may also hear or see a word but not be able to understand its meaning or have trouble getting others to understand what they are trying to say.

Autistic Spectrum Disorder (ASD)

Pupils with ASD find it difficult to:

- understand and use non-verbal and verbal communication
- understand social behaviour – which affects their ability to interact with children and adults
- think and behave flexibly – which may be shown in restricted, obsessional or repetitive activities.

4. Sensory and/or physical needs

Visual Impairment (VI)

Visual impairment refers to a range of difficulties from partial sight through to blindness. A pupil is considered to be VI if they require adaptations to their environment or specific differentiation of learning materials in order to access the curriculum.

Hearing Impairment (HI)

Pupils with a hearing impairment range from those with a mild hearing loss to those who are profoundly deaf. Pupils are regarded as having a hearing impairment if they require hearing aids, adaptations to their environment and/or particular teaching strategies in order to access the concepts and language of the curriculum.

Multi-Sensory Impairment (MSI)

Pupils with multi-sensory impairment have a combination of visual and hearing difficulties. They are sometimes referred to as deaf blind but may have some residual sight and/or hearing. Many also have additional disabilities but their complex needs mean that it may be difficult to ascertain their intellectual abilities.

Physical Disability (PD)

A wide range of physical disabilities fall into this category.

Some pupils are able to access the curriculum and learn effectively without additional educational provision. They have a disability but do not have a special educational need. For others, the impact on their education may be severe.

There are a number of medical conditions associated with physical disability which can impact on mobility, such as cerebral palsy, spina bifida and muscular dystrophy. Pupils with physical disabilities may also have associated sensory impairments, neurological problems or learning difficulties.

The Inclusion Debate

Types of provision for pupils with special needs

Once a child has been diagnosed as possessing a learning or other disability (different procedures for this exist in different countries), schools need to provide the necessary support for these children. Several options exist, for example placing children in 'special schools' explicitly designed to accommodate children with special needs; placing them in regular so-called 'mainstream' schools, but in special separate classrooms; placing them in mainstream schools in regular classrooms, but have them taken out of class for special education; or 'full inclusion' in mainstream classrooms (in this latter case, the necessary adjustments to this classroom will have to be made to meet children's special educational needs). In recent years, there has been a clear shift towards inclusion and away from placement in special schools or classrooms, often for philosophical reasons pertaining to pupils' human rights, as well as because of arguments concerning pupils' social growth. One of the arguments goes that included pupils will have enhanced self-esteem as they are not being labelled and secluded from peers to the same extent as when placed in special schools or classrooms.

Furthermore, non-disabled pupils will get used to being around disabled peers, leading them to be less likely to discriminate against them in adulthood. In this way it is hoped disabled pupils will be able to develop into active and respected members of the community.

Effects of inclusion on the academic achievement of pupils with special needs

One of the main questions argued over by supporters and opponents of the inclusion of pupils with special needs is whether integration into mainstream classrooms will benefit or harm pupils' academic progress. Supporters of placement in special schools/units usually argue that the smaller class sizes and specific attention given to special needs pupils by experts will aid their academic progress (Gartner and Lipsky, 1987). Furthermore, as we saw in the previous chapter, frame of reference effects may mean that pupils in special schools have higher academic self-concepts than when they are in mainstream schools (Marsh and Craven, 2002). Some teachers also feel that the performance of their non-SEN pupils will decrease because of inclusion (Dyson and Millward, 2000). On the other hand, proponents of integration argue that pupils in special schools/units may suffer from a lack of academic press and may benefit from interaction with higher-achieving peers. Furthermore, typical practices in special units/schools have often been found not to be in accordance with effective classroom practices, being characterized by lower cognitive demands, little use of higher-order cognitive skills, slower pacing, little time devoted to academic tasks and little direct instruction (Gartner and Lipsky, 1987; Walberg, 1993; Zigmond and Baker, 1997). Proponents of programmes in which pupils spend most of their time in mainstream classrooms but are pulled out for one or two hours a day to follow lessons in a special unit generally see this as a good compromise between mainstreaming and segregation, while opponents claim that this process leads to them missing parts of the mainstream programme, making it more difficult for them to follow the curriculum, especially as there often seems to be scant coordination between regular classroom teachers and teachers in these so-called pull-out programmes (Zigmond and Baker, 1997).

In their review of studies up to the mid-1980s (described as small in number and often methodologically flawed), Slavin and Madden (1986) report that while some studies found pupils in full-time special placement to do as well as pupils in mainstream settings, and others found them to do worse (according to Slavin and Madden, these latter tended to be the better designed studies), no studies reported that pupils in full-time placement did better academically than pupils in mainstream settings. Some evidence emerged that pupils who did not receive any support in mainstream classrooms did worse, however (Madden and Slavin, 1983; Slavin and Madden, 1986). No clear differences emerged between pupils in part-time placement and pupils in mainstream settings. A meta-analysis conducted by Wang and Baker (1986) (reviewing 11 studies conducted between 1975 and 1984) reports a slightly favourable effect of mainstreaming over full-time placement for academic outcomes. Sixty-five per cent of measured effects were positive, and mainstream pupils seemed to make more progress than segregated peers did. These results were consistent across grade levels and when controlling for contextual variables. When full-time mainstreaming was compared to pull-out programmes, the former was found to be non-significantly more effective. In an earlier meta-analysis, Carlberg and Kavale (1980) found 'educable mentally retarded' pupils to do worse in special classes than in mainstream classes. A review of three meta-analyses by Baker et al. (1995) found small positive effects for inclusion. Gartner and Lipsky (1987), reviewing a large number of studies, found that the mean academic performance of special needs pupils in mainstream settings was on average in the 80th percentile compared to non-special needs pupils, while the performance of pupils in segregated settings was in the 50th percentile. In three studies using a reading test as the outcome measure, Zigmond and Baker (1997) found inconclusive results; half the pupils with learning difficulties educated in mainstream settings made reliable gains, while 40 per cent made gains of less than half the magnitude of their peers. As these pupils were not compared with special needs pupils in segregated settings, this does not tell us much about the relative effectiveness of mainstreaming, however.

A review by Manset and Semmel (1997) looked at the effects of a number of integration programmes for pupils with special needs in the USA. Three out of the five reviewed programmes (Success for All, Adaptive Learning Environments Model, and an untitled programme by Jenkins et al.) reported significantly higher achievement gains for pupils in the programme than for pupils in 'pull-out' programmes (pupils spend most of their time in mainstream classrooms, but are removed from class for one or two hours a day for teaching in a special unit). These programmes seemed to share the common feature of highly focused instruction with individual basic skills tuition. Deno et al. (1990) compared pupils in three integrated programs (Adaptive Learning Environments Model, the Comparison Reading Program and Data-based Intervention) with pupils in resource room programmes, and found that low achievers and pupils with mild learning difficulties who participated in the programmes scored higher on the Basic Academic Skills Survey.

Lipsky and Gartner (1997) reported few differences between special needs pupils in mainstream education and in pull-out programmes. They also reported that the gap in achievement between pupils with mild learning difficulties and their mainstream peers did not widen as fast when these pupils were mainstreamed as when they were in pull-out programmes. In a study using the Metropolitan Achievement Test to compare learning disabled pupils in two schools, Jenkins et al. (1994) found that pupils in the integrated schools showed significantly higher overall gains than pupils in a school using a pull-out resource room method. In a small-scale study, Banerji and Dailey (1995) reported that 2nd to 5th grade pupils with specific learning difficulties achieved better in a mainstream classroom than in a pull-out programme. Schulte, Osborne and McKinney (1990) studied elementary school pupils with learning difficulties who spent:

- one hour per day in a resource room setting
- two hours per day in a resource room setting
- the whole day in mainstream classrooms in which a special education teacher provided some additional instruction to the child
- the whole day in mainstream classrooms where special education teachers provided technical assistance to the mainstream teacher, but no instruction in class.

It was found that pupils in the mainstream classroom with extra teaching did significantly better overall (though not in specific subjects) than pupils who spent one hour a day in the resource room. No other significant differences were found. A recent study of inclusion in early years, in which parents were interviewed with regards to their views, found that most parents felt that inclusion helped their child's cognitive and social development, although some were concerned about lack of teacher attention to their child and negative reactions of other children (Brown,

2001). However, another study reports that teachers in inclusive schools have significantly more positive attitudes towards pupils with special needs than teachers who taught at non-integrated mainstream schools (McLeskey et al., 2001).

In a review of reviews focusing on pupils with moderate learning difficulties, Williams (1993) reported that studies seemed to slightly favour mainstreaming. However, the deficiencies of the studies led the author to state that a no-effects conclusion was safest. Galloway (1985) reaches a similar conclusion.

Generally then, these studies seem to point to the positive effects of mainstreaming over full-time, and, to a lesser extent, part-time placement in special units. However, many studies were methodologically flawed and sample sizes were small. Conclusions must therefore be highly tentative, although there does seem to be some cumulative evidence for the higher effectiveness of mainstreaming over full-time placement for special needs pupils in general. The picture with regards to pull-out programmes must be considered inconclusive, however. Also, it seems clear that whether inclusion or placement are preferable may also depend on the nature and seriousness of the disability. As Lindsay (2003) points out, there is a need for more rigorous research on the effectiveness of different forms of provision for pupils with special educational needs.

A related question is that of the effects of inclusion on the achievement of the non-SEN pupils in the classroom. One study, looking at the effects of inclusion on the graduation test results in Indiana, found no effects (Bibler and Gilman, 2003). However, another study found that while there was no overall effect, low achievers' performance improved following inclusion of pupils with special needs, while the performance of high achievers was depressed (Huber et al., 2001). This suggests that the fact that a larger group of low-performing pupils was present led to teachers focusing more on this group, to the detriment of the highest ability pupils. In a study using national databases in England, a very weak negative relationship was found whereby more inclusive schools showed lower achievement. However, this was explained by the fact that the more inclusive schools served more socio-economically disadvantaged communities (Dyson et al., 2004). One problem for schools can be that if they are perceived as being too successful with pupils with SEN, they may buckle under the demands from their parents to take on their children, thus leading to an imbalance in the area. It is therefore necessary that schools in an area coordinate inclusion policies and practice (MacBeath et al., 2006).

In terms of overall school effectiveness, there appear to be a number of advantages to inclusion. In one qualitative study in England, teachers claimed that inclusion had:

- social benefits to pupils with SEN who were more accepted by their peers and by adults
- social benefits to mainstream pupils who develop a better understanding and acceptance of people with special needs

- a broader professional awareness of diversity of needs and learning difficulties
- improved skills of teachers and LSAs in dealing with a diversity of special needs.

However, some teachers felt that they lacked skills and expertise in dealing with these pupils, and that attention to SEN pupils could go at a cost of less attention to the needs of non-SEN pupils (MacBeath et al., 2006).

When does inclusion work?

In order for inclusion to work, a number of conditions need to be met. Teachers must believe the included pupils can succeed, and must prepare the other pupils in the class to accept the disabled pupils. This is often something that requires professional development, as teachers may often start off with very low expectations of special needs pupils, and may even be reluctant to teach them, sometimes palming them off on classroom assistants (Weiner, 2003).

The classroom and school need to be physically prepared if necessary, and all school staff need to understand the needs of the pupils with disabilities. Staff development needs to take place to prepare staff to support the pupil, and good working relationships need to be established with the special educators in the school. In many studies, it appears that inclusion is attempted without providing this level of professional development, a state which may be very disadvantageous to the integrated pupils (King and Edmunds, 2001; McLeskey and Waldron, 2002). It seems essential that all teacher training programmes include a substantial special needs module if teachers are to be fully prepared for the realities of today's classrooms.

The use of special needs coordinators is key to making sure that sufficient attention is paid to pupils with special needs, though in one Dutch study it was found that having such a coordinator could lead to other teachers detaching themselves from special needs issues and not developing their skills in this area (Imants et al., 2001). One issue that teachers need to be especially attuned to is a tendency, found in some studies, to address the special needs pupils and interact with them less than with non-SEN pupils in mainstreamed classes (Cawthon, 2001). One way in which teachers and schools try to accommodate pupils with special needs in mainstream classrooms is by giving them support through the use of classroom assistants. These are typically members of the community who have received limited pedagogical training. Recent studies (Blatchford et al., 2008; Muijs and Reynolds, 2003) suggest that this approach is not effective in improving performance, but none of these studies have looked specifically at support for pupils with SEN. What is clear is that if classroom assistants are going to be able to work effectively with pupils with SEN, they will require adequate training for this role.

Teaching Pupils with Learning Difficulties

Reading difficulties

According to extensive studies carried out by the National Institute for Child Health and Development in the USA, the main predictor of *reading difficulties* is problems with phonemic awareness. Vocabulary deficits, inadequate background knowledge of material presented in the text, lack of similarity with semantic and syntactic structures that help us to predict the meanings of words and sentences, and lack of understanding of author purposes (e.g. humour) were other significant factors. One of the most important aspects of treating reading disabilities, therefore, is teaching these pupils word–sound correspondences to decipher reading codes (the *phonics system*). This approach has been found to be effective in a number of studies (Lyon, 1994; McElgunn, 1996). This decoding skill needs to become automatic so memory capacity that should be used for strong comprehension of the text to occur isn't wasted on the decoding process. Strong comprehension is also influenced by pupils' background knowledge and vocabulary. Thus, both direct structured instruction in phonics and a literature-rich environment can help pupils with reading difficulties (Lyon, 1999).

Another problem that pupils with reading difficulties seem to have is an inability to properly self-monitor while reading a text. They fail to understand that they must pay attention to how well they understand the text and that they should reread a paragraph or sentence if they don't understand it. Pupils with this problem can be taught a number of self-monitoring skills, such as asking themselves questions while they read and summarizing what they have read. However, once taught, these pupils often experience difficulties in generalizing these skills to other situations (Gersten, 1999).

Learning difficulties

More generally, a meta-analysis of research on pupils with learning disabilities but of average intelligence looking at studies conducted over a 30-year period found that the most effective strategy for teaching these pupils combined elements of direct instruction (see Chapters 1–3) with components focusing on the teaching of learning and mnemonic strategies. The main components of this strategy include:

- sequencing (breaking down the task, providing step-by-step prompts)
- a drill-repetition-practice sequence
- segmentation (breaking down the task into small segments and then synthesising them as a whole)
- directed questioning and response
- use of technology

- modelling
- small group instruction.

The most important factor was found to be control of task difficulty, proceeding from simple to more difficult aspects in small, teacher-directed steps. The effectiveness of this combined direct instruction–strategy approach was strongest in reading, and somewhat less strong in mathematics and social skills (Swanson, 1999).

Use of small (3 to 10 pupils), teacher-directed groups rather than the whole class was found to be beneficial to learning disabled pupils in a meta-analysis of 20 studies. Peer tutoring was likewise found to be effective. Smaller groups (3 to 5 pupils) appeared more effective than larger groups. These grouping procedures could most usefully be combined with whole-class instruction (Erlbaum et al., 1999). One model which combined a number of these elements, such as guided reading, phonics instruction, cooperative learning and language support was found to have been successful in raising the achievement of pupils with reading difficulties in one small-scale study (Angell, 2001).

A problem for many LD pupils is a negative self-concept. As mentioned in Chapter 10, there are two possible approaches to dealing with this: a skills development approach, that aims to enhance pupils' academic achievement which should in turn enhance their self-concept; and a self-enhancement approach, which uses a therapeutic approach to change self-concept. A meta-analysis on the effectiveness of these two approaches among LD pupils concluded that an approach that combined the two worked best. Collaborative work appeared to be a factor that enhanced self-concept in many interventions (Erlbaum and Vaughn, 1999). This is a key issue in inclusive classrooms, as we have seen that pupils may experience decreased self-concept as they compare their achievement to that of non-SEN peers (Marsh and Craven, 2002).

Attention disorders

Pupils with *attention disorders*, which some evidence suggests are becoming increasingly prevalent, can be particularly problematic during lessons as these pupils can easily disrupt lessons and disturb other pupils.

There are a number of things a teacher can do to help maintain the attention of all and, in particular, attention-disabled pupils. Employing a range of introductory attention grabbers and stressing the importance of the topic to pupils' daily lives could help, as could presenting material in small steps, explaining the relevance of each step along the way. Pupils should be encouraged to learn from their mistakes, and be actively involved in the lesson. Helping pupils to set short-term goals that are not too hard to reach can also be beneficial. Using a variety of teaching methods and a quick succession of activities can help focus pupils' attention and keep them from becoming bored too quickly (Fulk, 2000).

Pupils with attention disorders often seem to suffer from disorganization as well. They may have difficulty remembering dates and assignments, bringing required materials into class and may incorrectly record assignments, use time inefficiently, fail to properly structure essays and written work, fail to express themselves in an organized fashion and fail to plan. It is important to provide these pupils with a clear structure and routines, and specify exactly what they are expected to bring to class at each point in the day. The teacher needs to give pupils clear and simple directions, and have her/him repeat these. Assignments need to be clearly presented and written on the same place of the board each time. Pupils must be made to copy these assignments. Teachers should try to minimize clutter on handouts and assignments.

Modelling problem-solving and essay-writing skills can help, especially when pupils are given large assignments, which they may find confusing. Various ways of storing material and being tidy need to be presented to them. They can be taught mnemonic techniques and the use of memory aides, such as a note attached to the pupils' backpack or satchel. Furthermore, pupils should be praised and rewarded for improvements in their organization, but they should also receive the consequences of their disorganization in order to provide them with an incentive to do better (Shore, 1998). Recently, researchers have begun to advocate using ICT with learners with attention disorders, and have reported some promising findings. Assistive reading software, for example, has been found to help pupils to attend better to their reading, become less easily distracted, read with less stress and read for longer periods of time (Hecker et al., 2002). However, the short time span of most of these studies does beg the question of whether this is merely the effect of novelty and will wear off after some time.

Children suffering from ADHD have been found to have problems dealing with change. Consistency is therefore important. They should, where possible, be placed at the front of the class, where they have the least chance of observing other children move as they write things down and answer questions. However, some hyperactive children can, when seated at the front, disturb their classmates through their constant movement and fidgeting. These pupils clearly are not best left at the front (Stevens, 1997). Pupils with ADHD should be surrounded by pupils who can act as positive behaviour models. They should not be placed near possibly distracting objects, such as heaters, windows and doors.

The US State Department of Education (2003: 15) issued the following tips for educators with regards to pupils with ADHD:

- work on the most difficult concepts early in the day
- give direction to one assignment at a time instead of directions to multiple tasks all at once
- vary the type and pace of activity to maximize pupils' attention

- structure the pupil's environment to accommodate her/his special needs. For example, the pupil can be seated away from distracting areas (such as doors, windows or computers) or seated near another pupil who is working hard on a shared assignment.

Other behavioural difficulties

When pupils suffer from *behavioural difficulties*, the first step is to identify exactly what it is that the pupil is doing that makes her/him cause problems in the classroom. Then one has to identify what it is that one wants the pupil to do instead, and what means could be used to get there. Teachers should try to avoid focusing on the undesired behaviour and try to focus on the desired behaviours instead. Opportunities should be provided for the pupil to practise the desired behaviours, such as interacting appropriately with peers and adults.

There are two possible problems that may need to be addressed with pupils with behavioural disorders: skills deficits and performance deficits. Which of these two situations is present can be assessed by having the pupil role play various situations or by asking them what they would do in a certain situation, such as if the teacher reprimanded them. If they can give the correct response to this type of question or can perform the appropriate behaviour in role play but not display the appropriate behaviour in actual classroom situations, then the problem is one of performance deficit. If they are not able to give an appropriate response to the question, then the problem may be a skills deficit. In the latter case, direct instruction in the required skill will be necessary before proceeding to practise the skill. In particular, in many cases, social skills instruction may be appropriate (Lo et al., 2002). If the problem is one of performance, providing more situations to practise the appropriate response may be sufficient.

Giving pupils choices (for example, about what activities they want to do), peer tutoring on desired behaviours and providing interesting activities have been found to limit behaviour problems (Jolivette et al., 2001; Kern et al., 2002; Nelson et al., 2002).

Deaf and hard of hearing pupils

Deaf or *hard of hearing* pupils can be educated in a number of ways. One of these is the *auditory–oral* approach. This method attempts to get deaf children to acquire spoken language in an environment in which spoken language is used exclusively, including both the classroom and the school. The home environment is crucial in this process, as is the use of hearing amplifiers, such as hearing aids and cochlear implants, depending on the seriousness of the hearing problem. As well as listening skills, pupils are taught speech production skills starting at the phonetic level (individual syllables), and proceeding from there to the phonological level (whole words and sentences) immediately. If successful, this approach will allow hard of hearing children to communicate with a wide range of others (Nielsen and Luetke-Stahlman, 2002). Some research (Geers and Moog, 1989) found that 16–17 year olds who had been taught using this technique had a reading age of about 13–14 years, which is almost double that of US deaf pupils in general. A possible problem may be that the hearing loss is too serious to be overcome, even with the use of cochlear implants (Stone, 1997).

The *auditory–verbal* approach works from a similar idea. In this approach, hearing problems are identified at the earliest possible stage and the best possible medical treatment or amplifier is then sought out. Then children are taught listening and speech skills. The idea is to identify the child's problems as soon as possible and to intervene by teaching the necessary strategies to the parents of young children (Goldberg, 1994, 1997). Therefore, more than a teaching approach, this is an approach that targets parents.

The *cued speech* method is basically a sound-based hand supplement to speechreading, designed to improve the literacy development of deaf children. It can be used by both parents and teachers to teach pupils phonics and articulation. The system is easy to learn and can be used to teach words for which there isn't a sign language equivalent (Caldwell, 1997). According to research by Wandel (quoted in Caldwell, 1997), pupils taught using this method read at the same grade level as their non-deaf peers.

A different option is using a *sign language* (Gustasson, 1997). Like spoken languages, sign languages differ from country to country, American Sign Language for example differing from British Sign Language. Most sign languages have developed naturally in the deaf community, but some have been specifically developed to more closely resemble the spoken version of the language, adding grammatical features of that language to the sign language. These systems are often used by parents and teachers to teach deaf children, as they allow them to more easily learn their home language. However, some deaf parents feel this practice negates their culture. According to some researchers, there is a need to concentrate on teaching hand development in the early years to enhance the communication skills of deaf pupils (Miles, 2001).

Summary

Among the most prevalent of special needs are learning difficulties. *Learning difficulties* are connected to problems with linking information in different parts of the brain. Learning difficulties can be more or less severe, and take a

(Continued)

(Continued)

number of different forms, making it hard to develop global approaches to teaching these pupils.

As well as learning needs, some pupils can suffer from behaviour, emotional and social development needs, communication and interaction needs or sensory and physical needs. These will all require specific approaches to creating a classroom environment that fosters the learning of all pupils.

For social and philosophical reasons, there has been a move away from teaching pupils with special needs in separate schools and classrooms and towards integrating them into regular classrooms – a process known as 'inclusion'. A question that has been asked is whether this is beneficial to their academic development. Most studies seem to point to positive effects of mainstreaming over full-time and, to a lesser extent, part-time placement in special units, although the number of studies is small and many are methodologically flawed.

One of the main problems for pupils with reading difficulties appears to be a lack of phonemic awareness. These pupils therefore need to receive explicit phonics instruction. Bad readers have also been found to have problems self-monitoring while reading, and these skills need to be improved as well.

Using attention grabbers, a variety of visual aids, proceeding in small steps and using a variety of teaching methods can help pupils with attention disorders. As these pupils are often disorganized, enhancing their organizational skills can be necessary.

A variety of approaches has been proposed for the teaching of deaf and hard of hearing pupils, such as the auditory–oral approach, the auditory–verbal approach, the cued speech approach and the use of sign language.

Reflective Questions

1. What teaching methods do you think work best for pupils with learning difficulties?
2. What is your view on inclusion? How does it affect non-SEN pupils?
3. Think of a lesson you have recently taught, observed or been a pupil in. Were there any pupils with behavioural difficulties? How were they dealt with? Was this appropriate?
4. What kind of training do you think classroom assistants would need to be able to effectively help pupils with learning difficulties?
5. How would you arrange your classroom to minimize disruption from students with behavioural difficulties?

CHAPTER 15

TEACHING GIFTED PUPILS

Key Points

In this chapter, you will learn about:

- how to identify gifted children, and what distinguishes them from bright children
- how to help gifted pupils fulfil their potential
- the advantages and disadvantages of different methods used to help gifted and talented pupils
- what parents can do to help their gifted offspring
- the characteristics of gifted learning disabled pupils.

Introduction

As was mentioned in Chapter 14, where we discussed pupils with special educational needs, the school system is inevitably geared towards the majority of pupils which means that additional provisions need to be made for pupils with special needs. Another group that differs from the norm, and that therefore may need special provisions, are gifted or highly able pupils. In this chapter, we will discuss how best to teach these pupils.

What is giftedness?

First of all, though, it is necessary to define exactly what is meant by gifted, especially compared to 'merely' bright pupils. The term gifted is usually used to refer to pupils who score significantly above average on ability tests such as the WISC III, Raven's Progressive Matrices or the Cognitive Ability Test. As a rule of thumb, a score in the top 2 per cent of the range of these tests (usually corresponding to a score of over 125) is considered to indicate giftedness. Within schools, a number of other factors are also taken into account in decision making on whether or not to include a certain pupil in 'gifted' programmes. These include pupils' grades, teachers' professional opinion and sometimes views of parents and pupils themselves.

Bright Versus Gifted Children

A number of elements that have been proposed as distinguishing bright and gifted children are listed below:

Bright child	Gifted child
Knows the answers	Asks the questions
Interested	Extremely curious
Pays attention	Gets involved physically and mentally
Works hard	Plays around, but still gets good test scores
Answers questions	Questions the answers
Enjoys same-age peers	Prefers adults or older children
Good at memorization	Good at guessing
Learns easily	Gets easily bored because s/he already knows the answers
Listens well	Shows strong feelings and opinions
Self-satisfied	Highly perfectionistic and self-critical

While use of cognitive ability tests is probably the best way of identifying gifted pupils at present, it can be important to identify gifted pupils early on in their school career. For kindergarten-aged pupils, sitting a cognitive ability test would not be either valid or practical, and therefore a number of signs indicating giftedness in young children have been proposed:

1. The child uses an advanced vocabulary for her/his age.
2. The child has the ability to make interesting or unusual shapes or patterns using various media.
3. The child has an early understanding of abstract concepts such as death and time.
4. The child can master new skills with few repetitions.

5. The child demonstrates advanced physical skills.
6. The child demonstrates advanced reasoning skills through explanation of occurrences.
7. The child uses spontaneous verbal elaboration with new experiences.
8. The child demonstrates a sense of humour during normal conversation.

When using tests, it is important to remember that children do develop at different rates and that therefore scores on a test taken at one particular time are not set in stone. Giftedness at a particular age could just be the result of more rapid development which ceases to exist once other children's development has caught up. One also has to remember that scores on ability tests do not simply reflect innate ability, but also result from environmental influences such as parents' cultural capital and their ability to provide their children with an intellectually stimulating environment. Scores on ability tests can also be influenced by a child's education. Identification of giftedness is therefore an empirical question at one particular moment in time, and will need to be reviewed.

Giftedness can be general, extending to a wide range of school subjects, or specific, limited to one particular area such as mathematics, creative writing or science. Specifically gifted pupils will achieve very well in that subject, while being average or able in other subjects. They will usually also be particularly interested in that area.

Apart from being intellectually gifted, pupils can be gifted in a number of other ways. Typical examples include pupils who are artistically gifted, or who are gifted footballers. These pupils are not necessarily intellectual high achievers, but obviously do have specific gifts, and in England are often referred to as talented rather than gifted. In this chapter, we will concentrate on academically gifted pupils.

Gifted Pupils in Classrooms and Schools

As has probably become clear from the above, teaching gifted pupils in regular classrooms can lead to a number of problems. The key one here is that gifted pupils need to be continually challenged. If they are not challenged, they are liable to find the content of lessons boring and will not be stretched by the regular curriculum. They will not benefit to the full from their classroom experience, and will not be able to work to their potential (Rogers, 2007). Their boredom can make them lose interest in school altogether, in some cases leading to truancy and disruptive behaviour, and more often to underachievement. Research has shown that for these pupils a lot of what they learn in school can be a waste of time, as they already know large parts of the curriculum (Kantrowitz and Wingert, 1992; Ness and Latessa, 1979; Parke, 1992). A number of measures have therefore been proposed to deal with gifted pupils, which will be discussed below.

Ability grouping

A first way of offering gifted pupils a more suitable education is through *ability grouping*. A lot of studies (discussed in more detail in Chapter 17) have looked at the effect of ability grouping on pupils' achievement. The conclusion most reach is that ability grouping overall does not significantly affect achievement, but that it does have a small negative effect on the achievement of low-ability pupils and a small positive effect on the achievement of high-ability pupils. It is therefore not surprising that this method has been advocated as a way of teaching gifted pupils. Obviously, being taught in a high-ability set will allow the teacher to teach higher-level content at greater speed, and thus counter some of the problems with regular whole class teaching of gifted pupils such as boredom. There is some research evidence that flexible ability grouping can indeed be beneficial to gifted and talented pupils in terms of achievement (Tieso, 2003). There is also some evidence of positive social and emotional effects of ability grouping on highly gifted students (Neihart, 2007). However, there is also evidence of a negative impact on self-concept, because of the frame of reference effect discussed in Chapter 13. This means that because pupils compare their achievement to their direct peers when developing academic self-concept, pupils in a class full of other gifted pupils have lower academic self-concepts than pupils in heterogeneous classes (Preckel et al., 2006). Some authors suggest gender grouping for gifted pupils, especially in those cases where they are gifted in areas that are traditionally seen as the preserve of the other gender, such as maths for girls and English for boys. This is seen as being beneficial to their self-esteem and achievement (Gavin and Reis, 2003). The evidence in support of this practice is limited at present, though there is some evidence that gifted girls' self-concept is lower when the majority of their class is made up of boys (Preckel et al., 2006).

A variation on ability grouping is *cluster grouping*. This means that the small number of gifted pupils in a year are put in the same class. The other pupils in the class remain of mixed ability. This will more easily allow the teacher to provide the gifted pupils with the learning opportunities they need (e.g. an enriched curriculum – see below) than when they are all in separate classes. Another advantage is the fact that the gifted pupils will have the chance to interact with other pupils of the same ability. For the other teachers, it obviates the need to have to deal with the one precocious child in their class (Winebrenner and Devlin, 1996). Disadvantages can be pressure from parents to have their children placed in a 'cluster' class, and the fact that dealing with a cluster of gifted pupils in a mixed-ability classroom can make classroom management more complex.

Cooperative learning

Another practice that has been posited as helpful to gifted pupils is *cooperative learning*. Cooperative group work was discussed in Chapter 4, but it is posited to have specific advantages for gifted pupils. The main advantage is said to be the fact that gifted pupils can work as mentors to their less able pupils, thus allowing them to take on responsible roles in the class, which will make them less likely to get bored by the lesson content as they are busy teaching others. Learning something with the expectation of teaching it to others is also said to lead to learning at a higher cognitive level (Johnson and Johnson, 1989).

This approach is not without problems, however. Gifted pupils can dominate the group to the extent that they start to take over rather than cooperate. Also, they can end up doing all the work themselves, not allowing lower-ability pupils to experience the full benefits of cooperative group work. Gifted pupils can also find it difficult to understand why other pupils don't grasp the material as quickly as they do, and can get impatient with them (Robinson and Noble, 1991; Rogers, 1991). They can at times feel exploited, in that they feel they are doing all the hard intellectual work while other pupils are benefiting from the results (Huss, 2006). Therefore, if this approach is used, it is best not to let the cooperative groups become too heterogeneous.

Huss (2006) identified a number of elements that need to be in place for cooperative learning to benefit gifted students:

- There needs to be mutual dependence in the group, in that group members must feel that they can only succeed through cooperation in which everyone contributes. The task can be structured to help achieve this, by, for example, giving each student part of the information needed to succeed or by giving each group member a specific goal (see Chapter 4).
- The activity must be structured in such a way that pupils have to ask each other for help and information, and cannot be completed without face-to-face interaction between pupils.
- The task needs to be structured so that there is both group and individual accountability for the outcome (see Chapter 4).
- Pupils in the group need to assess and discuss how well the group is doing in reaching its goals and what has been helpful and less helpful.

Curriculum adaptation

The problem of gifted pupils mastering the curriculum faster than average pupils and not needing to revisit learned parts of the curriculum as much can be countered through *curriculum compacting*. This means that curricular material that has already been learned is eliminated from the curriculum and replaced by more demanding new material for pupils identified as gifted or highly able. Reis et al. (1998) found that they were able to eliminate up to half of the curriculum in this way in their study of gifted primary-age pupils. Using a basic skills test, they found that this practice did not harm pupils' achievement, as achievement of pupils who had used the compacted curriculum did not differ from achievement of matched pupils who had used the full curriculum.

Another curriculum adjustment is the use of an *enriched curriculum*. This means that the curriculum is adapted to the needs of gifted pupils by adding activities that require more higher-level thinking, enquiry, exploration and discovery. An enriched curriculum should include more elaborate, complex and in-depth study of major ideas or themes and should encourage pupils to generate new knowledge or to reconceptualize existing knowledge. A curriculum for the gifted and talented should include a large knowledge base, be inter-disciplinary wherever possible and explore new developments in the field (Van Tassel-Baska, 1994). It should contain open-ended activities and complex questions with multiple solution paths (McAllister and Plourde, 2008). Some studies have shown that gifted pupils in enriched classes significantly outperform gifted pupils in non-enriched classes (Kulik, 1992). Increasingly, enrichment can be offered through online programmes, that can incorporate principles such as general research activities, strategic enrichment activities, creative enrichment activities, and self-reflection and evaluation (Sun-Wang and Bong-Hyun, 2009).

While enrichment and curriculum compacting can sometimes occur in the regular classroom, use is often made of some form of *withdrawal group*, whereby the gifted pupils will be withdrawn from their regular classroom for some part of the day to enable them to participate in enrichment activities there. This can be effective as gifted students are far more likely to enjoy and benefit from individual activities and research than their non-gifted peers (Rogers, 2007).

An enrichment activity that shows some promise is *mentoring*. The gifted pupil will be linked to an expert or a person experienced in a particular field from outside the school. This is particularly suited to pupils who have shown strong independent learning abilities and are highly motivated to work on a particular project or programme. The mentor, apart from being knowledgeable in his or her field, will have to be enthusiastic about the subject, have good communication skills, and be willing and able to work with young people. Mentors can be parents, former pupils or people from the community, such as members of local arts organizations. When these conditions are met, a mentoring arrangement can be a highly enriching experience for the pupil (Rogers, 2007).

Summer Schools and Academies

An alternative form of enrichment for gifted and talented pupils are summer schools and gifted and talented centres where they can go for additional activities and tuition outside of school time. Examples include the National Academy for Gifted and

Talented Youth in England, and the Centre for Talented Youth at Johns Hopkins University in the USA.

These centres aim to provide guidance for teachers as well as summer school programmes. All operate extensive talent search programmes, aimed at unearthing gifted and talented pupils from all social backgrounds. The extent to which they truly achieve that aim is contested, however (Lindsay et al., 2002).

They are often connected to universities, and employ university staff to help enthuse and challenge pupils. While one could question to what extent these lecturers are suited to teaching adolescents, results from the evaluation of the National Academy for Gifted and Talented Youth's summer school in England were very positive. Pupils seemed to have greatly enjoyed the experience, and felt they had learned a lot from the experience. They also felt far more challenged than at their schools. One problem in this respect is that this might lead them to be (even more) bored when they return to their regular classrooms. The fact that they could interact with other gifted children without the cultural stigma attached to giftedness in many schools was seen as another major advantage by the pupils (Lindsay et al., 2002).

Accelerated learning

Accelerated learning is another option for gifted pupils. This concept usually refers to the practice of allowing gifted pupils to move through the curriculum at a faster rate than their peers. This can take a number of forms, such as early entrance to school or to secondary school or university, grade skipping or grade advancement, placing the pupil with pupils in a higher grade for part of the day for one or more subjects, placing pupils in a class in which one or more grades are combined, and advanced placement in which primary pupils are put on a course at a local secondary school where they can study a more advanced topic for part of the week. Alternatively, secondary pupils can be placed on a course in a higher education institution (Gallagher, 1985; Southern and Jones, 1991).

This range of practices means that it is difficult to reach overall conclusions on the effectiveness of acceleration. However, a number of advantages have been proposed (Davis and Rimm, 1988; Southern and Jones, 1991). These include:

- increased learning efficiency
- increased learning effectiveness
- matching the curriculum to pupils' needs
- exposure of the pupil to a new (more mature) peer group
- increased options for academic exploration
- avoiding boredom
- avoiding alienation from less gifted peers.

Gifted Pupils with Learning Difficulties

A paradoxical finding is the existence of pupils who are gifted and have learning difficulties at the same time. These pupils exhibit great talents or strengths in one area, while simultaneously showing disabling weaknesses in others.

Baum (1990) identified three categories of gifted pupils with learning difficulties: (1) identified gifted pupils who have subtle learning disabilities; (2) unidentified pupils whose gifts and disabilities may be masked by average achievement; and (3) identified learning disabled pupils who are also gifted.

Identified gifted pupils with subtle learning difficulties are usually high achievers, or pupils with high IQ scores marking them out as gifted. However, as they grow older, their actual performance may increasingly fail to live up to their talents. Often this can be because their spelling or handwriting do not live up to their verbal ability. These pupils will often be told that they are not putting enough effort in, but sometimes teachers may be overlooking subtle learning difficulties which have not been diagnosed due to the pupil's overall giftedness. This however does not mean that underachievement in gifted pupils necessarily results from subtle learning difficulties. More often the cause will be motivational issues.

In *unidentified pupils,* disability and gifts mask each other. These pupils may often be struggling to achieve at their grade level, their giftedness compensating for their learning difficulties. An example of such a disability can be dyslexia. These pupils are often only identified when their giftedness comes out in a different context, often at a later age.

Identified learning disabled pupils who are also gifted are often failing at school and have been identified as learning disabled. However, sometimes their talent can be discovered within that group. More often, though, little attention is paid to the pupil's strengths as attention is focused on her/his problems.

However, outside of school, these pupils often demonstrate high-level interests, the ability to deal with complex matters or high levels of creativity. Because of this, they tend to be acutely aware of their problems at school, and can become increasingly pessimistic and negative about their school experience.

A number of guidelines to help these pupils in the classroom are the following:

- Focus attention on the development of the gift. As well as providing pupils with the remediation needed to overcome their learning difficulty, it is important to focus on their talent as well. This will help improve their self-esteem, and can in some cases lead to stronger gains than focusing on their disability (Whitmore and Maker, 1985).
- Encourage compensation strategies. While remediation will help the learner improve her/his skills in the area of weakness, it will usually not totally overcome them. Thus, pupils who have difficulty spelling can be encouraged to use computer

spellchecks and pupils who have problems writing can be encouraged to use different means of expressing their ideas.

- Pupils who are gifted and learning disabled should be helped to understand what their abilities and gifts, as well as their weaknesses, are. This can help them make the right choices with respect to education and career.
- Some authors suggest providing these pupils with challenge and differentiation in the areas of their strengths while using direct instruction of learning strategies to help develop their areas of weakness (Winebrenner, 2003).

Disadvantages have also been proposed, however. One of the most important of these is that although pupils may be academically more advanced than other pupils of their age, they may not necessarily be equally advanced socially. Therefore, putting them in a group with older peers may have negative social consequences, with the gifted child finding it difficult to fit in with the group. Older pupils may also be less likely to allow the younger, grade-advanced child to participate in their peer group, as associating with younger children does not convey prestige in the peer group. Giftedness can in some cases be the result of temporary faster development rather than permanent pupil characteristics. Acceleration can also be organizationally complicated for schools, especially with respect to timetabling.

A number of studies have found acceleration to have positive effects on the achievement of gifted pupils, both in the short term and in the long term (Benbow, 1991; Brody and Stanley, 1991; Rogers, 2007; Van Tassel-Baska, 1992). A longitudinal study conducted in Australia that looked at people with an IQ score over 160 over a 20-year period found that those who had been accelerated by two years or more at school showed greater professional success (in that they were in higher-status jobs) and higher levels of life satisfaction than their counterparts who had not been allowed acceleration or had only been allowed to accelerate by one year (Gross, 2006). There is not much evidence that acceleration has negative effects on pupils' social–emotional development either, although it is reasonable to expect that these effects will differ somewhat depending on which form of acceleration is used. Thus, advanced placement is unlikely to have detrimental effects, whereas grade skipping may, depending on the child. A recent review of research shows some mixed effects, with no overall impact of grade acceleration on gifted pupils evident. However, a minority of pupils did experience adaptation difficulties. This appeared to be linked to the way in which gifted pupils were defined and selected, with pupils who were selected purely on measures such as IQ without reference to emotional maturity most likely to suffer negative effects (Neihart, 2007). However, many gifted pupils have been found to be more socially mature as well and often seek out older friends (Gallagher, 1985; Janos and Robinson, 1985; Robinson and Noble, 1991; Southern and Jones, 1991).

A number of researchers (e.g. Benbow, 1991) have proposed guidelines to take into account before a decision to accelerate is taken:

- The child's intellectual abilities should be comprehensively examined, using a variety of measures including ability tests and academic achievement tests to make sure that the child is intellectually capable of being accelerated.
- The child's social–emotional readiness should be assessed by a psychologist. The child should have demonstrated an absence of adjustment problems and a high motivation to learn.
- Both the child and her/his parents should be involved in the decision to accelerate. Both must be willing to do this, and there must be no coercion.
- The receiving teacher must be enthusiastic about acceleration and be willing to help the child adjust.
- Grade advancement should occur at a natural transition point, such as the start of a new school year.
- Grade advancement should be arranged on a trial basis (e.g. one to two months). After the trial period, the child should be able to return to her/his original grade if s/he wants to do so.
- Teachers should try not to create excessive expectations of grade advancement, so that if it does not work out, the child does not consider her/himself to have failed.
- Sometimes grade advancement can lead to gaps in pupils' knowledge when they have missed certain topics. Arrangements need to be made to cover these. However, as most curricula revisit topics and gifted children learn fast, this is not usually a major problem.

Rogers (2007) suggests that it is best if acceleration is done on a subject-by-subject basis adapted to the gifted pupil's specific areas of strength.

Parents and Gifted Children

Parenting a gifted child can be quite a challenge as these children often have different interests from their peers, and will, from an early age, constantly ask questions. They can also challenge parental authority and it will be necessary to explain the reasons for decisions as 'because I said so' doesn't hold much water with gifted children.

Spending time reading to children from an early age and offering them an intellectually stimulating environment will help them both intellectually and emotionally. Children should be encouraged to develop their interests, even if they may seem unusual for a child of that age. Exposing them to the parents' own interests can also help them.

Gifted infants have been found to sleep less than other babies, and require extra stimulation when awake. This can obviously be very tiring for parents, who may need some other family member to help them at times (Silverman, 1992).

Parents can also help by placing their child in a school with good provision for gifted children.

A caveat here is that it is easy to overestimate the ability of one's own children, and therefore it is important to take into account all the elements of giftedness mentioned above before putting pressure on teachers to treat your child as gifted.

Summary

Gifted pupils are usually defined as pupils who score well above average on standardized achievement tests, who achieve much higher than their peers, and who are identified by teachers as gifted. Giftedness can be global or limited to a specific subject. Apart from being academically gifted, pupils can also be gifted in a number of non-academic fields, such as arts and sports.

Gifted pupils in regular classrooms are often insufficiently challenged by the regular curriculum. They can become bored and disenchanted with school, which can lead to underachievement.

For these reasons, a number of strategies have been proposed to cater for the needs of gifted pupils.

Ability grouping has been found to slightly improve the achievement of high-achieving pupils in some studies, but may be detrimental to low-achieving pupils. A variant of this is cluster grouping, in which gifted pupils are grouped in one class, which is mixed ability for the rest. This can have the advantage that it allows gifted pupils to interact with one another and that the teacher can more easily cater to their needs.

Cooperative learning allows gifted pupils to assume a monitoring role, which can motivate them and allows them to exploit their giftedness. Possible disadvantages are that gifted pupils become too dominating in the group, and that their presence can lead to free-rider effects occurring.

Other approaches have looked at adjustments to the curriculum. Curriculum compacting is the practice whereby parts of the curriculum are skipped for gifted pupils. Curriculum enrichment on the other hand means adding more challenging content to the curriculum.

Acceleration is the practice of allowing gifted pupils to move through the curriculum faster than their peers. This approach has been found to be quite effective, as long as certain conditions are met. These include ensuring that the pupil is not only intellectually but also socially–emotionally sufficiently advanced to be able to cope with acceleration, and that the pupil, her parents and the receiving teacher are all motivated to make acceleration work.

Reflective Questions

1. How would you try to alleviate the disadvantages of acceleration?
2. Do you know any children labelled gifted by their school? Do you think they were truly gifted, or bright? How do you know?
3. What strategy would you choose to help gifted pupils in your school?
4. What adjustments to the curriculum would you make to help gifted pupils in your school?
5. Why could gifted pupils pose a problem for teachers if nothing is done to cater to their needs?
6. Do you think provision for gifted pupils can disadvantage other pupils in school?

CHAPTER 16

TEACHING IN THE EARLY YEARS

Key Points

In this chapter, you will learn about:

- the importance of early childhood education
- differing views on how to teach in pre-school, and what research has to say about these methods
- how best to promote pupils' school-readiness in pre-school settings
- the importance of play and what children learn from it
- how to involve parents in their children's early years education.

Introduction

The early years of childhood are probably the most important developmental period in human life. Childhood experience shapes development in many ways. As we mentioned in Chapter 1, most learning theories claim that important cognitive developments take place in the early years, such as the transition from the sensori-motor stage to the pre-operational stage in Piagetian theory. Young children are learning through interaction with their parents and their environment long before they enter any kind of formal schooling. Brain research has shown that up to 85 per cent of all the neurological pathways that people acquire develop during the first six years of life (Rutter and Rutter, 1992).

At this age, large differences start to emerge between children caused by their social background. An excellent example of this is a longitudinal study by Hart and Risley (1995), which found that by the age of 48 months, children of parents from a professional background would have heard their parents use five times as many words as children of parents living on welfare benefits, and almost twice as many words as children of parents from a working-class background. Children of parents from a professional background would also have received 560,000 more instances of encouraging than of discouraging feedback, children of working-class parents 100,000 more instances of encouraging than discouraging feedback, and children from parents on welfare 125,000 more instances of discouraging feedback than of encouraging feedback by age four. This means that differences between children from different social backgrounds will already have accrued, both with respect to self-esteem and ability. If no intervention happens, these differences will increase over time, leading to large differences once pupils enter primary school.

This is clearly an argument to intervene before primary school, and to encourage children from lower social backgrounds to enter some form of pre-primary schooling. Most countries therefore encourage pre-school education, with enrolment in nursery education being almost universal in places like France, Belgium and the Scandinavian countries. This still leaves the question of how formal this schooling should be. This question will be discussed below.

Early Years Teaching: What Research Has to Say

The impact of pre-school education

That pre-school education does indeed have positive effects on children's subsequent achievement in primary school is demonstrated by research showing that children who take part in pre-school education perform better at primary school than pupils who have had no pre-school education. Some research even suggests that pupils benefit most if pre-school education starts before the age of three (the age that pre-school education starts in most countries) (Wylie, 1998).

Pre-school programmes have been found to have both short-term and long-term benefits, such as higher academic achievement, lower levels of grade retention, higher graduation rates and lower levels of delinquency later in life (Kagan and Hallmark, 2001; Stipek and Ogana, 2000). Research in New Zealand has shown that children who had experienced at least three years of pre-school education had higher scores on competency tests than their peers at age 10 (Wylie and Thompson, 2003). In research in the USA, Ramey et al. (2000) found that African Americans from at-risk families who had attended high-quality early care were twice as likely to report that they were still in education at age 21 than peers who had not attended high-quality early childcare programmes. They also reported having fewer children of their own.

As well as participation in early years programmes, the quality of the experience is important, with one review finding that children who had attended higher-quality early childhood centres showed better academic outcomes, more positive pupil–teacher relationships, better behaviour and better social skills than children who had attended lower-quality programmes. Key elements of quality were found to be effective centre leadership, creating a language-rich environment, sensitive teachers, child-focused communication with the child's home, higher levels of teacher/carer education, smaller child/adult ratios and lower staff turnover (Stipek and Ogana, 2000). A recent study likewise found both that attendance in early years programmes was related to gains in academic skills, and that children showed larger gains in academic outcomes when they experienced higher-quality instruction or closer teacher–child relationships (Howes et al., 2008). Petrogiannis (2002) reports similar findings in Greece.

Formal and informal approaches to early years education

Pupils starting nursery education have often been found to have difficulty with the transition from home to kindergarten. A survey of over 3500 teachers in the USA found that almost half of all children entering kindergarten had problems with this transition. Children had difficulties with following directions, academic skills, working independently, working in a group and communicating. These are clearly crucial skills that children will need during the course of their education from primary school onwards, and getting pupils ready for primary school therefore has to be one of the key goals of pre-school education (Wylie, 1998).

The main discussion among early years educators is whether to go for a mainly formal academic approach, starting early with the teaching of basic skills through instruction, or a more informal approach that stresses children's learning from interacting with their environment and other adults and children.

In the UK, there has been a clear move away from a play and group orientation to more direct teaching of basic skills in recent decades as a result of government strategies (Kwon, 2002; Siraj-Blatchford, 1999).

A focus on learning basic skills has been shown to be positively related to achievement on standardized tests, and it has been argued that this method is particularly important for children from less advantaged backgrounds in light of the fact that they in particular may be lacking these basic skills. There is good evidence that early intervention in teaching phonics to pupils with reading difficulties in the later early years can be effective, and that this needs to be delivered in a formal way in 30-minute blocks (Al Otaiba et al., 2007; Simmons et al., 2007), and in one longitudinal study academic skills in kindergarten were related to long-term outcomes, while socio-emotional skills weren't (Claessens et al., 2009). There is also some indication that children are less likely to be off task during structured teacher-directed activities than during other activities with less teacher direction (Rimm-Kaufman et al., 2005). In numeracy, there is evidence that children who possess early numeracy skills when they enter early years settings do better in primary numeracy than their peers, suggesting that pupils lacking these skills need some formal numeracy to be taught to them (Aubrey et al., 2006). Doubts have been expressed over whether this method is the best one over the long term, however, as a number of studies show that this type of instruction may lessen pupils' disposition to learn and cause them too much stress (Katz, 1999; Schweinhart and Weikart, 1997). In order to promote school-readiness, it may well be better to focus on social skills, creating a disposition to learn and developing 'school-readiness' skills. A number of studies have shown that over the long term young children taught in this more child-centred way (known as a developmentally appropriate practice) performed better (Miller and Bizzell, 1983; Schweinhart and Weikart, 1997). A longitudinal study comparing the active learning model devised in the High/Scope programme with an academic approach found better results for the High/Scope approach, and these more positive outcomes persisted up to age 23. Pupils in this type of classroom have also been found to score higher on measures of creative thinking (Hirsch-Pasek et al., 1990) and to show better language development (Marcon, 1992). Overall then, the evidence suggests that a combination of formal academic teaching and more general school readiness preparation is the best approach for effective early years teaching.

In a number of non Anglo-Saxon countries, the 'academic' approach to nursery education is far less prevalent. Thus, in Flanders, most nursery education centres around play, and literacy and numeracy teaching are not started until primary school. In Hungary, another educationally high-ranking country, formal numeracy and literacy teaching is likewise only started in primary school, with nursery teaching concentrating on school readiness skills such as listening and paying attention. In both Hungary and Flanders, primary education only starts at age six. A similar approach is taken in Scandinavia, where children are encouraged to learn by play and discovery.

Active learning in the early years

Research has shown that young children learn best when they are actively interacting with others and their environment rather than being passive recipients of information (Wood and Bennet, 1999). This means that early years teaching should be highly interactive, and pupils should be allowed to explore their environment. They should have the chance to record their learning in a variety of ways – verbally, written, through painting, drawing and building things (Katz, 1999).

Early years education needs to balance pupil discovery of their environment with structured activity designed to get the most from these experiences educationally. Teachers should emphasize the connections between the classroom and pupils' everyday experiences. As young children learn best through hands-on activities, these should be plentiful in the nursery classroom. A wide variety of easily accessible resources need to be provided. Children enjoy imitating adults, therefore activities such as peeling potatoes, washing the pots or cooking can be used to great effect.

Siraj-Blatchford (1999) identifies three main elements necessary for effective early years teaching:

1. Creating the learning environment. This includes organizing materials and resources, providing relevant, interesting and novel experiences and providing opportunities for active exploration and questioning, including a lot of pupil–pupil and pupil–adult talk to allow linguistic competency to develop.
2. Direct instruction, including demonstration, description, answering questions, directing the child's attention and constructive criticism and reinforcement.
3. Scaffolding, including directing children's attention to new aspects of a situation, helping the children to sequence activities and managing complex tasks by breaking them down into smaller, more manageable parts.

Promoting school readiness

Research thus seems to indicate that one of the main purposes of pre-school education is to promote school-readiness. School-readiness skills have been found to be related to growth in learning throughout primary school, and appear to be important to later pupil achievement, as demonstrated in a longitudinal study conducted in the USA (McClelland et al., 2006). Key school-readiness skills include the following:

- *Social skills*, such as the ability to respect others, to work cooperatively, to express emotions and feelings in an appropriate way, to listen to others, to follow rules and procedures, to sit attentively and to work independently
- *Communication skills*, such as asking for assistance in an appropriate way, verbalizing thoughts and feelings, answering open and closed questions, participating in class discussion and relating ideas and experiences
- *Task-related behaviours* such as not disrupting other pupils during the lesson, monitoring one's own behaviour, finding the materials necessary to complete

a task, following teacher directions, generalizing skills across situations, being on task during whole-class work, making choices, beginning and completing work at an appropriate time without teacher direction and trying different problem-solving strategies. Teaching pupils these types of skills in kindergarten was found to be quite strongly related to behaviours and achievement in primary school in one recent study in Germany (von Suchodoletz, 2009).

How can school readiness be developed? A wide number of recommendations exist, but these are some of the most common ones:

1. *Play.* One of the main aspects of early years education is play. Play is important, and can help develop children's receptive and expressive language, as well as their skills at joint planning, negotiation, problem solving and goal seeking (Bergen, 2001). Teachers should provide pupils with an environment in which they can play with each other using a variety of materials designed to facilitate their learning and development. Teachers can in some cases usefully join in children's play in order to extend it. The teacher needs to make sure that all children are joining in the activities, and needs to introduce the children to new ideas and situations. This can sometimes be done in the course of play, by observing children's problems and helping them to overcome them. For example, when building using blocks, children will initially pile them on top of each other, and will find that their structure quickly falls down. The teacher can point to how the walls of the classroom are built to help them pile up the blocks better (Edelman Borden, 1997).
2. *Drama and short plays* are another way of allowing children to take part in an activity they enjoy which has strong educational benefits, especially in developing their talk and language skills. The fact that drama activities allow children to engage in talk that is different from what they do day-to-day will also help develop their thinking more widely (Hendy and Toon, 2001).
3. *Small group or class discussion* is another method that has been proposed for early years education. One way to do this is for teachers to introduce an idea or topic, and then allow the children to give all the possible answers, ideas and relevant words they can come up with. All children should be encouraged to participate and should be made to listen to others. This will help develop listening skills and the skills to generate ideas, to verbalize ideas and to respect each other's opinions. The main ideas can then be written down on the board. These discussions can be more or less guided by the teacher, depending on the topic and goals of the discussion.
4. *Categorizing objects*, like toys or other materials in the classroom according to criteria such as colour, shape or size, will help the children to develop their classification skills and mathematical ability. The teacher needs to make sure that the children explain the criteria they have used to classify the objects and that all children understand what criteria can be used.
5. *Paired or group work*, in which children work together on a project or assignment, has been successfully employed in nursery schools as well, and

has been found to allow even young, at-risk children to take initiative (Helm and Katz, 2001). To ensure effectiveness, it is necessary to make all children contribute to the completion of the task. The teacher needs to closely monitor interaction between the children, modelling cooperative behaviour and correcting behaviour where necessary. This should help develop the children's cooperative learning skills, help them to verbalize what they are doing and develop their problem-solving skills. Working in large groups is not always suitable with very young children.

6. At the beginning of the lesson, the teacher can start with a *discussion* of a particular topic (known as 'circle time'). This can be a project they are going to work on or are working on, but may also be a game to help the children learn each other's names at the beginning of the year, a discussion of objects brought into the class by the children, singing, or discussing children's recent out-of-school experiences. This will help the children to learn to organize their thinking, and verbalize experiences in a structured way (i.e. telling a story with a beginning, middle and end).

Some research has shown that if a child has not achieved minimal social competence by age six, s/he will find it hard to develop that competence later in life (Katz, 1997). Children can easily slip into negative recursive relationships, in that their own behaviour patterns will cause reactions in others that will strengthen those patterns. It is therefore important that teachers try to counteract these forces by having high expectations of all pupils and by trying to draw shy and socially dysfunctional children out and develop their competences, for example through role-play and group activities.

Assessment in Early Years Education

As in primary and secondary education, activities need to be matched to the child's capabilities. This means that teachers need to be aware of what these capabilities are for each individual child and for their class as a whole. Standardized testing can be unsuitable for young children, whose performance on standardized tests can change from day to day, leading to highly unreliable results. Therefore, alternative methods have been proposed to assess the progress of young children. One of these methods is structured observation of children's behaviour. For example, in the High/Scope programme, teachers use a child observation record on which they take daily notes of children's developmentally significant behaviours. Another possibility is the use of portfolios. These contain a record of a child's work at different times of the year, including the child's drawings, teachers' notes and photographs of the child's work. This allows the teacher to look at progress over time, and can also help the children to develop forms of self-reflection, by allowing them to look at their own progress with the help of the teacher, who can ask questions such as 'What would you do differently if you did it now?' In order for this effect to be strongest, portfolios must be easily accessible to the children (Cohen, 1999).

What Children Learn From Play

As has been mentioned above, a lot of countries use a play-based approach to pre-school education. That this does not mean that no learning takes place is illustrated by the following examples, taken from Edelman Borden (1997).

As most play activities involve verbal interaction with other pupils, they can aid the development of social skills, verbal skills and cooperation, although teacher input will be necessary to develop these skills.

Outdoor play, such as running, digging and climbing, refines a child's gross-motor skills, including cross-lateral movements (using right arm with left leg, for example) that are important to later writing and reading. It also gives children the chance to manipulate their environment.

Indoor play activities, which are often more structured as the environment has usually been designed by the teacher for teaching purposes, likewise offer children a wide range of learning opportunities.

Block building develops children's small motor skills, and can help them learn about mathematical concepts like depth, width, height, volume, area and measurement, as well as scientific concepts like gravity, stability and weight. Shape recognition, differentiation of shapes and size are also involved in block building.

Dramatic play, such as dressing up, cooking or having a little shop helps pupils make sense of the adult world and helps develop children's vocabulary. Dramatic play helps pupils to concentrate, to be attentive and to use self-control. For example, when setting up a shop, the child must set up the counter, invite friends to shop, use the 'cash register' and bag the groceries, all of which develops children's concept of sequential acts. Imaginative play can contribute to children learning how to express their emotions and think abstractly. Imaginative play has an important role in developing children's creativity.

Solving *puzzles* requires abstract thinking to enable pupils to know where to fit the pieces and fine motor skills to allow them to actually do this.

Playing with *manipulative toys* such as Lego likewise develops children's fine motor skills and sometimes their abstract thinking as well. This type of play can encourage children's creativity, being incorporated into imaginative play in novel ways.

In contrast to adults, young children will also consider *cleaning up* after play to be a fun activity. Doing this is a useful educational activity, requiring children to sort, classify, match and organize when they put building blocks, toys and other materials in place.

A *sand or water basin* with containers that pupils can fill up and empty will allow pupils to develop pre-mathematical skills such as fractions, as well as developing fine motor skills.

Play can also be important in developing children's social skills, and one study found that allowing more child-initiated play in early years settings reduced aggression (Broadhead, 2009).

Involving Parents

One factor that is common to most successful early years intervention programmes, especially in areas of social disadvantage, is involving parents. As we saw earlier, the home environment has a very strong influence on children's development, and research has shown that parents who actively promote learning in the home, have direct and regular contact with school, and experience fewer barriers to involvement have children who demonstrate positive engagement with their peers, adults and learning (McWayne et al., 2004). This means that while work in schools and childcare centres is important, getting parents involved with the programme in ways that can help improve their child's development and education can be crucial (Hujala, 2002; Talay-Ongan, 2001).

Programmes like Head Start in the USA and Sure Start in the UK therefore aim to take a holistic approach, which includes work with families and health care professionals as well as educators. Achieving this is not always easy, which is why most programmes start off by providing parents with information about the programme, often in settings where young parents are likely to go anyway, like health care centres or doctors' surgeries. Any information provided needs to be free of jargon. A flexible approach, where parents are allowed to be involved to the extent that suits them rather than being forced into a particular pattern, appears to be the most effective way of reaching them.

Helping parents to help their children, through encouraging activities like getting parents to read to their children, mirroring experience through language whereby parents verbally reflect back to children what they are doing, asking for their children's opinions and showing interest in what children are doing, has been shown to be effective in fostering children's cognitive and social development (Talay-Ongan, 2001)

A further advantage of involving parents is that early involvement with education providers may lead to parents becoming accustomed to being involved with their children's education, an attitude that may lead to higher levels of involvement with school throughout their child's school years.

High/Scope and Reggio Emilia – Two Influential Early Years Programmes

The High/Scope project

The High/Scope project, developed in the USA, is based on principles of active learning emphasizing direct experience with real objects. Through active learning, children are supposed to engage in 58 key experiences set out by the High/Scope programme. These are grouped into 10 categories: creative representation, language and literacy, initiative and social relations, movement, music, classification, seriation, number, space and time. The school day is organized around the 'plan–do–review sequence'. The children plan what to do during that session, do the activity and then reflect on the results. Adults are supposed to interact with the children, taking part in the activities and generally helping to facilitate pupils' learning and interactions. The physical environment is organized around a number of 'interest areas', each focusing on a specific kind of play such as block play or art activities. Materials are made suitably accessible so children can work with them independently.

In High/Scope, academic skills aren't directly taught. Rather, experiences and an environment are provided that help children develop broad abilities which can form the basis of academic learning in primary school. This is done by providing them with relevant experiences (based on the 58 key experiences identified) through, for example, providing materials that allow children to use their beginning skills in counting (High/Scope, 2000).

Reggio Emilia

Another influential programme has been that adopted by the district of Reggio Emilia in Italy.

Nursery schools in this district follow a thematic, project-based approach developing an emergent curriculum that follows from the interaction between teachers and children. Teachers record children's discussion on a topic and their reactions to questions put to them by the teacher, and develop the curriculum based on their transcript of the tapes. This means that each year the curriculum is adapted to children's interests. Usually, children work in groups on a particular project over a number of days or weeks, not necessarily working on it every day, but returning to the project at regular intervals (Abbott and Nutbrown, 2001; Siraj-Blatchford, 1999).

An important aspect of the programme is documentation, which is seen as an important aid to children's learning. Children are encouraged to express the feelings and experiences they have during their work through drawings, in written form or through 3-D representations. These are then displayed, providing parents with a chance to see their children's work and what is being done in school, and allowing children to revisit past experiences and see themselves and their peers from a different point of view. Seeing their work displayed in this way also validates it for the children and can thus enhance their self-esteem. Looking at this documentation can also help teachers to refine their own work (Edwards et al., 1993).

The programme is well resourced, with schools employing specialist staff such as an 'atelierista' (resident artist) and a 'pedagogista' (child development specialist). Teachers usually work in teams of two.

Summary

Pre-school education is of crucial importance to the development of children, particularly those from disadvantaged backgrounds. Therefore, pre-school education is encouraged in most countries, with participation rates near to 100 per cent in a number of them.

A discussion point in early years education is whether it should be mainly academic and geared to teaching basic skills or use more informal, often play-based methods in order to foster school-readiness skills, leaving the actual acquisition of numeracy and literacy until later. The academic option does tend to show some positive results on short-term standardized tests. However, longitudinal studies show more positive effects for students taught in less academic ways in nursery school, such as those enrolled in settings taking part in the High/Scope project.

Ways to encourage the acquisition of school-readiness skills include the use of more or less structured play, small group or class discussion, paired or group work and circle time.

Assessment is another issue in early years, in that standardized testing is not suitable for pupils of this age group. Therefore, alternative forms of assessment need to be used, such as observation of pupils' behaviour in the classroom or portfolios of pupils' work.

Two programmes which have been influential in recent years are the High/Scope project in the USA and the Reggio Emilia project in Italy. The High/Scope project is based on principles of active learning, emphasizing direct experience with real objects. The Reggio Emilia project follows a thematic, project-based approach, developing an emergent curriculum that follows from the interaction between teachers and pupils. An important element of the project is documenting pupils' work.

Reflective Questions

1. At what age do you think children should receive formal education, and why?
2. How could you assess pupils' learning in pre-school?
3. Do you think there should be a stronger emphasis on play in early years education? Why/why not?
4. Do you think the approach taken in Reggio Emilia would work in your country?
5. To what extent do you think an academic approach to pre-school education is appropriate and necessary?
6. What school-readiness skills should children acquire in pre-school?
7. Can you think of some teaching strategies that can help children to acquire these school-readiness skills?

CHAPTER 17

PERSONALIZED LEARNING

Key Points

In this chapter, you will learn about:

- the principle of personalized learning
- the advantages and disadvantages of different grouping methods
- how to limit the negative effects of setting if it is used
- various ways of individualizing instruction
- the practice of personalized learning in schools and classrooms.

Introduction

One of the most controversial aspects of teaching is dealing with the many differences between pupils in the classroom. Traditionally, these differences have mainly been conceptualized in terms of differences in ability, though more recently they have been conceptualized in terms of personalized learning or personalization. The principle of personalization is to offer education that is tailored to the learner, within systems responsive to learner needs, rather than expecting the learner to adapt to existing systems within the school (West and Muijs, 2009).

In this chapter, we will look first at the main ways in which educators have tried to deal with differences in 'ability', and then explore how personalization could affect classroom practice.

Selection, Streaming and Setting

Selection

A method that has traditionally been used to deal with the fact that pupils may differ in ability is selection. In some countries, the whole education system is selective. This means that at some point in the pupil's school career s/he will be tested on a national test which will determine her/his entry into different types of schools. The '11-plus' exam, used in Northern Ireland and in the past in the whole of the United Kingdom, is an example of this. A second method is for individual schools to select their pupils by interview or testing.

There is not much reliable research comparing systems using selection to those that don't, but what research there is doesn't seem to suggest that selection leads to higher achievement once pupils' prior achievement has been taken into account. One recent study that compared achievement in countries that used early selection with those that didn't found that early selection was associated with both greater inequality and lower achievement (Woessmann and Hanushek, 2005). There are a number of reasons to suspect that selection is not the best approach to take for dealing with pupil differences. The first issue is that selection may lead to a waste of talent. In a selective system, the basic underlying principle is one of allowing only a minority of the school population to enter the 'academic' schools which will lead to higher education. This does not accord with the needs of societies in the information age that will require an ever larger proportion of people to acquire higher-order skills and go through higher education.

Furthermore, there is a clear equity issue here in that pupils from lower socio-economic status backgrounds, who tend to do worse on national tests, are likely to be excluded from the chance to participate in academic education and therefore in higher education. In essence, this argues against the thesis that schools can make a difference and can improve the skills of pupils from all social backgrounds. It has in fact been found that pupils at the bottom end of the achievement spectrum in selective schools will tend to do worse than if they studied at non-selective schools. Selection is also likely to be inefficient, as no selection mechanism will be 100 per cent accurate (some estimates suggest that any selection mechanism will inaccurately include 10 per cent and inaccurately exclude another 10 per cent). According to Maaz et al. (2008), there are two key mechanisms whereby the allocation of students to different types of schools or curricula at the beginning of secondary level increases the strength of the link between socio-economic background and student achievement. Firstly, there is a relationship between likelihood of being in a selective school and social background. The more educationally advantaged the parents, the higher a student's chance of being enrolled in a high-track school. Second, ability grouping at the secondary level produces relatively homogeneous developmental environments, with higher learning rates in high tracks.

Finally, the idea that one could select pupils who are to receive an academic education is based on the view that pupils' ability is both unidimensional and fixed. Both positions have been contradicted by research. Firstly, it has become increasingly clear that intelligence is a multidimensional concept. Furthermore, the idea that intelligence in any area is fixed and unchanging has been disproved by research (Gould, 1996). One of the factors that affects intelligence as measured through IQ tests is education. Therefore, it would seem that selection is not the best way to deal with pupil differences.

Streaming

A second way of dealing with pupil differences is streaming. This is a procedure whereby pupils are segregated into different classes according to ability within their school. This could have the advantage of allowing teachers to teach pupils of similar ability, which makes it easier to pitch lessons at the right level. By putting pupils in appropriate streams, all pupils could experience success.

However, there are a number of problems associated with streaming. Underlying streaming is still the assumption that intelligence is unidimensional enough to be able to predict pupils' achievement in all subjects based on some prior measure. This is not supported by research, which points to differences in pupil performance over different subjects. While correlations between performance in different subjects are significant, they are not high enough to suggest that one is measuring the same underlying concept (Muijs, 1998b). Like selection, streaming assumes that ability is basically fixed and unchanging, which, especially among rapidly developing teenagers, is a questionable assumption. Furthermore, streaming and selection both assume that ability is *the* determining factor in achievement. However, while this view is strongly engrained in our culture, this is not necessarily the case in non-Western societies. Thus, in other cultures, such as a number of South East Asian countries, effort is stressed more strongly, and the belief that anyone who puts in the effort can succeed is often cited as a reason for the educational success of these countries (Reynolds and Farrell, 1996). Other aspects, such as motivation and self-esteem, have also been found to affect achievement quite strongly, and a large number of studies show that being streamed into the lower streams has a negative effect on pupils' self-esteem (Hansell and Karweit, 1983; Muijs, 1997). This can clearly lead to self-fulfilling prophecies, as low self-esteem leads to low achievement and disaffection from school.

Research has also shown that pupils in lower streams are often taught an 'impoverished' curriculum, which does not engage pupils' thinking or understanding and is limited to simple drill and practice exercises (e.g. Hansell and Karweit, 1983). While in theory designed to teach pupils at their level, this practice can further widen the gap between the high and low streams and fails to give all pupils access to a rich, full curriculum, thus creating equity issues. This is another unfortunate consequence of streaming as many educators have found that 'low ability' pupils can pleasantly surprise them when allowed to engage with a high-level curriculum (Muijs et al., 2004). Furthermore, critical thinking skills are crucial to all in modern society, not just to a 'high ability elite'.

As with selection, there is a tendency for pupils from lower socio-economic status backgrounds and from ethnic minorities to be put in the lower streams whether or not they are able, thus presenting clear equity problems (Sorenson, 1985; Ireson et al., 2002; Secada, 1992).

Overall, then, streaming does not seem to be a particularly effective way of dealing with pupil differences.

Setting

A third way of dealing with pupil differences is through setting. In contrast to streaming, in setting pupils are assigned to 'same ability' groups on a subject by subject basis. Setting solves a number of the problems associated with streaming, in that in setting pupils it is acknowledged that pupils can be at different levels in different subjects. Thus, depending on her/his results, a pupil can be in the top group for maths and in one of the lower groups for English.

However, a number of problems do remain. The possibility of harming a pupil's self-concept in a certain subject still exists when that pupil is put into a lower set, although if that pupil is in a higher set for other subjects this should not necessarily harm her/his overall attitude to school. Also, as with streaming, it is extremely difficult for teachers to have high expectations of classes which they know to have been formed explicitly from pupils who are not particularly good at the subject. This is also a problem for the pupils themselves. In one qualitative study, for example, Latino pupils placed in both high- and low-ability groups thought that pupil performance in high-ability classrooms needed to meet more demanding standards and self-accountability than in low-ability classrooms (Wright-Castro et al., 2003). These expectancy effects among both teachers and pupils can clearly lead to a vicious circle among pupils in the low set. Furthermore, setting does not allow lower-ability pupils to benefit by learning from higher-ability pupils. All this does not necessarily mean that pupils themselves dislike setting. High-ability pupils in particular prefer working in homogeneous sets, and at least one study shows that this is the case for the majority of pupils (Davidson, 2001).

Streaming in Secondary Schools

One of the first major studies of the effects of streaming in schools occurred in England in the 1960s. This ethnographic study looked at the effect of both selection between schools – one school studied being one for pupils who had passed an IQ test at 11 years of age, the other catering for pupils who had failed this test – and at the effects of streaming within the schools. Both had similar effects, called 'differentiation and polarisation' by the two authors, Lacey (1970) and Hargreaves (1967).

Lacey's (1970) analysis of peer relations in a boys' grammar school (secondary school to which the pupils who performed best at '11+ exams' usually went) revealed the development of an anti-school subculture in the lower streams by the end of the second year, friendship choices being made almost exclusively within either the highest two or the lowest two streams, antagonism choices being made almost exclusively from the higher to the lower streams and vice versa. Lower-stream pupils were more strongly oriented to the out-of-school adolescent subculture and were expected to leave school earlier than higher-stream pupils. This process was even more strongly evident in the third year. Pupils who failed to ally themselves to either group became isolates. Extreme anti-school behaviour was not evident in this (elite) school, as pupils who went too far could be removed from school. This was not the case in the secondary modern school (for pupils with poorer results in the 11+ exam) studied by Hargreaves (1967), where the lower streams were much more extreme in their anti-school attitudes, resulting in the formation of a delinquent group among the anti-school group. The four streams in that school in general were differentiated in a similar way to those in the grammar school, the highest stream boys valuing academic norms and neat dressing, and being opposed to fighting, 'messing' in class and copying. They also tended to attend organized leisure time activities and more often visited the public library. Pupils from the lower streams considered school to be a waste of time and valued aggression and messing around in class. They were more likely to attend unorganized clubs, such as billiard halls and the 'beat' club. The two streams differed strongly in absenteeism, late arrivals and general school commitment. As in the grammar school studied by Lacey (1970), there was clear antagonism between the groups as evidenced by the friendship choices made.

On the positive side, setting can make teaching easier, as the attenuation of the range of ability in the lesson will make it less difficult for the teacher to pitch the lesson at the right level for pupils. In a set class, lower-ability pupils will not be left behind not understanding the lesson and becoming demoralized. Higher-ability pupils are on the other hand less likely to become bored in a group of similar ability, as the lesson is more likely to be sufficiently challenging for them. This is particularly relevant when whole-class teaching is employed in schools with a particularly heterogeneous intake with regards to pupil performance which is often the case in the most deprived areas.

However, setting is by no means an exact science. In one study, for example, MacIntyre and Ireson (2002) found that standardized test scores of children in high-, middle- and low-ability groups overlapped with one another to quite a considerable extent.

Looking at the effects of setting on pupil achievement, the results are somewhat indecisive and do not seem to be uniform across subjects. Most research in mathematics, for example, shows small positive effects (Askew and William, 1995; Ireson et al., 2002; Leonard, 2001). However, when the data are studied more closely, this seems to result from the fact that high-ability pupils perform better in sets than in mixed-ability classrooms, while low-ability pupils do worse in sets than in mixed-ability classrooms. There is no strong effect for average pupils. For English, the overall effect is usually slightly negative, but with similar results for high- and low-ability pupils. Some recent research appears to suggest that the relationship between setting and achievement among high-ability pupils is a little bit more complex than it first appears, however, in that whether or not high-ability pupils do better in homogeneous than in heterogeneous groups seems to depend on patterns of interaction in those heterogeneous groups. It would appear that if the heterogeneous group is functioning well, with no ill behaviour, high-ability pupils performed as well in these as in homogeneous groups. Where the heterogeneous groups functioned less well, high-ability pupils performed less well. In this study, all heterogeneous high-ability groups were characterized by on-task behaviour and prosocial interaction (Webb et al., 2001). A key problem with setting, as with streaming and selection, is the equity issue. One study in England, for example, found that pupils from low socio-economic status (SES) backgrounds were more likely to end up in lower sets regardless of their achievement, or, in other words, a pupil from a lower SES background is more likely to end up in a lower set than a pupil of equal ability from a high SES background (Muijs and Dunne, 2008)

All this means that whether or not to set is a difficult decision, for which there are arguments both for and against. These will need to be weighed against each other in each individual case.

If setting is to be used, there are a number of things that can be done to alleviate the most negative effects resulting from this practice. Firstly, to be effective, setting needs to be flexible with pupils being able to change from one group to

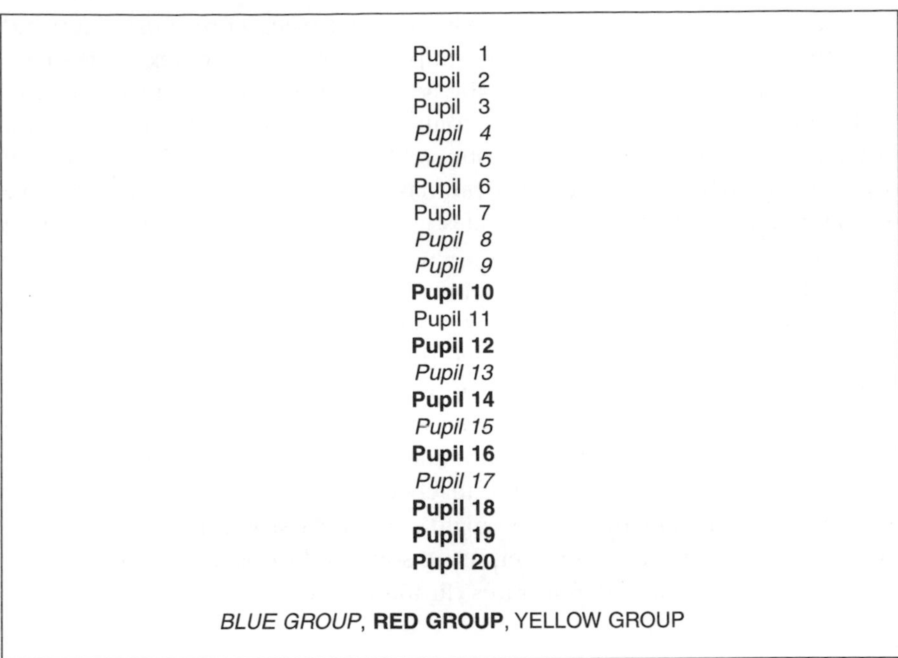

FIGURE 17.1 Setting using the 'zip method'

another when their achievement seems to call for this. This can help teachers keep in mind that ability is not fixed, and can also stop setting becoming too much of a self-fulfilling prophecy.

Another way of helping to avoid teacher expectancy effects, and also of preserving some of the advantages of having pupils of different ability levels helping one another in class while simultaneously decreasing the ability range in a subject, is using the 'zip method'. This method works as follows: pupils in a subject are listed by achievement in that subject (for example, on a standardized test) from high to low, and groups are then formed in the following way (see Figure 17.1).

While the range of ability in each of these three groups is reduced, in every case there is at least one pupil who has scored higher than the lowest scoring pupil in the other groups. This means that teachers can less easily assume that these are the 'worst' pupils.

Individual Learning

Rather than changing grouping arrangements in the school, teachers can also try to take individual differences into account as much as possible in their classroom teaching.

One way to do this is to allow all pupils to work through previously prepared schemes or worksheets at their own tempo, going on to the next worksheet/page/exercise when they are ready. The teacher's role is then primarily one of facilitating this individual learning by going round the class helping pupils with problems and answering their questions. This approach has been tried, in particular in Anglo-Saxon countries, but has not been found to be an effective teaching strategy. A large number of studies, discussed in Chapter 2, have found that when too much time is spent letting pupils work on their own, their achievement is lower (e.g. Brophy and Good, 1986; Mortimore et al., 1988; Rosenshine, 1979b). This is largely the result of the fact that this style of instruction doesn't allow many teacher–pupil contacts, or indeed pupil–pupil contacts (research has shown that the number of pupil–teacher contacts is lower in this type of classroom than in classrooms in which whole-class teaching predominates), and thus does not allow pupils to express and articulate their ideas. Scaffolding by either the teacher or other pupils is also less likely to occur. Using this method as the main part of classroom teaching is therefore not usually effective. However, using some individualized work in which pupils can progress at different rates during the seatwork part of the lesson may be useful.

Personalized Learning

In September 2003, the DfES (2003) set out what it saw as the key components of personalized learning. These are:

- **Assessment for learning** – the use of evidence from pupil assessment and dialogue between pupils and teachers to identify every pupil's learning needs.
- **Teaching and learning strategies** – that develop the competence and confidence of every learner by actively engaging them in the learning process and in activities that stretch them.
- **Curriculum entitlement and choice** – that delivers breadth of study, personal relevance and flexible learning pathways through the system.
- **A student-centred approach to school organization** – with school leaders and teachers thinking creatively about how to support high-quality teaching and learning.
- **Strong partnerships that extend beyond the school** – to reinforce and drive forward progress in the classroom, to remove barriers to learning and to support pupil well-being.

The principle of personalization is, then, to offer education that is tailored to the learner, within systems responsive to learner needs, rather than expecting the learner to adapt to existing systems within the school.

A range of developments are currently taking place in schools around these four main aspects of personalization.

Schools are experimenting with curricula that are better adapted to the needs of their individual learners. Developing a suitably tailored offering for pupils is key to this process (West and Muijs, 2009).

More pupil choice is evident in initiatives aimed at increasing the range of subjects available to older pupils. In particular, greater access to vocational options has been a clear trend in education over the past few years, and in England several new initiatives, such as the promotion of work-based diplomas, are meant to increase the number of options for pupils. Increased collaboration between schools has aided this process, by allowing pupils to follow different curriculum options in different schools. Not only is there a wider range of choice as pupils can study parts of their curriculum in nearby schools, but the different facilities in different schools (for example, an industrial kitchen in one school, and an electronics workshop in another) can be used more efficiently (West et al., 2006).

Assessment for learning is another important element of personalization, which we will discuss in more detail in Chapter 20.

Acknowledging and valuing the different strengths that pupils bring to the classroom can be interpreted in a number of ways. On the one hand, the move towards greater vocational provision can be seen as an acknowledgement that the academic curriculum is not the most appropriate pathway for all students. On the other hand, an increasing number of schools have been influenced by constructs such as multiple intelligence, and have been mapping 'learning styles' in an attempt to provide more suitable learning environments for students with different characteristics and abilities. Typically, instruments 'measuring' learning styles or intelligence are used to determine the characteristics of the individual pupil, with teaching then, in principle, adapted to coincide with the learning preferences of the pupils. This, however, is not an approach supported by evidence, in that learning styles themselves have little or no support, and methods of adapting instruction to them even less so (Coffield et al., 2004; West and Muijs, 2009).

One good way of individualizing teaching is the use of 'Individual Learning Plans'. In this strategy, used in several countries for pupils with special needs or learning difficulties, teachers will develop specific individual learning plans for pupils, which set out the goals that pupils should be able to acquire and the means by which teachers can help pupils acquire these goals. A more sophisticated version of this is known as *personalized instruction.* Personalized instruction has the aim of tailoring teaching provision to the individual needs of each pupil. According to Jenkins and Keefe (2002), personalized instruction has the following elements:

1. A *dual teacher role* of coach and adviser – this involves teachers acting as tutors of individual pupils. Pupils and teachers meet at least weekly, and weekly and longer-term individual goals are set and monitored. An individual timetable may be recommended and set up in conjunction with subject tutors.
2. Relevant pupil learning characteristics – these are *diagnosed,* and an individual learning plan of the type mentioned above is constructed.
3. A *collegial* school culture – this is encouraged, in which both pupils and teachers work in teams. Pupils regularly work together to solve problems, while teachers engage in common planning.
4. An *interactive* learning environment – one secondary school cited by Jenkins and Keefe (2002) used a series of learning guides for each course, written by teachers and addressing the major course objectives through a variety of activities between which pupils could choose. Open learning centres were a feature of this school, and pupils are expected to engage in independent reading and learning around the text.
5. Teaching which is *flexibly scheduled and paced* – group teaching is scheduled when needed, and individual pupils' weekly roster is decided in the meetings between advisors and pupils.
6. *Authentic assessment* methods – these are regularly used (see Chapter 23), and testing takes place when pupils are ready for it.

This is clearly a radical overhaul of the traditional school format, and Jenkins and Keefe (2002) report that pupils claim they work harder and learn more. In a somewhat artificial, quasi-experimental study, pupils undertaking a personalized maths programme did better on a maths post-test than pupils who had not done this (Ku and Sullivan, 2001). However, the evidence for the effectiveness of this approach, though interesting, is at present very limited, and a number of caveats need to be taken into account. Firstly, this process takes a lot of time and effort, and probably if applied to all pupils would require more staff than is usual in schools at present. Secondly, focusing too much on individual plans may disadvantage some pupils who are not able to access a full and rich curriculum, and may also exacerbate possible negative expectation effects. Finally, the question of how well this approach would work with less intrinsically motivated pupils is an open question at present.

Splitting the class into a number of small groups engaged in different tasks can also help the teacher to deal with pupil differences. This solves some of the problems involved with individualized instruction as it allows pupils to interact with each other and allows the teacher to teach different groups in turn, thus allowing more pupil–teacher and pupil–pupil contacts. However, arrangements in which different groups are engaged in different activities are complex from a classroom management point of view, and usually lead to more time being spent on routine classroom management activities at the expense of academic learning time. Teachers still have less contact with each individual pupil than in whole-class teaching. It is therefore not surprising that Mortimore et al. (1988) found that classrooms in which more time was spent teaching different small groups had lower gains in achievement. Differentiated group work can be useful during seatwork sessions, however.

Summary

In this chapter, we have learnt about some ways in which we can deal with individual differences between pupils.

Grouping practices have traditionally been proposed to deal with differences in ability.

Selection is the grouping of pupils into different schools which are supposed to cater for pupils of different aptitude. Selection is usually based on pupils' performance on a test of ability. This presupposes that ability is both fixed and unchanging, a theory that has been widely disproved, and that access to higher education should be limited to an elite of highly able pupils.

Streaming refers to selection within schools, where pupils are put into classes according to their 'ability'. While giving more pupils a chance, this method suffers from many of the disadvantages of selection.

A final grouping method is setting, in which pupils are put in different classes for different subjects according to ability. This still has a number of the disadvantages associated with streaming, but does allow different levels for different subjects, and can more easily be used in a flexible manner.

Recently, the concept of personalization has become increasingly popular. Personalization is meant to address the individual differences that exist between pupils through assessment for learning, teaching and learning strategies – that develop the competence and confidence of every learner by actively engaging them in the learning process and in activities that stretch them, curriculum entitlement and choice and a student-centred approach to school organization – with school leaders and teachers thinking creatively about how to support high-quality teaching and learning.

A more radical approach is that of personalized instruction. In personalized instruction, teaching provision is tailored to the individual needs of each pupil. Teachers act as advisers for individual pupils, and goals as well as instructional tasks are set at weekly meetings between pupils and their advisers.

Reflective Questions

1. What do you see as the main advantages and disadvantages of streaming and selection?
2. How could you help to dispel some of the negative effects of setting?
3. What forms of personalization have you come across in your experience in school? How effective do you think these were?
4. What effect do you think personalization could have on teachers' classroom practice?
5. Do you think personalized instruction is a feasible way to reform education?
6. Why do you think individual learning is not usually found to be effective?
7. Would you set your class, under which circumstances, and why?

PART 4

TEACHING SPECIFIC SUBJECTS, ASSESSMENT AND OBSERVATION

CHAPTER 18

LITERACY

Key Points

In this chapter, you will learn about:

- how children learn to read
- the main characteristics of the phonics, whole-language and collaborative approaches to reading instruction
- the main findings of the largest review of reading research undertaken to date
- the main characteristics of two popular early reading intervention strategies
- the importance of a balanced approach to reading instruction.

Introduction

The most important skill children acquire at school is learning to read. Literacy forms the basis of most other learning. Children and adults who cannot read proficiently will experience significant difficulties at school and will often fail to reach their potential both at school and in life (Basic Skills Agency, 1997). Although some commentators have posited that the growth of ICT will lead to a 'post-literate' society, this can easily be overstated. Most technology, even if not explicitly literate, assumes that literacy is there as a prior condition, and the importance of reading and language has certainly not diminished through the advent of largely language-based information and communication technologies.

In light of the crucial importance of literacy, it is not surprising that many different approaches to teaching reading have been developed and that controversy is rife in this area. While it falls outside the province of this book to discuss in detail all the existing literacy teaching strategies, we will discuss a number of key ones and the controversy surrounding them.

The Main Approaches to Teaching Children to Read

The main debate in literacy instruction in recent years has been between two approaches known as *phonics* and *whole language*. This debate has often been so heated (in particular in the USA) that it has been described as a 'language war'. In this section, we will discuss the main features of these two approaches, while in the next section we will review some research on this matter. However, while the phonics–whole-language debate has been fierce, we will also discuss the collaborative approach, the merits of which should not be ignored.

How Children Learn to Read

A first important thing to note is that reading, in contrast to oral speech development, is not a process that develops naturally through interaction with significant others. Most children have to be explicitly taught to read. Learning to read is a process that starts early in children's development, before they enter formal schooling in most cases, and takes a long time to complete. Frequent exposure to language and literacy from the earliest age is crucial to literacy development. Two main features of reading development are the acquisition of phonemic awareness and the acquisition of the alphabetic principle. Phonetic awareness refers to the knowledge that words and syllables are made up of small units of sound (phonemes). The problem with acquiring this awareness is that in speech specific phonemes often cannot be heard, e.g. the word cat is made up of three phonemes c/a/t, but sounds like one. Learning readers therefore need to learn that spoken words can be divided into phonemes, letters and combinations of letters that represent these phonemes, and that written words have the same number and sequence of sounds as are heard in spoken words (Adams, 1990; Ehri, 1987; Foorman et al., 1996; Lyon, 1999; Torgesen, 1993). The alphabetic principle refers to the knowledge that the 26 letters of the Western alphabet correspond to specific phonemes, in English 44. These principles must become automatic and fluent for reading with comprehension to occur. Research by the National Institute for Child Health and Development (NICHD) in the

USA has shown that poor readers often have difficulty developing these principles (Lyon and Kameenui, 2000).

Other factors that influence reading comprehension are the reader's vocabulary and background knowledge of the text.

Reading problems are often related to home background. Children who enter school with reading difficulties have often had limited exposure to language at home. They are often from poor backgrounds and have parents who themselves are not proficient readers. Therefore, raising parents' awareness of the importance of reading to their children and engaging in language-based play through rhymes, storybooks and later on early writing activities is crucial. Talking out loud to children will help develop their vocabulary and background knowledge, both crucial in reading development (Foorman et al., 1996; Lyon, 1999).

The phonics approach

The *phonics instruction* approach is supported by theories derived from cognitive psychology, research into the way pupils learn to read and research on the differences between pupils with and without reading difficulties. The basic supposition is that children learn to read by first making sense of the smallest component of the language and then progressing to larger wholes (Adams, 1990; Stahl et al., 1998). Phonics instruction focuses on teaching pupils sound–word correspondences, i.e. the correspondence of the 44 *phonemes* of the English language to the 26 alphabetic characters that represent them. There are a number of related approaches in phonics instruction.

In the *analytic phonics method*, the pupil first learns a number of words which encompass common phonic components, such as /p/ in pill, park and pot. This element is ideally discovered by the pupil him/herself, as s/he reads a number of words with the particular phoneme. During a second phase, pupils learn to discriminate this phoneme from a number of other phonemes, i.e. they read the words pan, bad, pop and then decide whether these begin with the same sound as the original words (in this example pill, park and pot). Pupils will then be asked to generate words that begin with the phoneme they are learning. Once pupils have mastered these steps, they will need to learn how to generalize from these known words to new words, and eventually apply this learning in actual reading situations, going on to sentences rather than single words. In this approach, the focus is on learning phonics through building up a bank of known words and creating new ones. Rather than learning the sounds in isolation, they are learned in context. This approach is *systematic* in that it consists of teaching children a planned sequence of phonics elements, rather than touching on phonics elements as and when they appear in a text.

Synthetic phonics instruction consists of teaching pupils to explicitly convert letters into phonemes and then blend the phonemes to form words. This is done through the use of *word families*, which are parts of a word that contain a vowel and a consonant element, to which one can add another consonant element to form different words. An example is the word family (or *grapheme*) it, which can become bit, hit, sit and so on. The basic principle here is that once a pupil has learned the phonemic principle and its relationship to the alphabet, s/he can use this principle to decode unknown words, thus helping her/him to learn to read. The teacher will usually start with a known word, the phonemic elements of which are explored. The word family can then be combined with new consonants to generate new words and sounds (nonsense words are also encouraged, as they can be sounds that form elements of larger words that the pupil may encounter later). The word family may be used as an end, beginning or middle of newly formed words. As well as starting off with a number of known words, pupils must know or be made aware of the rhyming principle, i.e. the fact that words can sound the same at the end, and be able to recognize that words which look the same at the end usually sound the same. There are a large number of commercial schemes available which can aid teachers in phonics teaching.

There is little evidence to support a preference for either analytic or synthetic phonics, as both appear to be similarly effective (Torgerson et al., 2006).

The whole-language approach

In contrast to phonics, which is a reading strategy based on research on reading, and cognitive psychology, *whole language* is a philosophy that draws on knowledge of child development. Advocates of this approach believe that children learn to read and write, as well as speak and listen, through trial and error and practical and authentic uses of language. They believe that rather than going from the smallest element to the whole, learning to read progresses from the whole to the part and from the familiar to the unfamiliar (Goodman and Goodman, 1982). As language is an aggregate of many language functions, these are best learnt as a whole rather than being disaggregated. Learning in this view is not about learning to read words, but about learning to make meaning from text. Therefore, rather than having specific lessons focusing on decoding skills teaching, reading will occur through communication and natural activities throughout the day. Any phonics instruction (which can be included in a whole-language approach if necessary) should take place in the context of a particular meaningful text and not on its own (Goodman and Goodman, 1982; Tierney and Readence, 2000).

One of the main factors to influence reading development is seen to be internal motivation, which means that building up children's enthusiasm is crucial.

Whole language is essentially a meaning-based approach, which sees reading as finding meaning in written language. This is evident, for example, when children can read a word in a familiar book, but not outside of that context. Skilful readers, according to this philosophy, 'skip, skim and guess' rather than reading exactly what is on the page. Both children's motivation and their learning through context are enhanced by letting them read interesting, authentic literature, and not artificial 'basal readers'. Word recognition skills should be picked up by the child in the context of actual reading, writing and immersion in a print-rich classroom. Learning to read should occur through pupil discovery, not teacher instruction, and learning in school should in this respect not be different from learning outside of school. Silent and oral reading are encouraged (Church, 1994; Goodman and Goodman, 1982; Weaver, 1990).

However, the view that skilled readers skim and guess what's on the page has been disputed by eye movement and brain scan research, that has shown that skilled readers tend to read meticulously, word to word and line by line, and translate print to speech while they are doing this (Adams, 1990).

Whole-language teachers will attempt to provide a stimulating classroom environment, consisting of a variety of print resources and artwork, designed to stimulate children's interest. Reading areas, literature circles and writing centres are often in evidence. Shared book experiences (children gather round an oversized 'big book' which they read and discuss cooperatively) are considered important, and children will be encouraged to write stories themselves and to read real literature and each other's writing (Tierney and Readence, 2000). There are a number of similar holistic reading instruction approaches, such as the 'real books' approach, which similarly focuses on learning to read by reading literature rather than using basal readers. A criticism of this approach is the fact that children can encounter a word in context, but then not encounter that word again for a long time. This is obviously not the case in basal readers, where words are introduced systematically.

Collaborative approaches

While most of the recent debates on teaching reading have focused on the phonics–whole-language divide, a number of other interesting approaches exist. One of the methods that is best supported by research is teaching reading in collaborative small groups. There are a wide number of collaborative programmes in existence (e.g. CIRC, Discussion Web, Language Circles). As an example, two collaborative approaches are discussed below.

One of these is *collaborative strategic reading*. In this approach, pupils are taught reading comprehension strategies while working collaboratively. The first step consists of the teacher presenting the comprehension strategies to the whole class using direct instruction, modelling and role playing. After practice has shown that the pupils have attained a sufficient level of mastery of the strategies, they are then asked to form groups (of heterogeneous composition) in which the pupils collaboratively implement the strategies, each pupil fulfilling a particular role (Johnson and Johnson, 1989; Palincsar and Brown, 1984). The approach has shown good results both with pupils with reading difficulties and with average and high-achieving pupils (Klinger and Nelson, 1996). The main comprehension strategies taught are:

1. Preview – this phase takes place before reading. Pupils have to discuss what they already know about the topic and then predict what they think they will learn about it.
2. 'Click and clunk' – pupils have to reflect on which parts of the text were hard to understand, and what they can do to 'fix' these 'clunks', such as by rereading the sentence and the sentences before and after the one they are having difficulty with, or breaking the word down into smaller parts.
3. Get the gist – this occurs by reflecting on what the most important ideas, persons or places in the text were, and what is most important about these places, persons or things.
4. Wrap up – after reading, pupils should ask questions showing they understand what the most important information in the text is, give the answers to those questions, and finally review what they have learnt from the text.

Another example of a cooperative approach is *Jigsaw*, in which pupils are supposed to become experts on a particular aspect of the text or lesson and then teach it to their peers, a method that is known as *peer tutoring*. Each pupil receives an expert sheet that tells them what they are to read, gives them some questions and tells them which group (which should be heterogeneous with respect to gender and ability) they will work with. They will then read their assigned text, and discuss with their expert group (other pupils from different cooperative groups who are to become experts on the same subject) what the most important aspects of that topic are. They then return to their cooperative group to tell the other children what they have learnt in their expert group. At the end of the activity, the teacher should give a short test (Slavin, 1983).

In general, cooperative learning has proved to be an effective teaching method in a wide variety of studies conducted over several decades (Johnson and Johnson, 2000; Slavin, 1983, 1996).

The NICHD Studies and the Evidence for Phonics

Probably the most extensive body of research on reading has come from studies conducted under the auspices of the National Institute of Child Health and Human Development (NICHD) in the USA. This organization has, since 1965, systematically studied reading development through a network of 41 research sites across North America, Europe and Asia. Over the past decades, researchers working with NICHD have studied the reading development of almost 35,000 children and adults, both with (about 1/3) and without (about 2/3) reading difficulties. This research has led to the development of a number of intervention projects, in which almost 8000 children have participated since the mid 1980s.

A number of important findings on effective teaching of literacy have emerged from these studies. Firstly, for both parents and teachers, reading out loud to children is highly effective in developing vocabulary, language expression, and expressive and receptive language skills (Lyon, 1999). Early intervention with pupils with reading difficulties is crucial.

Direct and systematic instruction in phoneme awareness and phonics skills was likewise found to be important, and should be continued until children can automatically process this information. Direct instruction in reading comprehension strategies was found to be effective, and children's reading development is also aided by a literature-rich environment and practice in reading authentic literature and familiar materials. While important, authentic literature and rich contexts are not a suitable replacement for explicit teaching of phonics decoding skills according to this research (Lyon, 1999; Moats, 1996). The NICHD research has shown that guessing words from their context (the text in which they are embedded) is only accurate about 10 to 20 per cent of the time. Thus, according to Lyon and Kameenui (2000), children need to be taught:

- phonemic awareness (the sounds that make up words such as c/a/t)
- the sound–spelling relationships in words
- how to say the sounds that make up words
- by using texts that are made up of words that use the sound–spelling correspondences children have learnt
- by using interesting and authentic stories to develop vocabulary and language comprehension.

Early intervention with pupils with reading difficulties is crucial as the intensity and duration of reading interventions needs to increase exponentially as children get older (Lyon, 1999). While some research shows that for the majority of children sound–word correspondence will be learnt through most teaching methods, for between 30 and 40 per cent this is not the case. Explicit phonics instruction is particularly crucial for this group.

Recently at the behest of the American Congress, NICHD reviewed the scientific literature on the most effective strategies to teach children to read. Out of the more than 100,000 studies published, the panel reviewed those that followed an experimental or quasi-experimental approach and reached rigorous scientific criteria.

The panel concluded that research strongly supported the explicit and systematic teaching of the manipulation of phonemes and phonemic awareness (the knowledge that words are made up of small segments of sound, e.g. go = two phonemes). There was also clear evidence that phonics teaching was beneficial for children from pre-school through to sixth grade, as well as for older children who are having reading problems.

For most children, *systematic phonics teaching* showed the strongest effects, but for low-achieving children and pupils with learning disabilities this could best be combined with *synthetic phonics teaching*. Synthetic phonics teaching was also found to be effective with pupils from low socio-economic status backgrounds and improves all pupils' spelling ability (NICHD, 2000).

Guided oral reading, where pupils read out loud to the teacher, a classmate or another adult who corrects their mistakes and provides feedback was found to develop pupils' reading fluency, and helped pupils to recognize new words, read accurately and improve their reading comprehension. The results on *silent reading* were inconclusive (NICHD, 2000).

The panel also looked at research on reading comprehension, focusing in particular on how best to teach vocabulary, text comprehension and comprehension strategies instruction. According to their review, *vocabulary* can best be taught both directly (apart from a particular text) and indirectly (as words occur in a particular text). Repetition and multiple exposure will help develop vocabulary, and use of ICT was also found to be effective. No single best teaching method could be identified, suggesting that a combination of methods is more appropriate. *Reading comprehension* itself can best be facilitated by teaching pupils a variety of techniques and systematic strategies to assist them with recall of information, question generation and summarizing of information (NICHD, 2000).

A recent British review of the evidence supports this conclusion, with the authors stating that: 'Of 100 children **not** receiving systematic phonics instruction, in a test 50 would score 50 per cent or more, compared with 62 children who would score 50 per cent or more if they **did** receive systematic phonics instruction' (Torgerson et al., 2006: 47). Phonics instruction would appear to be particularly beneficial to pupils from disadvantaged and ethnic minority backgrounds (Jeynes, 2007).

This research thus clearly supports the explicit teaching of phonics, while evidence supporting a whole-language approach does not seem to be this clear (Tierney and Readence, 2000). However, whole-language advocates reject these results, arguing that the standardized tests used in this type of research lack validity. They support a view of evaluation that focuses on pupil self-evaluation, teacher observation of classroom processes, periodic performance samples and dialogue journals (Church, 1994). It is clear, however, that the subjectivity inherent in this type of assessment precludes any scientific evaluation of the effectiveness of programmes and any objective assessment of pupils' progress.

A Balanced Approach

The research summarized above clearly points to the crucial importance of direct instruction in phonics in developing pupils' reading ability. This is especially important for pupils from lower SES backgrounds and pupils who are having difficulties reading. Both phonemic awareness and the alphabetic principle need to be explicitly taught until they become automatic.

Likewise, though, generating enthusiasm for reading and developing pupils' contextual understanding through exposure to interesting, authentic literature has clear merits. Spending too much time doing phonics in one session can be boring, and the materials used to teach it need to be as attractive and interesting as possible. Phonics teaching must not be reduced to meaningless skill and drill.

A balanced approach, in which both authentic, rich contexts and environments and explicit teaching of phonics coexist is therefore both possible and desirable. However, it has become clear that explicit phonics teaching must underlie teaching to read. Therefore, a balanced approach needs to consist of four components:

1. Explicit instruction in phonics skills and other skills such as spelling.
2. Direct and indirect teaching of reading comprehension strategies.
3. A focus on literature, language and authentic texts in a text-rich environment.
4. An effective early intervention programme for readers with problems, such as Reading Recovery (Chall, 1995). This type of balanced approach is becoming more and more common, and the English government's National Literacy Strategy is an attempt at such an approach, although the regimentation it produces has led to concerns about lack of creativity or flexibility with regards to differences in pupil ability (Williams, 2001), and some critics see it as being far closer to the phonics models than the whole-language approach.

This kind of balanced approach was found amongst effective teachers in one English study, in which the most effective literacy teachers were found to be more likely than the less effective teachers to emphasize children's knowledge of the purposes and functions of reading and writing and of the structures used to enable these processes; were more diagnostic in the ways they examined and judged samples of children's reading and writing; and paid attention to both the goals they had identified for reading and writing and to technical processes such as phonic knowledge, spelling, grammar and punctuation. They were also more likely to contextualize their teaching and stress the ways in which literacy skills were key to good communication (Wray and Medwell, 2001). In another English study, phonics embedded within whole-class teaching was found to have reduced the incidence of reading difficulties from 20 per cent in comparison schools to 5 per cent in intervention schools in which the approach was used (Shapiro and Solity, 2008). Similar findings were reported by Pressley et al. (2001) in their small-scale study of five classrooms. Analysis of National Reading Panel data in the USA likewise suggests that phonics is most effective when it is taught systematically, but embedded within broader approaches to reading instruction that emphasize other aspects such as context and culture (Stuebing et al., 2008). Teaching must also be adapted to the specific needs of the students. Connor et al. (2007), for example, found that spending more time on phonics instruction is beneficial to students weak in alphabetic skills, while spending more time on comprehension instruction leads to better outcomes in students weak in vocabulary.

Amidst all the thunder of the phonics–whole-language debate, it is easy to lose sight of other promising approaches, particularly in the field of collaborative learning. Hopefully, literacy instruction can move on from this debate and move forwards towards a more balanced and possibly more collaborative approach.

Early Intervention Programmes

As mentioned above, early intervention with pupils who are experiencing reading problems is crucial if these pupils are not to fall further behind other children in all subjects as they go through school. Two of the most successful intervention programmes are Reading Recovery and Success for All.

Reading Recovery, a programme devised in New Zealand by Marie Clay, combines direct phonics instruction with a rich, whole-language style environment. The programme runs for an average of 16 weeks, during which period specially trained teachers work with individual pupils for 30 minutes a day. Pupils are exposed to books that get gradually more difficult, mini writing lessons and plastic letters that children use to form words. Reading Recovery lessons have seven components:

1. Rereading of two or more familiar texts, i.e. stories the pupil knows (but doesn't know by heart) – the focus during this part is on comprehension of the text.
2. Using a running record on the previous day's new story – the teacher observes the child reading the text.
3. Letter identification and word formation using magnetic letters.
4. Writing a story and developing phonemic awareness – the pupil writes a story and phonics is used when children come up to a difficult word. Pupils are encouraged to divide words into their component sounds.
5. Pupils are then encouraged to cut up the story into its component parts, such as phrases, words, clusters of letters and single letters.
6. New book introduction – a new book is introduced which is not too difficult for the pupil to master, but which should contain a minimum of new elements the child needs to learn.
7. Reading the new book with help from the teacher (Clay, 1993).

In general, Reading Recovery, now used in most English-speaking countries, has proved effective with a wide range of pupils with learning difficulties, with gains in reading sustained over time and many students not requiring additional intervention (D'Agostino and Murphy, 2004; Potter, 2007). However, as up to a quarter of pupils may fail to make the necessary progress, some have doubted the cost-effectiveness of the method (Center et al., 1995; Geeke, 1988; Haen, 2000).

Success for All (SFA) is a highly successful school-wide programme designed for schools with disadvantaged intakes. As with Reading Recovery, SFA emphasizes both meaning and authentic texts and systematic phonics instruction. Direct instruction of reading strategies is another component of the programme.

The main programme components are:

- Trained reading tutors give one-to-one tutoring to pupils who are not performing up to the reading standards of their peers in 20-minute sessions. They also help teach the class during reading or literacy sessions, thus helping to reduce class sizes (see below). Pupils are continually assessed by their tutor.
- A 90-minute reading period is given every day, during which time the pupils are grouped by reading ability (possibly cross-age) in classes of at most 20 pupils. Direct instruction of phonics is used as are big books and reading stories to the class. By the time kindergarten children can read to primer level, they start cooperative work on reading and composition activities.
- Each eight weeks, pupils' progress is assessed, and tutor groups are re-evaluated.
- SFA schools provide half-day pre-school and a full day kindergarten, where pupils receive developmentally appropriate learning experiences and language development activities.
- A family support team works with pupils' families and provides what assistance is deemed necessary (Madden et al., 1993; Slavin, 1993; Tierney and Readence, 2000).

Success for All has been extensively evaluated, and has shown considerable success in raising reading levels and overall academic achievement compared to matched control schools (Slavin, 1995, 1997; Wasik and Slavin, 1993), and has been found to reduce achievement gaps between white and black students in the USA (Madden, 2006).

Other early intervention programmes, such as the 'Bright Beginnings' programme in Charlotte, NC, which contains a strong parental involvement and community elements, have also produced promising results (Smith et al., 2003), with many successful interventions combining use of phonics, measurement of reading progress and individually focused intervention for students experiencing particular problems reaching required reading standards (O'Connor et al., 2005).

Summary

Learning to read is probably the most important skill that children will pick up during the early years of schooling.

(Continued)

(Continued)

A range of approaches exist in reading instruction, but most controversy recently has focused on phonics instruction and the whole-language approach.

Phonics instruction focuses on teaching children the correspondence between the 44 phonemes (sounds) in the English language and the 26 letters of the alphabet. This is seen as essential to decoding language, the assumption being that the best way to learn to read is to proceed from the part to the whole. This approach is supported by research into how children learn to read.

The whole-language approach focuses on the importance of making meaning from texts. Motivation is seen as paramount, and using authentic, interesting literature and a text-rich environment to encourage pupils' motivation to read are seen to be crucial. According to the whole-language view, explicit teaching of phonics is usually unnecessary, as learning to read goes from the whole to the part, with guessing from context and skimming being prime strategies in reading.

The National Institute of Child Health and Development in the USA has conducted a series of studies over three decades, accumulating what is probably the most extensive evidence base on reading in the world. Their research clearly supports the importance of teaching phonics in an explicit way, although reading comprehension strategies were also found to be important. However, while this research clearly supports the importance of teaching phonics, meaning, motivation and the joy of reading as stressed by whole-language advocates are clearly important as well. This realization has led many to advocate a balanced approach, containing both phonics instruction and elements of the whole-language philosophy.

Reflective Questions

1. Do you think the whole-language philosophy is compatible with a balanced approach to reading instruction?
2. Why do you think phonics instruction has been found to be effective in the NICHD studies?
3. Does the NICHD research support the whole-language approach?
4. Do you think Reading Recovery is necessary if a balanced approach to literacy is used?
5. Is Success for All a balanced approach? Why?
6. Describe a collaborative approach to reading instruction.

CHAPTER 19

MATHEMATICS

Key Points

In this chapter, you will learn about:

- some findings from international studies on the mathematics achievement of children and adolescents
- what we know about how children learn mathematics
- the implications of research on how children learn mathematics to mathematics teaching
- other factors that can enhance the effectiveness of mathematics teaching.

Introduction

Mathematics is commonly seen as one of the most difficult subjects in the curriculum by pupils and adults alike. In a number of studies conducted by the Basic Skills Agency, for example, a large proportion of English adults were found not to possess basic numeracy skills (Bynner and Parsons, 1997; Bynner and

Steedman, 1995), a proportion that is larger than that of illiterate adults. In schools, a lot of pupils seem to become disenchanted with mathematics, and often question the relevance of the large amount of time spent teaching this subject. This notwithstanding, research has shown the importance of maths in adult daily life. According to the Basic Skills studies mentioned above, lack of numeracy was related to unemployment and low incomes among adults, over and above the effects of poor literacy among these same adults. Likewise, adults with a higher secondary school mathematics qualification (the 'A' level) in England had average earnings 10 per cent higher than people without this qualification (*The Economist*, 2003). Mathematics has importance over and above the application of basic numeracy skills. It is a prime vehicle for developing pupils' logical thinking and higher-order cognitive skills. Mathematics also plays a major role in a number of other scientific fields, such as physics, engineering and statistics. Mathematics as a subject is also strongly influenced by school and classroom effects. The impact of teachers and schools on mathematics outcomes is higher than on English language outcomes, for example, with one study using highly curriculum-relevant tests finding that 20 per cent of the variance in mathematics achievement was attributable to which school they went to and which teachers they were taught by, once factors such as pupil background and ability had been taken into account (Opdenakker et al., 2002).

In view of both the significance of maths and the problems many people have with the subject, it is not surprising that there is quite a lot of research into pupils' mathematical thinking and learning. In this chapter, we will review some of the main findings of this research.

What We Know about The Way Children Learn Mathematics

Children come to school with mathematical knowledge, skills and misconceptions

Even before they come to school, children engage in a number of activities that appear to be mathematical. They count, share out (things like sweets), and often manage to do simple addition and subtraction. However, the relationship between this prior out-of-school knowledge and children's maths learning in school is not straightforward, especially as some studies have found that pupils are in many cases actively discouraged from using that informal knowledge (Anghileri, 1995; Romberg and Kaput, 1999).

For example, while children can already to a large extent *count* before they come to school, their grasp of the meaning of number words and of *cardinality* (knowing that numbers are absolute amounts, and thus that, for example, four green sweets are as much as four red sweets) is shaky. *Sharing* is another activity that children master before they enter school, and in this case they seem to understand the concept well. Children have also been found to be able to *add and subtract* small numbers, though research has not yet established whether they understand that the two operations are *inverse*.

This early knowledge is important to children's learning and teaching in primary school as counting, sharing, adding and subtracting form the basis of much early in-school teaching and learning. Pupils build upon their existing knowledge to build up their mathematical competence and extend the breadth and understanding of that knowledge. Once pupils get older, they will continue to garner mathematical knowledge outside of school through such activities as shopping and reading the paper, and *this out-of-school learning* can usefully be incorporated into teaching. In this way, pupils will learn the relevance of maths to 'real life', and be able to *transfer* knowledge learned in the classroom to the outside world so they can actually use their maths in everyday situations.

The International Mathematics and Science Studies

The International Education Association has studied the maths performance of children from a large number of countries on three occasions. The First International Mathematics Study (FIMS) took place in the 1960s. More recently, the SIMS study in the 1980s and the ongoing TIMSS studies carried out in the past decade have produced valuable data on the comparative performance of children in different countries in various aspects of mathematics.

Most political interest has focused on the ranking of countries in the tests, which tend to show high performance by pupils from a number of South East Asian countries, such as Singapore, Korea and Hong Kong. In the USA and the UK, there is a perception that their pupils have done particularly badly. This is only partly true. In fact, pupils from both countries tend to get mediocre scores. Furthermore, these global rankings obscure some interesting differences in performance on different subsets of the tests. When one looks at these subsets, it appears that English pupils, for example, do quite well in geometry and very well in problem solving, but very poorly in basic number skills and arithmetic.

In both SIMS and TIMSS, researchers have attempted to look at factors that could explain these differences between countries, as well as the (usually larger) differences within countries. The main school-related factor that was found to be significant was opportunity to learn, i.e. the extent to which pupils in those countries and schools had encountered the questions on the test in their curriculum. Other findings relate to specific populations, such as the importance of pupils' beliefs about maths and the world in achievement in high-level maths (Koller, 2001).

Another set of international studies that have looked at mathematics achievement are the OECD-sponsored PISA studies. While again they are mainly used to rank countries, a lot of the more interesting findings relate to different school and classroom processes in participating countries.

While pupils' externally garnered knowledge forms one basis of their numeracy, it is important to remember that external knowledge may also provide them with misconceptions about the meaning of mathematical terms. Commonsense meanings of mathematical terms such as the '=' sign are not necessarily exactly the same as the mathematical meaning of these terms (Thompson, 1997). These misconceptions will need to be addressed by teachers, who therefore need to possess a good knowledge of their pupils' mathematical beliefs.

Numeracy is based on the application of logic

It seems like stating a truism to say that children need to be able to *think logically* to do mathematics. After all, don't they need this for whatever subject they do? However, logic is particularly important to mathematics learning. Even basic numerical operations such as counting rely on the application of logic.

One of the logical operations children must understand is *ordinality* – the fact that numbers are arranged in ascending order of magnitude (3>2, 2>1). This means that they need to understand not just this order, but also the fact that if 3>2, and 2>1, then 3>1 as well. They also need to know that if they are counting something (e.g. the number of sweets in a packet), they can count each one only once; that the order in which they are counted makes no difference; and that the final number they have counted to is the total number of objects in a *set* (in this case, the total number of sweets in the packet). These are all logical rules, and you can see that even a relatively simple operation like counting involves a lot of logical thinking on the part of the pupil!

Logic is equally important to more complex numerical operations. An example of this, taken from Piaget, is the following. Two children do a gardening job. One has worked for 10 hours, the other for 4 hours. They get 10 pounds between them. How to share this money? A fair share would clearly involve giving one child a larger share of the money than the other. Solving this kind of problem does not require much more advanced arithmetic than a simple sharing problem. However, as Piaget stated, the logic underlying this operation is far more complex, involving keeping the relationship between time and money constant. According to Piaget, this requires a *second-order operation*, or an operation on an operation (De Bock et al., 2003).

Numeracy means learning a conventional system

Numeracy doesn't just involve application of logic, however. It also involves acquiring a set of conventions that are needed for mastering mathematical techniques (such as long division, for example). These conventions provide us with ways of representing concepts, such as the *number set* (= the set of all possible numbers). These can differ between cultures, e.g. our base 10 number set or our measurement system differ from those in other countries (an example of this is the difference between the Imperial and the Metric measurement systems). These differences are essentially arbitrary. However, what they do share is that they encompass the logic needed to do mathematics. Both the Metric and the Imperial system share the concept of ordinality, for example.

Children obviously need to learn how to use these systems as well as master the logic behind mathematics. Initially, they may experience problems doing this. According to Bryant (1994), learning the conventional system may actually increase children's ability to think logically as well. An example he gives of this is use of a base number system, such as our base 10 system, in which 10 units make a decade, 10 decades a hundred etc. Such a base system is not inevitable, but number systems that have a base have been found to be more efficient than non-base systems. If a child has to learn number words in a fixed order (e.g. 0, 1, 2 etc.) in a non-base system, s/he will have to learn as many words as s/he can, the number of which is inevitably limited due to limitations in the capacity of memory. In a base 10 system, however, the children need to memorize all the words from one to 10, all the teen words (11, 12 etc.) and decade words (20, 30 …), as well as words such as hundred and thousand, but they will then be able to combine these to form new words. This allows them to easily count to high numbers without having to memorize a huge number of words. Therefore, once we have a base system, we possess a powerful tool for thought (Nunes and Bryant, 1996).

Effective Teaching: Maths-Specific Factors

Using effective teaching strategies

When discussing mathematics learning above, it was posited that the first thing one needs to do is look at applying what we know about learning in general. Similarly, when looking at how to teach mathematics, the first thing to do is to look at what have generally been found to be effective teaching strategies. These were discussed in Chapters 2 and 3.

It is important to point out here that this research is of particular relevance to mathematics. A lot of the American teacher effectiveness studies were carried out in mathematics classrooms and in many cases when we are saying that a certain behaviour is linked to achievement, it is therefore mathematics achievement that we are talking about. Similarly, a number of international studies point to the greater use of the direct instruction approaches found to be effective in these studies in countries where pupils do better in maths (Wang and Lin, 2005).

The structured teaching style advocated by the effective teaching researchers also corresponds well with the structured nature of mathematical knowledge as discussed above, and the emphasis on mastering relatively small chunks of content, before going on to the next step, could help counter the fear of maths and uncertainty about their mathematical ability that many people feel. It also ties in with the hierarchical nature of the subject itself. However, just using generic effective teaching strategies is not sufficient for effective mathematics teaching. There is clear evidence that knowledge and application of maths-specific teaching skills and knowledge are important to pupil outcomes. In one study, for example, mathematical knowledge used to carry out the *work of teaching mathematics* was significantly related to student achievement, after taking into account other characteristics of teachers such as their qualifications and experience (Hill et al., 2005).

From the above, it is also clear that effective maths teaching involves *both* teaching for understanding, using problem solving etc., and an element of rote learning, in that pupils need to master the conventional systems of maths and gain automaticity in the use of skills such as multiplication facts and times tables in order to allow them to work efficiently and to free memory space for more meaningful work (Merttens, 1996). An overemphasis on rote learning, however, may lead to pupils finding it hard to transfer their knowledge to other situations. A balanced approach, with a lot of emphasis on real-life contexts, is therefore essential (Yetkin, 2003).

Correcting misconceptions

As mentioned above, children can easily develop misconceptions about the meaning of mathematical concepts. It is important for teachers to address these from the start (Hiebert and Carpenter, 1992).

This implies that it is necessary to let pupils explain how they come to their answers, whether right or wrong, and in the second case to correct the wrong answer explicitly. This is especially important in mathematics as even right answers can sometimes result from inefficient or incorrect methods (which are incorrect because they can sometimes lead to the wrong answer). Teachers should also provide detailed justifications of the solutions they are using.

An example of a misconception that often occurs in the primary school is that pupils will acquire a rule and then overgeneralize it to situations in which it is not applicable. For example, pupils often acquire the rule that when multiplying a number by 10, one adds a zero. They will then use this rule in situations in which it is not correct, e.g. when multiplying decimals (e.g. 5.6 X 10 = 5.60). Also, pupils will often think that multiplication always makes things bigger, while division always makes things smaller and then choose wrongly to apply division or multiplication based on their perception of whether numbers need to get smaller or bigger.

As these misconceptions tend to be shared by a relatively large number of pupils, addressing them can improve pupils' mathematical achievement. It has been found to be more effective to let pupils make the mistake first and then to discuss it afterwards, rather than giving pupils examples of the misconception beforehand (Askew and William, 1995). Building on pupil mistakes has been found to be an effective method in developing pupils' reasoning and problem-solving skills (Eggleton and Moldavan, 2001).

One way of avoiding future misconceptions is to teach the exact meaning of mathematical terms right from the start. This may not seem immediately obvious, as in the lower years a less than exact definition or understanding of a term or symbol such as the '=' sign may be sufficient for children's mathematical problem solving at that stage. However, once they reach a higher stage of learning and need to know the exact mathematical meaning of the term, they will find it difficult to unlearn inexact meanings they have internalized. It is far more difficult to change pupils' understanding of a term later on than to teach them correctly in the first place (Askew and William, 1995). Another useful strategy is to get pupils to think about why a particular strategy doesn't work in particular situations. The example given above of 'adding a zero' when multiplying by 10 is a good example of a situation that can be used as the start of a discussion that will hopefully stimulate pupil interest as well as getting them to think about their misconceptions (Littler and Jirotkova, 2008).

Using real-life contexts

A specific difficulty of mathematics knowledge for pupils lies in its *abstract nature*. Pupils often find it hard to link mathematics learnt in the classroom to real-life situations, and also have difficulties making the connections between the mathematics knowledge they already possess and what they learn at school. These problems can be remedied by using real-life examples as much as possible and by validating pupils' existing mathematics knowledge. Use of real-life materials, such as shopping bills for the younger pupils, can enhance the making of these connections and the generation of informal mathematical knowledge. These materials can be brought to class by the pupils themselves, furthering involvement in the lesson (Gravemeijer, 1997).

A model that has been proposed is one in which the teacher starts off with a realistic example or situation, turns this into a mathematical model, leading to mathematical solutions, which are then reinterpreted as a realistic solution. This strategy would certainly be useful in linking mathematical and real-world knowledge and applications (Askew and William, 1995).

Examples given by the teacher should be as close as possible to the real world, and new mathematical concepts should be explained using a variety of representations, e.g. symbolic, graphic, through the use of materials, etc. In this way, the pupil can learn to think of the mathematical concept apart from its physical representation. Teachers do need to be aware, though, that in some cases real-life examples can lead to misconceptions among young children, especially if they don't fully represent the concept being studied. Also, mathematical symbols can take on slightly different meanings in different contexts, and overly limited real-life examples might actually militate against pupils using their knowledge in other contexts. Therefore, they should be provided with a variety of materials and be made aware of the contextual differences involved (Yetkin, 2003).

It is important to take into account here that using real-life examples is more than just using words from everyday life in a word problem that is, as a whole, unrealistic. An example of this is the following problem, taken from Pollack: 'Two bees working together can gather nectar from 100 hollyhock blossoms in 30 minutes. Assuming that each bee works the standard eight-hour day, five days a week, how many blossoms do these bees gather nectar from in a summer season of fifteen weeks?'. It is clear that this problem does not actually connect in any way to pupils' real-life experience. Use of this type of problem will not aid pupils' application of maths, or help them to connect informal maths learned outside the classroom to what they have to learn in school.

While this example may appear exaggerated, a lot of word problems resemble it, using a *context* which only at first sight appears realistic. To be effective, a real-life example needs to connect far more to pupils' actual experience.

Making connections

A subject already touched on in the chapter on pupils' learning is clearly linking different parts of the lesson and the curriculum. This has been found to be particularly important for maths, distinguishing teachers in China and other Asian countries with high levels of achievement in mathematics from teachers in the USA where mathematics achievement is comparatively lower (Wang and Lin, 2005). New knowledge needs to be linked to concepts learnt earlier and different parts of the lesson should be linked to each other, to knowledge acquired earlier and to the curriculum. Mathematical ideas should not be taught in isolation – a strong focus should be put on the relationship between ideas. This will enable pupils to be better able to retrieve knowledge from memory and to understand the hierarchical nature of mathematical knowledge. These linkages must be explicitly taught to pupils. Teachers can also use questions that ask a pupil to relate a newly taught concept to a previously learnt idea.

This means that teachers must themselves be aware of the connections between different aspects of the mathematics curriculum and the use and application of mathematics in different fields, and thus requires good subject knowledge from the teacher. This has been found to be linked to higher pupil achievement (Mandeville and Liu, 1997).

Summary

Mathematics and numeracy are a key part of schooling due to the importance of basic numeracy skills in everyday life, the role of mathematics in the acquisition of logical thinking skills, and the role of mathematics as a crucial component of other scientific fields.

Children come to school already possessing mathematical skills such as counting, simple addition and subtraction and cardinality, which need to be built on once they enter a formal school environment. From the earliest age, doing mathematics also requires use of logic, such as ordinality, and use of a formal system, such as the base 10 system. Children explicitly need to learn how to master these systems and develop their logical thinking.

A lot of the studies on which the findings on effective teaching reviewed in Chapters 2 and 3 are based were done in mathematics, so they are particularly relevant to this subject. However, there are a number of additional aspects that are specific to mathematics teaching. Pupils are often found to have misconceptions about maths which impede their learning of the subject. These need to be made explicit and need to be tackled in maths teaching. The abstract nature of maths often causes problems to both pupils' learning and their attitudes towards maths. This can be counteracted by using real-life contexts and examples as much as possible and by stressing the relevance of maths to daily life. Finally, it is particularly important to make sure that mathematical knowledge is linked and connected in pupils' minds.

Reflective Questions

1. In what ways can children's prior knowledge help or harm their classroom maths learning? What can teachers do about the latter?
2. Do you think the specific suggestions on teaching maths contradict or agree with the research on effective teaching discussed in Chapters 2 and 3?
3. Can you describe some specific problems that children face when learning maths, and make some suggestions to address these?
4. How important do you think it is for children to learn mathematical conventions?
5. Should maths teaching focus on understanding or on rote learning of basic skills?

CHAPTER 20

ASSESSMENT FOR LEARNING

Key Points

In this chapter, you will learn about:

- the main types of assessment used in schools and classrooms today
- the key characteristics of standardized tests
- the advantages and disadvantages of using teacher-made tests
- the most common forms of alternative assessment
- the importance of assessment for learning
- the main characteristics of assessment for learning.

Introduction

Assessment is probably one of the most important but also most contentious activities teachers engage in. Assessment occupies up to one third of teacher time according to research by Stiggins (1987). This is one of the reasons heavy use of assessment has been criticized, as some commentators have said that this time could be better spent on actual teaching. State accountability systems are exacerbating this trend, with teaching in some cases being geared almost entirely towards preparation for mandated tests (Berends et al., 2001). However, as we shall see below, assessment, and in particular assessment for learning, is an invaluable tool for teachers and education systems that allows teachers to better plan their lessons by taking into account the strengths and weaknesses of their pupils and helps teachers and schools to see whether pupils are actually learning what has been taught. Teachers can then adjust their teaching if this is not the case. Assessment can also allow teachers to see how well their pupils are doing relative to national norms.

What is assessment?

The term *assessment* refers to all information gathered about pupils in the classroom by their teachers, either through formal testing, essays and homework or informally through observation or interaction (Arends, 1998). The related term *evaluation* refers to the process of judging, valuing and ranking pupils (Arends, 1998; Scriven, 1999). In practice, giving a test is assessment (collecting data on a particular pupil), while assigning a grade or mark is evaluation.

Types of assessment

There are two main types of assessment: *formative* and *summative* assessment. *Formative* assessment, also known as *Assessment of Learning* is designed to inform the teacher about her pupils' performance, knowledge and skills, and this information is then used to plan lessons or remediation to improve pupils' performance. A key part of this type of assessment is feedback to pupils to help them to learn more effectively. Formative evaluation has been found to have a strong positive effect on achievement (Black and William, 1998). Summative evaluation is more useful for systemic quality control.

Summative evaluation is meant to give a picture of how well a pupil (or group of pupils) has done over a time period on a set of learning goals in a particular subject.

The three main types of assessment instruments in use today are standardized tests, teacher-made tests and alternative forms of assessment such as performance assessment and portfolio assessment. We will discuss each of these below.

Standardized Tests

Standardized tests have been developed by professional test developers (as opposed to classroom teachers) and have been designed to produce reliable results in a variety of settings. Examples include the California Achievement Test and the TAAS in the USA, and the CITO Schoolvorderingentoets in the Netherlands.

Standardized tests are widely used at school, local education authority, state and national levels, often for purposes of accountability. These tests cover a wide range of subjects and can be commercially purchased or developed specifically for state or national testing purposes. In many systems, the results of testing are used to make judgements on the effectiveness of schools and teachers.

Norm-referenced and criterion-referenced tests

The main types of standardized tests are *norm-referenced* and *criterion-referenced* tests. Norm-referenced tests are essentially comparative, in that they rank pupils and are designed to allow comparison of pupils' performance relative to that of other pupils, usually in a national sample. This means that these tests must be designed to discriminate pupils from one another, and thus must have enough variance in scores to allow this to happen. Usually, as well as the actual score of the pupil on the test (the *raw score*), this type of test provides users with an *age standardized score*, which has a mean of 100, corresponding to the average score of pupils of that age on the test, with a minimum of 70 and a maximum of 130. In order for this standardization to be reliable, the sample on which the test was originally *normed* must be representative of the population (for example, all grade 4 elementary school children in the Netherlands). This means the sample must include a percentage of pupils of different genders, different types of school and so on that corresponds to the distribution of these characteristics in the population.

Criterion-referenced tests are not designed to compare pupils with each other but to measure the performance of pupils on a particular pre-chosen criterion, for example being able to reach a particular level of mastery in a subject. This means that criterion-referenced tests need to be more specific than norm-referenced tests with respect to content, but will be less effective at distinguishing pupils from each other. For example, if the goal of the test is to measure whether pupils have mastered a particular topic in the curriculum, the test should be designed in such a way that the majority of pupils will pass the test if they have understood the subject. A good criterion-referenced test will give information on pupils' mastery of a wide range of topics in a subject or curriculum, such as addition with three digit numbers, place value or mental arithmetic in mathematics.

It is obviously important to decide before purchasing or designing a test what it is that you want it to do. For classroom use and for formative assessment more generally, criterion-referenced tests are usually most useful as they will allow the teacher to see whether pupils have attained specific learning goals. For some summative assessment purposes, especially where the performance of pupils is to be compared to that of peers, or where schools' or teachers' performance is to be compared, norm-referenced tests are more useful. It is important not to confuse the two, as designing tests for both purposes simultaneously often leads to poor tests.

It is important when choosing either a norm-referenced or a criterion-referenced test that the test has been either recently designed or recently re-normed (within the last five years). This is necessary because both pupils and teaching change over time, which means that older tests will have norms that may no longer be valid for the current cohort of pupils. Furthermore, curricula and textbooks change over time, so old criteria may no longer reflect schools' current curriculum.

Achievement and aptitude tests

A further distinction within standardized testing is that between *achievement tests* and *aptitude tests.* Achievement tests measure pupils' performance in a particular school subject or topic at a given time. Aptitude tests cover a broader area and are less closely tied to the school curriculum. They are designed to give an indication of the knowledge that a pupil brings to a situation with him or herself, and of the likelihood that the pupil will be academically successful during the course of the year (Macklem, 1990). As such, they can be a helpful diagnostic tool for teachers, giving a picture of the strengths and weaknesses of pupils and helping teachers to set (individual) targets for these pupils and the class as a whole.

Advantages and disadvantages of standardized tests

The main advantages of standardized tests lie in the high quality of the items, written by specialists in the subject and in item construction, the standardization of administration and scoring procedures, the fact that standardized tests allow comparison with national norms and pupils, and the good psychometric qualities (reliability and validity) of the test. Standardized multiple-choice tests in particular cover a wide range of topics, thus giving a good overview of pupils' knowledge of the curriculum (Sanders and Horn, 1994, 1995). Disadvantages lie in a possible mismatch between what pupils have learnt in class and what is measured by the test and in the lack of flexibility of these tests. They also offer less insight into pupils' thought processes than do a number of alternative assessment methods.

Computer Adaptive Testing

Computer adaptive tests (CAT) are, as the name suggests, performed on a computer, either via a connection to the World Wide Web or offline using software packages or CD-Roms. Essentially, these tests are standardized multiple-choice tests with the added advantage that (using so-called screening items) pupils will be presented with a selection of items suited to their ability level. The pupils will answer a number of preliminary questions, and on the basis of their performance on these items, they will take a test that is neither too easy nor too difficult for them – a problem that can often occur with written tests.

Computer adaptive tests also allow test developers to constantly update and add items to the test, so that items of similar difficulty can be randomly selected from large *item banks*. This means that tests are constantly changing and can be sat on several occasions without becoming unreliable through familiarity with the test items. Tests can also be immediately scored.

Technically, Item Response Models are used in order to calibrate new items and make sure that the difficulty levels of items are accurately known.

CAT tests increasingly include multimedia presentations and film. Audio versions for pupils with reading difficulties and touch-screens for people with impaired sight have already been developed.

Teacher-Made Tests

Rather than use standardized tests, teachers will often want to design their own tests, which may be better matched to their curriculum and their pupils' level of progress. Teacher-made tests allow for more frequent testing than non-computer adaptive standardized tests which can only be used occasionally because of item familiarity setting in and because the large range of topics covered makes them unsuitable to assess whether a particular recently taught topic has been learnt.

Effective teacher-made tests

Gronlund (1991) gives the following principles for effective teacher-made tests:

- Tests should be constructed to measure (as much as possible) all the learning goals that pupils are meant to reach, and not just a subset of these.
- A good test should encompass different types of knowledge, such as factual knowledge, procedural knowledge and thinking skills.

- Different types of test item are suitable for different purposes. Therefore, teachers need to consider whether they want to use open questions, multiple-choice questions or some other format based on their objectives.
- Tests should be used diagnostically. Pupils should be provided with feedback, and the teacher should go over problems in the test with pupils. Testing should be integrated with teaching. This is essential and far more important than giving marks or grades to pupils, according to a review of research by Black and William (1998). Feedback should be helpful and aim to improve pupils' learning rather than encouraging competition and comparison between pupils.

If these guidelines are followed, then this type of formative assessment has a strong positive effect on learning, especially among low achievers.

Types of questions

A major distinction in testing is between tests using *closed*, often *multiple-choice* questions and questions that are open, often requiring pupils to write a type of essay.

Both formats have advantages and disadvantages. The main advantage of multiple-choice tests are easy and quick scoring, objective marking (as there is only one possible right answer) and ease of varying questions according to difficulty based on statistical criteria. This type of test can also easily contain a large number of items, as closed questions take less time to answer than open questions. This means that a larger proportion of the topic can be covered. A disadvantage is that pupils are not able to explain their thinking, leading to a focus on outcomes rather than processes in scoring. A further problem is guessing the answer, although this problem can be lessened by techniques such as subtracting a point for a wrong answer.

Multiple-choice tests, while fast to administer and score, take longer to prepare as a lot of care has to be taken to develop unambiguous and clear items. The first part of the multiple-choice question is called the *stem* (e.g. 'King Leopold's rule over the Congo Freestate was highly controversial because...'). This should be clear and unambiguous, and provide sufficient context. The various (usually three) wrong answers are called *the distractors*. They need to be sufficiently plausible to be selected by pupils and should not contain formal clues that they are wrong, such as being significantly shorter than the right answer, being nonsensical and having a different grammatical structure (Arends, 1998; Borich, 2000).

Different forms of closed tests also exist, such as *matching* sets of items (an example of this is a vocabulary test in a foreign language, in which a list of words in the mother tongue needs to be matched to a list of words in the target language presented in a different order) and *cloze* tests, in which pupils have to fill in the blanks, for example 'The capital of France is_____').

Open questions have the advantage of allowing space for pupils to explain their answers and working out, and thus can be more useful diagnostically because teachers can see exactly where misconceptions are occurring. Open questions can cover a wider area or concept than multiple-choice questions. It has often been argued that multiple-choice questions don't allow process or higher-order questions. This argument is not entirely accurate, however, as multiple-choice tests covering a variety of learning objectives (and not just factual recall) have been successfully developed (Sanders and Horn, 1995). Usually, essay tests are better suited to testing higher-order thinking than multiple-choice tests, however.

Disadvantages of open questions include that they take longer to mark and that they are more difficult to mark objectively. In order to lessen this problem, clear and highly detailed marking schemes outlining exactly what elements are expected to be present or absent and how each element is to be marked are essential. 'Blind marking', where the teacher doesn't know whose test is being marked, can further enhance objectivity. This can be done by having pupils write their roll number rather than their name on the test, or by having them write their name on the back of the test sheet. In a classroom in which the teacher knows all the children personally and recognizes their handwriting, this can be problematic, however. Having a colleague mark the tests may be a solution here. Finally, it can be easy to mistake fluent and correct writing with knowledge and understanding of the topic to be assessed. Teachers need to make sure essay tests aren't turned into literacy tests, and should make sure they are not too strongly influenced by factors such as length and good handwriting, which can disadvantage certain pupils (Borich, 2000; Sanders and Horn, 1995).

In order for open essay style questions to be effective, they need to be clear and explain in a sufficiently detailed way exactly what is expected of pupils. If the goal of assessing higher-order thinking skills is to be reached, open questions need to require more than facts recall from pupils and preferably need to have more than one possible solution. Marking needs to set more store by the processes than by the outcomes of the question (Badger and Thomas, 1992).

Teacher-made tests are clearly suited to everyday classroom assessment. They can be made to fit exactly with the topics covered in class and the levels of pupils in a particular class. The main disadvantages are that it is harder to achieve good psychometric properties than with standardized tests designed over long periods of time and at some expense by a large team of experts, and the lack of a benchmark to compare the performance of pupils in the class to national norms.

Alternative Assessment Methods

Recently, a number of other assessment methods which aim to provide what is known as a more 'authentic' measure of pupils' learning have gained in popularity. Authentic in this context is usually taken to mean that pupil performance is measured directly on a realistic task, rather than indirectly using proxy items designed to measure an underlying latent trait (Wiggins, 1989). These types of assessment are intended to occur in a natural classroom context.

Performance assessment

The aim of *performance assessment* is to measure learning or performance directly instead of using a paper-and-pencil test. An obvious example of this can be found in physical education where performance is judged directly by the teacher in many instances. This method can also be used to measure higher-order cognitive processes.

To assess performance in this way, the teacher needs to establish a particular situation and then observe pupils solving problems, cooperating with other pupils and carrying out the tasks that the teacher wants to assess. The advantage of doing this is that it allows teachers to observe pupil behaviours in realistic situations rather than in the artificial test situation. This will allow teachers to study behaviours that may not occur under testing conditions, either because they are not explicitly tested or because test anxiety makes pupils not do them. An example is rating pupils while they are conducting a conversation in a foreign language or when they are conducting an experiment. Performance assessment can easily take place during a regular lesson (Brualdi, 1998; Moskal, 2000).

Developing a performance assessment is a deliberate and structured process that goes well beyond casual observation of pupils. When preparing a performance assessment, the teacher needs to start off by formulating the outcomes that s/he wants to measure, both at the cognitive and affective levels. Then a task needs to be designed that will allow pupils to use the skills, behaviours or performance the teacher wants to measure. These can include role plays, experiments or discussions. These tasks should be complex, allowing the teacher to assess a variety of skills, and do not necessarily have to lead to one particular 'right' outcome. The task should be sufficiently representative that it allows the teacher to make generalizations about the pupil's skills that are being assessed. As most performance assessments are administered to a single or small group of pupils, it is important that some standard procedure for presenting the task to the pupils is developed.

In order to assess pupils' performance, the teacher needs to develop a *scoring rubric* that clearly lists those elements that the teacher is wanting to assess, such as attitudes, skills and cognitive processes. The fact that there is a clear list of descriptions of what is expected can be very useful in providing feedback to pupils for formative purposes (Borich, 2000; Brualdi, 1998; Elliott, 1995; Moskal, 2000; Roeber, 1996).

Performance assessments are by their nature somewhat subjective, which means that teacher bias can be a problem. On the other hand, the ability to measure behaviours in realistic contexts and to assess processes that cannot easily be measured on paper (e.g. pupils' cooperative behaviour) makes this form of assessment potentially very powerful. Preparing and executing a performance assessment is very time-consuming, however, which means that usually only a few assignments can be graded. Performance assessment thus gives great depth, but not much breadth in assessing pupils' performance (Sanders and Horn, 1995).

Portfolio assessment

While performance assessment gives a picture of the pupil at one particular point in time, *portfolio assessment* is designed to give a picture of a pupil's performance over a longer period of time, such as a school year, by collating a collection of pupil work. As well as the finished essays, exercises and other specimens of pupil work, portfolios should also include drafts, early ideas and some indication of the processes the pupil used to arrive at the finished work.

As with performance assessment, the goals of the portfolio and what needs to be included in it need to be carefully defined at the outset and clearly agreed with the pupil. The contents of the portfolio need to match the goals that have been set out, and the teacher needs to prepare the pupil to be able to complete the portfolio successfully. The teacher needs to prepare a scoring rubric that outlines what criteria make for good, bad or average performance on each predefined goal and for each draft and final product in the portfolio. Finally, these grades will need to be aggregated, for example by adding the scores and averaging them, or by weighting one aspect (e.g. final products, structure) higher than others (e.g. drafts, spelling) (Borich, 1996).

One of the advantages of portfolios is that they show not just how pupils think and the processes they use to get to certain results, but how they, and their work, have evolved over the year. The main disadvantages of portfolio assessment lie in the considerable amount of work this involves from both teacher and pupils, problems with establishing reliability of this assessment method and the high demands portfolio assessment places on pupils' self-motivation. As with performance assessment, teacher bias can occur (Madaus and O'Dwyer, 1999; Sanders and Horn, 1995).

Information-rich Schools

In view of the large amount of assessment conducted, it is often surprising how little data is used at the school level. It could, however, be beneficial if schools were to become 'data-rich organizations' using pupil data to inform a range of school and department-level decisions. If test data on a variety of measures, from teacher-made tests to standardized tests and other achievement measures, are centrally stored and accessed, teachers, heads and heads of department will be able to immediately collect information, for example on a child that is having problems in her/his class. The teacher will be able to see whether the child is having problems in other subjects, has reading difficulties based on scores on a reading test, has performed well in her previous school and in previous classes, has scored well on aptitude tests or has self-esteem or school commitment problems as measured by attitude tests. This will help the teacher diagnose the problem.

At the school level, data can be used to set pupils in different subjects, to identify pupils who are underperforming relative to their potential as measured by the aptitude tests, to identify pupils with reading problems and to identify problems in the performance of subgroups of pupils (such as ethnic groups). Data can be used to look at the relative performance of different departments and subjects using value-added systems.

In order for this to be possible, schools need to collect and store all data centrally on an accessible database and teachers need to be trained both in data management and interpretation.

Assessment for Learning

Assessment for learning is a term that has been developed in the UK to describe forms of assessment that have been found to impact directly on pupil achievement and learning outcomes. Assessment for learning involves using assessment in the classroom to raise pupils' achievement. It is based on the idea that pupils will improve most if they understand the aim of their learning, where they are in relation to this aim and how they can achieve the aim (or close the gap in their knowledge) (QCDA, 2009). Black and William's (1998) study 'Inside the Black Box' was the impetus towards developing this concept, in which the authors of the study were themselves instrumental.

The key finding of that study was that formative assessment could have a strong, positive impact on pupil performance, especially if particular feedback strategies were used. Feedback elements that can help improve pupil performance are:

- *giving written feedback* – rather than just giving marks, teachers should provide written comments on pupils' work and assignments, in particular comments that focus on precise ways pupils can improve their work. This

has been found to lead to significant improvement in pupil learning. Many authors suggest not giving any numerical feedback at all, and concentrating solely on written comments instead
- considering the *timing of feedback* – in one experiment, a time-consuming task gave the pupils an incentive to think carefully and this greater 'mindfulness' led to more learning. When feedback was given before pupils had had a chance to work on a problem, they learned less
- using what Black and William (1999) call '*scaffolded responses*' – where pupils were given only as much help from the teacher as they needed when they got stuck was found to be more effective than giving them the complete solution and then giving them a new problem to work on
- developing pupils' self-assessment skills – this can help them become more self-regulated and effective learners. For pupils to be able to do that, three elements need to be in place:

    - clear goals or targets for pupils
    - clear information on where they stand in relation to those targets
    - some understanding of how they can close the gap between where they are now and their targets.

  Peer marking, whereby pupils assess each other's work, is one way of doing this that has been effectively used in schools.

To be effective, assessment for learning needs to become a central part of classroom practice. It starts off with learning goals that are shared by pupils and teachers, and it is therefore of key importance that pupils are aware of the learning goals of a particular lesson or set of lessons. This can be helped by involving learners in the setting of the learning goals themselves. Assessment criteria need to be clear to the learner (and not just the teacher), and again need to be communicated to them. Pupils need to know what teachers are looking for in a particular piece of assessed work or assessment, and on what basis any judgements will be made. The key thing here is to provide learners with effective feedback on their performance. According to the QCDA (2009), teachers should:

- pinpoint the learner's strengths and advise on how to develop them
- be clear and constructive about any weaknesses and how they might be addressed
- provide opportunities for learners to improve upon their work.

Assessment for learning is effective in alleviating some of the negative effects of assessment, such as anxiety and low self-esteem. Because this type of assessment is mainly about comparing the pupil's present progress with that of her previous level, the possible negative effects of comparison with other pupils is lessened. Also, if assessment becomes an everyday part of classroom experience and learning, and is used to help the pupil, the performance anxiety that comes with traditional testing will diminish.

In some cases, introducing assessment for learning may require a cultural change in schools and education systems, especially where assessment has traditionally been mainly about selection and sorting of pupils into high- and low-ability streams, different types of schools, or different higher education institutions (Kennedy, 2006).

The key elements of assessment for learning are:

1. Use of effective questioning methods
2. Feedback on assessed work
3. Sharing learning goals
4. Peer and self-assessment
5. Use of assessment to plan learning.

We will discuss each of these in turn.

Use of effective questioning methods

The use of effective questioning methods is a part of assessment for learning, but as we have already discussed this in Chapter 3, we will not repeat this here. However, use of higher-order questions in particular has been found to help develop pupils' understanding of their own learning.

In many cases, tasks can be followed up by the teacher with questions aimed specifically at measuring learning. The teacher needs to use questions to provoke thinking, and McCallum (2000) suggests they follow an 'observe, wait, listen, question' sequence during teaching, especially by organizing small group activities they can observe.

Feedback on assessed work

One of the most important elements of assessment for learning is giving formative feedback on assessed work. As mentioned above, Black and Willliam's (1998) work found that providing written feedback was far more conducive to learning than just providing a mark. It is important that this feedback provides suggestions for improvement, but not the full solution. Feedback should act as a 'scaffold' that allows pupils to find the right solution themselves given their current state of knowledge and skills. Pupils should also be encouraged to find alternative solutions, and feedback should be provided over time on different steps pupils have taken towards finding that solution.

Providing feedback that compares a pupil's performance to their own previous level rather than to other pupils can help them to see their own learning and develop appropriate targets. This is another advantage of using written feedback rather than marks.

Sharing learning goals

As we mentioned in our discussion of direct instruction in Part 1 of this book, it is important to make sure that pupils understand the objectives of the lesson. We said there that teachers need to put the objectives up and explain them at the start of the lesson. In terms of linking these to assessment, it needs to be clear not just what the content of the lesson will be, but what they are expected to learn from the various activities done during the lesson.

Peer and self-assessment

Peer assessment refers to methods whereby pupils assess each other's work. This can be a very effective way of encouraging pupils to reflect on their own learning, especially within a context of collaborative small group work. Pupils will be given clear assessment criteria with which to look at other's work, and must be taught how to give formative and constructive feedback before doing this.

Self-assessment can also be a very effective way of getting pupils to reflect on their own learning, and there is some evidence linking increased use of self-assessment to improved academic achievement (Noonan and Duncan, 2005). Getting pupils to judge their own work on the basis of clear criteria can help them to reflect on their own performance, and develop their metacognitive skills. Again, this requires very clear and pupil-friendly criteria, and some training to help them to do this. McCallum (2000) suggests the following strategy for teaching pupils the necessary skills in this area. During class sessions, teachers could:

- clarify what is meant by self-assessment
- explain 'learning objectives'
- describe different self-assessment strategies emphasizing how these can aid learning
- inform pupils that self-assessment will become part of classroom life
- explain that the pupil's own assessment will form part of assessment conversations with the teacher and that these conversations will be helpful because the teacher and the pupil will be looking for the best route to improve learning.

Another method that can help develop pupils' learning strategies is asking them to look at examples of other pupils' work that does and does not meet the assessment criteria. Looking at different responses can help pupils understand the different approaches they could have taken to the task and what areas they still need to develop.

The plenary session at the end of a direct instruction lesson can be used to get the class as a whole to reflect on the learning that has (hopefully) occurred during the lesson. Clarke (1998–2000) suggests that teachers use a poster of self-assessment questions during the plenary as the prompt for this reflection.

Use of assessment to plan learning

Assessment for learning is not just about what pupils do, but also about the way that teachers themselves use assessment. Teachers need to use assessment as a key way of planning lessons, adapting them to the needs of pupils, and reteaching where problems persist. This means that in many ways assessment will guide instruction more strongly than an existing curriculum, as the implication here is clearly that where assessment points to particular learning needs, these need to be the focus of the next lesson. According to McCallum (2000), the implications are that if formative assessment is to be effective, teaching needs to be planned so that the goal of teaching is subordinated to the goal of determining children's level of achievement.

To do this effectively requires that students are assessed at the start of a unit of learning, so that the tasks and instruction can be adapted to where students are. Assessment needs to be regularly repeated, and instruction adapted to the results of this assessment.

Assessment can inform the development of individual learning plans that are adapted to the specific learning needs of the pupils, which can help to personalize learning. A key element of this is the setting of individual targets, which need to be ambitious if pupils are to achieve to their full capability, but must of course also be realistic, and therefore based on assessment data. This target-setting process needs to consist of both long-term year targets and ongoing shorter-term targets that are based on the results of ongoing assessment. A good system of tracking how individual pupils are doing is important to this, and has become increasingly easy to implement using ICT. The English education ministry provides a convenient list of the characteristics of an effective tracking system:

- Individual pupils' progress is tracked, together with that of cohorts and specific groups, using a range of performance measures including a combination of periodic teacher assessments and test results.
- Strengths and weaknesses are identified, supporting planning and intervention.
- Data is collected on a regular basis, typically termly, and shared with staff and the pupils themselves.
- Pupils have regular opportunities to discuss their progress. Teachers actively involve pupils in setting and reviewing their progress towards their targets.
- Teaching programmes, intervention programmes and revision programmes are adjusted in the light of the progress the pupils are making.

- Parents and carers receive regular updates on their child's progress so that they can provide additional support and encouragement if necessary.
- Pupil progress data are managed through a school-wide system that all teachers can access.
- The process operates across the whole school to ensure consistency and is regularly evaluated by senior and middle leaders to ensure that the needs of all pupils are being met.
  (DCSF, 2009).

When looking at the types of assessment mentioned earlier in this chapter, we can see that assessment for learning requires a lot of use of teacher-made assessment and less formal methods, with a lot of use of questioning methods as an assessment technique. Standardized tests can be useful in assessing the level of pupils at the start of the school year in order to help to adapt instruction and individual learning plans. End of term and year tests are more useful for summative than for formative purposes.

Summary

Assessment is one of the main parts of the teacher's job, taking up almost a third of teacher time.

Formative assessment is designed to inform the teacher about their pupils' performance, prior knowledge and skills, and this information is then used to plan lessons or remediation to improve pupils' performance. Summative evaluation is meant to give a picture of how well a pupil (or group of pupils) has done over a time period on a set of learning goals in a particular subject.

Standardized tests have been developed by professional test developers and have been designed to produce reliable results in a variety of settings. There are two main types of standardized tests. Norm-referenced tests compare the performance of pupils to each other. Criterion-referenced tests assess whether pupils have reached a predefined level of mastery in a particular subject or topic.

Standardized tests should be reliable (dependable, giving the same result over time), valid (measure what they are supposed to measure) and recently designed or normed. The main advantages of standardized tests lie in their good psychometric properties, their easy scoring and use, the possibility of comparison to national standards and samples of pupils, and the breadth of coverage they can provide. Disadvantages include a lack of fit to the curriculum and a lack of flexibility.

(Continued)

(Continued)

Teacher-made tests can be made to link closely to the curriculum as covered in a particular classroom and can be tailored to the level of pupils in a particular class.

Multiple-choice questions have the advantage of being quick and unambiguous to mark and allow a large breadth of coverage as they can be answered quickly. They don't allow assessment of processes, however, and are often less suited to assessment of higher-level cognitive thinking. Open questions allow pupils to write down their thought processes and working out, and allow greater depth of coverage (but less breadth). Teacher bias and lack of standardization of scoring can be a problem with this type of test.

Recently, authentic assessment has gained in popularity. This type of assessment aims to study performance in natural circumstances rather than in the contrived pencil-and-paper test situation.

Assessment for learning is a term given to assessment practices that have been found to positively affect pupil learning. These include using comments rather than grades in feedback to pupils, using scaffolded feedback rather than telling pupils the answer and going on to the next task, and involving pupils themselves in assessing their own work.

Reflective Questions

1. What type of test (standardized, alternative . . .) would you prefer to use to assess pupils? Why?
2. Do you think portfolio assessment could replace the use of testing in accountability systems? Why/why not?
3. Do you think authentic assessment methods are truly 'authentic'?
4. What types of questions could a teacher ask to effectively assess learning?
5. In your experience of teaching and classrooms, can you think of any particularly good examples of assessment for learning? What did they look like?
6. Can you think of some examples of particularly helpful feedback you have come across as a learner? What made this feedback effective?

CHAPTER 21

CROSS-CURRICULAR TEACHING

Key Points

In this chapter, you will learn about:

- the key characteristics of cross-curricular teaching
- the advantages and disadvantages of cross-curricular teaching
- how to implement effective cross-curricular teaching
- challenges to cross-curricular teaching.

Introduction

Cross-curricular teaching is a method where teaching doesn't happen through the traditional subject-based lessons, but through topics that span boundaries between subjects. Cross-curricular teaching involves a conscious effort to apply knowledge, principles and/or values to more than one academic discipline simultaneously. The disciplines may be related through a central theme, issue, problem, process, topic or experience (Jacobs, 1989). The organizational structure of interdisciplinary/cross-curricular teaching is called a theme, thematic unit or unit, which is a framework with goals/outcomes that specify what students are expected to learn as a result of the experiences and lessons that are a part of the unit.

Cross-curricular and thematic teaching has a long history in education. In England, for example, the Plowden report in the 1960s led a move towards more thematic teaching in the late 1960s and 1970s. However, a perceived lack of rigour and a lack of basic skills in pupils led the government to introduce a subject-based National Curriculum in the late 1980s. However, schools have recently been given more freedom to experiment with the curriculum and with cross-curricular approaches (West and Muijs, 2009). For example, a recent report commissioned by the government stated that schools need to:

> recognise the continuing importance of subjects and the essential knowledge, skills and understanding they represent. As indicated in the interim report, the essential knowledge and skills all children should be taught, particularly in the middle and later phases of primary education, can be organised through clearly visible subject disciplines, such as history, geography and physical education. Subjects will be complemented by worthwhile and challenging cross-curricular studies that provide ample opportunities for children to use and apply their subject knowledge and skills to deepen understanding. (Rose Report, 2009, Executive Summary, Section 11)

The latter part of this statement clearly points to an encouragement for schools to engage in cross-curricular work alongside traditional subjects.

The main advantages of cross-curricular learning are seen as the fact that it provides a more realistic learning environment, as in the real world problems frequently need to be solved through recourse to insights and methods from different disciplines; and the opportunity it allows for independent exploration of a topic, and thus for learner-led approaches that can potentially lead to more metacognitive learning. Such topic-led approaches can also be engaging to pupils. Cross-curricular teaching can help pupils recognize the links between curriculum subjects. Emphasizing links between subjects helps children to make sense of what they are learning. Some proponents of cross-curricular learning also make the rather dubious claim that it helps learning because learning depends on being able to make connections between prior knowledge and experiences and new information and experiences (e.g. DfES, 2003) but, while the latter is true as we saw in Chapter 1, this does not necessarily imply that cross-curricular teaching is the best way to make these connections.

Critics point to a possible loss of rigour, a hit-and-miss approach to acquiring essential skills and the risk of inequitable outcomes, as allowing greater pupil discovery tends to advantage those from home backgrounds with greater educational resources.

Cross-curricular teaching typically takes the form of the exploration of a particular topic, through tasks aimed at discovery by pupils. Depending on the topic, one subject may be the 'lead subject', with elements of other subjects attached; in some cases, two subjects may equally lead on a topic, while in a third type of work, subjects form a strand of a more general overarching topic, such as 'the urban environment'.

The Research Evidence on Cross-Curricular Teaching

As mentioned above, the principle of cross-curricular teaching has gone through phases of popularity and unpopularity. In the late 1960s and 1970s, this method gained greatly in popularity, and many educators pioneered approaches in schools. However, a lot of this cross-curricular work was somewhat unfocused with little attention to learning goals and outcomes, and was heavily criticized as such by a report from the English inspectorate (HMI) in 1978, which was the precursor for the return to single-subject teaching mentioned above.

Overall, the research findings on the effectiveness of this type of approach are rather mixed.

An overview of research on integrated teaching of maths and science (Czerniak et al., 1999a) concluded that the research evidence in these areas at least was rather inconclusive, and that there was no real evidence that cross-curricular teaching was either more or less effective than subject-based methods.

In one review of research on Problem-Based Learning (PBL) approaches in secondary schools (this is a form of cross-curricular learning based on interdisciplinary approaches to solving real-life problems), Expeditionary Learning schools, where cross-curricular PBL approaches are linked to Outward Bound learning, showed strong gains in performance on standardized tests, with improvements being typically greater than the average for the US states in which they were based. These schools were also found to have a positive impact on teacher expectations of students and on student motivation. Co-nect, another US school reform programme that widely employs cross-curricular approaches, was also found to have positive effects in most but not all cohorts. There is also evidence that programmes which have translated PBL approaches from university to high-school level may be effective in improving achievement and problem-solving skills. However, the review also points to the challenges faced by schools in implementing these approaches, such as maintaining motivation for sustained investigation among pupils and pupils' lack of social skills. It was also found that some students have difficulties in benefiting from self-directed situations, especially in complex projects. Some pupils may have difficulties in directing investigations and managing time. The approach is also demanding for teachers, who have to engage in high levels of monitoring of learning and behaviour (Thomas, 2000). Teachers themselves, however, tend to be positive with regards to the possibilities of cross-curricular teaching, though they worry about watering down the curriculum and about the demands on their time

(Czerniak et al., 1999b). A recent study in Hong Kong similarly saw teachers generally positive, but found that they felt frustrated by the workload involved in cross-curricular teaching and were unclear as to how to assess learning in this context (Leung, 2004).

Studies that compare direct instruction to cross-curricular approaches also show conflicting and inconclusive results (Anderson, 2002). An issue that has been found to occur where curricula, such as maths and science, are fully integrated with one another, is that the scope of what is taught is limited because only those topics that can be integrated are included (Czerniak et al., 1999b).

A recent qualitative study in Germany where science and maths were integrated in a cross-curricular theme that used scientific experiments as the basis for the teaching of mathematical concepts, found that the scientific activities and their connection with reality led to valuable discussions on the mathematical concepts. Students were able to make the connections between the phenomenon and the mathematical model (Hofer and Beckman, 2008).

These findings therefore suggest that cross-curricular teaching can be an effective approach, but that it does depend on the incorporation of a range of supports to help students learn how to learn. Furthermore, it is also clearly not a method suited for all situations or parts of learning, and is best integrated into a varied approach to teaching that includes subject-oriented direct instruction and cooperative learning.

Effective Cross-Curricular Approaches

Much of the best cross-curricular teaching happens when a concept can be explored through pupil-centred activities that can take place over a longer period, such as a week or two weeks.

Cross-curricular work is found in a wide range of subjects, such as work combining maths, physics and biology, or English, drama and art. Some interesting projects combine less immediately obvious areas, like science and history. Historical approaches can be used, for example, to highlight ethical issues and changes in methodologies and insights in science, leading to a more rounded understanding of scientific method and concepts. Data-handling skills learnt in maths can be applied in geography and science, and experiencing and describing processes in geography and science can offer children relevant experiences and enhanced understanding when learning how to write explanations in English (DfES, 2003).

Doing a cross-curricular topic requires a fair amount of planning, and the following elements need to be thought through first:

1. What are the key learning goals that I want pupils to grasp?

If this is not carefully kept in mind in the planning stages, there is a risk that the activity can become a bit of a free-for-all, with uncertain learning outcomes. Therefore, you need to plan both what the learning goals are and how they will be achieved. It is a good idea to build milestones and events that will lead to the acquisition of those learning goals into these plans, and to carefully map when and what learning goals have been achieved. Working with key concepts can be helpful here, for example the concept of evolution in science, which can then be divided into its constituent parts around which activities can be organized, such as recognizing patterns of difference and similarity. These can then be taught thematically, by for example getting pupils to research Darwin's voyages, looking at his methods, and studying reactions and consequences, thus integrating science, history and religious education. When designing a cross-curricular activity, we need to make sure that we focus on a limited number of key learning goals, so the work doesn't become bitty and diffuse.

2. How does the topic I want to explore fit in with the broader curriculum?

It is important to keep in mind how our topic fits in with the curriculum more generally. In particular, it is useful to consider how much time is spent on achieving the learning objectives, and what other learning relevant to the curriculum may occur whilst studying the topic. One risk with cross-curricular teaching is that exploring topics may take time and that may lead to a lack of coverage of other important curriculum topics, and we need to plan carefully to ensure that this doesn't happen.

3. Does the topic lend itself to cross-curricular teaching?

Some topics lend themselves to cross-curricular work, while some don't. It is therefore important to look at which topics seem to naturally lend themselves to this, and will make sense to pupils as a cross-curricular theme. Don't try to shoehorn topics into a cross-curricular approach for the sake of using this approach. Where cross-curricular work can't be made to fit, this is a clear indication that this topic is best taught through a single subject. Cross-curricular approaches must contribute to learning, and that must be the case for all subject areas involved. Therefore, getting pupils to draw a picture about the topic in art may not be a particularly useful way of doing cross-curricular work if it doesn't move their learning in aspects of art itself forward.

4. What vocabulary do pupils need?

Most subjects work to a large extent through language. This is both an advantage and a problem for cross-curricular working. The advantage is that this allows us to look for common language as a starting point for doing cross-curricular work. The disadvantage is that each subject tends to have its own jargon and technical vocabulary, and we must make sure that pupils understand the suitable vocabulary for the fields the cross-curricular theme encompasses. This can be confusing, as similar terms may have somewhat different meanings in different fields (think of the term 'significant', for example), and similar concepts may be called different things. These aspects may therefore require some direct teaching during cross-curricular work.

5. What is my role as a teacher?

When planning the schedule, the teacher's role should also be considered. At times, the teacher's role is to facilitate, at others to provide explicit instruction, and sometimes simply to serve as a resource. Activities may be directed by the teacher or, occasionally, by the students themselves. Whether an activity is more effective with whole-class, small-group or individual instruction depends upon the topic, the nature of the activity and, of course, the abilities and interests of the students.

6. How am I going to assess learning?

As we saw in Chapter 20, assessment is an essential part of effective teaching and learning. This is equally true for cross-curricular teaching as for single-subject approaches. The mistake that is sometimes made in project work is to assume that doing something means that pupils have learnt. This is not necessarily the case – the activity itself is not the learning. Formative assessment for learning approaches needs to be built into cross-curricular work every bit as much as it does into any other aspect of teaching, and summative forms of assessment following the topic can be important to test for learning as well (Meijer, 2007).

An interesting example of a cross-curricular programme has been developed by the Nuffield Curriculum Programme in Science for Key Stage 3 (the first three years of secondary schooling in England). They have developed a cross-curricular approach around sustainable living that integrates maths, science and design and technology. The project starts with a session where students are introduced to the concepts of recycling and consumption, where the natural process of regeneration is contrasted with the model of production–consumption–dumping that has become common in our society, and to the learning and learning activities they will be doing. In a second activity, pupils learn about farms and forests and the production of food. This activity is led by the science department. In the third activity, led by the maths department, pupils think about recycling and waste; collecting, processing, and presenting data about this to others. In a third activity, led by design and technology, pupils learn about and reflect on the materials and processes used in producing familiar products. They reflect on where things come from, whether alternatives are possible and explore some of these alternatives. The final activity involves pupils working collaboratively around a problem of their choice, using a collaborative learning framework of the type we discussed in Chapter 4. They then present their work, demonstrating what they have learnt and what skills they have acquired (Nuffield Curriculum Programme, 2009).

Challenges in Cross-Curricular Teaching

One of the key challenges in doing cross-curricular work may be getting teachers from different subjects to work together, particularly in secondary schools. Subject departments tend to have their own specific cultures, pedagogies and goals. Bringing together a suitable team to engage in developing a cross-curricular activity therefore requires positive relations between departments, shared goals and the opportunities to plan and teach jointly. It is clear that to be able to do this, support from senior management is important, as they will have an important role in facilitating these activities. If successful, one of the useful learning points for teachers comes from learning about and from the different pedagogical approaches in different subjects, but compromise may be necessary in developing an approach that suits all.

Another challenge is time. Cross-curricular teaching is time- and labour-intensive. It takes extra time to replace lessons based strictly on textbooks or workbooks with something new, have meetings with other teachers to coordinate the activities and work on timetabling and planning.

As mentioned above, keeping in mind clear learning objectives and assessing whether these have been learnt are crucial if the activity is to actually make a clear contribution to learning.

A further challenge is to assess the readiness of pupils to participate in these tasks. In particular, motivation to undertake these prolonged tasks and lack of social skills may be a problem. As with cooperative learning approaches, some prior training in the processes involved may be necessary.

Summary

Cross-curricular teaching is an approach where teaching doesn't happen through the traditional subject-based lessons, but through topics that span boundaries between subjects.

(Continued)

(Continued)

The main advantages of cross-curricular learning are seen as the fact that it provides a more realistic learning environment, as in the real world problems frequently need to be solved through recourse to insights and methods from different disciplines; and the opportunities it allows for independent exploration of a topic, and thus for learner-led approaches that can potentially lead to more metacognitive learning. Such topic-led approaches can also be engaging to pupils. Cross-curricular teaching can help pupils recognize the links between curriculum subjects. Overall, the research findings on the effectiveness of this type of approach are rather mixed, however.

Doing a cross-curricular topic requires a fair amount of planning, and the following elements need to be thought through first:

1. What are the key learning goals that I want pupils to grasp?
2. How does the topic I want to explore fit in with the broader curriculum?
3. Does the topic lend itself to cross-curricular learning?
4. What vocabulary do pupils need?
5. What is my role as a teacher?
6. How am I going to assess learning?

Key challenges include collaboration with other teachers, finding the time to plan and implement cross-curricular teaching and making sure pupils possess the necessary skills to engage in cross-curricular teaching.

Reflective Questions

1. How would you build assessment for learning into a cross-curricular topic?
2. Which topics in your subject do you think lend themselves to cross-curricular teaching? Why? What benefits would this have?
3. Which topics in your subject don't lend themselves to cross-curricular teaching? Why not?
4. Can you remember any cross-curricular teaching you have done or experienced? How successful was this? What made it successful or less successful?

CHAPTER 22

PEER CLASSROOM OBSERVATION

Key Points

In this chapter, you will learn about:

- why classroom observation can be a powerful staff development tool
- the main types of classroom observation
- some examples of the use of general and specific classroom observation instruments
- factors that determine the effectiveness of classroom observation
- the use of classroom observation in educational research.

Introduction

In many countries, teaching has traditionally taken place 'behind closed doors'. While collegial discussion between teachers has always existed in the staff room, teachers have rarely observed colleagues teach. In many schools, even management has traditionally not observed teachers teach. Recently, this has changed significantly, however. Outside agencies, usually school inspection bodies sent out to observe lessons for purposes of accountability by state or national government, have invaded the classroom, leading managers of schools to start to observe their teachers as a quality control measure. This is good management practice, as seeing what is actually going on in classrooms will allow management to put in place tailored interventions aimed at improving teaching. Managers will be able to see whether new programmes and approaches are being implemented effectively, and whether teaching is consistent within (and across) subjects.

Classroom Observation and School Improvement

Observation by outside agencies

Outsiders observing lessons can give a wider perspective, having observed teaching in a variety of schools and classrooms, and should be able to give useful comparative information to teachers. However, this type of observation, especially high-stakes observation by school inspection agencies, can be somewhat problematic. Teacher stress is likely to be considerable and feedback based on observations of just one (or, in some cases, even just a part of one) not necessarily representative lesson is not necessarily valid.

Unsurprisingly, where observations are likely to have practical consequences for the school and teachers, such as in the Ofsted inspections in the UK, observed lessons can become 'performances' that are carefully set up for the benefit of the observer in an attempt to incorporate all the criteria used by the inspection agency. It is clear that the formative advantages of observations conducted under these circumstances will be very limited.

Observation by school management

These problems can exist to a greater or lesser extent when observations are done by the school management, depending on relations in the school and the goal of the observation (e.g. controlling teacher quality or staff development).

Peer observation

While classroom observation by management (and sometimes by inspectors) can be effective, it is a shame that in many schools this has become the dominant form of classroom observation, largely 'crowding out' observation by peers of each other's teaching.

Peer observation can be highly beneficial to both observer and observed. For the observed teacher, peer observation, which should, if done properly, occur without the pressures of management and inspection observations, can provide highly useful information on her strengths and weaknesses, which should be able to help her improve her teaching. For the observer, watching colleagues teach can provide ideas to use in his or her own classroom, and help reflect on the strengths and weaknesses in his or her own practice.

Peer classroom observation can also encourage discussion on classroom practice between teachers. Both peer and management observations can be used to help prepare teachers for external observations by, for example, school inspection bodies. However, while peer observation is the most useful form of observation for formative professional development, using it for public accountability or performance assessment purposes is likely to be less effective, as some research has shown that the ratings between colleagues vary strongly, correlations being only .26. in one study. Peer ratings have also been found to show a positive bias, with peers generally rating colleagues more positively than neutral observers (Centra, 1975, 1979).

A particularly interesting form of classroom observation is the use of 'research lessons' in Japan. In that country, teachers will regularly present research lessons to colleagues, in which they demonstrate some innovative practice in the subject they are teaching. Colleagues and the teacher will then discuss the lesson. These lessons are very well prepared beforehand, with teachers participating in this preparation. Usually, the whole school faculty is invited to attend. Some schools are designated 'research schools' in a particular subject, and will present research lessons to teachers from schools in the area or in some cases nationally (Lewis and Tsuchida, 1997).

Classroom Observation Instruments

To be effective, classroom observation needs to be done using some kind of standard instrument on which the observer notes those things s/he is meant to observe. This is essential in view of the complexity of the classroom and the many activities occurring in it, which makes it unrealistic to try and observe (and remember) everything. Therefore, at the outset, a number of decisions need to be made. Who is going to be observed? The teacher or the pupils, or maybe a classroom auxiliary? What is going to be observed? The overall quality of the lesson? Teachers' questioning behaviour? Classroom management? Whether or not boys and girls participate equally? Once these decisions have been made, an observation instrument needs to be chosen that fits in with these goals. All aspects of teaching can form the object of classroom observation.

Behavioural and value-oriented instruments

One of the main distinctions in classroom observation is that between behaviourally oriented observation instruments and instruments that require value judgements from the observer (*value-oriented instruments*).

Behavioural instruments are designed to look at the occurrence or not of often very specific behaviours without passing global judgements on whether the teaching or the behaviour observed were 'good' or otherwise.

At the opposite end, *value-oriented instruments* aim to provide global value judgements on large parts of the lesson.

Many instruments fall in between these two extremes. When instruments require too much subjective judgement from the observer (such as when observers need to judge the overall quality of the lesson on a scale from 'excellent' to 'inadequate'), they can become highly problematic. The reliability of these judgements will be hard to establish even with extended training of the observers, and the meaning of the judgements (what is 'good') will make this type of observation hard to use formatively. For professional development purposes, this kind of global measure also provides too little detail for teachers to use to improve their practice.

High and low inference measures

A related distinction is that between high and low inference measures.

Low inference measures require the minimum of judgement from the observer. An example of this is to count the number of times a teacher asks a question or to count the number of minutes that the teacher waits for the pupil to answer after asking a question.

High inference measures require more judgement from the observer. An example of this is 'the teacher gave clear explanations'. The observer needs to make a judgement on whether explanations were clear, and ultimately what 'clear' means in this case. High inference scales are often rating scales and will require training of the observer on the meaning of the items (e.g. 'behaviour has occurred frequently' to 'behaviour did not occur').

General and specific instruments

A final distinction is that between *general instruments*, which aim to look at a wide range of teaching behaviours, and *specific instruments*, which look at one particular part of teaching such as classroom management. One possible sequence in peer classroom observation is to start off with a relatively general measure and then, based on what that has revealed with respect to the main problems, proceed to more detailed schedules looking at those particular areas.

Some Examples of Classroom Observation Instruments

Global classroom observation schedules aim to look at the totality of classroom practices of a particular teacher. This can help to pinpoint general strong and weak points of a teacher's teaching which can form the basis of a conversation about suggested improvements or professional development activities. Alternatively, one can move on from the findings of this observation to observing certain areas (such as questioning or classroom management) in more detail using a specific instrument. As an example we will discuss two global classroom observation instruments in this chapter, QAIT and MECORS.

MECORS

The MECORS Mathematics Enhancement Classroom Observation Record System (see Figure 22.1)instrument (Schaffer et al., 1998) was designed for the evaluation of a primary mathematics programme in the UK, but most items refer to more general teaching characteristics and the scale can therefore easily be adapted to other subjects. The scale was inspired by the SSOS and Virgilio scales (Schaffer et al., 1998). It is a high inference scale that contains both qualitative and quantitative components.

The first part of the instrument is the actual observation sheet. This is filled in during the observation. Every time the teacher does a particular activity, the observer writes down the time that activity starts. On the left, the observer fills in a code indicating whether teaching of that activity was whole-class interactive (direct instruction), whole-class lecture, individual review and practice, assessment or classroom management (i.e. changes from one part of the classroom to the other, distribution of worksheets and purely administrative activities such as collecting school trip money). If the activity involves cooperative group work, the code b is added. Observers then write down exactly what is occurring during that part of the lesson in the mid-section of the sheet.

The observer also needs to count the number of pupils on task or off task every five minutes – a method known as 'time sampling'. The results are filled in on the right-hand side of the sheet. Only pupils visibly off task (who are, for example, looking outside, fiddling with displays or talking about yesterday's television with peers) are rated off task, as the assumption is that observers cannot look inside the heads of pupils. The category 'waiting' refers to pupils waiting for the teacher to help them. An average on-task rate of over 80 per cent is adequate, while over 90 per cent is good in most cases.

The second section of the instrument is the actual rating scale. This consists of 59 items, based on the effective teaching research discussed in Chapters 1 to 6.

Observers are asked to rate whether behaviours occurred rarely, occasionally, often, frequently or constantly. Training is necessary to ensure that observers rate consistently. When trained, observers have been found to produce reliable ratings (inter-observer reliability being high) (Muijs and Reynolds, 2000b). This scale can be used to highlight general strengths and weaknesses of teachers, although the level of detail may be insufficient for specific interventions. Once problems have been identified using this scale, one can use a more fine-grained and specific scale to look at the problem area.

QAIT

One of the instruments that MECORS is based on is QAIT (the acronym refers to the different elements of the scale: Quality of instruction, Appropriate level of interaction, Incentive and Time, (see Figure 22.2)). his instrument is similar to MECORS in that it consists of two parts – a qualitative part and a rating scale. The qualitative part is similar to MECORS, the only difference being that there are 15 instead of 7 activity codes (teacher presentation of content, recitation/discussion, directions for assignment, small group work, tests, checking, individual seatwork, pair or group seatwork, pupil presentations, procedural behavioural presentation, administrative routines, transitions, non-academic activities, waiting time and discipline). The items in the rating scales are given in Figure 22.3.

This scale has been successfully used in international research, supporting its cross-cultural validity (Schaffer et al., 1994). As can be seen in Figure 22.3, this instrument highlights some different aspects to the MECORS scale. The scale is generally somewhat higher inference than MECORS, requiring more observer judgement.

There are numerous other general classroom observation scales available, such as Virgilio, SSOS and the Classroom Observation Instrument, and it may be necessary to adapt one or a number of these scales to the purposes of the observation and the teaching practices prevalent in the school or school system (Schaffer et al., 1994).

Once a general classroom observation instrument has highlighted areas that could be improved, it might be useful to follow up using a more fine-grained instrument to look at that particular area. Alternatively, it could be that one has made a decision beforehand to look at a particular part of teaching in the school.

An 'effective questioning' scale

An example of a more specific rating scale is the following scale (see Figure 22.1) for looking at effective questioning:

Uses Classroom Management Techniques

1. Rules and consequences are clearly understood	1	2	3	4	5	na
2. The teacher starts a lesson on time (within one minute)	1	2	3	4	5	na
3. The teacher uses time during class transitions effectively	1	2	3	4	5	na
4. The teacher takes care that tasks/materials are ready and papers and materials are collected and distributed effectively	1	2	3	4	5	na
5. There are limited disruptions in the class	1	2	3	4	5	na

Maintains Appropriate Classroom Behaviour

6. The teacher uses a reward system to manage pupil behaviour	1	2	3	4	5	na
7. The teacher corrects behaviour immediately	1	2	3	4	5	na
8. The teacher corrects behaviour accurately	1	2	3	4	5	na
9. The teacher corrects behaviour constructively	1	2	3	4	5	na
10. The teacher monitors the entire classroom	1	2	3	4	5	na

Focuses and Maintains Attention on Lesson

11. The teacher clearly states objectives/purposes of the lesson	1	2	3	4	5	na
12. The teacher checks for prior knowledge	1	2	3	4	5	na
13. The teacher presents material accurately	1	2	3	4	5	na
14. The teacher presents material clearly	1	2	3	4	5	na
15. The teacher gives detailed directions and explanations	1	2	3	4	5	na
16. The teacher emphasizes key points of the lesson	1	2	3	4	5	na
17. The teacher has an academic focus	1	2	3	4	5	na
18. The teacher uses a brisk pace	1	2	3	4	5	na

Provides Pupils with Review and Practice

19. The teacher clearly explains tasks	1	2	3	4	5	na
20. The teacher offers effective assistance to individuals/groups	1	2	3	4	5	na
21. The teacher checks for understanding	1	2	3	4	5	na
22. The teacher or pupils summarize the lesson	1	2	3	4	5	na
23. The teacher reteaches if error rate is high	1	2	3	4	5	na
24. The teacher is approachable for pupils with problems	1	2	3	4	5	na

FIGURE 22.1. The MECORS (Mathematics Enhancement Classroom Observation Record) rating scale

(Continued)

(Continued)

Demonstrates Skills in Questioning

25. The teacher uses a high frequency of questions	1	2	3	4	5	na
26. The teacher asks academic questions	1	2	3	4	5	na
27. The teacher asks open-ended questions	1	2	3	4	5	na
28. The teacher probes further when responses are incorrect	1	2	3	4	5	na
29. The teacher elaborates on answers	1	2	3	4	5	na
30. The teacher asks pupils to explain how they reached their solution	1	2	3	4	5	na
31. Pupils are asked for more than one solution	1	2	3	4	5	na
32. The teacher uses appropriate wait time between questions and responses	1	2	3	4	5	na
33. The teacher notes pupils' mistakes	1	2	3	4	5	na
34. The teacher guides pupils through errors	1	2	3	4	5	na
35. The teacher clears up misconceptions	1	2	3	4	5	na
36. The teacher gives immediate academic feedback	1	2	3	4	5	na
37. The teacher gives accurate academic feedback	1	2	3	4	5	na
38. The teacher gives positive academic feedback	1	2	3	4	5	na

Demonstrates MEP Strategies

39. The teacher uses realistic problems and examples	1	2	3	4	5	na
40. The teacher encourages/teaches pupils to use a variety of problem-solving strategies	1	2	3	4	5	na
41. The teacher uses correct mathematical language	1	2	3	4	5	na
42. The teacher encourages pupils to use correct mathematical language	1	2	3	4	5	na
43. The teacher allows pupils to use their own problem-solving strategies	1	2	3	4	5	na
44. The teacher implements a quick-fire mental questions strategy	1	2	3	4	5	na
45. The teacher connects new material to previously learnt material	1	2	3	4	5	na
46. The teacher connects new material to other areas of mathematics	1	2	3	4	5	na

Demonstrates a Variety of Teaching Methods

47. The teacher uses a variety of explanations that differ in complexity	1	2	3	4	5	na
48. The teacher uses a variety of instructional methods	1	2	3	4	5	na
49. The teacher uses manipulative materials/instructional aides/resources (e.g. number lines, coins)	1	2	3	4	5	na

Establishes a Positive Classroom Climate

50. The teacher communicates high expectations for pupils	1	2	3	4	5	na
51. The teacher exhibits personal enthusiasm	1	2	3	4	5	na
52. The teacher displays a positive tone	1	2	3	4	5	na
53. The teacher encourages pupil interaction and communication	1	2	3	4	5	na
54. The teacher conveys genuine concern for pupils (empathic, understanding, warm, friendly)	1	2	3	4	5	na
55. The teacher knows and uses pupil names	1	2	3	4	5	na
56. The teacher displays pupils' work in the classroom (ample amount, attractively displayed, current)	1	2	3	4	5	na
57. The teacher prepares an inviting and cheering classroom	1	2	3	4	5	na

Key 1 = behaviour rarely observed
2 = behaviour occasionally observed
3 = behaviour often observed
4 = behaviour frequently observed
5 = behaviour consistently observed
na = not applicable

	Unlike this class				Like this class
I Quality of Instruction					
A. Lessons make sense to pupils. The teacher:					
1. Organizes information in an orderly way	1	2	3	4	5
2. Notes transitions to new topics	1	2	3	4	5
3. Uses many vivid images and examples	1	2	3	4	5
4. Frequently restates essential principles	1	2	3	4	5
B. Lessons relate to pupils' background. The teacher:					
1. Uses devices such as advanced organizers	1	2	3	4	5
2. Reminds pupils of previously learnt material	1	2	3	4	5
C. Teacher exhibits enthusiasm	1	2	3	4	5
D. Teacher shows a sense of humour	1	2	3	4	5
E. Teacher clearly specifies objectives of the lesson. The teacher:					
1. Conducts formal and/or informal assessments	1	2	3	4	5
2. Provides immediate and correct feedback	1	2	3	4	5
F. The teacher uses an appropriate pace to cover content	1	2	3	4	5
II Appropriate Level of Instruction					
A. Instructional strategies match pupils' abilities. The teacher:					
1. Accommodates pupils' level of prior knowledge	1	2	3	4	5
2. Accommodates pupils' different learning rates	1	2	3	4	5
B. Grouping strategies enable pupils to work together or alone. The teacher:					
1. Uses in-class ability grouping	1	2	3	4	5
2. Has a class that is homogeneous in ability	1	2	3	4	5
3. Bases instruction on mastery of skills and/or concepts	1	2	3	4	5
4. Uses individualized instruction	1	2	3	4	5
5. Uses cooperative learning arrangement	1	2	3	4	5
III Incentive					
A. Teacher arouses pupils' curiosity by:					
1. Presenting surprising demonstrations	1	2	3	4	5
2. Relating topics to pupils' lives	1	2	3	4	5

FIGURE 22.2 The QAIT rating scale

(Continued)

(Continued)

	Unlike this class				Like this class
3. Allowing pupils to discover information	1	2	3	4	5
4. Presenting intrinsically interesting material	1	2	3	4	5
B. Teacher uses extrinsic academic incentives, such as:					
1. Praise and feedback	1	2	3	4	5
2. Accountability	1	2	3	4	5
3. Homework checks	1	2	3	4	5
4. Waiting for responses	1	2	3	4	5
5. Guiding partial responses	1	2	3	4	5
6. Tokens and rewards	1	2	3	4	5
7. Communicating high expectations	1	2	3	4	5
8. Small groups with individual incentives	1	2	3	4	5
9. Pupils encourage one another to achieve	1	2	3	4	5
10. Group contingencies	1	2	3	4	5
C. Teacher uses extrinsic behavioural incentives such as:					
1. Praise	1	2	3	4	5
2. Tokens and rewards for improvement	1	2	3	4	5
3. Group contingencies	1	2	3	4	5
D. Teacher provides instruction appropriate for pupil abilities:					
1. Effort by the pupil leads to success	1	2	3	4	5
IV Time					
A. Allocated time					
1. Necessary time is allocated for instruction	1	2	3	4	5
B. Engaged rates					
1. Teacher uses effective management	1	2	3	4	5
2. Pupils attend to lessons	1	2	3	4	5

	Like this class				Unlike this class
1. The teacher asks a high number of questions	5	4	3	2	1
2. The teacher uses factual recall questions	5	4	3	2	1
3. The teacher uses higher-order questions	5	4	3	2	1
4. The teacher asks open-ended questions	5	4	3	2	1
5. The teacher asks closed questions	5	4	3	2	1
6. The teacher asks product questions	5	4	3	2	1
7. The teacher asks process questions	5	4	3	2	1
8. The teacher acknowledges correct responses	5	4	3	2	1
9. The teacher praises pupils who give the right answer	5	4	3	2	1
10. The teacher acknowledges incorrect answers	5	4	3	2	1
11. The teacher criticizes pupils who give incorrect answers	5	4	3	2	1
12. The teacher prompts the pupil when the answer is incorrect	5	4	3	2	1
13. The teacher gives verbal prompts before going on to gestural or physical prompts	5	4	3	2	1
14. The teacher acknowledges correct part of partially correct answers	5	4	3	2	1
15. The teacher prompts the same pupil to answer incorrect part correctly	5	4	3	2	1
16. The teacher uses an appropriate wait time after asking a question	5	4	3	2	1
17. The teacher only moves on to the next step once pupils have demonstrated mastery over the topic during questioning	5	4	3	2	1
18. The teacher makes sure all pupils are given the chance to answer questions	5	4	3	2	1
19. The teacher makes sure pupils don't shout out answers	5	4	3	2	1
20. The teacher allows pupils to ask questions themselves	5	4	3	2	1
21. Pupils freely volunteer answers during the lesson	5	4	3	2	1

FIGURE 22.3 High inference rating scale (based on effective interactive teaching behaviours – see Chapter 4)

Using low inference measures

Alternatively, rather than using a rating scale, one could use low inference measures to look at particular behaviours.

For example, if one wanted to look at the involvement of boys and girls in an interactive classroom, one could count the number of questions directed at boys and girls, measure the time boys and girls were talking during interactive sessions or discussions, or count the number of higher-order questions directed at the two genders.

From use of a general classroom observation instrument, one could have concluded that classroom climate was not as good as it might be. One could then decide to look at particular behaviours, such as types of praise and criticism or expressions of low and high expectations of pupils by the teacher by, for example, counting the number of times positive and negative feedback occur, the number of negative and positive comments directed at pupil effort, the number and type of expressions of either high or low expectations and other such measures. Likewise, most of the items in the rating scale given above could be made low inference by simply counting the number of times they occur.

Effective Classroom Observation: Some Pointers

For the observation to be useful to the observed teacher, a number of conditions need to be met. The most important thing is to provide feedback, preferably both some brief feedback immediately after the observation and more comprehensive feedback later on (though not too much later – 48 hours seems a reasonable period). It is good practice to allow the observed teacher the opportunity to say what s/he thought about the lesson. One can start off with questions such as:

- What did you think of the lesson?
- What were your objectives, and do you think you have met them?
- Did things go as you had intended?
- What did you think were the strong points of the lesson?
- What did you think were the weak points?
- What would you have done differently?
- What caused things to go as they did?
- Was this a typical class or lesson?

These initial questions should be open (e.g. 'Why did you send that boy out?') and the observer should avoid leading questions (e.g. 'Did you send that boy out because he was talking all the time?') in order to receive enlightening answers (Brown, 1990).

Shadowing Pupils

Another type of observation aims to look not at the teacher but at the experience of one or more pupils in school. One variant of this is for an observer to follow the school day of a particular pupil, following her or him from lesson to lesson. This can give valuable insights into how pupils experience school and can highlight problems such as impractical lesson transitions, inconsistent teaching or inconsistent behaviour management and rule enforcement. It can also allow one to see how the pupil reacts to different lessons and teaching styles and may help teachers deal with problem pupils. Teachers can find out whether the language they use is appropriate, whether there are hidden difficulties in texts or questions used, whether pupils are able to work independently in lessons, whether pupils get bored during certain parts of the lesson and what factors make particular pupils more likely to be on or off task during lessons.

Alternatively, the teacher can observe one or more pupils within her/his own lesson. Obviously this means that a colleague will need to take over teaching in the class while the teacher does the observations. The teacher can also ask a colleague to do the observing. As with observations of teaching, it is necessary to decide beforehand what it is one wants to observe; the pupil's interaction with other pupils, her/his behaviour or her/his motivation during different lessons. An observation schedule of some kind should be used here as well,

A problem with shadowing is obviously that pupils' behaviour is likely to be affected by the knowledge that they are being observed. When observing pupils in one's own class this can be partly solved by going about the observation in as subtle a way possible by sitting at the back of the class or joining a group as a kind of 'classroom assistant'. This obviously is not possible when pupils are actually followed through school.

The observer then needs to describe what he or she observed, starting off on a positive note by highlighting the strong points found during the observation. The observer should then point out what was less successful about the lesson, and allow the observed to comment on her/his observations.

Feedback needs to focus on the data collected and needs to be factual, whether delivered by peers or management. It should be concrete and focused towards practical issues, concentrating on the behaviours rather than on the person observed. Feedback should be neither anecdotal nor judgemental (Miles, 1989; Warwick University, 2000). For example, if the focus of the observation was the respective involvement of boys and girls during interactive lessons the observer will probably have counted the number of questions directed at girls and boys, the amount of times boys and girls were picked to answer questions, and possibly the length and types of questions answered by boys and girls. Observer and observed should go over and analyze the data and identify points that need to be worked on together. Observer and observed should then work out a strategy to solve these problems. It is important that the observer has some constructive suggestions to make (which can include advice on following external courses as well as practical tips), as the teacher can otherwise be left with the feeling that the criticism is purely there for its own sake and s/he can't really do anything to improve. Feedback should therefore be focused on behaviours which the observed teacher can change. Once the intervention has finished, the teacher will need to be observed again to see whether s/he has successfully changed her/his teaching practices. The feedback should concentrate on the main points and not overload the observed with information, as this can make the task of improving seem hopeless.

A relationship of trust between observer and observed is essential. The observing colleague needs to be a 'critical friend'. When using peer observation, the observer and observed should hopefully be people who trust one another and should establish a positive and supportive relationship (Aiex, 1993). The role of the observer needs to be agreed on beforehand, as does the purpose of the observation. The criteria on which the observation is based need to be clear from the start and feedback needs to be constructive and positive.

During the observation, the observer needs to be as unobtrusive as possible and should not intervene in the lesson by correcting the teacher, for example. S/he should stay focused on the goals of the observation and mainly concentrate on collecting information to be used later.

SUMMARY

Recently, as a result of increased calls for accountability, classroom observation by outside agencies such as the school inspectorate has become an increasingly common occurrence for teachers in many countries. Largely as a result of this outside pressure, observation by school management has become increasingly common as well.

While classroom observation by management has its uses, peer classroom observation during which teachers observe one another's lessons can be an even more effective tool. Peer observation can be highly beneficial to both observer and observed. For the observed, peer observation can provide formative feedback on her strengths and weaknesses. For the observer, watching colleagues teach can provide ideas to use in her/his own classroom.

Research and Classroom Observation

Apart from its use as a staff development tool, classroom observation has been widely used in educational research. A lot of the major effective teaching studies discussed earlier in this book used classroom observation as a

(Continued)

(Continued)

major research tool. Initially, a lot of these studies employed low inference instruments, looking purely at the quantity of behaviours occurring (Stallings and Kasowitz, 1974). Later on, increasing use was made of high inference instruments, with the aim of looking at quality as well as quantity of behaviours. Typically, these ratings or counts are correlated with achievement measures, usually scores on standardized tests or gain measures (changes in standardized test scores over a period of time), in order to ascertain which behaviours make a difference to pupil outcomes. It is this research that has led to much of our knowledge on effective teaching.

Nevertheless, a number of criticisms have been levelled at this type of observation-based 'process-product' research. Thus, this type of research has been said to insufficiently take into account the context in which the observation occurs with respect to factors such as subject matter, pupils' socio-economic background, school-level and socio-political factors (Schaffer et al., 1994). This problem can be alleviated by collecting more data on school-level factors and pupil-level factors such as pupils' socio-economic background and ethnicity to incorporate into researchers' models, and by incorporating interviews and qualitative research to provide richer contextual knowledge.

The generalizability of the findings has also been questioned, for example whether findings from primary studies are generalizable to secondary schools and whether findings in mathematics and reading are generalizable to other subjects. More research is needed to sort these matters out.

Finally, the practical use of these results in teacher training, while some successful examples are known (e.g. Good et al., 1983) remains, in the words of Schaffer, et al. (1994) 'spotty, inaccurate and difficult to implement'.

Classroom observation is best done using some kind of standard observation instrument. These observation instruments can be broadly ranged on a continuum between two poles. At one end, purely behavioural instruments are designed to look at the occurrence or not of often very specific behaviours without passing global judgements on the quality of teaching. At the opposite end are instruments which aim to provide global value judgements on large parts of the lesson. Many instruments fall in between these two extremes.

Low inference measures require the minimum of judgement from the observer, usually consisting of counting behaviours or measuring time. High inference measures require more judgement from the observer, and aim to take into account quality as well as quantity of behaviours.

Finally, observation instruments can be either general, aiming to look at a wide range of behaviours (such as MECORS and QAIT) or specific, looking at just one aspect of classroom teaching.

For the observation to be useful to the observed teacher, a number of conditions need to be met, the most important of which is the provision of feedback, preferably both immediate feedback after the observation and more comprehensive feedback later on.

Reflective Questions

1. Have you ever been observed teaching? Was the experience useful? Why/why not? What benefits could classroom observation have for the observer?
2. What do you think is most important in making observation useful for teachers?
3. What type of measure do you think is most useful – high or low inference measures? Why?
4. Do you think shadowing pupils will help you as a teacher?
5. Think about a teacher you would like to observe. What kind of instrument would you use?

CONCLUSION: TEACHING AND TEACHERS IN THE TWENTY-FIRST-CENTURY SCHOOL

What should have become clear to the reader is how much we now know about what makes for effective teaching. Obviously, we have only been able to present a summary of the range of research findings in the various areas discussed, and we would like to point the interested reader to the References given if she or he wants to find out more. Also, there are a number of areas that we have not touched upon, including subject-specific research in such areas as science and modern foreign languages, and research on differences in teaching pupils from different social backgrounds and ethnic groups. We have, however, reviewed what we think are the main findings of research in a very large number of teaching-related areas.

Our Contents Reviewed

Firstly, to take the most robust research areas initially, we have summarized the research on classroom and behaviour management, which has provided firm foundations for creating classroom environments in which learning can take place. Secondly, research on the direct instruction model has provided us with best practice for teaching basic skills, as well as a large amount of information on effective generic teaching behaviours in such areas as questioning, individual practice and structuring of the lesson. An increasingly robust body of knowledge now exists, thirdly, on the teaching of higher-order thinking skills, and we also know a lot about student self-esteem, enhancing social skills and, to a lesser extent, teaching gifted pupils and pupils with special needs. There are, fourthly, robust findings on the learning and teaching of reading and literacy, and an increasingly strong research base on the learning and teaching of mathematics (although this research base remains less strong than that on teaching literacy). Fifthly, assessment for learning provides another strong area of research and practice.

The research base is not as robust as on these five in all areas, however. The knowledge base on generic teaching behaviours discussed in Part 1 is probably the most firmly grounded in research of all. However, most of this research was conducted in a limited number of countries (mainly the UK, the USA and the Netherlands), in a limited number of subjects (mainly mathematics and reading) and often in the primary rather than in the secondary years. This clearly leaves question marks over the generalizability of this research to other subjects, years and countries. While arguments can be made for the universal nature of many of the findings, only further research will be able to resolve this question of generalizability. The research base on a number of other areas, such as personalizing learning and undertaking classroom observation, is weaker and needs further development.

The Need for More Research

Two areas particularly in need of more research are the effective use of IT within classrooms and the cost-effectiveness of various educational strategies and interventions. While a large number of IT interventions have been developed and IT use has been generally supported by politicians and educators alike, there is very little research that gives clear pointers on the most effective programmes in this area. In the first two editions of this book, we had a chapter on IT usage, but knowledge in this area has advanced so slowly on this by comparison with the other areas we reviewed in this present edition that there was simply no point in having an 'IT chapter' this time. Given the huge expenditure historically on IT, and given the real power that some IT applications have to transform knowledge generation and transmission in ways that play with the grain of young people's own cultures, it would be a great pity if IT were not potentiated by further research.

Another area that is in need of more research is the cost-effectiveness of educational interventions. Funding for education is not unlimited, which means that decisions about the best allocation of resources constantly have to be made at all levels. While obviously a first concern has to be to select practices and strategies that are educationally effective, attention has to be paid to the cost-effectiveness of educational strategies as well. At the system level, policymakers may need to choose between spending more money on providing schools with IT or spending more on in-service training. Similarly, when providing IT resources, how should these be allocated between, say, software and training of users? More research needs to be done on how cost-effective and cost-efficient (as well as educationally effective) various educational strategies are.

Even in those areas in which the research base is more developed, there are still weaknesses. More sophisticated methodologies need to be employed in many areas of teacher effectiveness research. Mixed methodologies, combining quantitative and qualitative research, seem to provide a fruitful way forward, combining quantitative rigour with qualitative depth (Tashakkori and Teddlie, 1998). Better collection of pupil background data is essential if research is to progress. Also, research in the various areas we have looked at is often done without consideration of the unintended consequences they may cause. For example, what is the effect of inclusion of pupils with special needs on the achievement of their more advantaged peers? Or how does the effective teaching of higher-order thinking skills impact on the effective teaching of basic skills?

Another methodological issue is that in most research an underlying, though often not acknowledged or even realized, assumption is that learning proceeds in a linear fashion. This is particularly the case in quantitative research, which usually applies linear models to educational phenomena, as this is the type of model underlying such common statistical methods as multiple linear regression or linear structural equation modelling. This assumption clearly does not accord with most theories and research on learning, or with the experience of teachers, who see students moving in distinctly non-linear ways, and it is high time educational researchers started to make more use of the non-linear methods now available.

Another of the key research needs is to explore the extent to which effective teaching is a set of 'generic' behaviours and attributes that 'work' across all kinds of educational contexts, or the extent to which a more differentiated model, in which effective teachers have to do different things in different contexts, may be necessary (Campbell et al., 2004). In this latter perspective, teaching effectiveness is seen as a multi-dimensional construct, and a variable factor, rather than a universal 'given'.

Generally, more and more evidence is accumulating of the need for differentiated explanations of good teaching, as shown in the following areas:

- Differences between subjects – the major studies on teacher effectiveness commissioned by the Teacher Training Agency (Askew et al., 1997; Wray and Medwell, 2001) showed that subject knowledge mattered less in teaching numeracy than literacy. Classroom grouping of tasks by ability was more prevalent in literacy teaching that was effective.
- Differences between pupils of varying SES – low SES students generally need teacher behaviours that generate a warm and supportive climate by letting children know help is available, elicit a response (any response) before moving on to the next bit of material, show how bits fit together before moving on, emphasize knowledge and applications before abstraction (putting the concrete first), give immediate help (through use of peers perhaps) and which generate strong structure, ground-flow and well-planned transitions.

Effective practices within middle socio-economic status classrooms, by contrast, involve requiring extended reasoning, posing questions that require associations and generalizations, giving conceptually difficult material, use of projects that require independent judgement, discovery, problem solving and use of original information, encouraging learners to take responsibility for their own learning and very rich verbalizing (from Borich, 1996).

- The effectiveness level of the school – with more effective institutions needing a more 'collegial' approach to performance enhancement by comparison with the teachers in less effective schools, who require more 'assertive' kinds of leadership (Hopkins and Reynolds, 2001).
- The trajectory that a school is on – with schools already on a steep curve of improvement needing less provision of basic or foundational material than those yet to start that journey (Hopkins and Reynolds, 2001).

We also need to have teacher effectiveness studies that take into account the need for the teaching behaviours related to the new, more contemporary outcomes of schooling to be measured, particularly the 'learning to learn' skills that are necessary for the existence of successful learning processes (De Corte et al., 1996). Many argue that these skills contribute to achievement outcomes (Wang et al., 1990, 1993), although it is not clear how large their contribution actually is (Palincsar and McPhail, 1993).

Also, new perspectives on the process of learning itself (Resnick, 1987) have, as we noted earlier in this book, reconceptualized it as an active process in which students construct knowledge and skills by working with the content, which differs from the passive role of the student to be 'instructed' that is in evidence in most teacher effectiveness research. Whereas older models of instruction aim at direct transfer, the new models consider learning as an active part of knowledge construction, in which the student plays the active part. Ideas about active learning also change the role of the teacher in that the student is responsible for learning. The teacher is seen as a manager, an orchestrator of that learning process, and is no longer seen as a person who delivers the content and the instruction, but as a supervisor and a counsellor. This implies teaching students how to learn (Weinstein and Mayer, 1986).

The new views on learning, especially the views on the responsibilities of teachers and students in the learning process, have resulted in new models for instruction, or at least adaptations of the direct instruction model we outlined earlier in this book (Veenman, 1992). The new models put more emphasis on the students as active, responsible learners in cooperation with their teachers and with other students in cooperative learning, classroom discourse and interactive instruction (Vermunt, 1992). Examples of the new instructional models are reciprocal teaching (Brown and Palincsar, 1989), modelling (Schoenfeld, 1985), procedural facilitation (Scardamalia and Bereiter, 1985) and cognitive apprenticeship (Collins et al., 1989), although the power of these models is still somewhat unclear.

The Future Policy and Practice Agenda

Our need for more research to cope with the 'holes' where existing knowledge has not been developed enough and to expand knowledge into areas like the possible need for greater variation by context, pales into insignificance in comparison with the need to cope – both at the level of the practice and research of teaching – with the very challenging educational policy agenda that is likely in the next decade.

This agenda is not just about the need to respond to the implications of new governmental policy priorities. It is about the likely responses to the existing educational research and also the revolutionary new bodies of knowledge that are emerging that have the potential to transform classroom and school practice for the benefit of all teachers and of all learners. We look at these instruments of change – from government and from the research community – for the remainder of this Conclusion.

There are, firstly, the major policy challenges. The educational system is being required to respond to the five *Every Child Matters* outcomes – be healthy, stay safe, enjoy and achieve, make a positive contribution, and achieve economic well-being. However, the volume of evidence about which teaching practices generate the four 'new' goals is a fraction of what exists about the conventional 'enjoy and achieve' outcome area (although here it must be admitted that 'enjoyment' has been researched much less than 'achievement' (Mortimore et al., 1988; Sammons et al., (1996)). As is the case currently with the social or affective outcome areas by comparison with the academic (Teddlie and Reynolds, 2000), it may also be the case that teaching effects are less in these new outcome areas, leaving teachers to attain goals where they have less educational 'leverage'.

Where is the knowledge about the new 'stretched' educational and teaching mission to come from? There are no existing plans in the UK for the major research and development work required to generate this. In the absence of this, no doubt the 'Pathfinder' or exemplary institutions and their teachers will be used to model and transmit good practice, but these 'early adopters' of new practices are likely to be very different kinds of persons to those more 'in the centre of the circle' (Fullan, 1991). Besides, policymaker use of these outlier teachers and schools is likely to continue to focus more on the persons than on their methods – and, indeed, with continued likely use of one-off case studies of successful 'superteachers' that conflate persons and their methods.

Further problems may also lie in:

- the likely relative independence of the new outcome measures from each other, which means that the practices that generate one 'new' measure may not generate the other

- the inadequate development of ways to measure all of the 'new' outcome areas
- the absence of proposals to 'value add' the new outcome measures, which would be essential if schools in disadvantaged areas are not to be unfairly judged
- the absence of any attempt to prioritize academic achievement outcomes, since there is abundant evidence that although there is a loose relationship between academic outcomes and social/affective/other outcomes, it is the academic outcomes that are causal of the social/affective rather than the other way around (Muijs and Reynolds, 2000b, 2002, 2003).

Secondly, there are the implications of research which are now being generally realized. Policy in the UK has historically been wrongly obsessed with 'the school' as the unit of measurement, accountability, policy change and improvement, and this needs to change. Although in the future it is currently acknowledged in general policy discourse that education will take place across multiple settings additional to schools, these settings are still seen in policy documentation in terms of their overall 'macro level' organizational provision and features, rather than their 'micro level' teaching and learning processes. However, as we have noted frequently in this volume:

- Young people do not learn in schools or other organizations. They learn in classrooms and in other face-to-face locations with their teachers. If we are truly interested in meeting their needs, we need educators to have educational perspectives and policies that look upward from their (probably highly varied) pupil experiences, rather than down from the school or 'organizational level'. We need a focus on education as *experienced,* not as *intended* by policy – two very different things.
- It is the teacher or educator in the classroom/learning setting that is the biggest source of influence over children, not the school. Indeed, in virtually all multilevel analyses conducted to date, in whichever country or sector, teacher or classroom effects on achievement outcomes are four to five times greater than school effects (see the Muijs and Reynolds' references above and our material in the Introduction).
- School-level organizational features do not appear to be very powerful determinants of anything at all, whether they are school size, formal school designation, governance or type of school or any other school-level variables. Yet if one reads the number of references to 'the school' in policy documents, it is much greater than the references to 'the classroom'. This is something that appears to be greatest in the Anglo Saxon countries rather than others, perhaps related to the way in which 'education' in our Anglo Saxon societies has become intensely politicized and the repository of simplistic political solutions. In most societies of the world – including the high-scoring Pacific Rim and Finnish ones – discussions about education are usually about teaching and the curriculum rather than about the school unit, and are therefore linked to the most powerful 'levers' of how children perform.

We have outlined in this book that teaching as a research and practice area is endlessly fascinating. There seem to be numerous teaching behaviours associated with student outcomes, most of which are weakly intercorrelated and with an absence of strong correlations, suggesting that good teaching is not about getting a few 'big things' right but a large number of 'little things' right. There is a relationship between the beliefs that teachers have – about themselves and their efficacy – and their students' progress, but their behaviours influence their attitudes as well as vice versa. Teaching can be modified, easily and effectively (Hopkins and Reynolds, 2001; Slavin, 1996).

In fairness, the concentration upon 'the school' is not solely the fault of the politicians and policymakers. From its beginning, the school effectiveness movement (Teddlie and Reynolds, 2000) researched and celebrated the 'school' rather than the classroom, leading to knowledge bases that were much depleted when it came to effective teaching behaviours, although this has changed in the past 10 years as we have noted earlier in this book.

But – whoever's fault it is – the future teaching and teachers of the twenty-first century that we need to see will not be generated by further focus on schools, their leadership or their management. Such a managerial focus means that many teachers will simply not be motivated, since their focal concerns are much more likely to be teaching and subject related. Such a managerial focus would also mean that policy will pull 'weak' levers rather than 'strong' ones at the learning level. We need, simply, learning-level policies.

Another example of research likely to change practice is that on variation in schools. Present managerial 'whole school' focus also means that we are neglecting a potential policy area – within school variation (WSV) – that may well transform our teaching of the future if it is to be focused upon, particularly if it is part of a range of 'disaggregated' school policies.

WSV is much larger than school-against-school variation, not surprisingly since school averages are an aggregation of multiple persons/departments. In the PISA 2006 study, England had amongst the highest levels of WSV in the participating countries. Only half (approximately) of WSV was explicable by prior attainment and background characteristics, leaving the remainder to be explained in all likelihood by variable teacher quality, and by other factors.

In existing Research and Development programmes for NCSL (2003–2007) and TDA (2008 to date), schools have shown that the reduction of WSV is linked to rises in Value Added. Additionally, a range of interventions proven to be successful have been codified into a programme designed to help schools learn from their best *within the school* and to make *their best practice their standard practice* (see NCSL, 2006; Reynolds, 2007). These intervention programmes involve attention to:

- ensuring school culture can support what is potentially difficult inter-professional collaboration to enable teachers to learn more from each other
- high-quality data systems to ensure best practice is recognized
- using student voice to inform discussions of what different departments and individuals can learn from each other (often delivered with shocking clarity)
- using Standard Operating Procedures to minimize variability, without sacrificing creativity
- focusing upon teaching and learning, not school-level organizational matters
- turning the middle leader 'level' into an engine of improvement, rather than merely of administration and management.

The twenty-first-century school needs therefore to be a disaggregated one – in its organization, conceptualization and functioning. Individuals (in the case of primary schools) and departments (in the case of secondary schools) are closer to the real business of education – teaching and learning. They are smaller and more malleable, additionally, than entire school staff groups. Learning from one's own colleagues is quicker than waiting for the arrival of the school-to-school transfer of persons and knowledge. It is also devoid of an excuse-making culture, since in the case of most subjects in schools, largely the same students will be studying in each one, meaning that differences will reflect on how students are educated rather than on only initial variation between them.

Whilst classrooms and schools of the future clearly need to connect more with other sources of valuable learning and experiences outside themselves, they also need to connect better with 'themselves' as it were. Conceptualizing and organizing education in smaller learning units would seem to be axiomatic here.

The New Kid on the Block: Cognitive Neuroscience

There is also likely to be a major challenge to existing teaching practice from emerging research in cognitive neuroscience. In British educational circles generally, there has been a muted response to some of the emerging findings, although they have been enthusiastically embraced abroad. Educationalists and teachers seem to need to believe in improvement through the systems of education (linked with ourselves) rather than remediation through involvement directly with the human physiology or genotype. The latter approaches cut against the grain of our discipline because there are widespread misunderstandings that the brain is a static, self-contained unit that begins the process of learning from a predetermined, immutable set of attributes with high genetic heritability. In fact, the brain is at certain younger ages highly 'plastic' and billions of neurones in the brain are capable of connecting with each other or not (what is referred to as the 'wiring'). It is also inherently social and learners' brains need opportunities to clarify, discuss and question to enhance memory and retrieval. Brains are as much a product of the environment as of inherited predispositions.

It is clear that the extent to which a person feels they belong to a group profoundly influences their ability to focus, remember, respond and mature intellectually, socially, emotionally and cognitively. Interestingly, given the very positive effects we noted earlier for formative assessment approaches, the brain likewise is self-referencing and so also relies heavily on feedback to develop. What have we learned, and what are the implications for policies?

The first set of insights concerns the neglected role of the cerebellum. We know that skill acquisition occurs in several stages – one is the 'declarative' stage in which a person learns what to do; another is the 'procedural' stage in which a person learns how to do it, and then there is the 'automatic' stage where the skill is exercised without conscious control. The cognitive neuroscience revolution has demonstrated that there are two circuits in the brain – one for declarative learning (the frontal lobe and hippocampus) and the other for procedural learning (the frontal lobe, cerebellum and motor areas). The cerebellum functions for physical skill and mental skill, and is central to language acquisition, temporal processing and with clear connectivity to the frontal cognitive regions. Nicolson, Fawcett and Dean (2001) have outlined a Cerebellar Deficit Theory (CDT), believing that inadequate development of the cerebellum is implicated in such learning problems as dyslexia, dyspraxia and ADHD/ADD, because of the inability of those children affected to make their learned skills 'automatic'. They believe that Cerebellar Developmental Delay (CDD) is at the heart of much avoidable educational failure. The thesis is controversial, and indeed work showing considerable achievement gains from an exercise-based intervention designed to potentiate the cerebellum (the famed 'balancing on a wobble board' and the 'throwing of bean bags from one hand to the other') has been criticized by some for small sample sizes, and for inappropriate statistics (see *Dyslexia* volume 9 for multiple criticisms and Nicolson and Reynolds, 2003, for a defence). Nevertheless, it remains possible that the teaching of the future needs to give as much attention to finding processes that can potentiate the cerebellum as to those which are aimed, more conventionally, at the 'thinking brain'.

The second set of insights is concerned with how to potentiate skill development for the brain as a whole. We have known for a long time that 'distributed' practice is more effective than 'mass' practice – it is better to learn a skill in six ten-minute sessions rather than in a one-hour time slot. This is probably because there are different stages in skill acquisition – from storing in an easily alterable EEG (electroencephalogram) form, to – in a few more hours – a more stable form (that can still be influenced) and then to a more fixed and concrete form, often produced with sleep. In the longer term, the neural pathways get further established. In these processes, sleep is of major importance. These stages need time to operate as the brain is stimulated. Simply, the brain needs space, to open new neural pathways and to shut those that are redundant. However, it is mass learning and non-distributed practice that remains the conventional educational method. Subjects are taught for an hour or longer, merely meaning that the information presented later in a long lesson interferes with that presented earlier. Then – compounding error upon error – nothing is done for a day or two in the same subject so that there is no developmental 'fine tuning'.

Existing practices contrast with evidence about what we should be doing. An American, Fields, arrived at the importance of a temporal pattern of activity when investigating the intracellular switches for DNA synthesis during development (Fields, 2005). His studies suggested that the activation of CREB (the c AMP responsive element protien), a key transcription factor involved in memory, was optimized by three pulses of stimulation separated by 10-minute intervals. (This material is taken from Kelley, 2007, who reviews this literature extensively.) The highly publicized 'spaced learning' experiments conducted at Monkseaton High School (Barkham, 2009), in which a spaced learning teaching session of short bursts of intellectual stimulation lasting only 90 minutes generated equivalent results to four months conventional teaching, show the potential for radical redesign of teaching and learning in the twenty-first-century school. Admittedly, the 'spaced learning' material was taught by an outstanding teacher, it was 'new' and therefore interest was high, the Powerpoints were multicoloured and of high quality, and the cerebellum may have also been potentiated by the fact that the ten-minute gaps between teaching were filled with sessions involving the dribbling of a football between cones in the school gymnasium. Nevertheless, there is nothing in the existing literature that could even partially explain gains of this size as due to these factors alone. One must begin to ask very serious questions of 'mass education' if these results are shown elsewhere, and begin to believe in the need for radical redesign of teaching and learning.

The third insight from contemporary cognitive neuroscience concerns the possibility of optimizing brain function through appropriate resourcing. There are the hints about the positive effects of fish oil supplements – the major dietary change of the British population since the 1950s has been the decline in per capita fish consumption of approximately two thirds, and the argument is that neural connectivity can be enhanced artificially by these supplements replacing what would have been naturally generated through diet. Water is another important supplement argued to be implicated in improving learning outcomes. The classroom of the future may need to be nutritionally nourishing as well as emotionally nourishing.

The fourth insight from contemporary neuroscience comes in the work looking at sleep patterns and the effects of the different patterns of circadian rhythms that are evidenced by children of different ages (Foster, 2007). Teenagers are heavily sleep deprived – they show delayed sleep and fewer hours of sleep once in bed. Sustained periods of reduced sleep generate poor performance in terms of increased errors, impaired vigilance, poor memory, reduced mental/physical reaction times, reduced motivation, reduced risk taking and increased depression. The practice of starting school early and of putting more demanding subjects in the morning timetable is disliked by teenagers and generates lower p[illegible]e, which improves for this group later in the day. Unfortunately, adult perf[illegible]of the teachers – is likely to be *higher* in the morning, which is of [illegible]y schools start early and the 'difficult' subjects are timetabled for th[illegible]s. Ways of squaring this circle need to be found! The dramatic gains shown by approaches influenced by cognitive neuroscience – from exercise to fish oils to spaced learning – may be because they are from enthusiasts, on often small samples in atypical situations. Alternatively, it may be that they are, simply, more powerful interventions than our conventional educational 'weak' levers. Further large-scale research in these areas is clearly urgently necessary.

The Future of Teaching

It should be clear from our discussion so far that the next decade may see major challenges from government about their policy needs, from the increased knowledge of existing research and from the very new research knowledge that is now beginning in the key area of cognitive neuroscience. However, responding to these challenges through utilization of conventional methods of teacher education and professional development is unlikely to be adequate, since these rely on an 'apprenticeship' orientation in which teachers learn at the foot of the 'master' (or sometimes 'mistress') teacher and pick up the methods and approaches that have been seen to be effective and valid historically.

But such methods of training, of professional development and of upskilling the teaching profession cannot be adequate in a world where the old knowledge, approaches and methods are rapidly redundant because of policy changes and the arrival of the new, more valid knowledge bases that we have outlined in this Conclusion. More useful is a rational, empirical model of teaching in which the members of the profession are seen as research-based problem solvers, taking whatever policy demands or intellectual changes they are given and experimenting, based upon existing and new knowledge, to see how the problems may be solved.

In this latter model, teachers are skilled to be able to respond to anything that policy or intellectual changes may throw at them. They are not merely ciphers of past approaches, or adherents to what they were once told 'worked'. Developments such as the introduction of the Masters in Teaching and Learning (MTL) course to make the entire teaching profession research based are a useful start, but there is much more yet to do to create the teachers that can effectively respond to the challenge of the future by being the excellent researchers of their own classrooms.

REFERENCES

Abbott, L. and Nutbrown, C. (eds) (2001) *Experiencing Reggio Emilia: Implications for Pre-School Provision*. Ballmoor, Bucks: Open University Press.

Adams, M. (1990) *Beginning to Read: Thinking and Learning About Print*. Cambridge, MA: MIT Press.

Adey, P. and Shayer, M. (1994) *Really Raising Standards: Cognitive Intervention and Academic Achievement*. London: Routledge.

Adey, P. and Shayer, M. (2002) Cognitive Acceleration Comes of Age. In M. Shayer and P. Adey (eds) *Learning Intelligence: Cognitive Acceleration Across the Curriculum 5–15*. Ballmoor, Bucks: Open University Press.

Aiex, N. K. (1993) *A Communicative Approach to Observation and Feedback*. ERIC Digest ED364926.

Akin-Little, K. A., Little, S. G. and Laniti, M. (2007) Teachers' Use of Classroom Management Procedures in the United States and Greece: A Cross-Cultural Comparison. *School Psychology International* 28(1), 53–62.

Al Otaiba, S., Connor, C., Lane, H., Kosanovich, M., Schatschneider, D., Dyrlund, A., Miller, M. and Wright, T. (2007) Reading First Kindergarten Classroom Instruction and Students' Growth in Phonological Awareness and Letter Naming–Decoding Fluency. *Journal of School Psychology* 46(3), 281–314.

Anderson, A., Hamilton, R. and Hattie, J. (2004) Classroom Climate and Motivated Behavior in Secondary Schools. *Learning Environments Research* 7, 211–25.

Anderson, R., Greene, M. and Loewen, P. (1988) Relationships Among Teachers' and Students' Thinking Skills, Sense of Efficacy and Student Achievement. *Alberta Journal of Educational Research,* 17, 86–95.

Anderson, R. (2002) Reforming Science Teaching: What Research Says About Inquiry. *Journal of Science Teacher Education* 13(1), 1–12.

Anderson-Butcher, D., Newsome, W. and Nay, S. (2003) Social Skills Intervention during Elementary School Recess: A Visual Analysis. *Children and Schools* 25(3), 135–46.

Ang, R. P. and Hughes, J. N. (2002) Differential Benefits of Skills Training with Antisocial Youth Based on Group Composition: A Meta-Analytic Investigation. *School Psychology Review* 31(2), 164–85.

Angell, C. (2001) *I Can Read! Reading Strategies That Work for Students at Risk*. Chicago, IL: St Xavier University.

Anghileri, J. (ed.) (1995) *Children's Mathematical Thinking in the Primary Years: Perspectives on Children's Learning. Children, Teachers and Learning*. London: Cassell.

Arends, R. I. (1998) *Learning to Teach*. Boston, MA: McGraw-Hill.

Aronson, E. and Patnoe, S. (1997) *Cooperation in the Classroom: The Jigsaw Method*. New York: Longman.

Arsenault, D. J. (2001) *Behavioral, Social, and Cognitive Predictors of Adolescent Academic Self-Concept: A Longitudinal Investigation*. Paper presented at the Annual Meeting of the Society for Research in Child Development, Minneapolis, MN, 19–22 April.

Askew, M. and William, D. (1995) *Recent Research in Mathematics Education 5–16*. London: Office For Standards in Education, 53.

Askew, M., Rhodes, V., Brown, M., William, D. and Johnson, D. (1994) *Effective Teachers of Numeracy. Report of a Study Carried Out for the Teacher Training Agency*. London: King's College London, School of Education.

Au, K. H. and Carroll, J. H. (1997) Improving Literacy Achievement through a Constructivist Approach: The KEEP Demonstration Classroom Project. *Elementary School Journal* 97(3), 203–21.

Aubrey, C. (2007) *Leading and Managing in the Early Years*. London: Sage.

Aubrey, C., Dahl, S. and Godfrey, R. (2006) Early Mathematics Achievement and Later Development: Further Evidence. *Mathematics Education Research Journal,* 18(1), 27–46.

Ausubel, D. P. (1968) *Educational Psychology: A Cognitive View*. New York: Holt, Rinehart and Winston.

Badger, E. and Thomas, B. (1992) Open-Ended Questions in Reading. *Practical Assessment, Research and Evaluation* 3(4).

Baker, E. T., Wang, M. C. and Walberg, H. J. (1995) The Effects of Inclusion on Learning. *Educational Leadership* 52(4), 33–5.

Bamburg, J. D. (1994) *Raising Expectations To Improve Student Learning. Urban Monograph Series.* CS: North Central Regional Educational Lab., Oak Brook, IL. PY: 1994.

Bandura, A. (1985) *Social Foundations of Thought and Action*. Englewood Cliffs, NJ: Prentice-Hall.

Banerji, M. and Dailey, R. A. (1995) A Study of the Effects of an Inclusion Model on Students with Learning Disabilities. *Journal of Learning Disabilities* 28(8), 511–22.

Barak, M. and Shakman, M. (2008) Fostering Higher-Order Thinking in Science Class: Teachers' Reflections Fostering Higher-Order Thinking in Science Class: Teachers' Reflections. *Teachers and Teaching: Theory and Practice* 14(3), 191–208.

Barber, M. and Mourshed, M. (2007) *How The World's Best Performing School Systems Come Out On Top*. London: McKinsey & Co.

Barkham, P. (2009) Can You Really Do a GCSE in Just Three Days? *The Guardian, G2 section.* 13 February, pp. 4–7.

Barron, B. (2003) When Smart Groups Fail. *The Journal of the Learning Sciences* 12 (3), 307–59.

Basic Skills Agency (1997) *International Numeracy Survey. A Comparison of the Basic Numeracy Skills of Adults 16–60 in Seven Countries*. London: The Basic Skills Agency, 26.

Bates, L., Luster, T. and Vandenbelt, M. (2003) Factors Related to Social Competence in Elementary School among Children of Adolescent Mothers. *Social Development* 12(1), 107–24.

Battistich, V., Solomon, D. and Delucchi, K. (1993) Interaction Processes and Student Outcomes in Cooperative Learning Groups. *Elementary School Journal* 94, 19–32.

Baum, S. (1990) *Gifted But Learning Disabled: A Puzzling Paradox*. Reston, VA: The ERIC Clearinghouse on Disabilities and Gifted Education, Digest E479.

Baumeister, R. F., Campbell, J. D., Krueger, J. I. and Vohs, K. D. (2003) Does High Self-esteem Cause Better Performance, Interpersonal Success, Happiness, or Healthier Lifestyles? *Psychological Science in the Public Interest* (4), 1–44.

Baumrind, D. (1991) The Influence of Parenting Style on Adolescent Competence and Substance Use. *Journal of Early Adolescence* 11(1), 56–95.

Beattie, M. (1995) New Prospects for Teacher Education: Narrative Ways of Knowing Teaching and Teacher Learning. *Educational Research* 37(1), 53–70.

Benbow, C. P. (1991) Meeting the Needs of Gifted Students Through Use of Acceleration. In M. C. Wang, M. C. Reynolds and H. J. Walberg (eds) *Handbook of Special Education: Research and Practice*. Oxford: Pergamon Press.

Bennett, N. (1976) *Teaching Styles and Pupil Progress*. London: Open Books.

Bennett, N., Desforges, C., Cockburn, A. and Wilkinson, B. (1981) *The Quality of Pupil Learning: Interim Report*. Lancaster: University of Lancaster, Dept. of Education.

Benzwie, T. (1987) *A Moving Experience*. Tucson, AZ: Zephyr Press.

Berends, M., Chun, J., Schuyler, G., Stockly, S. and Briggs, R. (2001) *Challenges of Conflicting School Reforms: Effects of New American Schools in a High-poverty District*. Santa Monica, CA: RAND.

Bergen, D. (2001) *Pretend Play and Young Children's Development*. ERIC Digest ED458045. Washington, DC: Office of Educational Research and Improvement.

Bernstein, B. (1968) Education Cannot Compensate for Society, *New Society*, 87.

Best, J. (2000) The Role of Context on Strategic Actions in Mastermind. *Journal of General Psychology* 52(3), 451–87.

Beyer, B. K. (1985) Critical Thinking: What is it? *Social Education* 49, 270–6.

Bibler, T. and Gilman, D. A. (2003) *The Effects of the Inclusion of Special Needs Student Scores on ISTEP: Indiana's Graduation Qualification Exam*. Indianapolis, IA: ISTEP.

Black, P. and William, D. (1998) Inside the Black Box: Raising Standards Through Classroom Assessment. *Phi Delta Kappan*, October.

Black, P. and William, D. (1999) *Assessment for Learning*. Cambridge: University of Cambridge School of Education.

Black, S. (1997) Doing Our Homework on Homework. *American School Board Journal* 183, 48–51.

Blatchford, P., Bassett, P., Brown, P., Koutsoubou, M., Martin, P., Russell, A. and Webster, R. with Rubie-Davies, C. (2009) *The Impact of Support Staff in Schools. Results from the Deployment and Impact of Support Staff (DISS) Project. Strand 2 Wave 2. DCSF online*. Available at: http://www.dcsf.gov.uk/research/data/uploadfiles/DCSF-RR148.pdf (accessed 07 June 2009).

Blay, J. and Ireson, J. (2009) Pedagogical Beliefs, Activity Choice and Structure, and Adult-Child Interactions in the Nursery Classroom. *Teaching and Teacher Education,* 1–12.

Blum, L. (1980) *Friendship, Altruism, and Morality*. Boston, MA: Routledge and Kegan Paul.

Boers, D. and Caspary, P. (1995) Real-life Homework. *Executive Educator* 17(3), 37–8.

Bohn, C., Roerig, A. and Pressley, M. (2004) The First Days of School in the Classrooms of Two More Effective and Four Less Effective Primary-Grades Teachers. *The Elementary School Journal* 104(4), 269–87.

Borich, G. (1996) *Effective Teaching Methods* (third edition). New York: Macmillan.

Borich, G. (2000) *Effective Teaching Methods* (fifth edition). Upper Saddle River, NJ: Prentice Hall.

Brandt, M. and Christensen, R. (2002) Improving Student Social Skills through the Use of Cooperative Learning, Problem Solving, and Direct Instruction. ERIC Digest ED465929.

Broadhead, P. (2009) Conflict Resolution and Children's Behaviour: Observing and Understanding Social and Cooperative Play in Early Years Educational Settings. *Early Years* 29(2), 105–18

Brody, L. E. and Stanley, J. C. (1991) Young College Students: Assessing Factors that Contribute to Success. In W. T. Southern and E. D. Jones (eds) *The Academic Acceleration of Gifted Children*. London: Teachers College Press.

Brooks, M. G. and Brooks, J. G. (1999) The Courage to be Constructivist. *Educational Leadership* 57(3), 18–24.

Brophy, J. (1981) Teacher Praise: A Functional Analysis. *Review of Educational Research*, Spring, 5–32.

Brophy, J. (1992) Probing the Subtleties of Subject-matter Teaching. *Educational Leadership* 49 (April), 4–8.

Brophy, J. (1996) *Teaching Problem Students*. New York: Guilford.

Brophy, J. E. and Good, T. L. (1986) Teacher Behaviour and Student Achievement. In M. C. Wittrock (ed.) *Handbook of Research on Teaching*. New York: Macmillan, 328–75.

Brown, A. L. and Palincsar, A. S. (1989) Guided, Cooperative Learning and Individualised Knowledge Acquisition. In L. B. Resnick (ed.) *Knowing, Learning and Instruction*. Hillsdale, NJ: Lawrence Erlbaum.

Brown, K. T. (2001) *The Effectiveness of Early Childhood Inclusion (Parents' Perspectives)*. Research paper presented at the Special Education Seminar, Loyola College, Baltimore, MD, 25 April.

Brown, S. (1990) *Getting the Most from Observing Teaching*. Spotlights, the Scottish Council for Research in Education. Available at: www.scre.ac.uk/spotlight/spot-light32.html

Brualdi, A. (1998) Implementing Performance Assessment in the Classroom. *Practical Assessment, Research and Evaluation* 6(2).

Bruner, J. S. (1962) *On Knowing: Essays for the Left Hand*. Cambridge, MA: Harvard University Press.

Bryan, T. and Sullivan, K. (1995) *A Teacher's Guide to Homework*. Phoenix, AZ: Planning for Success.

Bryan, T. and Sullivan-Burstein, K. (1997) Homework How-To's. *Teaching Exceptional Children* 29(6).

Bryant, P. (1994) Children and Arithmetic. *Journal of Child Psychology and Psychiatry* 36(1), 3–32.

Burns, D., Johnson, S. and Gable, R. (1998) Can We Generalize about the Learning Style Characteristics of High Academic Achievers? *Roeper Review* 20(4), 276–81.

Burns, R. B. (1979) *The Self-concept in Theory, Measurement and Behaviour*. London: Longman.

Byer, J. L. (2001) *The Effects of College Students' Perceptions of Teaching and Learning on Academic Self-Efficacy and Course Evaluations*. Paper presented at the 30th Annual Meeting of the Mid-South Educational Research Association, Little Rock, AR, 14–16 November.

Bynner, J. and S. Parsons (1997) *Does Numeracy Matter? Evidence From the National Child Development Study on the Impact of Poor Numeracy on Adult Life*. London: The Basic Skills Agency, 48.

Bynner, J. and Steedman, J. (1995) *Difficulties with Basic Skills: Findings from the 1970 British Cohort Study*. London: The Basic Skills Agency.

Byrne, B. and Shavelson, R. (1986) On the Structure of Adolescent Self-Concept. *Journal of Educational Psychology* 78(6), 473–81.

Caldwell, B. (1997) *Educating Children Who Are Deaf or Hard of Hearing: Cued Speech*. Reston, VA: ERIC Clearinghouse on Disabilities and Gifted Education. ERIC Digest E555.

Campbell, J., Kyriakides, L., Muijs, D. and Robinson, W. (2004) *Assessing Teacher Effectiveness: Developing a Differential Model*. London: RoutledgeFalmer.

Canter, L. (1976) *Assertive Discipline: A Take Charge Approach for Today's Educator*. Seal Beach, CA: Canter and Associates.

Canter, L. (1989) Assertive Discipline: More than Names on the Board and Marbles in the Jar. *Phi Delta Kappan* September, 57–61.

Carlberg, C. and Kavale, K. (1980) The Efficacy of Special Placement for Exceptional Children: A Meta-Analysis. *The Journal of Special Education* 14(31), 295–309.

Carter, L. D., Coleman, L. D., Haizel, M. D. and Michalowski, L. A. (2001) *Improving Social Skills through Cooperative Learning*. Winnebago, IL: St Xavier University.

Cawthon, S. W. (2001) Teaching Strategies in Inclusive Classrooms with Deaf Students. *Journal of Deaf Studies and Deaf Education* 6(3), 212–25.

Center, Y., Wheldall, K., Freeman, L. and Outhred, L. (1995) An Evaluation of Reading Recovery. *Reading Research Quarterly* 30(2), 240–63.

Centra, J. A. (1975) Colleagues as Raters of Classroom Instruction. *Journal of Higher Education* 12(3), 237–337.

Centra, J. (1979) *Determining Faculty Effectiveness: Assessing Teaching, Research, and Service for Personnel Decisions and Improvement*. New Jersey: RIE.

Centre for Academic Practice, University of Warwick (2000) *Observing Teaching, Guidance Notes for Departments*. Available at: www.warwick.ac.uk

Chall, J. (1995) *Stages of Reading Development*. Fort Worth, TX: Harcourt Brace.

Chang, M., Romisowski, A. and Grabowski, B. (1994) *Constructivist and Objectivist Approaches to Teaching Chemistry Concepts to Junior High School Students*. Paper presented at the Annual Meeting of the American Educational Research Association, New Orleans, LA, April.

Chapman, J. W. and Tunmer, W. E. (1995) Development of Young Children's Reading Self-concepts: An Examination of Emerging Subcomponents and their Relationship with Reading Achievement. *Journal of Educational Psychology* 87, 154–67.

Chen, W. (2001) Description of an Expert Teacher's Constructivist-Oriented Teaching: Engaging Students' Critical Thinking in Learning Creative Dance. *Research Quarterly for Exercise and Sport* 72(4), 366–75.

Chen, M. and Ehrenberg, T. (1993) Test Scores, Homework, Aspirations and Teachers' Grades. *Studies in Educational Evaluation* 19, 403–19.

Church, S. (1994) *Is Whole Language Really Warm and Fuzzy? Facts on Myths About Whole Language Education*. Available at: http://toread.copm/myths.html

Claessens, A., Duncan, G. and Engel, M. (2009) Kindergarten Skills and Fifth-grade Achievement: Evidence from the ECLS-K. *Economics of Education Review* 28(4), 415–27.

Clark, C. M., and Peterson, P. L. (1986) Teachers' thought processes. In Wittrock, M.C. (ed.). *Handbook of research on teaching* (third edition) pp. 255–96. New York: Macmillan.

Clarke, S. (1998–2000) *In-service Materials for Teachers*. London: Institute of Education.

Clay, M. M. (1993) *Reading Recovery: A Guidebook for Teachers in Training*. Portsmouth, NH: Heinemann.

Cloer, T. Jr. and Dalton, S. R. (2001) Gender and Grade Differences in Reading Achievement and in Self-Concept as Readers. *Journal of Reading Education* 26(2), 31–6.

Coffield, F., Moseley, D., Hall, E. and Ecclestone, K. (2004) *Learning Styles and Pedagogy in Post-16 Learning: A Systematic and Critical Review*. London: Learning and Skills Research Centre.

Cohen, L. (1999) The Power of Portfolios. *Early Childhood Today*, February.

Coleman, J. S., Campbell, E., Hobson, C., McPartland, J., Mood, A., Weinfeld, F. and York, R. (1966) *Equality of Educational Opportunity*. Washington, DC: US Government Printing Office.

Collins, A., Brown, J. S. and Newman, S. E. (1989) Cognitive Apprenticeship: Teaching the Crafts of Reading, Writing and Mathematics. In L. B. Resnick (ed.) *Knowing, Learning and Instruction*. Hillsdale, NJ: Lawrence Erlbaum.

Connor, C. M., Morrison, F. J., Fishman, B. J., Schatschneider, C. and Underwood, P. (2007) Algorithm-guided Individualized Reading Instruction. *Science* 315, 464–5.

Cooper, H. (1989) Synthesis of Research on Homework. *Educational Leadership* 47, 58–91.

Cooper, H. (1994) *The Battle over Homework: An Administrator's Guide to Setting Sound and Effective Policies*. London: Corwin Press.

Cooper, H. (2006) *The Battle Over Homework: Common Ground for Administrators, Teachers, and Parents*. London: Corwin.

Cooper, H., Robinson, J. C. and Patel, E. A. (2006) Does Homework Improve Academic Achievement? A Synthesis of Research, 1987–2003. *Review of Educational Research* 76(1), 1–62.

Cooper, J. O., Heron, T. E. and Heward, T. L. (1987) *Applied Behavior Analysis*. Upper Saddle River, NJ: Merrill/Prentice Hall.

Coopersmith, S. (1967) *The Antecedents of Self-Esteem*. San Francisco: W. H. Freeman.

Costa, A. L. and Garmston R. J. (1994) *Cognitive Coaching: A Foundation for Renaissance Schools*. Norwood, MA: Christopher-Cordon.

Cotton, K. (1997) *Educating for Citizenship*. Portland, OR: Northwest Regional Education Laboratory.

Covington, M. C. and Beery, R. G. (1976) *Self-worth and School Learning*. New York: Holt, Rinehart and Winston.

Creemers, B. P. M. (1994) *The Effective Classroom*. London: Cassell.

Creemers, B. P. M. and Reezigt, G. J. (1999) The Role of School and Classroom Climate in Elementary School Learning Environments. In H. J. Freiberg (ed.) *School Climate. Measuring, Improving and Sustaining Healthy Learning Environments*. London: Falmer Press.

Croll, P. (1996) Teacher–pupil Interaction in the Classroom. In P. Croll and N. Hastings (eds) *Effective Primary Teaching*. London: David Fulton.

Croll, P. and Moses, D. (1988) Teaching Methods and Time on Task in Junior Classrooms. *Educational Researcher* 30(2), 90–7.

Czerniak, C., Weber, W. B., Sandmann, A. and Ahern, J. (1999a) A Literature Review of Science and Mathematics Integration. *School Science and Mathematics* 99(8), 421–30.

Czerniak, C., Lumpe, A. and Haney, J. (1999b) Science Teachers' Beliefs and Intentions to Implement Thematic Units. *Journal of Science Teacher Education* 10(2), 123–45.

D'Agostino, J. V. and Murphy, J. A. (2004) A Meta-Analysis of Reading Recovery in United States Schools. *Educational Evaluation and Policy Analysis* 26(1), 23–8.

Dai, D. Y. (2001) A Comparison of Gender Differences in Academic Self-Concept and Motivation between High-Ability and Average Chinese Adolescents. *Journal of Secondary Gifted Education* 13(1), 22–32.

Dall'Alba, G. (2006) Learning Strategies and the Learner's Approach to a Problem Solving Task. *Research in Science Education,* 16(1), 11–20.

Dana, T. M. and Davis, N. T. (1993) On Considering Constructivism for Improving Mathematics and Science Teaching and Learning. In K. Tobin (ed.) *The Practice of Constructivism in Science Education*. Hillsdale, NJ: Lawrence Erlbaum.

Danielson, C. and Phelps, C. (2003) The Assessment of Children's Social Skills through Self-Report: A Potential Screening Instrument for Classroom Use. *Measurement and Evaluation in Counseling and Development* 35(4), 218–29.

Darling-Hammond, L. (2000) Teacher Quality and Student Achievement: A Review of State Policy Evidence. *Education Policy Analysis Archives*, 8(1). Available at: http://epaa.asu.edu/epaa/v8n1/

Davidson, J. (2001) Images of Setting in the Primary Classroom. *Scottish Educational Review* 33(2), 183–91.

Davis, G. A. and Rimm, S. B. (1988) *Education of the Gifted and Talented*. Englewood Cliffs, NJ: Prentice Hall.

Davis, J. (1990) *On Matching Teaching Approach with Student Learning Style: Are We Asking the Right Question*. Memphis, TN: University of Memphis.

Dawkins, R. (1989) *The Selfish Gene* (new edition). Oxford: Oxford University Press.

Day, C., Stobart, G., Kington, A., Gu, Q., Smees, R. and Mujtaba, T. (2006) *Variation in Teachers' Work, Lives and Effectiveness (VITAE).* Nottingham: DCFS Publications.

DCSF (2009) *Tracking and Target Setting*. Available at: http://nationalstrategies.standards.dcsf.gov.uk/node/156785?uc=force_uj (accessed 14 October 2009)

De Bock, D. Verschaffel, L. Janssens, D. Van Dooren, W. and Claes, K. (2003) Do Realistic Contexts and Graphical Representations Always Have a Beneficial Impact on Students' Performance? Negative Evidence from a Study on Modeling Non-Linear Geometry Problems. *Learning and Instruction* 13(4), 441–63.

De Corte, E., Greer, B. and Verschaffel, L. (1996) Mathematics Teaching and Learning. In D. C. Berliner and R. Calfee (eds) *Handbook of Educational Psychology*. New York: Macmillan.

Deci, E.L., Koestner, R. and Ryan, M.R. (1999) A Meta-analytic Review of Experiments Examining the Effects of Extrinsic Rewards on Intrinsic Motivation. *Psychological Bulletin* 125, 627–68.

De Fraine, B., Van Damme, J. and Onghena, P. (2006) A Longitudinal Analysis of Gender Differences in Academic Self-concept and Language Achievement: A Multivariate Multilevel Latent Growth Approach. *Contemporary Educational Psychology* 32(1), 132–50.

De Jager, B. (2002) *Teaching Reading Comprehension: The Effects of Direct Instruction and Cognitive Apprenticeship on Comprehension Skills and Metacognition*. Groningen: Proefschrift GION.

De Jager, B., Janssen, N. and Reezigt, G. (2005) The Development of Metacognition in Primary School Learning Environments. *School Effectiveness and School Improvement* 16(2), 179–96.

Denissen, J., Zarrett, N. and Eccles, J. (2007) I Like to Do It, I'm Able, and I Know I Am: Longitudinal Couplings Between Domain-Specific Achievement, Self-concept, and Interest. *Child Development* 78(2), 430–47.

Deno, S., Maruyama, G., Espin, C. and Cohen, C. (1990) Educating Students with Mild Disabilities in General Education Classrooms: Minnesota Alternatives. *Exceptional Children* Oct–Nov., 150–61.

Department for Education and Employment (DfEE) (1999) *The Structure of the Literacy Hour*. Available at: www.standards.dfee.gov.uk/literacy/literacyhour

Department for Education and Employment (DfEE) (2000a) *Definition of SEN*. Available at: www.dfee.gov.uk/sen/sengloss.htm

Department for Education and Employment (DfEE) (2000b) *A Model of Teacher Effectiveness: Report by Hay McBer to the Department for Education and Employment – June 2000*.

Department for Education and Skills (DfES) (2003) *Excellence and Enjoyment.* London: HMSO.

DeRosier, M. E., Kupersmidt, J. B. and Patterson, C. J. (1994) Children's Academic and Behavioral Adjustment as a Function of the Chronicity and Proximity of Peer Rejection. *Child Development* 65, 1799–1813.

Dettmers, S., Trautwein, U. and Ludtke, O. (2009) The Relationship Between Homework Time and Achievement is not Universal: Evidence From Multilevel Analyses in 40 Countries. *School Effectiveness and School Improvement* 20(3), 1–31.

Dewey, J. and Bento, J. (2009) Activating Children's Thinking Skills (ACTS): The Effects of an Infusion Approach to Teaching Thinking in Primary Schools. *British Journal of Educational Psychology* 79(2), 329–51.

Dharmadasa, I. (2000) *Teachers' Perspectives on Constructivist Teaching and Learning*. Paper presented at the Annual Conference and Exhibition of the Association for Childhood Education International, Baltimore, MD, 17–20 April.

Dodge, K., Petit, G., McClaskey, C. and Brown, M. (1986) *Social Competence in Children*. Monographs of the Society for Research in Child Development, 51(2).

Dohrn, L., Holian, E. and Kaplan, D. (2001) *Improving Social Skills at the Elementary Level through Cooperative Learning and Direct Instruction*. PhD Dissertation, University of Illinois.

Duffy, T. M. and Jonassen, D. H. (1992) *Constructivism and the Technology of Instruction: A Conversation*. Hillsdale, NJ: Lawrence Erlbaum.

Dunn, R. and Dunn, K. (1978) *Teaching Students Through Their Individual Learning Styles*. Reston, VA: Reston Publishing.

Dunn, R., Dunn, K. and Price, A. (1985) *Learning Styles Inventory*. New York: CUNY.

Durlak, J. and Weissberg, R. (2007) *The Impact of After School Programs that Promote Personal and Social Skills*. Chicago, IL: CASEL.

Dyson, A. and Millward, A. (2000) *Schools and Special Needs: Issues of Innovation and Inclusion*. London: Paul Chapman.

Dyson, A., Farrell, P., Polat, F. and Hutcheson, G. (2004) *Inclusion and Pupil Achievement*. London: Department for Education and Skills.

The Economist (2003) Hard Numbers. Failing Maths and Science, 17 April.

Edelman Borden, M. (1997) *What Are Children Leaning When They Play*. Available at: http://users.stargate.net/~cokids/borden.html (accessed 13 March 2001).

Edwards, C., Gandini, L. and Foorman, G. (1993) *The Hundred Languages of Children: The Reggio Emilia Approach to Early Childhood Education*. Norwood, NJ: Ablex.

Edwards, J. (1991) The Direct Teaching of Thinking Skills. In G. Evans (ed.) *Learning and Teaching Cognitive Skills*. Hawthorn, Victoria: Australian Council for Educational Research.

Eggleton, P. J. and Moldavan, C. C. (2001) The Value of Mistakes. *Mathematics Teaching in the Middle School* 7(1), 42–7.

Ehri, L. C. (1987) Learning to Read and Spell Words. *Journal of Reading Behavior* 19, 5–31.

Elliott, S. N. (1995) *Creating Meaningful Performance Assessments*. Reston, VA: ERIC Clearinghouse on Disabilities and Gifted Education. ED381985.

Elliott, S. N., Malecki, C. K. and Demaray, M. K. (2001) New Directions in Social Skills Assessment and Intervention for Elementary and Middle School Students. *Exceptionality* 9(1–2), 19–32.

Emmer, E., Evertson, C., Clements, B. and Worsham, M. (1997) *Classroom Management for Secondary Teachers*. Upper Saddle River, NJ: Prentice Hall.

English, L. (1993) Children's Strategies for Solving Two- and Three-Dimensional Combinatorial Problems. *Journal for Research in Mathematics Education* 24(3), 255–73.

Erlbaum, B. and Vaughn, S. (1999) *Can School-Based Interventions Enhance the Self-Concept of Students with Learning Disabilities?* Available at: www.ncld.org/summit99/osep2.htm

Erlbaum, B., Watson Moody, S., Vaughn, S., Shumm, J. S. and Hughes, M. (1999) *The Effects of Instructional Grouping Format on the Reading Outcomes of Students with Disabilities: A Meta-Analytic Review*. Available at: www.ncld.org/summit99/osep2.htm

Erlbuam, J. (2002) The Effect of Self-appraisals on Ability of Academic Performance. *Journal of Personality and Social Psychology* 47, 944–52.
Ernest, P. (1999) *Social Constructivism as a Philosophy of Mathematics: Radical Constructivism*. Available at: www.exeter.ac.uk
Evertson, C. M. (1995) Classroom Management in the Learning Centered Classroom. In A. Ornstein (ed.), *Teaching: Theory and Practice*. Boston, MA: Allyn & Bacon.
Evertson, C. and Emmer, E. (1982) Effective Management at the Beginning of the School Year in Junior High Classes. *Journal of Educational Psychology* 74, 485–98.
Fang, Z. (1996) A Review of Research on Teachers' Beliefs and Practices. *Educational Research* 38(1), 47–65.
Faulkner, J. and Blyth, C. (1995) Homework: Is It Really Worth All the Bother? *Educational Studies* 21(3), 447–54.
Feuerstein, R., Rand, Y., Hoffman, M. and Miller, M. (1980) *Instrumental Enrichment: An Intervention Programme for Cognitive Modifiability*. Baltimore, MD: University Park Press.
Fields, R. D. (2005) Making Memories Stick. *Scientific American* 29(2), 58–65.
FitzGibbon, C. T. (1988) Peer Tutoring as a Teaching Strategy. *Educational Management and Administration* 16, 217–29.
Fitzpatrick, K. A. (1982) *The Effect of a Secondary Classroom Management Training Program on Teacher and Student Behavior*. Paper presented at the AERA Annual Meeting, New York.
Flynn, J. R. (1994) IQ Gains Over Time. In R. J. Sternberg (ed.) *Encyclopaedia of Human Intelligence*. New York: Macmillan, 617–23.
Foorman, B. R., Fletcher, J. and Francis, D. (1996) *A Scientific Approach to Reading Instruction*. Available at: www.ldonline.org/ld–indepth/reading/cars.html
Fosnot, C. T. (1996) *Constructivism: Theory, Perspectives, and Practice*. New York: Teachers College, Columbia University.
Foster, R. G. (2007) Teenagers, Body Clocks, Health and Learning. *The Times Higher Educational Supplement*, 5 January.
Foyle, H. C. and Bailey, G. D. (1988) Research on Homework Experiments in Social Studies: Implications for Teaching. *Social Education* 52(4), 292–8.
Fraser, B. J. (1994) Research on Classroom and School Climate. In D. Gabel (ed.) *Handbook of Research on Science Teaching and Learning*. New York: Macmillan.
Fraser, B. J. (1999) Using Learning Environment Assessments to Improve Classroom and School Climates. In H. J. Freiberg (ed.) *School Climate: Measuring, Improving and Sustaining Healthy Learning Environments*. London: Falmer Press.
Freiberg, H. J. (1999) Three Creative Ways to Measure School Climate and Next Steps. In H. J. Freiberg (ed.) *School Climate: Measuring, Improving and Sustaining Healthy Learning Environments*. London: Falmer Press.
Freiberg, H. J. and Stein, T. A. (1999) Measuring, Improving and Sustaining Healthy Learning Environments. In H. J. Freiberg (ed.) *School Climate: Measuring, Improving and Sustaining Healthy Learning Environments*. London: Falmer, 11–29.
Fullan, M. G. (1991) *The New Meaning of Educational Change*. London: Cassell
Fulk, B. (2000) 20 Ways to Make Instruction More Memorable. *Intervention in School and Clinic* 35(3), 183–4.
Furtwengler, W. J. (1996) Improving Secondary School Discipline by Involving Students in the Process. *NASSP Bulletin* 80(581), 36–44.
Gaby, C. (forthcoming) *Stress and Resilience among Secondary School Teachers.* Manchester: University of Manchester.
Gagne, R. M. (1965) *The Conditions of Learning*. New York: Holt, Rinehart & Winston.

Gales, M. J. and Yan, W. (2001) *Relationship between Constructivist Teacher Beliefs and Instructional Practices to Students' Mathematical Achievement: Evidence from TIMMS*. Paper presented at the Annual Meeting of the American Educational Research Association, Seattle, WA, 10–14 April.

Gallagher, J. J. (1985) *Teaching the Gifted Child*. Boston: Allyn & Bacon.

Galloway, D. (1985) *Schools, Pupils and Special Educational Needs*. Beckenham: Croom Helm.

Galton, M. (1987) An ORACLE Chronicle: A Decade of Classroom Research. *Teaching and Teacher Education* 3(4), 299–313.

Galton, M. and Croll, P. (1980) Pupil Progress in the Basic Skills. In M. Galton and B. Simon (eds) *Progress and Performance in the Primary Classroom*. London: Routledge.

Gardner, H. (1983) *Frames of Mind*. New York: Basic Books.

Gardner, H. (1993) *Multiple Intelligences: The Theory in Practice*. New York: Basic Books.

Gardner, H. (1995) Reflections on the Multiple Intelligences: Myths and Messages. *Phi-Delta Kappan* 77(3), 200–9.

Gardner, H. (2003) *Multiple Intelligences After 20 Years*. Presentation delivered at the Annual Meeting of the American Educational Research Association, Chicago, IL, April.

Garner, I. (2000) Problems and Inconsistencies with Kolb's Learning Styles. *Educational Psychology: An International Journal of Experimental Educational Psychology* 20(3), 341–8.

Gartner, A. and Lipsky, D. K. (1987) Beyond Special Education: Toward a Quality System for All Students. *Harvard Educational Review* 57(4), 367–95.

Gavin, M. K. and Reis, S. M. (2003) Helping Teachers To Encourage Talented Girls in Mathematics. *Gifted Child Today* 26(1), 32–44.

Geeke, P. (1988) *Evaluation Report on the Reading Recovery Field Trial in Central Australia*. Centre for Studies in Literacy, University of Wollongong.

Geers, A. and Moog, J. (1989) Factors Predictive of the Development of Literacy in Profoundly Hearing-Impaired Adolescents. *Volta Review* 91, 69–86.

Gersten, R. (1999) Lost Opportunities: Challenges Confronting Four Teachers of English-Language Learners. *Elementary School Journal* 100(1), 37–56.

Gipps, C. and McGilchrist, B. (1999) Primary School Learners. In P. Mortimore (ed.) *Understanding Pedagogy and its Impact on Learning*. London: Paul Chapman.

Glasser, W. (1998) *Choice Theory: A New Psychology of Personal Freedom*. New York: HarperCollins.

Goldberg, D. (ed.) (1994) Auditory–verbal Philosophy: A Tutorial. *Volta Review* 95(3), 181–262.

Goldberg, D. (1997) *Educating Children Who Are Deaf or Hard of Hearing: Auditory–Verbal*. Reston, VA: ERIC Clearinghouse on Disabilities and Gifted Education. Digest E552.

Goldman, G. and Newman, J. B. (1998) *Empowering Students To Transform Schools*. Thousand Oaks, CA: Corwin Press.

Good, R. G., Wandersee, J. H. and St. Julien, J. (1993) Cautionary Notes on the Appeal of the New 'ism' (Constructivism) in Science Education. In K. Tobin (ed.) *The Practice of Constructivism in Science Education*. Washington, DC: AAAS Press, 71–87.

Good, T. L. and Brophy, J. E. (1986) *Looking in Classrooms* (sixth edition). New York: Harper Row.

Good, T.L., and Grouws, D.A. (1979) The Missouri Mathematics Effectiveness Project in Fourth-grade Classrooms. *Journal of Educational Psychology* 71, 355–62.

Good, T. L., Biddle, B. J. and Brophy, J. E. (1975) *Teachers Make a Difference*. Washington, DC: University Press of America.

Good, T. L., Grouws, D. A. and Ebmeier, D. (1983) *Active Mathematics Teaching*. New York: Longman.

Good, T., McCaslin, M. and Reys, B. (1995) Investigating Work Groups to Promote Problem Solving in Mathematics. In J. Brophy (ed.) *Advances in Research on Teaching* (Vol. 3). Greenwich, CT: JAI Press.

Goodman, K. S. and Goodman, Y. (1982) A Whole Language Comprehension Centred View of Reading Development. In L. Reed and S. Louis (eds) *Basic Skills: Issues and Choices*. St Louis, MO: CEMREL.

Gould, S. (1983) *The Mismeasure of Man*. London: Penguin.

Gould, S. J. (1996) *The Mismeasure of Man*. New York: Norton.

Gravemeijer, K. (1997) Mediating Between Concrete and Abstract. In T. Nunes and P. Bryant (eds) *Learning and Teaching Mathematics: An International Perspective*. Hove: Psychology Press, 315–45.

Gredler, M. E. (1997) *Learning and Instruction: Theory into Practice*. Upper Saddle River, NJ: Prentice Hall.

Griffin, G. A. and Barnes, S. (1986) Using Research Findings to Change School and Classroom Practice: Results of an Experimental Study. *American Educational Research Journal* 23(4), 572–86.

Gronlund, N. E. (1991) *Constructing Achievement Tests*. Englewood Cliffs, NJ: Prentice Hall.

Gross, M. U. M. (2006) Exceptionally Gifted Children: Long-Term Outcomes of Academic Acceleration and Nonacceleration. *Journal for the Education of the Gifted* 29(4), 404–29.

Grossen, M. and Bachman, K. (2000) Learning to Collaborate in a Peer-tutoring Situation: Who Learns? What is Learned? *European Journal of Psychology of Education* 15(4), 491–508.

Grugnett, L. and Jaquet, F. (1996) Senior Secondary School Practices. In A. J. Bishop, K. Clements, C. Keitel, J. Kilpatrick and C. Laborde (eds) *International Handbook of Mathematics Education*. Dordrecht: Kluwer.

Guay, F., Marsh, H. W. and Boivin, M. (2003) Academic Self-Concept and Academic Achievement: Developmental Perspectives on Their Causal Ordering. *Journal of Educational Psychology* 95(1), 124–36.

Gueldenzoph, L. and May, G. (2002) Collaborative Peer Evaluation: Best Practices for Group Member Assessments. *Business Communication Quarterly* 65(9), 9–20.

Gustasson, G. (1997) *Educating Children Who Are Deaf or Hard of Hearing: English-Based Sign Systems*. Reston, VA: ERIC Clearinghouse on Disabilities and Gifted Education. ERIC Digest E556.

Gut, D. M. and Safran, S. P. (2002) Cooperative Learning and Social Stories: Effective Social Skills Strategies for Reading Teachers. *Reading and Writing Quarterly: Overcoming Learning Difficulties* 18(1), 87–91.

Guthrie, L. F., Guthrie, G. P., Van Heusden, S. and Burns, R. (1989) *Principles of Successful Chapter 1 Programs*. San Francisco: Far West Laboratory for Educational Research and Development.

Haen, J. F. (2000) *Reading Recovery: Success for How Many?* Paper presented at the Annual Meeting of the American Educational Research Association, New Orleans, April.

Hair, E. C., Jager, J. and Garrett, S. (2001) *Background for Community-Level Work on Social Competency in Adolescence: Reviewing the Literature on Contributing Factors*. Washington: Child Trends Inc. Available at: www.childtrends.org/PDF/KnightReports/ KSocial.pdf

Hall, J. D. and Bramlett, R. K. (2002) Screening Young Children's Social Behaviors: An Examination of Decision Reliability with Alternative Measures. *Special Services in the Schools* 18(1–2), 83–93.

Hallam, S. (2004) *Homework: The Evidence*. London: Institute of Education.

Hallam, S. and Cowan, R. (1999) *Is Homework Important for Increasing Educational Achievement?* LDE-Online Publications-Homework.

Hallinan, M. T. and Sorensen, A. B. (1985) Ability Grouping and Student Friendship. *American Educational Research Journal* 22(4), 485–99.

Hamers, J. H. M. and Csapo, B. (1999) Teaching Thinking. In J. M. H. Hamers, J. E. H. Van Luit and B. Csapo (eds) *Teaching and Learning Thinking Skills*. Lisse: Swets & Zeitlinger.

Hanley, S. (1994) *On Constructivism*. Available at: www.inform.umd.edu/UMS;State/UMD-Projects/MCTP/Essays/Constructivism.txt

Hannafin, M. J., Hill, J. R. and Land, S. M. (1997) Student-centered Learning and Interactive Multimedia: Status, Issues, and Implications. *Contemporary Education* 68(2), 94–7.

Hansell, S. and Karweit, N. (1983) Curricular Placement, Friendship Networks and Status Attainment. In J. L. Epstein and N. Karweit (eds) *Friends in School, Patterns of Selection And Influence*. New York: Academic Press.

Hansford, B. C. and Hattie, J. A. (1982) The Relationship Between Self and Achievement/Performance Measures. *Review of Educational Research* 52(1), 123–42.

Hargreaves, D. H. (1967) *Social Relations in a Secondary School*. London & Henley: Routledge & Kegan Paul.

Harman, P., Egelson, P., Hood, A. and O'Connell, D. (2002) *Observing Life in Small-Class Size Classrooms*. Paper presented at the Annual Meeting of the American Educational Research Association, New Orleans, LA, 1–5 April.

Hart, B. and Risley, T. R. (1995) *Meaningful Differences in the Everyday Experience of Young American Children*. Baltimore, MA: Paul Brookes Publishing.

Hartup, W. W. and Moore, S. G. (1990) Early Peer Relations: Developmental Significance and Prognostic Implications. *Early Childhood Research Quarterly* 5 (March), 1–17.

Heath, J. and Vik, P. (1994) Elementary School Student Councils: A Statewide Survey. *Principal* 74(1), 31–4.

Hecker, L., Burns, L., Elkind, J., Elkind, K. and Katz, L. (2002) Benefits of Assistive Reading Software for Students with Attention Disorders. *Annals of Dyslexia* 52, 243–72.

Helm, J. H. and Katz, L. G. (2001) *Young Investigators: The Project Approach in the Early Years*. Early Childhood Education Series. Williston, VT: Teachers College Press.

Hembree, R. (1992) Experiments and Relational Studies in Problem-Solving: Meta-Analysis. *Journal for Research in Mathematics Education* 23(3), 242–73.

Hendy, L. and Toon, L. (2001) *Supporting Drama and Imaginative Play in the Early Years: Supporting Early Learning*. Florence, KY: Taylor & Francis.

Henson, R. K. (2001) *Teacher Self-Efficacy: Substantive Implications and Measurement Dilemmas*. Keynote Address given at the Educational Research Exchange, Texas A7M University, 26 January.

Hiebert, J. and T. P. Carpenter (1992) Learning and Teaching with Understanding. In D. A. Grouws (ed.) *Handbook of Research on Mathematics Teaching and Learning*. New York: Macmillan, 65–97.

High/Scope (2000) *The High/Scope Approach*. High/Scope Educational Research Foundation. Available at: www.high/scope.org

Hilgard, E. (1995) *Theories of Learning*. New York: Appleton.

Hill, H., Rowan, B. and Loewenberg Ball, D. (2005) Effects of Teachers' Mathematical Knowledge for Teaching on Student Achievement. *American Educational Research Journal* 42(2), 371–406.

Hirsch-Pasek, K., Hyson, M. and Recorla, L. (1990) Academic Environments in Preschool: Do They Pressure or Challenge Young Children? *Early Education and Development* 1(6), 401–23.

HMI (1978) Primary education in England: A survey by HM Inspectors of Schools. London: Her Majesty's Stationery Office.

Hodges, H. (1994) A Consumer's Guide to Learning Style Programs. *School Administrator* 51(1), 14–18.

Hofer, T. and Beckman, A. (2008) Supporting Mathematical Literacy: Examples From a Cross-curricular Project. *ZDM Mathematics Education* (41), 223–30.

Hogan, K., Nastasi, B. K. and Pressley, M. (1999) Discourse Patterns and Collaborative Scientific Reasoning in Peer and Teacher-Guided Discussions. *Cognition and Instruction* 17(4), 379–432.

Hoge, D. R., Smit, E. K. and Crist, J. T. (1995) Reciprocal Effects of Self-concept and Academic Achievement in Sixth and Seventh Grade. *Journal of Youth and Adolescence* 24(3), 295–314.

Hong, Z.-R., Veach, P. and Lawrenz, F. (2002) *An Investigation of Self-Esteem and School Achievement of Taiwanese Secondary Students*. Hong Kong: Institute of Education.

Hoover-Dempsey, K. V., Bassler, O. C. and Burow, R. (1995) Parents' Reported Involvement in Students' Homework: Strategies and Practices. *Elementary School Journal* 95(5), 435–50.

Hopkins, D. and Reynolds, D. (2001) The Past, Present and Future of School Improvement: Towards the Third Age. *British Educational Research Journal* 27(4), 459–75.

Horcones, J. (1991) Walden Two In Real Life: Behavior Analysis in the Design of the Culture. In W. Ishag (ed.) *Human Behavior in Today's World*. New York: Praeger.

Horcones, J. (1992) Natural Reinforcement: A Way to Improve Education. *Journal of Applied Behavior Analysis* 25(1), 71–5.

Howe, M. J. A. (1997) *IQ in Question: The Truth About Intelligence*. London: Sage.

Howes, C., Burchinal, M., Pianta, R., Bryant, D., Early, D., Clifford, R. and Barbarin, O. (2008) Ready to Learn? Children's Pre-academic Achievement in Pre-Kindergarten Programs. *Early Childhood Research Quarterly* 23(1), 27–50.

Huber, K. D., Rosenfeld, J. G. and Fiorello, C. A. (2001) The Differential Impact of Inclusion and Inclusive Practices on High, Average, and Low Achieving General Education Students. *Psychology in the Schools* 38(6), 497–504.

Hujala, E. (2002) The Curriculum for Early Learning in the Context of Society. *International Journal of Early Years Education* 10(2), 95–104.

Huss, J. A. (2006) Gifted Education and Cooperative Learning: A Miss or a Match? *Gifted Child Today* 29(4), 19–23.

Hyson, M. C. and Van Trieste, K. (1987) *The Shy Child*. ERIC Clearinghouse on Elementary and Early Childhood Education, ED295741.

Imants, J., Van der Aalsvoort, G., De Brabander, C. and Ruijssenaars, A. (2001) The Role of the Special Services Coordinator in Dutch Primary Schools: A Counterproductive Effect of Inclusion Policy. *Educational Management & Administration* 29(1), 35–48.

Ireson, J., Hallam, S., Hack, S., Clark, J. and Plewis, I. (2002) Ability Grouping in English Secondary School: Effects on Attainment in English, Mathematics, and Science. *Educational Research and Evaluation* 8(3), 299–318.

Jacobs, H. (1989) The Inter-Disciplinary Concept Model: A Step-by-Step Approach to Integrated Units of Study. In H. Jacobs (ed.) *Interdisciplinary Curriculum: Design and Implementation.* Alexandria, VA: Association for Supervision and Curriculum Development.

Janos, P. M. and Robinson, N. M. (1985) The Performance of Students in a Radical Acceleration at the University Level. *Gifted Child Quarterly* 29, 175–80.

Jencks, C., Smith, M., Acland, H., Bane, M. J., Cohen, D., Gintis, H., Heyns, B. and Michelson, S. (1972) *Inequality: A Reassessment of the Effects of Family and Schooling in America*. New York: Basic Books.

Jenkins, J. M. and Keefe, J. W. (2002) Two Schools: Two Approaches to Personalized Learning. *Phi Delta Kappan* 83(6), 449–56.

Jenkins, J. R., Jewell, M., Leicester, N., O'Connor, R. E., Jenkins, L. M. and Troutner, N. M. (1994) Accommodations for Individual Differences Without Classroom Ability Groups: An Experiment in School Restructuring. *Exceptional Children* 60(4), 344–58.

Jeynes, W. (2007) A Meta-Analysis of the Relationship Between Phonics Instruction and Minority Elementary School Student Achievement. *Education and Urban Society* 23(3), 256–71.

Joachim, S. (2002) Accentuate the Positive: Improving the Classroom Climate in Developmental Classes. *Research and Teaching in Developmental Education* 19(1), 66–8.

Johnson, D. W. and Johnson, R. T. (1989) Cooperative Learning: What Special Educators Need to Know. *The Pointer* 33, 5–10.

Johnson, D. W. and Johnson, R. T. (1994) *Joining Together. Group Theory and Group Skills*. Englewood Cliffs, NJ: Prentice Hall.

Johnson, D. W. and Johnson, R. T. (2000) *Cooperative Learning*. Presentation given at the Annual Meeting of the American Educational Research Association, New Orleans, April.

Johnson, D. W., Johnson, R. T. and Smith, K. A. (1998) Cooperative Learning Returns to College: What Evidence is There That it Works? *Change* 30(4), 26–35.

Johnsson-Smaragdi, U. and Jonsson, A. (1995) Self-evaluation in an Ecological Perspective: Neighbourhood, Family and Peers, Schooling and Media Use. In K. E. Rosengren (ed.) *Media Effects and Beyond*. London: Routledge.

Jolivette, K., Wehby, J., Canale, J. and Massey, N. G. (2001) Effects of Choice-Making Opportunities on the Behavior of Students with Emotional and Behavioral Disorders. *Behavioral Disorders* 26(2), 131–45.

Joyce, B. and Weil, M. (1996) *Models of Teaching* (fifth edition). Boston: Allyn & Bacon.

Joyce, B., Weil, M. and Calhoun, E. (2000) *Models of Teaching.* New York: Allyn & Bacon.

Kagan, S. L. and Hallmark, L. G. (2001) Early Care and Education Policies in Sweden: Implications for the United States. *Phi Delta Kappan* 83(3), 237–45.

Kamps, D., Greenwood, C., Arreaga-Mayer, C., Veerkamp, B., Utley, C., Tapia, Y., Bowman-Perrott, L. and Bannister, H. (2008) The Efficacy of Class Wide Peer Tutoring in Middle Schools. *Education and Treatment of Children* 31(2), 119.

Kantrowitz, B. and Wingert, P. (1992) An 'F' in World Competition. *Newsweek*, 17 February, p. 57.

Katz, L. G. (1997) Tomorrow Begins Today: Implications from Research. *ERIC/EECE Newsletter* 9(4).

Katz, L. G. (1999) Another Look at What Young Children Should be Learning. *ERIC/EECE Newsletter* 11(2), 1–3.

Keith, T. Z. (1987) Children and Homework. In A. Thomas and J. Grimes (eds) *Children's Needs: Psychological Perspectives*. Washington, DC: National Association of School Psychologists.

Kelley, P. (2007) *Making Minds.* London: Routledge.

Keltikangas-Jarvinen, L. (1992) Self-esteem as a Predictor of Future School Achievement. *European Journal of Psychology of Education* 7(2), 123–30.

Kemple, K. M. (1992) *Understanding and Facilitating Preschool Children's Peer Acceptance*. ERIC Clearinghouse on Elementary and Early Childhood Education, ED345866.

Kennedy, K. J. (2006) *Barriers to Innovative School Practice: A Socio-Cultural Framework for Understanding Assessment Practices in Asia.* Paper prepared for the Symposium: 'Student Assessment and its Social and Cultural Contexts: How Teachers Respond to Assessment Reforms'. Redesigning Pedagogy – Culture, Understanding and Practice Conference, Singapore, 28–30 May.

Kern, L., Bambara, L. and Fogt, J. (2002) Class-Wide Curricular Modification to Improve the Behavior of Students with Emotional or Behavioral Disorders. *Behavioral Disorders* 27(4), 317–26.

Kim, J. S. (2005) The Effects of a Constructivist Teaching Approach on Student Academic Achievement, Self-concept, and Learning Strategies. *Asia Pacific Education Review* 6(1), 7–19.

King, W. and Edmunds, A. (2001) Teachers' Perceived Needs To Become More Effective Inclusion Practitioners: A Single School Study. *Exceptionality Education Canada* 11(1), 3–23.

Kirschner, P., Sweller, J. and Clark, R. (2006) Why Minimal Guidance During Instruction Does Not Work: An Analysis of the Failure of Constructivist, Discovery, Problem-Based, Experiential and Inquiry-Based Teaching. *Educational Psychologist* 41(2), 75–86.

Klahr, D. and Nigam, M. (2004) The Equivalence of Learning Paths in Early Science Instruction: Effects of Direct Instruction and Discovery Learning. *Psychological Science* 15, 661–7.

Klein, P. D. (1997) Multiplying the Problems of Intelligence by Eight: A Critique of Gardner's Theory. *Canadian Journal of Education* 22(4), 377–94.

Klieme, E. and Clausen, M. (1999) *Identifying Facets of Problem Solving in Mathematics Instruction*. Paper presented at the Annual Meeting of the American Educational Research Association, Montreal, Quebec, 19–23 April.

Klinger, B. and Nelson, D. (1996) *Improving Academic Achievement of At-Risk Students in English*. Winnebago, IL: St Xavier.

Koebley, S. C. and Soled, S. W. (1998) *The Effects of a Constructivist-Oriented Mathematics Classroom on Student and Parent Beliefs about and Motivations towards Being Successful in Mathematics*. Paper presented at the Annual Meeting of the American Educational Research Association, San Diego, CA, 13–17 April.

Kolb, D. A. (1995) The Process of Experiential Learning. In M. Thorpe, R. Edwards and A. Hanson (eds) *Culture and Processes of Adult Learning*. Milton Keynes: Open University Press.

Kolb, K. and Weede, S. (2001) *Teaching Prosocial Skills to Young Children to Increase Emotionally Intelligent Behavior*. Paper presented at the Annual Meeting of the American Educational Research Association, New Orleans, LA, April.

Koller, O. (2001) Mathematical World Views and Achievement in Advanced Mathematics in Germany: Findings from TIMSS Population 3. *Studies in Educational Evaluation* 27(1), 65–78.

Kotulak, R. (1996) *Inside the Brain*. Kansas City, MO: Universal Press Syndicate.

Kounin, J. (1970) *Discipline and Groups Management in the Classroom*. New York: Holt, Rinehart & Winston.

Ku, H.-Y. and Sullivan, H. J. (2001) *Effects of Personalized Instruction on Mathematics Word Problems in Taiwan*. 24th Annual Proceedings of Selected Research and Development [and] Practice Papers Presented at the National Convention of the Association for Educational Communications and Technology, Atlanta, GA, 8–12 November.

Kulik, J. A. (1992) *An Analysis of Research on Ability Groupings: Historical and Contemporary Perspectives*. Storrs, CT: The National Research Center on the Gifted and Talented, University of Connecticut.

Kunter, M., Baumert, J. and Koller, O. (2007) Effective Classroom Management and the Development of Subject-related Interest. *Learning and Instruction* 17(4), 494–509.

Kupersmidt, J. B. and Coie, J. D. (1990) Preadolescent Peer Status, Aggression, and School Adjustment Predictors of Externalising Problems in Adolescence. *Child Development* 61, 1350–62.

Kwon, Y.-I. (2002) Changing Curriculum for Early Childhood Education in England. *Early Childhood Research & Practice* 4(2), 13–25.

Lacey, C. (1970) *Hightown Grammar. The School as a Social System*. Manchester: Manchester University Press.

Lackney, J.A. (1999) Twelve Design Principles for Schools Derived from Brain-based Learning Research. *Schoolhouse Journal* 2(2), 1–12.

LaConte, R. T. (1981) *Homework as a Learning Experience: What Research Says to the Teacher*. Washington, DC: NEA.

Laird, R. D., Pettit, G. S., Mize, J., Brown, E. G. and Linsey, E. (1994) Parent–Child Conversations About Peer Relationships: Contributions to Competence. *Family Relations* 43, 425–32.

Lane, K., Wehby, J. and Cooley, C. (2006) Teacher Expectations of Students' Classroom Behavior across the Grade Span: Which Social Skills are Necessary for Success? *Exceptional Children* 72(2), 153–67.

Lane, K. L., Wehby, J., Menzies, H. M., Doukas, G. L., Munton, S. M. and Gregg, R. M. (2003) Social Skills Instruction for Students At Risk for Antisocial Behavior: The Effects of Small-Group Instruction. *Behavioral Disorders* 28(3), 229–48.

Lave, J. and Wenger, E. (1991) *Situated Learning: Legitimate Peripheral Participation*. Cambridge: Cambridge University Press.

Lavoie, R. D. (1997) *The Teacher's Role in Developing Social Skills*. LDA-CA. Available at: www.kidsource.com/LDA-CA/teacher.html

LaVoie, R. (2005) *Social Skill Autopsies: A Strategy to Promote and Develop Social Competencies*. Downloaded from LD Online, 12/09/2009. http://www.ldonline.org/article/Social_Skill_Autopsies%3A_A_Strategy_to_Promote_and_Develop_Social_Competencies.

Leithwood, K. and Steinbach, R. (2002) Successful Leadership for Especially Challenging Schools. *Journal of Leadership in Education* 79(2), 73–82.

Lemlech, J. K. (1988) *Classroom Management: Methods and Techniques for Elementary and Secondary Teachers* (second edition) New York: Longman.

Leonard, J. (2001) How Group Composition Influenced the Achievement of Sixth-Grade Mathematics Students. *Mathematical Thinking and Learning* 3(2–3), 175–200.

Lester, K. K. Jr. (1994) Musings About Mathematical Problem-Solving Research: 1970–1994. *Journal for Research in Mathematics Education* 25(6), 660–75.

Leung, W. H. A. (2004) *Teaching Integrated Curriculum: Teachers' Challenges*. Paper presented at the Pacific Circle Consortium, 28th Annual Conference, Hong Kong Institute of Education, 21–23 April.

Lewis, C. and Tsuchida, I. (1997) Planned Educational Change in Japan: The Case of Elementary Science Instruction. *Journal of Educational Policy* 12(5), 313–31.

Lindsay, G. (2003) Inclusive Education: A Critical Perspective. *British Journal of Special Education* 30, 3–12.

Lindsay, G., Muijs, D., Hartas, D. and Phillips, E. (2002) *National Academy for Gifted and Talented Youth Evaluation of Summer School 2002*. Coventry: CEDAR, University of Warwick.

Linn, M. C. and Burbules, N. C. (1993) Construction of Knowledge and Group Learning. In K. Tobin (ed.) *The Practice of Constructivism in Science Education*. Washington, DC: American Association for the Advancement of Science.

Linn, M. C., Lewis, C., Tsuchida, I. and Butler Songer, N. (2000) Beyond Fourth-Grade Science: Why Do US and Japanese Students Diverge? *Educational Researcher* 29(3), 4–14.

Linsey, E. W., Mize, J. and Pettit, G. S. (1997) Mutuality in Parent–Child Play: Consequences for Children's Peer Competence. *Journal of Social and Personality Relationships* 14(4), 523–8.

Lipsky, D. and Gartner, A. (1997) *Inclusion and School Reform: Transforming America's Classrooms*. Boston, MA: RIE.

Littler, G. and Jirotkova, D. (2008) Highlighting the Learning Process. In A. D. Cockburn and G. Littler (eds) *Mathematical Misconceptions*. London: Sage.

Litzinger, M. E. and Osif, B. (1993) Accommodating Diverse Learning Styles: Designing Instruction for Electronic Information Sources. In L. Shirato (ed.) *What is Good Instruction Now? Library Instruction for the 90s*. Ann Arbor, MI: Pierian Press.

Liu, W. C. and Wang, C. K. J. (2008) Home Environment and Classroom Climate: An Investigation of their Relation to Students' Academic Self-Concept in a Streamed Setting. *Current Psychology* 27(4), 242–56.

Lo, Y.-Y., Loe, S. A. and Cartledge, G. (2002) The Effects of Social Skills Instruction on the Social Behaviors of Students at Risk for Emotional or Behavioral Disorders. *Behavioral Disorders* 27(4), 371–85.

Lyon, G. R. (1994) *Research in Learning Disabilities at the NICHD*. Bethesda, MD: NICHD Technical Document/Human Learning and Behavior Branch.

Lyon, G. R. (1999) *The NICHD Research Program in Reading Development, Reading Disorders and Reading Instruction*. NICHD: Keys to Successful Learning Summit. Available at: www.nichd.org/summit99/keys99-nichd.htm

Lyon, G. R. and Kameenui, E. J. (2000) *National Institute of Child Health and Development (NICHD) Research Supports America Reads Challenge*. Available at: www.ed.gov/inits/americareads/nichd.html

Maaz, K., Trautwein, U., Ludtke, O. and Baumert, L. (2008) Educational Transitions and Differential Learning Environments: How Explicit Between-School Tracking Contributes to Social Inequality in Educational Outcomes. *Child Development Perspectives* 2(2), 99–106.

MacBeath, J., Galton, M., Steward, S., MacBeath, A. and Page, C. (2006) *The Cost of Inclusion*. Cambridge: University of Cambridge, Faculty of Education.

MacIntyre, H. and Ireson, J. (2002) Within-Class Ability Grouping: Placement of Pupils in Groups and Self-Concept. *British Educational Research Journal* 28(2), 249–63.

Macklem, G. L. (1990) Measuring Aptitude. *Practical Assessment, Research and Evaluation* 2(5) Available at: //PAREonline.net/getvn.asp?v=2&n=5

Madaus, G. F. and O'Dwyer, L. M. (1999) A Short History of Performance Assessment. *Phi Delta Kappan* 80(9), 688–95.

Madden, N. (2006) Reducing the Gap: Success for All and the Achievement of African American Students. *Journal of Negro Education* 75(3), 389–400.

Madden, N.A. and Slavin, R. E. (1983) Mainstreaming Students with Mild Handicaps: Academic and Social Outcomes. *Review of Educational Research* 53(4), 519–69.

Madden, N. A., Slavin, R. E. and Simons, K. (1999) *MathWings: Effects on Student Mathematics Performance*. Baltimore, MD: CRESPAR, Johns Hopkins University, Center for Social Organization of Schools.

Madden, N. A., Slavin, R. E., Karweit, N. L., Dolan, L. J. and Wasik, B. A. (1993) Success for All: Longitudinal Effects of a Restructuring Program for Inner-City Elementary Schools. *American Educational Research Journal* 30, 123–48.

Magliaro, S., Lockee, B. and Burton, J. (2005) Direct Instruction Revisited: A Key Model for Instructional Technology. *Educational Technology Research and Development* 53(4), 41–9.

Malecki, C. K. and Elliott, S. N. (2002) Children's Social Behaviors as Predictors of Academic Achievement: A Longitudinal Analysis. *School Psychology Quarterly* 17(1), 1–23.

Mandeville, G. K. and Liu, Q. (1997) The Effect of Teacher Certification and Task Level on Mathematics Achievement. *Teaching and Teacher Education* 13(4), 397–407.

Manset, G. and Semmel, M. I. (1997) An Inclusive Program for Students with Mild Disabilities: A Comparison Review of Model Programs. *The Journal of Special Education* 31(2), 155–80.

Maqsud, M. and Rouhani, S. (1991) Relationships Between Socio-economic Status, Locus of Control, Self-concept and Academic Achievement of Bophutatswana Adolescents. *Journal of Youth and Adolescence* 20(1), 107–113.

Marcon, R. A. (1992) Differential Effects of Three Preschool Models on Inner-city 4-Year-Olds. *Early Childhood Research Quarterly* 7(4), 517–30.

Marsh, H. W. (1990) Causal Ordering of Academic Self-concept and Academic Achievement: A Multiwave, Longitudinal Panel Analysis. *Journal of Educational Psychology* 82(4), 646–56.

Marsh, H. W. and Craven, R. G. (2002) The Pivotal Role of Frames of Reference in Academic Self-Concept Formation: The 'Big Fish-Little Pond' Effect. In *Academic Motivation of Adolescents*. Greenwich, CT: Information Age Publishing.

Marsh, H. W. and Craven, R. G. (2006) Reciprocal Effects of Self-Concept and Performance from a Multidimensional Perspective: Beyond Seductive Pleasure and Unidimensional Perspectives. *Perspectives on Psychological Science* 1(2), 133–63.

Marsh, H. W. and O'Mara, H. (2008) Reciprocal Effects Between Academic Self-Concept, Self-Esteem, Achievement, and Attainment Over Seven Adolescent Years: Unidimensional and Multidimensional Perspectives of Self-Concept. *Personality and Social Psychology Bulletin* 34(4), 542–52.

Marsh, H. W., Relich, J. D. and Smith, I. D. (1983) Self-concept: The Construct Validity of Interpretations Based on the SDQ. *Journal of Personality and Social Psychology* 45(1), 213–31.

Marsh, H. W., Parker, J. and Barnes, J. (1985) Multidimensional Adolescent Self-concepts: Their Relationship to Age, Sex and Academic Measures. *American Educational Research Journal* 22(3), 422–44.

Marsh, H. W., Hau, K.-T. and Kong, C.-K. (2002) Multilevel Causal Ordering of Academic Self-Concept and Achievement: Influence of Language of Instruction (English Compared with Chinese) for Hong Kong Students. *American Educational Research Journal* 39(3), 727–63.

McAllister, B. and Plourde, E. (2008) Enrichment Curriculum: Essential for Mathematically Gifted Students. *Education* 129(1), 40–9.

McCallum, B. (2000) *Formative Assessment: Implications for Classroom Practice*. London: Institute of Education.

McClelland, M., Acock, A. and Morrison, F. (2006) The Impact of Kindergarten Learning-related Skills on Academic Trajectories at the end of Elementary School. *Early Childhood Research Quarterly* 21(4), 471–90.

McDavitt, D. S. (1994) *Teaching for Understanding: Attaining Higher Order Learning and Increased Achievement through Experiential Instruction*. Charlottesville, VA: University of Virginia.

McElgunn, B. (1996) *Critical Discoveries in Learning Disabilities: A Summary of Findings by the National Institute of Health. Research Centres Report at the LDA 1996 Conference*. Newsbriefs, July–August, 1996, LDA Home Page (accessed 08 June 2009).

McGuinness, C. (2006) *ACTS (Activating Children's Thinking Skills): A Methodology for Enhancing Thinking Skills across the Curriculum (with a Focus on Knowledge Transformation)*. Paper presented at the ESRC TLRP First Programme Conference, 9–10 November.

McIntyre, T. (2003) *Teaching Social Skills to Kids who don't Yet Have Them.* Available at: www.ldonline.org/article/Teaching_Social_Skills_to_Kids_Who_Don%27t_Yet_Have_Them (accessed 12 September 2009).

McLeskey, J. and Waldron, N. L. (2002) School Change and Inclusive Schools: Lessons Learned from Practice. *Phi Delta Kappan* 84(1), 65–72.

McLeskey, J., Waldron, N. L., So, T.-S., Swanson, K. and Loveland, T. (2001) Perspectives of Teachers toward Inclusive School Programs. *Teacher Education and Special Education* 24(2), 108–15.

McWayne, C., Hampton, V., Fantuzzo, J., Cohen, H. and Sekino, Y. (2004) A Multivariate Examination of Parent Involvement and the Social and Academic Competencies of Urban Kindergarten Children. *Psychology in the Schools* 41(3), 363–77.

Mead, G. H. (1934) *Mind, Self and Society from the Standpoint of a Social Behaviorist*. Chicago: Chicago University Press.

Meijer, J. (2007) Cross-Curricular Skills Testing in the Netherlands. *The Curriculum Journal* 18(2), 155–73.

Merrell, K. W. (2001) *Helping Students Overcome Depression and Anxiety: A Practical Guide*. New York: Guilford Press.

Merttens, R. (ed.) (1996) *Teaching Numeracy: Maths in the Primary Classroom*. Primary Professional Bookshelf. Leamington Spa: Scholastic.

Meyer, D. K. and Turner, J. C. (2006) Re-conceptualizing Emotion and Motivation to Learn in Classroom Contexts. *Educational Psychology Review* 18: 377–90.

Miles, B. (2001) *Die Sprache der Hande zu den Handen sprechen* ('Talking the Language of the Hands to the Hands'). Available at: www.tr.wou.edu/dblink/handgerman

Miles, P. L. (1989) *A Communication Based Strategy to Improve Teaching: The Continuous Feedback Technique*. Paper presented at the Annual Meeting of the Speech Communication Association. University of Texas, Austin, April, ED 314 787.

Miles, S. B. and Stipek, D. (2006) Contemporaneous and Longitudinal Associations Between Social Behavior and Literacy Achievement in a Sample of Low-income Elementary School Children. *Child Development* 77(1), 103–17.

Miller, L. B. and Bizzell, R. P. (1983) Long-Term Effects of Four Preschool Programs: Sixth, Seventh and Eighth Grades. *Child Development* 54(3), 727–41.

Moats, L. C. (1996) *Neither/Nor: Resolving the Debate Between Whole Language and Phonics*. Lecture given at the 1996 Washington Summit Conference of Learning Disabilities. Transcript available at: www.greenwoodinstitute.org/resources/res-nor.html

Moll, L. (1992) Literacy Research in Community and Classrooms: A Sociocultural Approach. In R. Beach, J. Green, M. Kamil and T. Shanahan (eds) *Multidisciplinary Perspectives on Literacy Research*. Urbana, IL: National Council of Teachers of English, 211–44.

Monk, D. H. (1994) Subject Matter Preparation of Secondary Mathematics and Science Teachers and Student Achievement. *Economics of Education Review* 13(2), 125–45.

Moore, W. and Esselman, M. (1992) *Teacher Efficacy, Power, School Climate and Achievement: A Desegregating District's Experience.* Paper Presented at the Annual Meeting of the American Educational Research Association, San Francisco, CA.

Moran, P. B. and Eckenrode, J. (1991) Gender Differences in the Costs and Benefits of Peer Relations During Adolescence. *Journal of Adolescent Research* 6(4), 396–409.

Morgan, H. (1996) An Analysis of Gardner's Theory of Multiple Intelligence. *Roeper Review* 18, 263–9.

Mortimore, P., Sammons, P., Stoll, L., Lewis, D. and Ecob, R. (1988) *School Matters*. Wells, Somerset: Open Books.

Mosher, R. (1994) *Preparing for Citizenship: Teaching Youth To Live Democratically*. Westport, CT: Praeger.

Moskal, B. M. (2000) Scoring Rubrics: What, When and How? *Practical Assessment, Research and Evaluation* 7(3), 88–96.

Mosley, J. (1999) Circle Time: A Whole Class Peer Support Model. In S. Decker, S. Kirby, A. Greenwood and D. Moore (eds) *Taking Children Seriously: Application of Counselling and Therapy in Education*. London: Cassell, 171–83.

Muijs, R. D. (1997) *Self, School and Media: A Longitudinal Study of the Relationship Between Self-Concept, School Achievement, Peer Relations and Media Use among Flemish Primary School Children*. Leuven: K.U. Leuven, Department of Communication Science.

Muijs, R. D. (1998a) The Reciprocal Relationship Between Self-Concept and School Achievement. *British Journal of Educational Psychology* 67(3): 263–77.

Muijs, R. D. (1998b) *The Relationship Between KS Test Results in HRS Schools and the CAT*. Unpublished research paper, Newcastle University, Department of Education.

Muijs, R. D. (2000) *Three Innovative Uses of ICT in the Primary Classroom*. Loughborough: Educational Effectiveness Centre.

Muijs, R. D. (2008) Educational Effectiveness and the Legacy of Bert P. M. Creemers. *School Effectiveness and School Improvement,* 19(4), 463–72.

Muijs, D. and Dunne, M. (2008) *Setting by Ability, Or Is It?* Paper presented at the Annual Meeting of the American Educational Research Association, New York, March.

Muijs, R. D. and Reynolds, D. (1999) *School Effectiveness and Teacher Effectiveness: Some Preliminary Findings from the Evaluation of the Mathematics Enhancement Programme*. Presented at the American Educational Research Association Conference, Montreal, Quebec, 19 April.

Muijs, R. D. and Reynolds, D. (2000a) *Learning Psychology*. Part 3 of Distance Learning Material. London: CfBT.

Muijs, R. D. and Reynolds, D. (2000b) School Effectiveness and Teacher Effectiveness: Some Preliminary Findings from the Evaluation of the Mathematics Enhancement Programme. *School Effectiveness and School Improvement* 11(2), 247–63.

Muijs, R. D. and Reynolds, D. (2000c) *Effective Mathematics Teaching: Year 2 of a Research Project*. Paper presented at the International Conference on School Effectiveness and School Improvement, Hong Kong, 8 January.

Muijs, D. and Reynolds, D. (2001) Student Background and Teacher Effects on Achievement and Attainment in Mathematics: a Longitudinal Study. Presentation at the International Congress for School Effectiveness and School Improvement, Toronto, 7 January.

Muijs, D. and Reynolds, D. (2003) The Effectiveness of the Use of Learning Support Assistants in Improving the Mathematics Achievement of Low Achieving Pupils in Primary School. *Educational Research* 45(3), 219–30.

Muijs, R. D. and Reynolds, D. (2002) Teacher Beliefs and Behaviors: What Matters. *Journal of Classroom Interaction* 37(2), 3–15.

Muijs, R. D. and Reynolds, D. (2003) Student Background and Teacher Effects on Achievement and Attainment in Mathematics. *Educational Research and Evaluation* 9(1), 289–313.

Muijs, D., Harris, A., Chapman, C., Stoll, L. and Russ, J. (2004) Improving Schools in Socio-Economically Disadvantaged Areas: An Overview of Research. *School Effectiveness and School Improvement* 15(2), 149–76.

Muijs, D., Chapman, C., Armstrong, P. and Collins, A. (2010) The Impact of Teach First on Leadership and Classroom Practice: A Mixed Methods Study of the Impact of an Alternative Teacher Certification Programme on Schools Serving Disadvantaged Areas. Paper Presented at the International Congress for School Effectiveness and School Improvement, Kuala Lumpur, 3–6 January.

Murray, L., Woolgar, M., Martins, C., Christaki, A., Hipwell, A. and Copper, B. (2006) Conversations around Homework: Links to Parental Mental Health, Family Characteristics and Child Psychological Functioning. *British Journal of Developmental Psychology* 24(1), 125–49.

National College for School Leadership (NCSL) (2006) *Narrowing the Gap: Reducing Within School Variation in Pupil Outcomes.* Nottingham: NCSL.

National Institute of Child Health and Human Development (NICHD) (2000) *Report of the National Reading Panel – Teaching Children to Read: An Evidence-Based Assessment of the Scientific Research Literature on Reading and its Implications for Reading Instruction – Reports of the Subgroups*. Washington, DC: NIH.

Nattiv, A. (1994) Helping Behaviors and Math Achievement Gain of Students Using Cooperative Learning. *The Elementary School Journal* 94(3): 285–97.

Neihart, M. (2007) The Socio-Emotional Impact of Acceleration and Ability Grouping: Recommendations for Best Practice. *Gifted Child Quarterly* 51(4), 330–41.

Nelson, J., Martella, R. and Marchand-Martella, N. (2002) Maximizing Student Learning: The Effects of a Comprehensive School-Based Program for Preventing Problem Behaviors. *Journal of Emotional and Behavioral Disorders* 10(3), 136–48.

Ness, B. and Latessa, E. (1979) Gifted Children and Self-Teaching Techniques. *Directive Teacher* 2, 10–12.

Newcomb, A. F. and Bagwell, C. L. (1996) The Developmental Significance of Children's Friendship Relations. In W. M. Bukowski, A. F. Newcomb and W. W. Hartup (eds) *The Company They Keep: Friendship in Childhood and Adolescence*. Cambridge: Cambridge University Press.

Nickerson, R. S., Perkins, D. N. and Smith, E. E. (1985) *The Teaching of Thinking*. Hillsdale, NJ: Lawrence Erlbaum.

Nicolson, R. and Reynolds, D. (2003) Science, Sense and Synergy – Response to Commentators. *Dyslexia* 9(3), 48–71.

Nicolson, R., Fawcett, A. and Dean, P. (2001) Developmental Dyslexia: The Cerebellar Deficit Hypothesis. *Trends in Neuroscience* 24(9), 508–11.

Nielsen, D. C. and Luetke-Stahlman, B. (2002) Phonological Awareness: One Key to the Reading Proficiency of Deaf Children. *American Annals of the Deaf* 147(3), 11–19.

Noonan, C. and Duncan, C. R. (2005) Peer- and Self-Assessment in High Schools. *Practical Assessment, Research and Evaluation* 17(10), 12–20.

Nuffield Curriculum Programme (2009) *KS3 STEM Project*. Available at: www.nuffieldcurriculumcentre.org/go/minisite/OtherScienceProjects/Page_210.html/ (accessed 25 October 2009).

Nunes, T. and Bryant, P. (1996) *Children Doing Mathematics*. Oxford: Blackwell.

Nunn, G. D. and Parish, T. S. (1992) The Psychological Characteristics of At-risk High School Students. *Adolescence* 27(106), 435–40.

Nye, B., Konstantopoulos, S. and Hedges, L. V. (2004) How Large are Teacher Effects?. *Educational Evaluation and Policy Analysis* 26(3), 237–57.

O'Connor, R., Fulmer, D., Harty, K. and Bell, K. (2005) Layers of Reading Intervention in Kindergarten Through Third Grade: Changes in Teaching and Student Outcomes. *Journal of Learning Disabilities* 38(5), 440–55.

O'Donnell, A. M. (2006) The Role of Peers and Group Learning. In P. Alexander and P. Winne (eds) *Handbook of Educational Psychology* (second edition). Mahwah, NJ: Lawrence Erlbaum.

O'Donohue, W. and Ferguson, K. (2001) *The Psychology of B. F. Skinner*. Thousand Oaks, CA: Sage.

OFSTED (1995) *Primary Matters*. London: HMSO for OFSTED.

Ogden, T. (2003) The Validity of Teacher Ratings of Adolescents' Social Skills. *Scandinavian Journal of Educational Research* 47(1), 63–76.

Opdenakker, M.-C., Van Damme, J., De Fraine, B., Van Landeghem, G. and Onghena, P. (2002) The Effect of Schools and Classes on Mathematics Achievement. *School Effectiveness and School Improvement* 13(4), 399–427.

Organisation for Economic Cooperation and Development (OECD) (1994) *Teacher Quality: Synthesis of Country Studies*. Paris: OECD.

Organisation for Economic Cooperation and Development (OECD) (2005) *Teachers Matter: Attracting, Developing and Retaining Effective Teachers*. Paris: OECD.

Ornstein, A. C. (1994) Homework, Studying and Role-Taking: Essential Skills for Students. *NASSP Bulletin* 78(558), 58–70.

Orr, E. and Dinur, B. (1995) Social Setting Differences in Self-esteem: Kibbutz and Urban Adolescents. *Journal of Youth and Adolescence* 24(1), 3–27.

Orton, A. (1992) *Learning Mathematics: Issues, Theory and Classroom Practice* (second edition). London: Cassell.

O'Sullivan, R. G., Puryear, P. and Oliver, D. (1994) *Evaluating the Use of Learning Styles Instruction to Promote Academic Success Among At-risk 9th Graders*. Paper presented at the annual meeting of the American Educational Research Association, New Orleans, LA. March.

Palincsar, A. S. and Brown, A. L. (1984) The Reciprocal Teaching of Comprehension-fostering and Comprehension-monitoring Activities. *Cognition and Instruction* 1, 117–75.

Palincsar, A. S. and McPhail, J. C. (1993) A Critique of the Metaphor of Distillation in 'Toward a Knowledge Base for School Learning'. *Review of Educational Research* 63(3), 327–34.

Panitz, T. and Panitz, P. (1996) Assessing Students and Yourself by Observing Students Working Cooperatively and Using the One Minute Paper. *Cooperative Learning and College Teaching* 6(3), 21–7.

Parke, B. (1992) *Challenging Gifted Students in the Regular Classroo*m. ERIC EC Digest E513.

Parker, J. G. and Asher, S. R. (1987) Peer Relations and Later Social Adjustment: Are Low-Accepted Children At Risk? *Psychological Bulletin* 102, 357–89.

Parker, J. and Asher, S. (1993) Friendship and Friendship Quality in Middle Childhood: Links with Peer Group Acceptance and Feelings of Loneliness and Social Dissatisfaction. *Developmental Psychology* 29(4), 611–21.

Patall, E., Copper, H. and Robinson, J. C. (2008) Parental Involvement in Homework: A Research Synthesis. *Review of Educational Research* 78(4), 1039–101.

Pekrun, R. (1990) Social Support, Achievement Evaluations and Self-concepts in Adolescence. In L. Oppenheimer (ed.) *The Self-Concept: European Perspectives on its Develoment, Aspects and Applications*. Berlin: Springer.

Perkins, D. N. and Salomon, G. (1989) Are Cognitive Skills Context Bound? *Educational Researcher* 18(1), 16–25.

Petrogiannis, K. (2002) Greek Day Care Centres' Quality, Caregivers' Behaviour and Children's Development. *International Journal of Early Years Education* 10(2), 137–48.

Piaget, J. (1970) *Science of Education and the Psychology of the Child* (trans. Derik Coltman). New York: Orion Press.

Piaget, J. (2001) *The Child's Conception of Physical Causality*. New Brunswick, NJ: Transaction Publishers.

Podesta, C. (2001) *Self-Esteem and the 6-Second Secret* (updated edition). Thousand Oaks, CA: Corwin Press.

Pollard, A., Broadfoot, P., Croll, P., Osborn, N. and Abbott, D. (1994) *Changing English Primary Schools?* London: Cassell.

Potter, W. (2007) *An Analysis of the Achievement Gap of Discontinued Reading Recovery Students: A Longitudinal Study of Reading Recovery Students*. ETD collection for University of Nebraska–Lincoln. Paper AAI3258776.

Powell, A. M. (1997) *Peer Tutoring and Mentoring Services for Disadvantaged Secondary School Students*. Sacramento, CA: California Research Bureau, 2(4).

Pratt, N. (2006) Interactive Teaching in Numeracy Lessons: What do Children Have to Say? *Cambridge Journal of Education* 36(2), 221–35.

Preckel, F., Zeidner, M., Goetz, T. and Schleyer, E. J. (2006) Female 'Big Fish' Swimming Against the Tide: The 'Big-fish-little-pond effect' and Gender-ratio in Special Gifted Classes. *Contemporary Educational Psychology* 33(1), 78–96.

Pressley, M., Allington, R. L., Wharton-McDonald, R., Block, C. C. and Morrow, L. M. (2001) *Learning To Read: Lessons from Exemplary First-Grade Classrooms. Solving Problems in the Teaching of Literacy*. New York: Guilford.

Prins, F.J., Veenman, M. J. and Elshout, J. J. (2006) The Impact of Intellectual Ability and Metacognition on Learning: New Support for the Threshold of Problematicity Theory. *Learning and Instruction* 16, 374–87.

Qualifications and Curriculum Development Agency (QCDA) (2009) *Assessment for Learning Guidance.* Available at: www.qcda.gov.uk/4334.aspx (accessed 15 October 2009).

Ramey, S., Ramey, C., Phillips, M., Lanzi, R., Brezausek, C., Katholi, C., Snyder, S. and Lawrence, F. (2000) *Head Start Children's Entry into Public School: A Report on the National Head Start/Public School Early Childhood Transition Demonstration Study*. Birmingham, AL: Alabama University, Civitan International Research Center.

Rand, Y., Mintzker, Y., Miller, R., Hoffman, M. and Friedlender, Y. (1981) The Instrumental Enrichment Program: Immediate and Long-term Effects. In P. Mittler (ed.) *Frontiers of Knowledge in Mental Retardation*, Vol. 1. Baltimore, MD: University Park Press, 141–52.

Reis, S. M., Westberg, K. L., Kulikowich, J. M. and Purcell, J. H. (1998) Curriculum Compacting and Achievement Test Scores: What Does the Research Say? *Gifted Child Quarterly* 42(2), 56–66.

Resnick, L. B. (1987) *Education and Learning to Think*. Washington, DC: National Academy Press.

Reynolds, D. (1992) School Effectiveness and School Improvement: An Updated Review of the British Literature. In D. Reynolds and P. Cuttance (eds) *School Effectiveness: Research, Policy and Practice*. London: Cassell.

Reynolds, D. (2006) *Schools Learning From Their Best: The Within School Variation Project.* Nottingham: The National College for School Leadership.

Reynolds, D. (2007) School Effectiveness and School Improvement (SESI): Links with the International Standards/Accountability Agenda. In T. Townsend (ed.). *International Handbook of School Effectiveness and Improvement*. Berlin: Springer.

Reynolds, D. and Farrell, S. (1996) *Worlds Apart? A Review of International Studies of Educational Achievement Involving England*. London: HMSO.

Reynolds, D. and Muijs, R. D. (1999a) The Effective Teaching of Mathematics: A Review of Research. *School Leadership and Management* 19(3), 273–88.

Reynolds, D., Sammons, P., Stoll, L., Barber, M. and Hillman, J. (1996) School Effectiveness and School Improvement in the United Kingdom. *School Effectiveness and School Improvement* 7(2), 133–58.

Rimm-Kaufman, S., La Paro, K., Downer, J. and Pianta, R. (2005) The Contribution of Classroom Setting and Quality of Instruction to Children's Behavior in Kindergarten Classrooms. *The Elementary School Journal* 105(4), 377–94.

Ritter, J. T. and Hancock, D. R. (2007) Exploring the Relationship Between Certification Sources, Experience Levels, and Classroom Management Orientations of Classroom Teachers. *Teaching and Teacher Education* 23(6), 1206–16.

Rittle-Johnson, B. (2006) Promoting Transfer: Effects of Self-Explanation and Direct Instruction. *Child Development* 77(1), 1–15.

Robinson, N. M. (1993) *Parenting the Very Young Gifted Children*. Storrs, CT: The National Research Center on the Gifted and Talented, University of Connecticut.

Robinson, N. M. and Noble, K. D. (1991) Social–Emotional Development and Adjustment of Gifted Children. In W. T. Southern and E. D. Jones (eds) *The Academic Acceleration of Gifted Children*. London: Teachers College Press.

Roe, K. (1983) *Mass Media and Adolescent Schooling: Conflict or Coexistence*. Stockholm: Almquist & Wiksell International.

Roeber, E. D. (1996) Guidelines for the Development and Management of Performance Assessments. *Practical Assessment, Research and Evaluation* 5(7) //PAREonline.net/getvn.asp?v=5&n=7

Rogers, C. R. (1967) Some Observations on the Organisation of Personality. In R. S. Lazarus and E. M. Opton (eds) *Personality, Selected Readings*. Harmondsworth: Penguin Books.

Rogers, K. B. (1991) *The Relationship of Grouping Practices to the Education of the Gifted and Talented*. Storrs, CT: The National Research Center on the Gifted and Talented, University of Connecticut.

Rogers, K. B. (2007) Lessons Learned About Educating the Gifted and Talented: A Synthesis of the Research on Educational Practice. *Gifted Child Quarterly* 51(4), 382–96.

Romberg, T. and Kaput, J. (1999) Mathematics Worth Teaching, Mathematics Worth Understanding. In E. Fennema and T. Romberg (eds) *Mathematics Classrooms that Promote Understanding*. Mahwah, NJ: Erlbaum, 3–32.

Rose, D. and Meyer, A. (2002) *Teaching in the Digital Age.* Alexandria, VA: ASCD.

Rose, J. (2009) *Independent Review of the Primary Curriculum.* London: Department for Children Schools and Families.

Rosenberg, M., Schooler, C., Schoenbach, C. and Rosenberg, F. (1995) Global Self-esteem and Specific Self-esteem: Different Concepts, Different Outcomes. *American Sociological Review* 60, 141–56.

Rosenshine, B. (1979a) Content, Time and Direct Instruction. In P. L. Peterson and H. J. Walberg (eds) *Research on Teaching*. Berkeley, CA: McCutchan.

Rosenshine, B. (1979b) Instructional Principles in Direct Instruction. *Theory into Practice* 17(3), 267–71.

Rosenshine, B. (1983) Teaching Functions in Instructional Programs. *Elementary School Journal* 83(4), 335–51.

Rosenshine, B. and Furst, N. (1973) The Use of Direct Observation to Study Teaching. In R. W. M. Travers (ed.) *Second Handbook of Research on Teaching*. Chicago: Rand McNally.

Rosenshine, B. and Stevens, R. (1986) Teaching Functions. In M. C. Wittrock (ed.) *Handbook of Research on Teaching* (third edition). New York: Macmillan, 376–91.

Rosenthal, R. and Jacobson, L. (1968) *Pygmalion in the Classroom: Teacher Expectations and Pupils' Intellectual Growth*. New York: Holt, Rinehart and Winston.

Rowe, M. B. (1986) Wait Time: Slowing Down May be a Way of Speeding Up. *Journal of Teacher Education* 37, 43–50.

Rudduck, J. and Flutter, J. (2003) *How to Improve your School: Giving Pupils a Voice*. Continuum Press: London and New York.

Rutter, M. and Rutter, M. (1992) *Developing Minds: Challenge and Continuity Across the Life Span*. New York: Basic Books.

Rutter, M., Maughan, B., Mortimore, R. and Ouston, J. (1979) *Fifteen Thousand Hours: Secondary Schools and their Effects on Children*. London: Open Books.

Salomon, G. and Perkins, D. N. (1989) Rocky Roads to Transfer: Rethinking Mechanism of a Neglected Phenomenon. *Educational Psychologist* 24, 113–42.

Sammons, P., Mortimore, P. and Thomas, S. (1996). Do Schools Perform Consistently across Outcomes and Areas? In J. Gray, D. Reynolds, C. FitzGibbon and D. Jesson (eds) *Merging Traditions: The Future of Research on School Effectiveness and School Improvement.* London: Cassell.

Sammons, P., Sylva, K., Melhuish, E., Siraj-Blatchford, I., Taggart, B., Barreau, S. and Grobbe, S. (2008) *Effective Pre-School and Primary Education 3–11 Project (EPPE): The Influence of School and Teacher Quality on Children's Progress in Primary School*. Nottingham: DCSF.

Sanders, W. L. and Horn, S. P. (1994) The Tennessee Value-Added System: Mixed Model Methodology in Educational Assessment. *Journal of Personnel Evaluation in Education* 8, 299–311.

Sanders, W. L. and Horn, S. P. (1995) Educational Assessment Reassessed: The Usefulness of Standardised and Alternative Measures of Student Achievement as Indicators for the Assessment of Educational Outcomes. *Educational Policy Analysis Archives*, 3(6) Available at: //epaa.asu.edu/ojs/article/viewFile/649/771.

Scardamalia, M. and Bereiter, C. (1985) Development of Dialectical Processes in Composition. In D. R. Olson, N. Torrance and A. Hildyard (eds) *Literacy, Language and Learning*. Cambridge: Cambridge University Press.

Schaffer, E. (1997) *Effective Teaching*. Notes for HRS training. Newcastle: Newcastle University School of Education.

Schaffer, E. C., Nesselrodt, P. S. and Stringfield, S. (1994) The Contributions of Classroom Observation to School Effectiveness Research. In D. Reynolds, B. P. M. Creemers, P. S. Nesselrodt, E. C. Schaffer, S. Stringfield and C. Teddlie (eds) *Advances in School Effectiveness Research and Practice*. Oxford: Pergamon.

Schaffer, E. C., Muijs, R. D., Kitson, C. and Reynolds, D. (1998) *Mathematics Enhancement Classroom Observation Record*. Newcastle: Educational Effectiveness and Improvement Centre.

Scheerens, J. and Creemers, B. P. M. (1996) School Effectiveness in the Netherlands: The Modest Influence of a Research Programme. *School Effectiveness and School Improvement* 7(2), 181–95.

Schippen, M., Houchins, D., Steventon, C. and Sartor, D. (2005). A Comparison of Two Direct Instruction Reading Programs for Urban Middle School Students. *Remedial and Special Education* 26(3), 175–82.

Schoenfeld, A. H. (1985) *Mathematical Problem Solving*. New York: Academic Press.

Schoenfeld, A. H. (1987) What's All the Fuss About Metacognition? In A. H. Schoenfeld (ed.) *Cognitive Science and Mathematics Education*. Hillsdale, NJ: Lawrence Erlbaum.

Schoenfeld, A. H. (1992) Learning to Think Mathematically: Problem Solving, Metacognition and Sense Making in Mathematics. In D. A. Grouws (ed.) *Handbook of Research on Mathematics Teaching and Learning*. New York: Macmillan.

Schraw, G., Crippen, K. and Hartley, K. (2006) Promoting Self-Regulation in Science Education: Metacognition as Part of a Broader Perspective on Learning. *Research in Science Education* 36, 111–29.

Schulte, A. C., Osborne, S. S. and McKinney, J. D. (1990) Academic Outcomes for Students with Learning Disabilities in Consultative and Resource Room Programs. *Exceptional Children* Oct–Nov. 162–72.

Schunk, D. H. (2000) *Learning Theories: An Educational Perspective* (third edition). Upper Saddle River, NJ: Prentice-Hall.

Schutte, N. S., Malouff, J. M., Bobik, C., Coston, T. D., Greeson, C., Jedlicka, C., Rhodes, E. and Wendorf, G. (2001) Emotional Intelligence and Interpersonal Relations. *Journal of Social Psychology* 141(4), 523–36.

Schweinhart, L. J. and Weikart, D. P. (1997) *Lasting Differences: The High/Scope Preschool Curriculum Comparison Study Through Age 23* (High/Scope Educational Research Foundation Monograph no. 12). Ypsilanti, MI: High/Scope Press.

Scriven, M. (1999) The Nature of Evaluation. *Practical Assessment, Research and Evaluation* 11(6). Available at: PAREonline.net/getvn.asp?v=6&n=11

Secada, W. G. (1992) Race, Ethnicity, Social Class, Language, and Achievement in Mathematics. In D. A. Grouws (ed.) *Handbook of Research on Mathematics Teaching and Learning*. New York: Macmillan.

Shapiro, L. R. and Solity, J. (2008) Delivering Phonological and Phonics Training Within Whole-Class Teaching. *British Journal of Educational Psychology* 78, 597–620.

Shavelson, R. J. and Bolus, R. (1982) Self-concept: The Interplay of Theory and Methods. *Journal of Educational Psychology* 74(1), 3–17.

Shavelson, R. J., Hubner, J. J. and Stanton, G. C. (1976) Self-concept: Validation of Construct Interpretations. *Review of Educational Research* 46, 407–41.

Shayer, M. and Adey, P. (2002) *Learning Intelligence: Cognitive Acceleration Across the Curriculum from 5–15*. Ballmoor, Bucks: Open University Press.

Shayer, M. and Adhami, M. (2007) The Impact of a Thinking Skills Approach (CAME) on Students' Mathematical Ability. *Educational Studies in Mathematics* 64, 265–91.

Shayer, M. and Beasley, F. (1989) Dow Instrumenter Lunchinad Work. *British Educational Research Journal* 13(2), 101–19.

Shechtman, Z. (2002) *Aggression and Classroom Climate: Relations and Applications.* Paper presented at the 110th Annual Meeting of the American Psychological Asssociation, Chicago, IL, 22–25 August.

Shore, K. (1998) *Special Kids Problem Solver: Ready-to-Use Interventions for Helping Students with Academic, Behavioural and Physical Problems*. Upper Saddle River, NJ: Prentice Hall.

Short, P. and Greer, J. (1993) *Empowering Students: Variables Impacting the Effort*. Paper presented at the Annual Meeting of the University Council for Educational Administration, Houston, TX, October.

Shymansky, J. A., Yore, L. D. and Anderson, J. O. (1999) *A Study of the Impact of a Long-Term Local Systemic Reform on the Perceptions, Attitudes, and Achievement of Grade 3/4 Students.* Paper presented at the Annual Meeting of the National Association for Research in Science Teaching, Boston, MA, 28–31 March.

Shymansky, J. A., Yore, L. D. and Anderson, J. O. (2000) *A Study of Changes in Students' Science Attitudes, Awareness and Achievement Across Three Years as a Function of the Level of Implementation of Interactive–Constructivist Teaching Strategies Promoted in a Local Systemic Reform Effort*. Arlington, VA: National Science Foundation.

Silverman, L. K. (1992) *How Parents Can Support Gifted Children*. Reston, VA: The ERIC Clearinghouse on Disabilities and Gifted Education, Digest E515.

Simmons, D., Kame'enui, E., Harn, B., Coyne, M., Stollmiller, M., Santoro, L., Smith, S., Beck, C. and Kaufman, N. (2007) Attributes of Effective and Efficient Kindergarten Reading Intervention: An Examination of Instructional Time and Design Specificity. *Journal of Learning Disabilities* 40(4), 331–47.

Siraj-Blatchford, I. (1999) Early Childhood Pedagogy: Practice, Principles and Research. In P. Mortimore (ed.) *Understanding Pedagogy and its Impact on Learning*. London: Paul Chapman Publishing.

Skaalvik, E. M. and Hagtvet, K. A. (1990) Academic Achievement and Self-concept: An Analysis of Causal Predominance in a Developmental Perspective. *Journal of Personality and Social Psychology* 58(2), 292–307.

Skinner, B. F. (1974) *About Behaviorism.* New York: Random House.

Slavin, R. E. (1983) *Cooperative Learning*. New York: Longman.

Slavin, R. E. (1993) *Student Team Learning: An Overview and Practical Guide*. Washington, DC: National Education Association.

Slavin, R. E. (1995) A Model of Effective Instruction. *The Educational Forum* 59, 166–76.

Slavin, R. E. (1996) *Education For All*. Lisse: Swets & Zeitlinger.

Slavin, R. (1997) *Success for All*. Lisse: Swets & Zeitlinger.

Slavin, R. E. and Madden, N. A. (1986) The Integration of Students with Mild Academic Handicaps in Regular Classrooms. *Prospects* 16(4), 443–61.

Smith, E. J., Pellin, B. J. and Agruso, S. A. (2003) *Bright Beginnings: An Effective Literacy-Focused PreK Program for Educationally Disadvantaged Four-Year-Old Children*. Arlington, VA: Educational Research Service.

Smith, F., Hardman, F., Wall, K. and Mroz, M. (2004) Interactive Whole Class Teaching in the National Numeracy and Literacy Strategies. *British Educational Research Journal* 30(3), 395–411.

Smith, L. K. (2005) The Impact of Early Life History on Teachers' Beliefs: In-School and Out Of School Experiences as Learners and Knowers of Science. *Teachers and Teaching: Theory and Practice* 11(1), 5–36.

Sosniak, L. A. and Etherington, C. A. (1994) When Teaching Problem Solving Proceeds Successfully in US 8th Grade Classrooms. In I. Westbury, C. A. Etherington, L. A. Sosniak and D. P. Baker (eds) *In Search of Effective Mathematics Education*. Norwood, NJ: Ablex.

Sousa, D. (1998) Brain Research Can Help Principals Reform Secondary Schools. *NASSP Bulletin* 82(598), 21–8.

Southern, W. T. and Jones, E. D. (1991) Academic Acceleration: Background and Issues. In W. T. Southern and E. D. Jones (eds) *The Academic Acceleration of Gifted Children*. London: Teachers College Press.

Spiro, R. and DeSchryver, M. (2009) Constructivism: When it's the Wrong Idea and When it's the Only Idea. In S. Tobias and T. Duffy (eds) *Constructivist Education: Success or Failure?* New York: Routledge.

Sprod, T. (1998) 'I Can Change Your Opinion on That': Social Constructivist Whole Class Discussions and their Effect on Scientific Reasoning. *Research in Science Education* 28(4), 463–80.

Stahl, S. (1999) Different Strokes for Different Folks? A Critique of Learning Styles. *American Educator* 23(3), 27–31.

Stahl, S. A., Duffy-Hester, A. M. and Stahl, K. A. D. (1998) Everything You Wanted to Know About Phonics but Were Afraid to Ask. *Reading Research Quarterly* 35, 338–55.

Stallings, J. and Kasowitz, D. (1974) *Follow Through Classroom Observation Evaluation*. Menlo Park, CA: SRT International.

Stevens, S. H. (1997) *Classroom Success for the LD and ADHD Child*. Stephen H. Blair, publisher.

Stiggins, R. J. (1987) *Profiling Classroom Assessment Environments*. Paper presented at the Annual Meeting of the National Council on Measurement in Education, San Francisco, April.

Stipek, D. and Ogawa, T. (2000) *Early Childhood Education: Building Community Systems for Young Children*. Los Angeles, CA: University of California at Los Angeles, Center for Healthier Children, Families and Communities.

Stone, P. (1997) *Educating Children Who Are Deaf or Hard of Hearing: Auditory–Oral*. Eric Clearinghouse on Disabilities and Gifted Education. Reston, VA: Digest E551.

Stringfield, S., Millsap, M.A., Herman, R., Yoder, N., Brigham, N., Nesselrodt, P., Schaffer, E., Karweit, N., Levin, M. and Stevens, R. (with Gamse, B., Puma, M., Rosenblum, S., Beaumont, J., Randall, B. and Smith, L.) (1997) *Urban and Suburban/Rural Special Strategies for Educating Disadvantaged Children. Final Report.* Washington, DC: U.S. Department of Education.

Stuebing, K. K., Barth, A. E., Cirino, P. T., Francis, D. J. and Fletcher, J. M. (2008) A Response to Recent Reanalyses of the National Reading Panel Report: Effects of Systematic Phonics Instruction are Practically Significant. *Journal of Educational Psychology* 100(1), 123–34.

Sun-Wang, K. and Bong-Hyun, S. (2009) The Development of e-Learning Platform for Gifted Children Education. *International Journal for Educational Media and Technology* 3(1), 39–51.

Swanson, H. L. (1999) *Intervention Research for Students with Learning Disabilities: A Meta-Analysis of Treatment Outcomes*. Available at: www.ncld.org/summit99/osep2.htm

Swartz, R. and Parks, S. (1994) Infusing the Teaching of Critical and Creative Thinking into Content Instruction: A Lesson Design Handbook for the Elementary Grades. Pacific Grove, CA: Critical Thinking Press.

Talay-Ongan, A. (2001) Early Intervention: Critical Roles of Early Childhood Service Providers. *International Journal of Early Years Education* 9(3), 221–8.

Tashakkori, A. and Teddlie, C. (1998) *Mixed Methodology: Combining Qualitative and Quantitative Approaches*. Applied Social Research Methods Paper 46. Newbury Park, CA: Sage.

Taylor, A., Peterson, C., McMurray-Schwartz, P. and Guillou, T. (2002) Social Skills Interventions: Not Just for Children with Special Needs. *Young Exceptional Children* 5(4), 19–26.

Teddlie, C. and Reynolds, D. (eds) (2000) *The International Handbook of School Effectiveness Research*. London: Falmer Press.

Teddlie, C. and Stringfield, S. (1993) *Schools Make a Difference: Lessons Learned from a 10-Year Study of School Effects*. New York: Teachers College Press.

Thomas, J. W. (2000) *A Review of Research on Problem-Based Learning*. San Rafale, CA: Autodesk.

Thomason, J. E. (2003) *Improving Bilingual Student Learning and Thinking Skills through the Use of the Constructivist Theory*. University of Illinois, PhD dissertation.

Thompson, A. (1992) Teachers' Beliefs and Conceptions: A Synthesis of the Research. In D. A. Grouws (ed.) *Handbook of Research on Mathematics Teaching and Learning* (pp. 127–46). New York: Macmillan.

Thompson, I. (1997) The Early Years Curriculum Tomorrow. In I. Thompson (ed.) *Teaching and Learning Early Number*. Buckingham: Open University Press.

Thomson, N. and Zand, D. (2002) The Harter Self-Perception Profile for Adolescents: Psychometrics for an Early Adolescent, African American Sample. *International Journal of Testing* 2(3–4), 297–310.

Tierney, R. J. and Readence, J. E. (2000) *Reading Strategies and Practices: A Compendium.* Needham Heights, MA: Allyn & Bacon.

Tieso, C. L. (2003) Ability Grouping is Not Just Tracking Anymore. *Roeper Review* 26(1), 29–36.

Tizard, B., Blatchford, P., Burke, J., Farquar, C. and Plewis, I. (1988) *Young Children at School in the Inner City*. Hove: Lawrence Erlbaum.

Topping, K. J. (2005) Trends in Peer Learning. *Educational Psychologist* 25(6), 631–45.

Topping, K. J. and Bryce, A. (2004) Cross-age Peer Tutoring of Reading and Thinking: Influence on Thinking Skills. *Educational Psychology* 25(5), 595–621.

Topping, K., Nel, C. and Van Kraayenoord, C. (2006) Enhancing Reading in Different Worlds: South Africa and Australia. *The Reading Teacher* 60(3), 300–2.

Torgerson, C. J., Brooks, G. and Hall, J. (2006) *A Systematic Review of the Research Literature on the Use of Phonics in the Teaching of Reading and Spelling.* DFES Research Report no 711. Sheffield: University of Sheffield.

Torgesen, J. K. (1993) Variations on Theory in Learning Disability. In G. R. Lyon, D. B. Gray, J. E. Kavanagh and N. A. Krasnegor (eds) *Better Understanding of Learning Disabilities: New Views from Research and their Implications for Education and Public Policies*. Baltimore, MD: Brookes.

Trautwein, U. (2007) The Homework–Achievement Relation Reconsidered: Differentiating Homework Time, Homework Frequency, and Homework Effort. *Learning and Instruction* 17(3), 372–88.

Trautwein, U., Ludtke, O., Koller, O. and Baumert, J. (2006) Self-esteem, Academic Self-concept, and Achievement: How the Learning Environment Moderates the Dynamics of Self-concept. *Journal of Personality and Social Psychology* 90(2), 334–49.

Tryon, G. S., Soffer, A. and Winograd, G. (2001) *Relationship of Social Skills, Depression, and Anxiety in Adolescents*. Paper presented at the 109th Annual Conference of the American Psychological Association, San Francisco, CA, 24–28 August.

Tymms, P. B. and Fitz-Gibbon, C. T. (1992) The Relationship of Homework to A-level Results. *Educational Research*. 34: 3–10.

U.S. Department of Education (2003) *Identifying and Implementing Educational Practices Supported by Rigorous Evidence: A User Friendly Guide.* Washington, DC: U.S. Department of Education.

Uzuntiriyaki, E., Bilgin, I. and Geban, O. (2003) *The Effect of Learning Styles on High School Students' Achievement and Attitudes in Chemistry*. Paper presented at the Annual Meeting of the National Association for Research in Science Teaching, Philadelphia, PA, 23–26 March.

Van Petegem, K., Aelterman, A., Van Keer, H. and Rosseel, Y. (2008) The Influence of Student Characteristics and Interpersonal Teacher Behaviour in the Classroom on Students' Wellbeing. *Social Indicators Research* 85(2), 279–91.

Van Tassel-Baska, J. (1992) Educational Decision Making on Acceleration and Grouping. *Gifted Child Quarterly* 36(2), 68–72.

Van Tassel-Baska, J. (1994) *Comprehensive Curriculum for Gifted Learners*. Boston, MA: Allyn & Bacon.

Veenman, S. (1992) Effectieve instructie volgens het directe instructiemodel. *Pedagogische Studien* 69(4), 242–69.

Veenman, S., Denessen, E., van den Akker, A. and van der Rijt, J. (2005) Effects of a Cooperative Learning Program on the Elaborations of Students During Help Seeking and Help Giving. *American Educational Research Journal* 42, 115–51.

Vermunt, J.D. (1992) *Leerstijlen en sturen van leerprocessen in het hoger onderwijs–Naar procesgerichte instructie in zelfstandig denken*. [Learning Styles and Regulation of Learning in Higher Education: Towards Process-oriented Instruction in Autonomous Thinking]. Amsterdam/Lisse: Swets & Zeitlinger.

Visser, B. A., Ashton, M. C., and Vernon, P. A. (2006) Beyond *g*: Putting Multiple Intelligences Theory to the Test. *Intelligence* 34(5), 464–83.

Von Glasersfeld, E. (1984) An Introduction to Radical Constructivism. In P. Watzlawick (ed.) *The Invented Reality*. New York: Norton.

Von Glasersfeld, E. (1987) *The Construction of Knowledge: Contributions to Conceptual Semantics*. Seaside, CA: Intersystems Publications.

Von Glasersfeld, E. (1989) Constructivism in Education. In T. Husen and N. Postlethwaite (eds) *International Encyclopedia of Education* (supplementary vol.). Oxford: Pergamon, 162–3.

von Suchodolelz, A., Tromssdorf, G., Heikamp, T. Wieber, F. and Gollwitzer, P. (2009) Transition to School: The Role of Kindergarten Children's Behaviour. *Learning and Individual Differences* 19(4), 561–6.

Walberg, H. J. (1993) Learning 'Disabilities' Revisited. *European Journal of Special Needs Education* 8(3), 289–302.

Walker, C. M. (1999) *The Effect of Different Pedagogical Approaches on Mathematics Students' Achievement*. Paper presented at the Annual Meeting of the American Educational Research Association, Montreal, Quebec, 19–23 April.

Wang, J. and Lin, E. (2005) Comparative Studies on US and Chinese Mathematics Learning and the Implications for Standards-Based Mathematics Teaching Reform. *Educational Researcher* 34(5), 3–13.

Wang, M. C. and Baker, E. T. (1986) Mainstreaming Programs: Design Features and Effects. *Journal of Special Education* 19(4), 503–21.

Wang, M. C., Haertel, G. D. and Walberg, H. J. (1990) What Influences Learning? A Content Analysis of Review Literature. *Journal of Educational Research* 84(1), 30–43.

Wang, M. C., Haertel, G. D. and Walberg, H. J. (1993) Toward a Knowledge Base for School Learning. *Review of Educational Research* 63, 249–94.

Wang, M. C., Haertel, G. D. and Walberg, H. J. (1997) Learning Influences. In H. J. Walberg and G. D. Haertel (eds) *Psychology and Educational Practice*. Berkeley, CA: McCutchan.

Wasik, B. A. and Slavin, R. E. (1993) Preventing Early Reading Failure with One-to-One Tutoring: A Review of Five Programs. *Reading Research Quarterly* 28, 179–200.

Waterhouse, L. (2006) Multiple Intelligences, the Mozart Effect, and Emotional Intelligence: A Critical Review. *Educational Psychologist* 41(4), 207–25.

Watson, S., Goodwin, M. and Ackerman, B. (2007) *Improving Instruction for Teacher Candidates in Classroom Management and Discipline Issues*. Paper presented at the AACTE Annual Meeting, New York, February.

Weaver, C. (1990) *Understanding Whole Language: From Principles to Practice*. Portsmouth, NH: Heinemann.

Webb, N. M. (1991) Task-Related Verbal Interaction and Mathematics Learning in Small Groups. *Journal for Research in Mathematics Education* 22(2), 366–89.

Webb, N. M. (2009) The Teacher's Role in Promoting Collaborative Dialogue in the Classroom. *British Journal of Educational Psychology* 79, 1–28.

Webb, N. M. and Mastergeorge, A. M. (2003) The Development of Students' Learning in Peerdirected Small Groups. *Cognition and Instruction* 21, 361–428.

Webb, N. M. and Moore Kendersky, C. M. (1984) Student Interaction and Learning in Small-Group and Whole-Class Settings. In P. L. Peterson, M. Wilkinson and M. Hallinan (eds) *The Social Context of Instruction*. Orlando, FL: Academic Press.

Webb, N. M., Welner, M. and Zuniga, S. (2001) *Short Circuits or Superconductors? Examining Factors that Encourage or Undermine Group Learning and Collaboration among High-ability Students*. Los Angeles, CA: Center for Research on Evaluation, Standards, and Student Testing, UCLA.

Weiner, H. M. (2003) Effective Inclusion: Professional Development in the Context of the Classroom. *Teaching Exceptional Children* 35(6), 12–18.

Weinstein, C. E. and Mayer, R. E. (1986) The Teaching of Learning Strategies. In M. C. Wittrock (ed.) *Handbook of Research on Teaching*. New York: Macmillan.

Weinstein, C., Tomlinson-Clark, S. and Curran, M. (2004) Toward a Conception of Culturally Responsive Classroom Management. *Journal of Teacher Education* 55(1), 25–38.

Wertsch, J. and Tulviste, P. (1992) L. S. Vygotsky and Contemporary Developmental Psychology. *Developmental Psychology* 28(4), 548–57.

West, C. K., Fish, J. A. and Stevens, R. J. (1980) General Self-concept, Self-concept of Academic Ability and School Achievement: Implications for 'Causes' of Self-concept. *Australian Journal of Education* 24(2), 194–213.

West, M. and Muijs, D. (2009) Personalized Learning. In C. Chapman and H. Gunter (eds) *Radical Reforms: A Decade of Educational Change*. Abingdon: Routledge.

West, M., Muijs, D. and Ainscow, M. (2006) *Improving Schools in Challenging Circumstances: A Study of School-to-school Collaboration*. Paper presented at the Australian Association for Research in Education Conference, Canberra, November.

Westerhof, K. J. (1992) On the Effectiveness of Teaching: Direct Versus Indirect Instruction. *School Effectiveness and School Improvement* 3(3), 204–15.

White, J. (1998) *Do Howard Gardner's Multiple Intelligences Add Up?* London: Institute of Education, University of London.

Whitmore, J. and Maker, J. (1985) *Intellectual Giftedness Among Disabled Persons*. Rockville, MD: Aspen Press.

Wiggins, G. P. (1989) A True Test: Toward More Authentic and Equitable Assessment. *Phi Delta Kappan* 70(9), 703–13.

Williams, G. A. and Asher, S. R. (1993) Children Without Friends. In C. M. Todd (ed.) *Day Care Connections*. Urbana-Champaign, IL: University of Illinois Cooperative Extension Service.

Williams, P. (1993) Integration of Students with Moderate Learning Difficulties. *European Journal of Special Needs Education* 8(3), 303–20.

Williams, M. (2001) Trainee Teachers' Perceptions of the Effectiveness of the Literacy Hour in Primary Schools in England. *Early Child Development and Care* 166, 53–61.

Wilson, B., Abbott, M. L., Joireman, J. and Stroh, H. R. (2002) *The Relations among School Environment Variables and Student Achievement: A Structural Equation Modeling Approach to Effective Schools Research*. Technical Report, Washington: Washington Assessment of Student Learning. Available at: www.spu.edu/wsrc

Wilson, H. K., Pianta, R. C. and Stuhlman, M. (2007) Typical Classroom Experiences in First Grade: The Role of Classroom Climate and Functional Risk in the Development of Social Competencies. *The Elementary School Journal* 108(2), 81–96.

Wilson, L., Andrew, C. and Below, J. (2004) A Comparison of Teacher/Pupil Interaction within Mathematics Lessons in St Petersburg, Russia and the North-East of England. *British Educational Research Journal* 32(3), 411–41.

Winebrenner, S. (2003) Teaching Strategies for Twice-Exceptional Students. *Intervention in School and Clinic* 38(3), 131–7.

Winebrenner, S. and Devlin, B. (1996) *Cluster Grouping of Gifted Students: How to Provide Full-Time Services on a Part-Time Budget*. Reston, VA: The ERIC Clearinghouse on Disabilities and Gifted Education, Digest E538.

Woessmann, L. and Hanushek, E. (2005) *Does Educational Tracking Affect Performance and Inequality? Differences-in-Differences Evidence across Countries*. CESifo Working Paper Series No. 1415. Available at SSRN: http://ssrn.com/abstract=668864

Wong, H. and Wong, R. (2004) It's All About Procedures. *New Teacher Advocate* Fall, 2–3.

Wood, E. and Bennett, N. (1999) Progression and Continuity in Early Childhood Education: Tensions and Contradictions. International Journal of Early Years Education 7(1), 5–16.

Woolfolk, A. (1997) *Educational Psychology*. Needham, MA: Allyn & Bacon.

Wray, D. and Medwell, J. (2001) *What Can Teachers of Literacy Learn from a Study of Effective Teachers*? Paper presented at the 12th European Reading Conference, Dublin, Ireland, 1–4 July.

Wright-Castro, R., Ramirez, R. and Duran, R. (2003) *Latino 6th Grade Student Perceptions of School Sorting Practices*. Paper presented at the Annual Meeting of the American Educational Research Association, Chicago, IL, 21–25 April.

Wubbels, T., Brekelmans, M. and Hooymayers, H. (1991) Interpersonal Teacher Behavior in the Classroom. In B. J. Fraser and H. J. Walberg (eds) *Educational Environments: Evaluation, Antecedents and Consequences*. Oxford: Pergamon Press.

Wylie, C. (1998) *Six Years Old and Competent: The Second Stage of the Competent Children Project – A Summary of the Main Findings*. Wellington, NZ: New Zealand Council for Educational Research.

Wylie, C. and Thompson, J. (2003) The Long-Term Contribution of Early Childhood Education to Children's Performance: Evidence from New Zealand. *International Journal of Early Years Education* 11(1), 69–78.

Wylie, R. C. (1974) *The Self-Concept: A Critical Survey of Pertinent Research Literature*. Lincoln, NE: University of Nebraska Press.

Yetkin, E. (2003) *Student Difficulties in Learning Elementary Mathematics*. ERIC Digest no. ED482727. Washington, DC: Office of Educational Research and Improvement.

Zigmond, N. and Baker, J. M. (1997) Inclusion of Pupils with Learning Disabilities in General Education Settings. In S. J. Peijl, C. J. W. Meyer and S. Hegarty (eds) *Inclusive Education: A Global Agenda*. London: Routledge.

Zimmerman, B. J. and Kitsantas, A. (2005) Homework Practices and Academic Achievement: The Mediating Role of Self-efficacy and Perceived Responsibility Beliefs. *Contemporary Educational Psychology* 30(3), 397–417.

INDEX

Added to a page number 'f' denotes a figure.